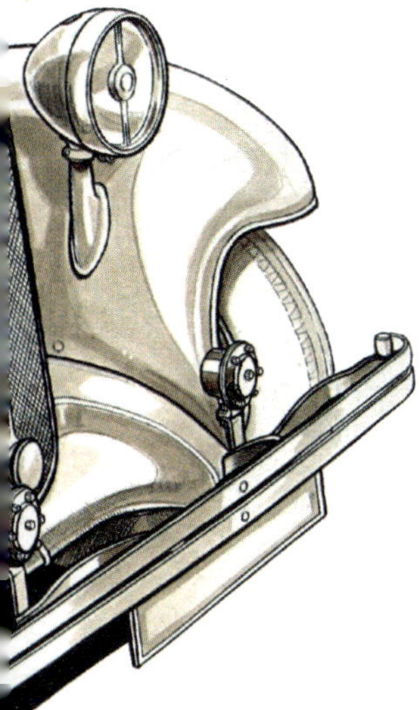

in association with The Michael Sedgwick Trust

THE BOOK OF THE STANDARD MOTOR COMPANY

Graham Robson

VELOCE PUBLISHING
THE PUBLISHER OF FINE AUTOMOTIVE BOOKS

Also from Veloce Publishing ...

Those Were The Days ... Series
Alpine Trials & Rallies 1910-1973 (Pfundner)
American 'Independent' Automakers – AMC to Willys 1945 to 1960 (Mort)
American Station Wagons – The Golden Era 1950-1975 (Mort)
American Trucks of the 1950s (Mort)
American Trucks of the 1960s (Mort)
American Woodies 1928-1953 (Mort)
Anglo-American Cars from the 1930s to the 1970s (Mort)
Austerity Motoring (Bobbitt)
Austins, The last real (Peck)
Brighton National Speed Trials (Gardiner)
British Drag Racing – The Early Years (Pettitt)
British Lorries of the 1950s (Bobbitt)
British Lorries of the 1960s (Bobbitt)
British Touring Car Racing (Collins)
British Police Cars (Walker)
British Woodies (Peck)
Café Racer Phenomenon, The (Walker)
Drag Bike Racing in Britain – From the mid '60s to the mid '80s (Lee)
Dune Buggy Phenomenon, The (Hale)
Dune Buggy Phenomenon Volume 2, The (Hale)
Endurance Racing at Silverstone in the 1970s & 1980s (Parker)
Hot Rod & Stock Car Racing in Britain in the 1980s (Neil)
Last Real Austins 1946-1959, The (Peck)
MG's Abingdon Factory (Moylan)
Motor Racing at Brands Hatch in the Seventies (Parker)
Motor Racing at Brands Hatch in the Eighties (Parker)
Motor Racing at Crystal Palace (Collins)
Motor Racing at Goodwood in the Sixties (Gardiner)
Motor Racing at Nassau in the 1950s & 1960s (O'Neil)
Motor Racing at Oulton Park in the 1960s (McFadyen)
Motor Racing at Oulton Park in the 1970s (McFadyen)
Superprix – The Story of Birmingham Motor Race (Page & Collins)
Three Wheelers (Bobbitt)

Enthusiast's Restoration Manual Series
Citroën 2CV, How to Restore (Porter)
Classic Car Bodywork, How to Restore (Thaddeus)
Classic British Car Electrical Systems (Astley)
Classic Car Electrics (Thaddeus)
Classic Cars, How to Paint (Thaddeus)
Jaguar E-type (Crespin)
Reliant Regal, How to Restore (Payne)
Triumph TR2, 3, 3A, 4 & 4A, How to Restore (Williams)
Triumph TR5/250 & 6, How to Restore (Williams)
Triumph TR7/8, How to Restore (Williams)
Volkswagen Beetle, How to Restore (Tyler)
VW Bay Window Bus (Paxton)
Yamaha FS1-E, How to Restore (Watts)

Essential Buyer's Guide Series
Alfa GT (Booker)
Alfa Romeo Spider Giulia (Booker & Talbott)
Austin Seven (Barker)
BMW GS (Henshaw)
BSA Bantam (Henshaw)
BSA 500 & 650 Twins (Henshaw)
Citroën 2CV (Paxton)
Citroën ID & DS (Heilig)
Corvette C2 1963-1967 (Falconer)
Fiat 500 & 600 (Bobbitt)
Ford Capri (Paxton)
Harley-Davidson Big Twins (Henshaw)
Hinckley Triumph triples & fours 750, 900, 955, 1000, 1050, 1200 – 1991-2009 (Henshaw)
Honda CBR600 (Henshaw)
Honda FireBlade (Henshaw)
Honda SOHC fours 1969-1984 (Henshaw)
Jaguar E-type 3.8 & 4.2-litre (Crespin)
Jaguar E-type V12 5.3-litre (Crespin)
Jaguar XJ 1995-2003 (Crespin)
Jaguar XK8 (1996-2005) (Thorley)
Jaguar/Daimler XJ6, XJ12 & Sovereign (Crespin)
Jaguar/Daimler XJ40 (Crespin)
Jaguar Mk2 (1955 to 1969) (Thorley)
Jaguar XJ-S (Crespin)
Land Rover Series I, II & IIA (Thurman)
MGB & MGB GT (Williams)
Mercedes-Benz 280SL-560DSL Roadsters (Bass)
Mercedes-Benz 'Pagoda' 230SL, 250SL & 280SL Roadsters & Coupés (Bass)
MG Midget & A-H Sprite (Horler)
MG TD, TF & TF1500 (Jones)
Mini (Paxton)
Morris Minor & 1000 (Newell)
Norton Commando (Henshaw)
Peugeot 205 GTi (Blackburn)
Porsche 911 (964) (Streather)
Porsche 911 (993) (Streather)
Porsche 911 (996) (Streather)
Porsche 911 SC (Streather)
Porsche 928 (Hemmings)
Rolls-Royce Silver Shadow & Bentley T-Series (Bobbitt)
Subaru Impreza (Hobbs)
Triumph Bonneville (Henshaw)
Triumph Spitfire & GT6
Triumph Stag (Mort & Fox)
Triumph TR6 (Williams)
Triumph TR7 & TR8 (Williams)
Vespa Scooters – Classic 2-stroke models 1960-2008 (Paxton)
VW Beetle (Cservenka & Copping)
VW Bus (Cservenka & Copping)
VW Golf GTI (Cservenka & Copping)

Rally Giants Series
Audi Quattro (Robson)
Austin Healey 100-6 & 3000 (Robson)
Fiat 131 Abarth (Robson)
Ford Escort MkI (Robson)
Ford Escort RS Cosworth & World Rally Car (Robson)
Ford Escort RS1800 (Robson)
Lancia Delta 4WD/Integrale (Robson)
Lancia Stratos (Robson)
Mini Cooper/Mini Cooper S (Robson)
Peugeot 205 T16 (Robson)
Saab 96 & V4 (Robson)
Subaru Impreza (Robson)
Toyota Celica GT4 (Robson)

WSC Giants
Ferrari 312P & 312PB (Collins & McDonough)
Gulf-Mirage 1967 to 1982 (McDonough)
Matra Sports Cars – MS620, 630, 650, 660 & 670 – 1966 to 1974 (McDonough)

Biographies
André Lefebvre, and the cars he created at Voisin and Citroën (Beck)
Cliff Allison, The Official Biography of – From the Fells to Ferrari – (Gauld)
Edward Turner: The Man Behind the Motorcycles (Clew)
Jack Sears, The Official Biography of – Gentleman Jack (Gauld)
Jim Redman – 6 Times World Motorcycle Champion: The Autobiography (Redman)
John Chatham – 'Mr Big Healey' – The Official Biography (Burr)
Pat Moss Carlsson Story, The – Harnessing Horsepower (Turner)
Virgil Exner – Visioneer: The Official Biography of Virgil M Exner Designer Extraordinaire (Grist)

From Veloce Publishing's new imprints:
Battle Cry!
Soviet General & field rank officer uniforms: 1955 to 1991 (Streather)
Red & Soviet military & paramilitary services: female uniforms 1941-1991 (Streather)

Hubble & Hattie
Animal Grief – How animals mourn for each other (Alderton)
Clever Dog! (O'Meara)
Complete Dog Massage Manual, The – Gentle Dog Care (Robertson)
Dinner with Rover (Paton-Ayre)
Dog Cookies (Schops)
Dog Games – Stimulating play to entertain your dog and you (Blenski)
Dogs on wheels (Mort)
Dog Relax – Relaxed dogs, relaxed owners (Pilguj)
Exercising your puppy: a gentle & natural approach – Gentle Dog Care (Robertson)
Fun and games for cats (Seidl)
Know Your Dog – The guide to a beautiful relationship (Birmelin)
Living with an Older Dog – Gentle Dog Care (Alderton & Hall)
My dog has cruciate ligament injury – but lives life to the full! (Häusler)
My dog has hip dysplasia – but lives life to the full! (Häusler)
My dog is blind – but lives life to the full! (Horsky)
My dog is deaf – but lives life to the full! (Willms)
Smellorama – nose games for dogs (Theby)
Swim to Recovery: Canine hydrotherapy healing (Wong)
Waggy Tails & Wheelchairs (Epp)
Walking the dog – motorway walks for drivers and dogs (Rees)
Winston ... the dog who changed my life (Klute)
You and Your Border Terrier – The Essential Guide (Alderton)
You and Your Cockapoo – The Essential Guide (Alderton)

www.veloce.co.uk

First published in May 2011 by Veloce Publishing Limited, Veloce House, Parkway Farm Business Park, Middle Farm Way, Poundbury, Dorchester, Dorset, DT1 3AR, England.
Fax 01305 250479/e-mail info@veloce.co.uk/web www.veloce.co.uk or www.velocebooks.com.

ISBN: 978-1-845843-43-4 UPC: 6-36847-04343-8

Readers with ideas for automotive books, or books on other transport or related hobby subjects, are invited to write to the editorial director of Veloce Publishing at the above address.
British Library Cataloguing in Publication Data – A catalogue record for this book is available from the British Library. Typesetting, design and page make-up all by Veloce Publishing Ltd on Apple Mac.
Printed in India by Imprint Digital Ltd.

THE MICHAEL SEDGWICK TRUST
This work is published with the financial assistance of the Michael Sedgwick Memorial Trust. This Trust was founded in memory of the famous motoring researcher and author, Michael Sedgwick, 1926-1983.
The Trust is a registered charity (charity no. 290841) set up to encourage the publication of new motoring research and the recording of motoring history. Full details and contact address can be found on the Trust's web site,
www.michaelsedgwicktrust.co.uk
The Trust welcomes suggestions for new projects, and financial donations to help with future work.

The Book of the Standard Motor Company

Contents

Introduction

In terms of British motoring history, an account of the birth, evolution and – finally – the death of Standard is long overdue. In Coventry, not only was Standard one of the most important motoring pioneers, it also eventually became one of the largest employers in the city. From the 1930s to the 1970s, indeed, the only rival of a similar size in Coventry was the Rootes Group (Hillman, Humber, Singer and Sunbeam), though Jaguar gained much of the publicity. Standard, along with Triumph, which it absorbed in 1944, was the most important of all these enterprises.

Now, with the motor industry all but dead in Coventry, and since the big factories have been demolished, the story of this ambitious enterprise ought to be told. Standard, like other businesses in the city, is a classic study of the way the British love affair with cars was born, waxed, stumbled, waned, and then finally disappeared. First there was individual enterprise, then hopeful (and under-financed) expansion. Next came a flirtation with financial disaster, rebuilding under the control of one visionary, vast expansion on the back of government contracts, and – finally – a descent towards financial oblivion.

Standard cars were built in the UK from 1903 to 1963, assembled in several overseas nations after 1945, and ended their days in India in 1987. Along the way, millions of customers bought machines as humble as the Little Nine of the late 1920s, as ruggedly successful as the Vanguards of the 1940s and 1950s, and of course as flamboyant and charismatic as the Triumph-badged sports cars of the postwar years.

But there was more – much more – and this is where no previous look at the company has ever done more than scratched the surface. Without the decision to build a new factory in 1916 to manufacture World War One fighters, then build hugely successful fighter-bombers (such as the Mosquito and Beaufighter) in the 1940s, along with the massive radial aero engines to match, there would not have been a post-World War Two company with such potential.

But there was more. After the war came the takeover and rescue of the much-respected Triumph motor car brand, the enormous Ferguson tractor-building project, and a short-lived excursion into the production of ultra-powerful jet aero engines. But it wasn't all good news, as the terrifying financial descent of 1960, into near-bankruptcy confirms. Say what you will about Leyland Motors, and its approach to motor car marketing (and, yes, many have done so in the past), but without its aid the Standard story would probably have ended, there and then.

Looking back, indeed, it's possible to see that Standard operated in four genuinely separate periods. First there was the setting up of a business by its founder 'Dick' Maudslay, second there was the revitalising period of 1929 to 1954 under John (later Sir John) Black, third was the exhilarating 'dash for growth' under Alick Dick, and finally (from 1961) there was the wind-up period when Leyland rescued the business, when Triumph came to dominate, and when Standard finally disappeared.

As any author and researcher will understand, when writing this book I found it difficult to compress all the information into a sensible, readable, package. In particular, I have had to restrict the coverage I gave to the 'Triumph' side of the operation, which became progressively more important as the 1950s and 1960s evolved. In addition, I have had to lay out much of the financial history involved, which means that at times I have had to be selective about some of the cars themselves.

All in all, though, my research through the annals of one of the most important of all British carmakers has been a fascinating journey, which tells us much about the company, about Coventry, and about the age in which it lived. I think I'm right in suggesting that it could never happen again.

Graham Robson

ACKNOWLEDGEMENTS

This will be difficult, as the number of contacts I have made over the years has been enormous. As a Standard-Triumph employee from the early 1960s, as a motoring writer from the mid-1960s, and as a budding historian from the start of the 1970s, I have been involved with the 'Standard' brand, and all its developments, for many years. In that time, a large number of people – starting at the top with Alick Dick (Managing Director of Standard from 1954), and with Harry Webster (Director of Engineering from 1957, but a long-time Standard employee for decades before that) – and a multitude of helpful, enthusiastic, knowledgeable and patient employees, consultants and observers, have all come to my aid.

Accordingly, the following may be an impressive list, but may not even be the total of all those who have helped me update all my knowledge, statistics, facts, figures and opinions in writing this dedicated Standard history. If so, I apologise to them, but offer the following:

The Michael Sedgwick Memorial Trust, for supporting the birth and compilation of a history that is long overdue in the annals of the British motor industry.

The Modern Records Centre, at the University of Warwick, where a mountain of vitally important Standard records is available for scrutiny, by appointment, to serious students. My thanks to them for agreeing that, perhaps, I am 'serious' ...

Companies House, for finding and providing so many invaluable financial details about the company and its business history.

The Reference Library at the National Motor Museum, which really does have most references to everything, and a mountain of expertise to back it all.

– And, of course:

Phil Homer and all his colleagues in the Standard Motor Club. Not only for reading every word, filtering it, and correcting my mistakes and assumptions, but also for finding, and providing, so many rare illustrations. It would certainly not have been possible to complete an authoritative job without them. Not forgetting their encouragement, to me to complete a task that other people have attempted before me ...

Anders Clausager, once running the archive at the British Motor Industry Heritage Trust, but now doing a similar magnificent job at Jaguar Daimler Heritage. It isn't only his knowledge, but his lateral insight, which I value so much ...

The AC Owners' Club – for information regarding the use of Standard-sourced chassis under ACs of the 1930s and 1940s.

Tony Beadle – the distinguished editor/joint founder of *Triumph World*, for his assistance in locating and using rare illustrations.

John Blunsden of Motor Racing Publications – for allowing me to quote extensively from Doug Nye's monumental three-volume work on BRM.

John Carlton, who really will be completing his own book on Flying Standards one day, for casting a critical eye over everything I wrote about the 1930s and 1940s when his beloved cars were on the scene at Canley.

Mike Cook, eminent USA-based historian, for his continuous insight into all things Standard and Triumph.

Ian Cornish, Vice President of the Triumph TR Register – for digging so far into the origins of the famous 'tractor engine' that it was above and beyond the call of duty.

Alan Crussell, of the Triumph 2000/2500/2.5 Register, for providing invaluable site plans of the fully developed Canley site.

Mrs Betty Dick – Alick Dick's gallant widow – who gave me a privileged and invaluable insight of her late husband's unpublished memoir about his life at Standard.

Stuart Gibbard, for probably knowing more about Ferguson tractors than any other historian, for sharing some of that knowledge, and for providing some rare illustrations.

Peter Lockley, then chairman of the Standard Motor Club, who originally did so much to encourage me to start this project, and who also provided invaluable illustrations of Banner Lane being ripped apart when its useful days were over.

– And, of course, the hundreds of Standard, and Triumph, owners I have met and talked to about their cars during the many years in which I have been connected with these marques.

TIMELINE

1903	Foundation of the Standard Motor Co Ltd
1903/1904	First cars delivered
1905	Launch of the very first six-cylinder Standard car. First deliveries in 1905/1906
1913	Launch of Model S – Standard's first-ever truly 'small' car
1916	A new factory was erected on the Canley site – originally to build fighter aircraft
1920	Introduction of new SLO – the first postwar Standard car.
1927	Launch of the Nine (later to become Little Nine), which started Standard's transformation.
1928	First appearance of the new straight-six cylinder engine, which underpinned Standard (and SS!) models until the late 1940s.
1929	Capt John Black joined Standard, originally as Assistant to R W Maudslay. He became a director in 1930.
1931	Launch of the first Coventry-built SS car, with chassis and all running gear made and supplied to SS by Standard
1934	December: Death of the company founder, 'Dick' Maudslay. From then until 1953/1954, John Black was in total executive control.
1935	Introduction of the first Flying Standards – the Twelve, Sixteen and Twenty models. Other 'Flying' types would follow in 1936, 1937 and 1938.
1937	Completion of the first Standard 'shadow' factory on the Canley site – intended to produce military Bristol aircraft engine components.
1939	Outbreak of the Second World War. Suspension of private car production to civilians. Erection of Banner Lane factory began.
1940	Completion of two further shadow factories to produce aircraft engine parts – at Banner Lane, and on the Canley site.
1942	Delivery of the first Beaufighter aircraft fuselage – 3000 would be built by 1945.
1943	Completion of the first De Havilland Mosquito fighter-bomber fuselage – 1066 would be built by the end of 1945.
1944	Standard took over the remnants of the Triumph car company. The first new 'Standard-Triumphs' would follow in 1946.
1945	Agreement with Harry Ferguson, to build Ferguson tractors at the Banner Lane factory.
	Launch of first postwar Standard cars – mildly revamped Eight, Twelve and (soon) Fourteen models. 'Flying' name now dropped.
1946	Launch of the original Standard-built Triumphs – the 1800 Saloon and 1800 Roadster Production of Ferguson tractors began.
1947	Official preview of the original Standard Vanguard.
1948	Sales of the postwar Vanguard began
1952	First showing of a Standard-designed Triumph sports car prototype, the '20TS.' Deliveries of the production type, the TR2, would begin in 1953. This brand's success would soon change the face of Standard.
1953	Launch of the new Standard Eight model – an all-new vehicle, with an all-new small engine.
1954	January: Sir John Black (Chairman and Managing Director) was ousted in a Boardroom coup. Alick Dick (aged 37) became managing director in his place.
	Failed merger talks with Rover.
1957	Failed merger talks with the Rootes Group.
1959	Launch of a new corporate small car, badged 'Triumph Herald, eventually to replace the Standard Eight/Ten range: this was the beginning of end for the Standard brand Final 'divorce' from Massey Harris Ferguson: Standard ceased to build tractors, and vacated the Banner Lane factory.
1960	Launch of the Vanguard Luxury Six – the first six-cylinder engined Standard to be put on sale since 1939. Standard hit serious financial trouble, and headed for bankruptcy. Leyland Motors put in a rescue bid.
1961	Rescue of Standard (-Triumph) by Leyland Motors.
	Alick Dick sacked by Leyland management. Stanley Markland succeeded him.
1963	(May.) Last-ever British-built Standard-badged private car (an Ensign De Luxe) built at Canley. Assembly of Triumphs continued, and increased.
1987	Assembly of Standard cars finally ended, in India. The final product was a Rover SD1-based machine.

CHAPTER 1

RAISING THE STANDARD 1903-1906

Where to start? Not, for sure, on 2 March 1903 when the Standard Motor Co Ltd was founded, or even a year or so earlier when the first Maudslay car was produced by another concern, but probably in the 1830s when Maudslay built its very first steam carriage. For without Maudslay there would have been no Standard, and without 'Dick' Maudslay the idea would never have got off the ground.

The fact that Coventry was the original home of the British motor industry tells us why Standard came to be there at all, but – why Coventry? Way back in the early 19th century, Coventry had been one of Britain's largest watch-making cities, but by the end of the 1850s those industries were being battered by competition from the Swiss. Entrepreneurs who looked around then settled on the idea of making pedal cycles, and within a decade this new industry had prospered, making Coventry its British manufacturing centre.

Rover, Singer, and several other companies all prospered, and motorcycles were an obvious progression from cycles, after which the city's very first motor cars, built by Riley and Daimler, followed in the 1890s. By the mid 1900s Daimler, Humber, Lea-Francis, Riley, Rover, Siddeley and Singer had all taken the plunge, so it was no wonder that a new company called the Standard Motor Co Ltd should also join in.

In the meantime, way back at the end of the 1700s, and

REGINALD WALTER ('DICK') MAUDSLAY (1871-1934)

'Dick' Maudslay (he was rarely known by his official given names of Reginald Walter) was the son of another Coventry entrepreneur. His father Walter H Maudslay originally set up the Coventry-based Maudslay Motor Company in the 1890s, initially to build marine engines. From 1902 the company began making engines for private cars, the first Maudslay cars followed in 1904, trucks followed, but from 1948 the business was subsumed into AEC.

Dick Maudslay was born in London in 1871, was educated at Marlborough (the noted public school), and was originally apprenticed to a civil engineering company. He left that concern in 1902, and set up his own business, the Standard Motor Co, in 1903, and ran it as founder and managing director until 1933 when, with his health failing, Captain John Black effectively replaced him. He died in December 1934, and within days was replaced as Standard's chairman by Charles Band.

just as the Industrial Revolution was gathering momentum, one Henry Maudslay (1771-1831) had set up a workshop in Lambeth, south London, where many of the foundations of the British machine tool industry were laid. Among the many innovations, which he inspired, were the Micrometer and the screw-cutting lathe, which led to the standardisation of threads, and the Whitworth screw thread.

Henry Maudslay's second son, Thomas Henry Maudslay (1792-1864), ran the business for years and built the steam engines for Brunel's SS Great Britain along the way. Eventually it was his grandson WH Maudslay who founded a company in Coventry to build internal combustion engines, initially for marine applications.

Although this was not the direct ancestor, now we are nearing the genesis of Standard as we know it, for it was WH's son Reginald ('Dick') and his cousin Cyril who set up the Maudslay Motor Co Ltd in 1901. Reginald Walter Maudslay (1871-1934, and almost universally known as 'Dick,' by the way ...) seems to have been what might be called a 'golden child' in a typically middle-class Victorian manner, blessed with an ambitious and indulgent family who presumed that he would eventually join the 'family business,' and who wanted him to have a thorough and high-level technical training.

Originally educated at the patrician boys' public school of Marlborough, in Wiltshire, with the family's influence he then became an articled pupil in the London-based civil engineering firm headed by Sir John Wolfe Barry (whose father had been the architect for the Houses of Parliament), and by Henry Marc Brunel (who was the son of the celebrated Isambard Kingdom Brunel), which had palatial offices in the West End of London.

Not that this was achieved without some financial pain for, as the records show, Maudslay's parents originally had to pay 500 Guineas (£525) for his five years engineering training – which was a very considerable sum of money in those Victorian days – though £50 was paid back to them in the fifth year when top management considered that he had earned such a remission!

The young Maudslay, therefore, found himself with a good grounding in engineering in general, though this was all on major civil works, and not on motor cars of any type. In his time in London, he was involved, or connected, with the new Tower Bridge, the Barry Docks in South Wales, and in the survey of the scenically spectacular West Highland railway line.

Motorcars, and the first-ever Standards

In 1901, however, the romance of getting involved in the new-fangled motor industry became compelling. Although motoring was still a relatively expensive business – there was no question, as yet, of serious mass production being started anywhere in Europe, though the French and the Germans were prominent – driving a motor car was already becoming a fashionable thing to do. With Maudslay's family already in Coventry (though Dick still lived, in some style, in 20 Victoria Square, London SW1, a mere stone's throw from Buckingham Palace), the attraction of this now-booming city was obvious, so the 31-year-old made haste to return, to join them.

It was at Maudslay that Dick first encountered Alexander Craig, a consulting engineer who is credited with the design of its first internal combustion engine for automotive use. Later, Craig was to play an important part in Standard's initial development. Ambitiously, it was the Maudslay company, which also pioneered the design of what is thought to be the first six-cylinder engine.

It was in Coventry, therefore, that Maudslay set out to build up his own car company, one which would be entirely separate from the Maudslay Motor Co Ltd, which was itself beginning private car manufacture in a small factory in Parkside, Coventry. Dick's previous employer, Sir John Wolfe Barry, fully supported his ex-pupil's enterprise, backing him with a cheque for no less than £3000. Alexander Gibb and Rustat Blake, both previously pupils of Barry, each made a contribution, with the balance made up to £5000 by Maudslay himself.

Cautious though, just as he would be in later life, Dick Maudslay started carefully. First of all he had to find premises (there was never any question of him sharing the same buildings as the existing Maudslay Motor Co), next he had to get up to speed with current automobile engineering practice, and finally he had to find a design engineer to do the job for him: he thought he already knew the man who could do that.

The company's very first Board meeting was held on 17 March 1903, there being just four directors present – Dick Maudslay, Guy Maudslay (Dick's brother), Alexander Craig, and the new company secretary, AJ Head: the latter took the notes of the meeting. The majority of the newly issued shareholding – 1600 £1 shares – went to RW Maudslay, though 500 shares were allocated to Craig.

At this juncture, the company's issued share capital was £5000 – modest by any standards for a potential manufacturing enterprise – and it was not long before Maudslay moved into an elegant house, Portland House, in Kenilworth. Company records showed that he moved several times in the next few years, but only to reflect his growing family, and the growing status of the tycoon, which he became.

All the notes for this inaugural meeting were kept in a small ledger (which survives), and written up by hand. It was a very modest start for a company, which would eventually become one of the largest car makers in the UK. Business transacted on this occasion was purely formal, and confined to financial details, there being no mention of the company's vision of the future, or even of its immediate plans.

Maudslay's very first achievement in Coventry was to find, and to lease, a small workshop in the Conduit Yard, at the back of Smithford Street. Hidden as it was in the teeming mass of Coventry's old-style, and over-crowded centre, no trace of these premises seems to have survived. As we will later see, this being spelt out in detail in chapter 6, much of the centre of Coventry was in any case obliterated in the Luftwaffe's bombing blitz of 14 November 1940 – and persistent postwar reconstruction did the rest.

From there he set out to buy a selection of small/medium-sized cars, which his soon-to-be rivals had already put on the market, have them stripped out, examined and assessed, and began to formulate a design of his own. He was, in fact, quite incapable of doing such a job himself, and had already found a competent engineer to do the job for him.

After a brisk search, and after taking family advice from his relations at the Maudslay company, he had hired Alexander Craig, who then settled down to interpret Maudslay's ideas. Not that Craig would stay long at Standard, for even though he was one of the founding directors, early in 1906 he moved off to design cars for, among other people, Lea-Francis, which was also a new-born Coventry car-making concern. By that time, in fact, Craig had been joined at Standard by John Budge, who went on to become Standard's de facto Chief Engineer (working to interpret the inspiration of Maudslay himself) for a number of years to come.

It was the choice of a brand name for the new car, that really laid the foundations for the new company. It was not long after his research began, that RW Maudslay concluded that other current cars clearly needed too much hand-building, fitting and fettling to make engineering or economic sense. His car, whatever it might be when finalised, would have to be manufactured accurately, and up to a certain level.

Was this a true story, or was it only apocryphal, that Maudslay once ended a spirited argument with Craig with these words:

"I don't want any of these new ideas, Mr Craig. I want my car to be composed purely of those components whose principles have been tried and tested and accepted as reliable standards. In fact, I will name my car the Standard car."

It was a name which became, at once, recognisable, but eventually controversial, as the motor industry changed its model-naming hierarchy.

Interestingly, over in the USA, Cadillac was about to take the same view on the way that it would also build cars – though at a considerably higher level of specification, output and prices. For years and years, of course, Standard would insist that its cars, and no one else's cars, were built up to a standard, a high standard that it had set, and would always maintain. It was not until the later years of this marque that in the British motor industry the word 'standard' would come to mean something which was built down to a level, and that 'de luxe,' or 'super,' was better. 'Standard,' in other words, came to equate with the modern phrase of 'entry level.'

Standards go on sale

Although Maudslay himself had schemed up the first car in January 1903 – this was what he called the 'Motor Victoria' – he and Alex Craig did not turn it into the metal until the middle of the year, for the premises chosen as a 'factory,' in Much Park Street, was only equipped with £400-worth of machinery, and was very simple and small. One hundred years later, incidentally, the Standard Motor Club sponsored the erection of a plaque on the site, which stated, proudly:

"The Standard Motor Company was founded on this site in March 1903 by Reginald Maudslay"

Because time has marched on so completely in Coventry, that plaque now finds itself on the wall of the civic Court building, which was erected in the 1960s.

It was in its issue of 6 June 1903 that *The Autocar* announced the existence of such a machine, and a five-page description finally appeared in December of the same year.

The 'Motor Victoria' model (Maudslay gave it that name) was a simple and modest little machine, built up on a simple chassis frame with a single-cylinder engine mounted low down at the front, under the front floorboards, a three-speed gearbox, and shaft drive to the rear wheels. Right away, one notes that it did not have chain final drive, though this was still normal practice in the early 1900s.

Although it was not an ambitious project – with a 6ft 6in wheelbase, and a side-valve engine which developed about 6bhp, it was never likely to be that – but there were, of course, signs of technical bravery. The shaft drive was one feature – not ground-breaking, but up-to-the-minute – and the use of a drastically 'oversquare' engine (it had a cylinder bore of five inches, and a stroke of only three inches) pointed to that.

At this point, of course, Standard was neither equipped nor financially able, to build complete cars. In the case of the 'Motor Victoria,' the engine had been machined and assembled in a first-floor workshop in Much Park Street, with the rolling chassis taking shape at ground level. Cars were then transported to Newport Pagnell, where the body was produced by Salmons (the company which would later be known as Tickford, and where, even later, Aston Martins were to be manufactured).

By the end of 1903, sources suggest that up to three prototypes had been completed, but these did not yet go on sale. When *The Autocar* ran its generous description in December 1903, it noted that the engine produced 8hp at 1200rpm, and that a twin-cylinder engine (with 'precisely similar dimensions to the single cylinder engine') was also now in existence, and that the construction was really of two independent single cylinders attached to an enlarged crankcase.

The design of both is credited to Craig, and it is acknowledged that he 'lifted' nothing at all from previous designs. It is noticeable that the car illustrated in *The Autocar* on 12 December is not the Motor Victoria, which indicates that it was not for sale. The illustrated car is quite different, and has a front-mounted two-cylinder engine. There is little doubt that this was the same two-cylinder car, which later appeared at the Motor Show in February 1904.

The fact that prices were not mentioned at that time confirms that these cars were not yet 'showroom ready,' but

This was the very first Standard of 1903 – no-one could have realised that it would found a great empire, and the biggest car-making company in Coventry in the 1920s and 1930s.

once the twin-cylinder 12/15hp machine went on show at the Crystal Palace Motor Show in February 1904, the enterprise began to look more serious. That model, priced at £367 10s 0d (£367.50) was purchased by Alexander Gibb, who therefore became famous as the first recorded private owner of a Standard car.

By 1904 the business had settled down, and expanded, though it would be some time before substantial profits could be recorded. With only twenty people on the payroll, production, of course, was still on an individual basis, though the company was reputedly able to produce a car every three weeks!

Ambition, though, soon swept commercial caution aside, for later in 1904 the company also launched (or previewed perhaps, for we have no authentic record of how many cars were actually delivered) three-cylinder and four-cylinder multiples of the same original engine, adding a longer-wheelbase chassis, and a four-speed transmission to what was now beginning to be a burgeoning range.

Although there was still no settled distributor chain (especially in the cities, notably London, where most car sales seemed to be made at first), Standard began to sell cars to the Maudslay family, to their friends, and to friends of friends – this being a normal way of drumming up business at the time! Maudslay's ambitions, it seemed, were also to start building bigger, better and more costly cars, which may explain why the first six-cylinder Standard (admittedly, not yet complete, and completely un-tested at the time ...) was put on show at the Olympia Motor Show of February 1905.

Here was the second-wave of technical innovation from Standard, for this engine had a more conventional under-square layout (80mm cylinder bore and 100mm stroke, the cylinder head layout being of what our Transatlantic cousins would call a 'T-head' design), with a line of exhaust valves on the left (nearside) of the unit, and a row of inlet valves (along with the carburettor) on the right. Although the cylinders were cast separately, there was a common crankcase. Naturally this was a considerably bigger car than previous Standards had been, for the wheelbase was 9ft 0in, and the tracks 4ft 6in.

By this time Alex Craig had had second thoughts on the dimensions of the original 'modular' engine, so the drastically oversquare piston dimensions were abandoned, the latest iteration having 4.0in bore and stroke dimensions.

Produced in 1905, when all such Standards were hand-built and very exclusive, this 16/20 model was very elegant and exclusive.

Naturally, this made the pistons considerably lighter than before, and allowed the engine to turn over faster. This became known as the 18/20 model.

Nowhere was this more obvious than in the single 'Works' car prepared by Standard to compete in the Tourist Trophy road race in the Isle of Man in September 1905. Although Maudslay, who proposed to drive the car himself, can be accused of taking a 'Don Quixote attitude,' and to tilt at windmills, the car itself, the very latest four-cylinder 16/20hp model proved to be competent, if only a mid-field runner.

As prepared for the race, the special 16-20hp engine developed 20hp at 1200rpm, and ran with a four-speed transmission. Although Maudslay himself was no race driver, he was no doubt competent behind the wheel of a car that might have been capable of a reputed 42mph (though, in fairness, repeated use of the brakes would still have been no match for even this limited velocity!), and was clearly set on putting up a show against the mass of other cars from Britain's fledgling motor industry, rather than trying to win outright.

The circuit itself was 52⅛th miles (83.7km) long, on public roads especially closed for the occasion. Much of what would later become famous as the legendary 'TT circuit' for motorcycles, with extra sections, and some of the road surfaces could best be described as rough-and-ready. The cars started at minute intervals so – as in a rally – they were racing as much against the clock as against each other. The Maudslay/Standard combination began at No 32 (there were 44 entrants), made a good start, and kept going where many rivals fell by the wayside.

In the end, he completed the test in 7hr 28min 2⅖sec (which equated to an average speed of 27.95mph), and took 11th place overall of 18 finishers. This was a good, if not startling, result – though the physical demands on the driver, and the intensity of the competition, presumably convinced Maudslay that he should not try to do it again. He never did.

Six-cylinder future?

By this time, it seems, Maudslay had decided to strike up-market, and to concentrate on the building of large-engined six-cylinder cars at a somewhat larger factory in Bishopsgate Green, after which the Much Park Street premises were relinquished.

By the end of 1905, the part-finished six-cylinder car, which had been seen at the Olympia Motor Show, had been finished off, and sales were about to begin. Standard had stopped playing at car-making, and was about to start fighting with the Big Boys.

CHAPTER 2

STANDARD AND THE UNION FLAG – BUILDING THE BRAND 1906-1914

From 1905 Dick Maudslay seemed to have fallen in love with the idea of producing massive and expensive six-cylinder-engined Standards: but surely he could not have immediately hoped to match the ambition of companies like Napier (and, soon, Rolls-Royce), who both had fine reputations for producing just such machinery?

It certainly looked like it. The first Standard 'six' to go on the market was the 24-30hp machine which was shown at the Olympia Motor Show in November 1905 (there were two Olympia Shows in that year), and in the next six years no fewer than eight different 'sixes' were listed, the largest of all being a 50hp behemoth of over 11.7-litres!

Not everyone connected with Standard, it seems, agreed with this policy, which was undoubtedly pushed along by the company founder himself, and definitely urged on him by one Charles Friswell. There is no doubt that, financially and commercially, these were turbulent times for Standard, but as Dick Maudslay was still the controlling personality in every way, there was no formal way in which he could be diverted.

This was, indeed, a time when important changes occurred to the Standard staff. This was the point when Maudslay appears to have been introduced to Charles Friswell, a thrusting London-based businessman with premises in Albany Street, London, who was looking for the opportunity to take complete control of the distribution of Standard cars in the nation's capital.

No sooner had Friswell visited the Standard stand at Olympia than he began a self-selling job, as to how proficient he was, how suitable were his premises in Albany Street (a highway close to the eastern boundary of Regent's Park), and how he could do a lot for the company. Friswell insisted that he could sell up to ten of the new 18/20hp 'sixes' every week, and proceeded to back his bombast by arranging, and guaranteeing, a £10,000 overdraft with Standard's bankers – Barclays – to make all this possible. It was on the back of this enterprise that new manufacturing premises in Bishopsgate Green, Coventry, had been acquired to provide more space. By this time, the company was employing more than 100 people – which was a far cry from the modest way in which Dick Maudslay had set up shop only three years earlier, in 1902. In fact, Standard would not remain long in Bishopsgate Green – a larger and (by the standards of the day) more spacious building in Cash's Lane would soon become the Edwardian-era centre of the business – for the premises would eventually be used only for coachbuilding purposes, before being sold off to Charlesworth (bespoke body coachbuilder), and were later still acquired by Lea Francis (car maker). Like most of the historic centre of Coventry that helped to make the British motor industry world-famous, however, these premises were later demolished.

Not that this concentration on big six-cylinder machines (there would be three different models, in short order ...) came about without dissent, and some technical confusion back in Coventry, where there seems to have been major disagreement within the company over the design and marketing of new models. It was Friswell, with his big ideas, and his London-based selling strategy, which seems to have tipped the balance.

At this point, by the way, is it worth mentioning two 'might-have-been' Standard models which surfaced, and were briefly described and supposedly ready to go on sale, but were never again seen in public. One was where the company dabbled with the launch of an air-cooled six-cylinder engine (this had been developed in concert with WH Bradburn of Wednesfield, Wolverhampton and no reference to it now survives in the company's archive), and another was when it also showed a small air-cooled four-cylinder '10 horsepower' model, which was glimpsed at Olympia in November 1906, but then disappeared completely, and permanently, from sight.

Looking back over more than a century, it is easy to see that at this point, Dick Maudslay's Standard really needed to be controlled by an older, wiser man – but that (as Maudslay was the founder and a major shareholder in the business, and did not need to take heed of democracy) never happened. Inescapably, therefore, the author is drawn to making a comparison (not a favourable one ...) with the developing fortunes of the Rootes Group in the 1920s and 1930s, when it became Standard's biggest business rival in Coventry. Throughout those years one of two brothers (William Rootes) was demonstrably the restless and innovative genius, while his younger brother (Reginald) was the 'sheet anchor.' In later life, 'Billy' Rootes once stated that; "I am the engine, and Reginald is the steering and brakes of the business ..."

Though Maudslay soon built up a relationship with Friswell (not necessarily to his, Maudslay's, advantage), Standard was still not selling enough cars. It was in this period that he developed the 'six-cylinder' model fixation, which would stay with him for some years, and hired a pliant engineer called John Budge to help him with this policy. Budge was well-known in Coventry, if not in the motor industry in general, having previously worked for the Triumph Cycle Company, which had just begun building very popular motorcycles.

Though John Budge had ostensibly been hired only to assist Alex Craig in the design and engineering of new cars (his original title was 'Chief Draughtsman'), he also found himself drawn in to the monitoring of company accounts, of chasing up unpaid bills, and generally putting the business on a more even footing. Perhaps it was this 'can-do' attitude, which eventually found him clashing with Craig, who soon resigned his directorship and left the company, eventually to work successfully with other Coventry-based concerns. Budge, however, would remain with Standard, would

In a real rush of blood to the head, Standard tested a Bradburn-designed, air-cooled six-cylinder engine of 5.6 litres in 1906. It was not a success.

become the company's general manager, and was on the Board until the end of the 1920s.

It was at about this time, incidentally, when the company claimed (many years later, one must admit) that its 200th car was completed during 1906. That claim was issued in 1951, incidentally, when one Albert Edward Smith retired from Standard, after forty-five years of continual service, which had begun in 1906 ...

Financially, the fact is that the company was by no means stable and sure-footed. Although Maudslay had agreed to inject a further £1200 into the business (thus taking up the balance of the so-far un-issued share capital), this disguised, rather than solved, the fact that the business was not yet consistently profitable.

In 1905, when Budge arrived, surviving company records, which are minimal to say the least, are shown to be at once boastful, but opaque. At the Annual General Meeting of 29 December 1905 (the meeting at which Maudslay had subscribed the aforesaid £1200 for more shares) he also boasted that: "... after expending a considerable sum on experiments, the Company had standardised their pattern, and the cars now being built appeared to be turning out satisfactory."

Nine weeks later, at a General Meeting, the balance sheet was presented, this presenting a less optimistic picture. The notes reported that:

Restored by Standard apprentices many years after it was built, SMC1 is a 1907 B-Type model with a 3.3-litre six-cylinder engine, and an extremely elegant Roi des Belges ('King of the Belgians') body style.

"It was reported to the Meeting that the Auditor had, with regard to the £1390 16s 3d net loss, shown ... had decided with the Managing Director that this amount would represent the goodwill of the business at the date of the balance sheet ..."

Although this was legal, in accountancy terms, the phrase 'smoke and mirrors' comes to mind, and it was not surprising, therefore, that within weeks Maudslay had proposed that the company's capital should be increased to £10,000 (it was currently £5000), though later in the year this proposal was not approved, and was therefore dropped. A vast expansion in Standard's capital base, though, would follow in the 1920s and 1930s.

For the moment, however, Maudslay (and, in due course, Charles Friswell) concentrated on building, launching and marketing large cars, almost all of them with six-cylinder engines. In 1906 and 1907 the company found itself selling not one, but three six-cylinder-engined cars in parallel. Such was the hand-built nature of Standard cars at this time that there was little commonisation of specifications.

As an example, the original 24-30hp prototype of 1905 had featured a side-valve engine with what the Americans always called 'T-head' layout – the inlet valves on one side of the block, the exhaust valves on the other, there being a wide and shallow combustion chamber up top which connected the two. That engine had a bore of 80mm and a stroke of 100mm, which gave a 3016cc capacity. By March 1906, however, when Mr Powys-Lybbe, whose very early example had been delivered to him in January, loaned his car to the media for trial, it was listed as being designed by 'J Budge,' still had a T-head side-valve layout, but this was considerably larger, with a 102mm bore, a 108mm stroke (which equated to 5192cc), and was rated at 30hp. This model, called the Model A, by the way, had a four-speed gearbox and retailed at £725. A previous writer on the Standard brand referred to this as an 'economy six-cylinder car,' which it might have been to a plutocrat, entrepreneur, or belted earl, but surely not to the rest of the world?

Later in the first year, though – revealed in September 1906 – there was more, much more. This was the arrival of the massive and expensive 50hp model. So important was it that *The Autocar*, which was of course based in Coventry, and therefore at the very heart of everything that stirred in that vibrant motor city, allocated no fewer than five pages to its description. No expense, it seemed, had been spared in the design of this behemoth, which was stated to be a joint effort between Dick Maudslay and John Budge (for Alex Craig had moved on ...).

Although the chassis and its suspension were strictly conventional for a Standard of this period, the engine was colossal. Six separate cylinders, each with the T-head side-valve arrangement, sat on top of a common crankcase. Each had a bore of 5.5in/139.7mm, and a stroke of 5.0in/127mm, which gave a swept volume of 11,679cc. The '50hp' model name looked very reasonable because of those dimensions, and to keep the crankshaft in check there was a main bearing between each big end, seven bearings in all.

With a choice of 132in or 144in wheelbases, and priced at no less than £850, this was always intended to be a flagship rather than a main-stream model, and as far as is known, very few such cars were sold. There are no survivors.

The third of the six-cylinder models, previewed in the autumn of 1906, but fully described in March 1907, was almost a complete contrast – not the largest, but the smallest, six-cylinder car, not only in Standard's range, but also of any other machine on sale in the UK. Although the incompletely developed prototype of 1906 supposedly had an engine of only 1893cc, running in an 87in wheelbase, the car, which actually appeared, was called a 15hp model, even though it had a 3.5 x 3.5in bore and stroke (88.9 x 88.9mm), which equated to 3724cc, and ran on a 116in wheelbase: this was the Model G.

Technically, it differed considerably from the '50hp,' because it had an 'L-head' side-valve engine layout, with cylinders cast in three pairs, with all the valves, inlet and exhaust, in a long line on the nearside (left side, that is) of the power unit, along with a single disc clutch running in oil, and a three-speed transmission.

New chairman, new policy

By 1907, not only was the company pushing ahead to produce, and sell, several different types of side-valve six-cylinder types, but also several management and factory changes were made to suit.

Most notable was the sudden appointment of Charles Friswell as the company's chairman. Up to that moment he had merely been the sales dynamo behind the company's expansion in London, but from a an Extraordinary General Meeting held on 1 January 1907, he was appointed a director

Perhaps the word 'automation' had not even been coined in the Edwardian era, for in pre-World War One days, at Standard this seemed to be a one man/one machine workshop. The mass of exposed drivebelts would surely not appeal to today's 'Health and Safety' enforcers.

of Standard, and immediately elevated to become Chairman of the Board.

Clearly Friswell was not in this for the monetary rewards it would bring, for his annual fee was fixed at £5 (£5, that is, for the year, and not the week, or month ...), a fee that would be raised to £50 in 1908. Dick Maudslay, on the other hand, was currently drawing £500/annum, which was a much more reasonable sum.

Only months later, the new Chairman reported that profits of £299 12s 5d (£299.62) had been made in the year ending 31 December 1906, and that those profits should be taken forward: "... towards extinguishing the item of £400 for 'Craig's drawings,'" which appeared among the assets in the published balance sheet.

In the meantime, Standard took a further step towards finding a larger, more permanent space, to assemble its cars. To do this, premises in Cash's Lane, to the north of the city centre, were bought from Pridmore & Co, whose business had been in elastic web weaving. This factory was actually bought on Standard's behalf by Charles Friswell, this being one more way in which the London-based chairman made himself a major corporate player at Standard, and it was here that the company's cars would be completed until after the outbreak of World War One (see *Interruption – World War One, and aircraft*) in 1914/1915.

The Bishopsgate Green factory already mentioned, was thereafter given over to coach-building – producing the bodyshells for the cars – while premises were also taken in Aldbourne Road, just off Widdrington Road, close to where Coventry-Climax, eventually an equally famous engine-manufacturing concern in the city, would prosper.

Incidentally, it was not only the company itself, but its model policy, which was somewhat restless at this time, for when the 1908 models were revealed in October 1907, it was baldly stated that just two types of Standard would be produced in the following year, both of them six-cylinder types, but to be called 20hp and 40hp models. One, the '20hp' was a development of the existing '15hp,' but the 30hp and 50hp types were both swept away.

For the next two or three years, therefore, something approaching stability came to the Standard range, though production was always at a pedestrian rate, and profits were still hard to come by. Those two cars, compared with the '30hp' model, which was discontinued, like this:

20hp	88.9 x 88.9mm, L-head side valves, 3724cc, 116in wheelbase
30hp	(obsolete) (Model B) 88.9 x 88.9mm, L-head side- valves, 3724cc, 116in wheelbase
40hp	(Model C) 101.6 x 127mm, L-head side valves, 6177cc, 132in wheelbase.

– note that the '20' was sometimes called the '15,' and that Standard insisted that it was the '40' which had taken the place of the '30.'

It was a Model B which, subsequently, became the first 'flag ship' by which the Standard heritage was recognised in modern times (1950 and 1960s, that is!), for a car carrying luxurious 'Roi des Belges' (King of the Belgians) convertible coachwork, later to carry the registration plate, took to the road in 1907.

Four-cylinder again

Market pressures then persuaded Standard to develop smaller cars than its patrician six-cylinder machines, the result being the launch of a new-generation 16hp 'four' in October 1908. Planning had started early in 1908 – Dick Maudslay had told his Board that he wanted to: "... get out designs and estimates for a 4-cylinder chassis, to be sold at £200, with a view to having one ready for exhibition in November."

Not that such a design seemed easy to pin down, for only a month later there was talk of 10hp machine, yet by mid-summer the new project had settled down to be a four-cylinder 16hp car – coincidentally, its engine output was quoted at 16bhp at 1000rpm. When launched, this new Model E was described as having: "... in effect, two thirds of the original six-cylinder engine," for it shared the same side-by-side side-valve (L-head) valve gear layout, the cylinders were cast in pairs on a separate crankcase, the same cylinder bore of 88.9mm, but had a longer stroke of 108mm. The same type of leather-faced cone clutch, and a three-speed gearbox, were also evident.

Although this new model seems to have established itself relatively quickly, a degree of commercial tension remained between Dick Maudslay and Charles Friswell. Founder and chairman disagreed on many matters, but since it was Friswell who brought most of the sales, and most of the financial stability, to the enterprise, this had to be sustained. The fact that the company announced profits of £1264 for the 15 months ending 30 September 1908 made things a little easier.

Dating from 1910, this 4-litre six-cylinder Model G, rated at 29.5hp, has now reached its centenary, and is still in regular use.

Before Standard changed its strategy in the 1910s, most of its cars were big, solid, costly and magnificently equipped. This was a gorgeous Model G Landaulet of 1909, complete with a four-litre six-cylinder engine.

Even so, we now know that Maudslay's strategy, of bringing back smaller-engined Standards with lower price tags, which would sell faster than before, was in direct opposition to Friswell's strategy, which was of having larger and more costly cars, built in small batches (and, by definition, almost all to be sold through his palatial premises in London) instead. Friswell's target audience was landed gentry, business people, and even members of the Royal family, whereas Maudslay was looking to infiltrate the middle classes, who were becoming more and more significant to the motor industry.

Friswell partly proved his point in mid-1909 when he arranged for Standard to provide a fleet of six-cylinder 20hp cars for the Imperial Press Conference, and as no major changes were made to the model line up later that year he seemed to be justified.

It was enough, incidentally, for him to see his annual Chairman's fee raised to £250 in the autumn, and by this time he had been knighted. Not only that, but Standard's annual profits continued to rise, those for 1909/1910 eventually being announced as £6915.

Upheaval

First the good news – that in 1911 Standard dominated the scene at the glittering Royal Durbar Coronation ceremonies in India. Now the bad news – relations between Maudslay and Sir Charles Friswell had virtually broken down, and a divorce, neither amicable nor easy, seemed to be inevitable.

Here at home, King Edward VII had died in 1910, to be succeeded by King George V, and as the new king was, by definition, the Emperor of India, it was decided to hold a Royal Durbar, in that country, in 1911. This, effectively, was an occasion where all the pomp and ceremony of the recent Coronation – crowns, robes and all – was duplicated

This is the fleet of new Standards gathered together in London before being shipped off to the famous Durbar in India. Chairman Charles Friswell took most of the credit for securing this deal.

This rare shot shows H M King George V, alongside a Standard 20hp with six-cylinder engine and Landaulette body, as used by the Royal party during the Durbar celebrations in India in 1911.

in India. Naturally, a fleet of motor vehicles would be needed to keep this show on the road – and to Standard's great joy, Sir Charles Friswell managed to swing the deal to make Standard cars dominant.

In April 1911, *The Autocar* had this to say about the forthcoming event:

"Sir Charles has entered into a contract with the authorities concerned, to provide all the cars necessary to the proper entertainment for the guests at the Durbar Coronation ceremonies in December [1911] next. He has also made a contract with the Vice-Regal department for the provision of Standard cars for the whole of the Royal Suite, and last, but assuredly not least, Sir Charles is to provide two Standard cars for the personal use of HM King George during the Durbar celebrations.

"Ten Standard lorries will be supplied for the carriage of beaters in connection with the tiger hunting expeditions which will, of course, form part of the Royal programme, and two more for the transportation of the general impedimenta. Adequately to carry out these undertakings, Sir Charles contemplates the despatch of no less than 100 Standard cars to India for this purpose."

When one considers that Standard's annual output at this time was certainly less than 500 cars a year, this represents an enormous undertaking, magnificent publicity for the marque by any standards, but one which assuredly must have put a heavy strain on the company's finances, 'work-in-progress' and factories for some time. It is strange that there seems to be no mention of this enterprise in the Board minute books.

We now know that 70 cars were actually sent – they were shipped out, of course, some weeks in advance of being needed – and that they were of several different types. Once arrived, and settled, in India, they were divided into four small 'fleets,' based in Delhi (the nation's capital), Bombay, Calcutta, and neighbouring Nepal. The actual Landaulette used by HM King George was a 20hp six-cylinder model, decked out in Royal Blue, and trimmed in blue, while cars for use by the Indian government were painted cream and upholstered in green.

All this pomp and circumstance helped to bring a major cause of friction between Dick Maudslay and Sir Charles Friswell to a head. It would not be too much to suggest that a major struggle for power brewed up. On the one hand, Maudslay and his Chief Designer/general factotum John Budge continued to press for the development of smaller-engined, cheaper-to-sell models, while Friswell, dazzled no doubt by his continuing, and indeed burgeoning, links with the aristocracy, wanted to stay up-market.

Matters came to a head before the end of 1911, the end result being that Friswell was cast adrift, and Standard carried on without him. Because little appears to have been published about this episode (and company records are strangely reticent on the subject), the details are not clear.

However, it seems that Friswell tried to take over Standard completely, yet could not settle his own London-based dealership's debts with the company. Two important new personalities now enter the story. One was Coventry solicitor Charles Band, whose sage and cautious legal advice in this matter was invaluable, and the other was

This 15hp model of 1913 was, effectively, the very last of Standard's Edwardian models, for all postwar cars would be of a simpler, cheaper-to-buy, type.

This is the only known portrait of the distinguished Coventry businessman Siegfried Bettman, who became Standard's chairman when Charles Friswell resigned in 1911. Not only was Bettman the founder of the successful Triumph motorcycle business at the start of the century, but for a time he was also the Lord Mayor of Coventry, which explains the robes he wears in this study.

Siegfried Bettman (who was the well-respected founder and major shareholder of the Triumph motorcycle making concern in the city). Bettman replaced Friswell who was ousted from the chair by the end of 1912.

Friswell now fades out of the company's history, but not without one final flare-up. In order to pay off its debts to him (effectively to buy out his shareholding), the Board minutes of 29 October 1912 recorded that it had agreed to supply thirty 15hp motor cars to Friswell's London company, and in a letter to him agreed that:

"Not at any time hereafter to use or mention in any advertisement or circular the name of Sir Charles Friswell or Friswells Limited ..."

A CHANGE OF STRATEGY

The principal reason for all this upheaval became apparent within months. Not only did the company arrange for a massive increase in issued capital (to £30,000, by an extra 25,000 in £1 shares, which was allocated to the United Counties Bank as security for the overdraft with that bank), but also for the launch of a brand-new car – for Standard, a brand-new type of car – which was the 9.5hp Model S. At the end of the year, therefore, it was no wonder that profits had slumped considerably – though the company was still in profit, to the tune of a measly £1950. In the following year the company was floated on the Stock Exchange, just thirteen years after coming into existence: after a suitable interval, during the 1920s and 1930s this finally gave Standard access to the new capital which it needed to expand.

Inspired by John Budge and Dick Maudslay (a development resisted, it seems, at every stage until he was ousted, by Sir Charles Friswell), the Model S was totally different from Standard's existing models. Small instead of vast, keenly priced instead of expensive, and a 'peoples' car rather than one for the landed gentry, it was clearly meant for a different clientele. Two stats alone tell their own story – the engine was a 1087cc unit, and the selling price was a mere £185 when previewed in March 1913, but £195 within weeks.

Designing the little S – a light car by any standards, but especially as it fell right into the middle of a 'light car' trend developing across the motor industry, one led most

This 1913 Model S was Chief Scout General Lord Baden-Powell's favourite mode of transport for some years.

Standard's first small 'peoples' car was the Model S, which featured a tiny side-valve four-cylinder engine. This would be the foundation stone for Standard's great expansion in the 1920s.

noticeably by the later-legendary 'bullnose' Morris – had been a real financial gamble, for almost every nut and bolt was new, the factory premises at Cash's Lane were bound to prove to be too small to cope with the increased flow, and the still-scanty dealership chain would have to rethink its methods, and find a new class of customer.

Technically, in fact, the S broke no new ground – but, as we now know, it set a trend at Standard, which would take the company securely into the 1920s. The chassis was a simple frame, with a 90in wheelbase, and 48in wheel tracks (we would get used to those dimensions), while the two seater 'Rhyl' version was only 126in long – not much longer, in fact, that a 1960s-type Mini!

It was the drive-train which was particularly novel – and which had taken up much of the development capital expended in developing the new car. Backed by a three-speed transmission with a single dry plate clutch (though as *The Autocar's* analysis so coyly put it: "Provision is also made to insert lubricant between the plates should they not engage quite smoothly ...") and a worm-drive axle, there was an ultra-simple L-head side-valve four-cylinder engine, with bore and stroke of 62 x 90mm, measuring 1087cc. Neither powerful nor temperamental – if it had a genuine 10bhp, the author would be surprised – it was none-the-less reliable. Incidentally, to keep down the costs, the Zenith carburettor was bolted up direct to the cylinder block, the inlet manifold as such being by way of internal passages in the block itself.

The little car's principal attraction, of course, was that it was simple, compact and, above all, it offered good value. Not only the £195 'Rhyl,' but a 'Rhyl Special' at £205 (with a superior hood, side-screens and two-piece windscreen) were the basic models, while the range also included a 'Hurlingham Victoria' coachwork version, available at £250, and Ranelagh' or 'Richmond' coupé styles for £275. 12-volt electric lighting was available as a 15 Guineas option. Commercial bodies were available for the first time, there being a canvas-top light van for £185 and a 'Tradesman' High Van for £205.

Not that Standard immediately put all its bets on the Model S from the start. The 1913 catalogue also included the 'Goodwood,' 'Bath,' 'Kenilworth' and 'Pytchley' body styles on the 15hp chassis, along with the 'Eastbourne,' 'Buxton' and 'Chester' types on the 20hp. Six-cylinder cars were no longer listed.

By mid-1914, therefore, Standard at last appeared to be thriving on a regular basis, with annual output in the region of 1000 cars a year. Although the big Standards were still available, these had virtually disappeared, for the entire Cash's Lane facility was now bursting at the seams with 9.5hp Model S production: some sources suggest that up to 50 cars a week were sometimes completed – and we do know that before prewar assembly closed down in May 1915, that 1936 such machines were built.

In August 1914, however, the civilised world was shocked, to be drawn, somewhat unwillingly, into a global conflict, which became known as the Great War (later, of course, the First World War). Although Standard was neither ready, nor outwardly enthusiastic, to get involved in producing military machinery, that soon changed.

It was this interruption, from 1915 to 1918, which helped propel Standard into the 'Big League' in the 1920s.

Even by 1914, Standard had virtually outgrown its Cash's Lane works in the north of Coventry. This explains why Canley was built, redeveloped, and enlarged so persistently in the 1920s.

WORLD WAR ONE AND AIRCRAFT 1914-1918

When Britain was drawn in to the First World War in August 1914, the government had few immediate plans to increase production of military machines to support the Army and the Navy. The smug statement that: "It will all be over by Christmas" was heard far too often, and soon proved to be horrifyingly wrong. As to the provision of aircraft – these were still unproven technology, their tactical use was still not understood, and only a few visionaries seemed to have considered their use at all ...

When War broke out, Standard was not involved with the military, though the government soon came shopping. Private cars in production at that time were still the 3.3-litre 20hp model, and the very promising little 9.5hp Model S, which had the 1087cc engine, and was the very first of a long and popular family of small Standards. None of the various Standard workshops and plants, which were scattered around the city, seemed to be suitable for expansion, all of them had the very minimum of modern machinery installed, though as soon as possible another new block was built at Cash's Lane.

It was not long before the initial opinion – that the war would not last long – was seen to be over-optimistic, so the government settled down to commissioning more and more of anything that could be hurled against the Central Powers. In particular, and not before time, it began to take an interest in the use of aircraft, first for use in aerial reconnaissance by the Royal Flying Corps (RFC, especially to aid the Royal Artillery), and later for use as fighters.

So, what could Standard do to aid the war effort? First of all, it had to wind down its assembly of cars for private customers, and it seems that the last of all, a 9.5hp Model S, was built in May 1915. By this time, incidentally, 1936 such cars had been produced, which made it Standard's most successful model to date, and it was also Standard's first volume-production model.

Except by supplying cars for use by the military staff (in which the government showed little interest at first) Standard could contribute very little at first. Shortly, though, the company was persuaded to start building – not designing, but building – military aircraft, beginning this process with assembly of the RAE (Royal Aircraft Establishment) BE-12 fighter aircraft, which was a flimsy-looking biplane with a tubular fuselage frame, and a 150bhp RAF Type 4 engine. The design of this plane had been inspired by Geoffrey de Havilland, and thus the very first links between Standard and that company were established – for in the Second World War the links would be renewed, and would become very close indeed.

Standard's first big expansion came during World War One, when the first sections of the new Canley factory were erected. Photo taken in 1916.

But not even in those simpler days (simpler, that was, in engineering terms) could a programme be rushed through in a matter of weeks, so although Standard became involved with the RAE in 1915, it did not deliver any aircraft until the end of that year, and BE-12s did not begin their RFC careers until mid 1916. Of military procurement, was it not Winston Churchill who once said; "In the first year, nothing, in the second year, a trickle, then in the third year, a flood!"

Standard's problem, and that of the British government, was that the existing Cash's Lane factory was close to the centre of Coventry, was surrounded by roads, railways and the canal, and its low roof layout had never been intended to assemble aircraft, so work in the main erecting shop was hampered by a lack of headroom. Encouraged by government, Standard then began to look around for new land – a lot of new land – on which to build new premises. Happily for it (but not necessarily for the environmentalists and 'tree-huggers' who were not at all prominent in those days) there were few planning restrictions in the 1910s, so when Standard's directors found a large, triangular area of undeveloped agricultural land to the west of the city centre, it seemed ideal for the purpose. The fact that the land was currently owned by Lord Leigh, a local grandee who was also a great patriot, was a huge advantage.

Although this land was totally undeveloped (and an even larger tract, next to it, would also be purchased from Lord Leigh in 1918) – it could perfectly be described as a 'greenfield' site – it was not well served by main roads: what would eventually become the A45 Coventry by-pass (which eventually swept across the western corner of the site) was still not even projected, and in fact was still 20 years into the future. The whole area was vast by British industrial standards, triangular in shape, and with the apex closest to Coventry itself. There were roads and railways defining the northern and southern boundaries, all within the parish boundaries of Canley, so this was invariably known within the business as the 'Canley' complex.

Nowadays, of course, and in the new century, this one-time Standard 'Canley' complex has been totally redeveloped for non-motor-industry usage, is tightly constrained by the A45 Coventry by-pass road to the west, by the main Coventry-Birmingham railway line to the south, and by Tile Hill Lane to the north. Many of the original geographical landmarks have long been obliterated by the redevelopment that followed the closure of the old Standard (by that time renamed as British Leyland) factory at the end of the 1980s.

One clear landmark remains, however, this being the modest little railway station once called Canley Halt. When Standard began building its expansive new factory on the Canley site, it was close to the Canley road, which crossed the line by a level crossing. The very first Standard buildings, including the iconic office block known as 'Ivy Cottage' (reasonably enough, because ivy was encouraged to grow up the side of the brand new building!), were erected close to the Canley Halt, and in the 1930s, 1940s and 1950s, Captain John Black's palatial offices were also located close to this facility.

[Not that this is still visible. In recent years, not only was the entire Canley factory site levelled then re-developed, but the railway line was electrified, the level crossing alongside the station was closed, a passenger footbridge was erected, car parks were added close to the platforms, and there is now no vehicular access from one side of the railway to the other. This is just as well, for at least four high-speed passenger trains, and four stopping trains, now pass through Canley station every hour, and there are plans to install quadruple tracks instead of the existing two ...]

After the government and the local authorities had made its policy clear, the first contact with Lord Leigh and his advisors came in 1915, and early in 1916 he formally sold the first tranche of this land area to Standard, totalling

Standard's new factory at Canley was set up in 1916 to build early-type BE-12 fighter aircraft just like this.

Canley was set up in 1916 specifically to build World War One fighter planes, and was soon a hive of activity. These aircraft, I believe, were Sopwith Pups.

Sopwith's Pup aircraft may look fragile and archaic today, but built by Standard during the First World War, it was a very effective little biplane.

30½ acres. This was neatly packaged to the north and north-east of Canley Halt railway station.

Originally called the 'Hearsall Land' (Hearsall Common adjoined it, as a buffer from Coventry city itself), it soon became familiarly and officially known as 'Canley' – and by the end of the War in 1918 it had quite outstripped the parent plant at Cash's Lane. In the years which followed, it would grow, and grow, and grow ...

The skeleton steelwork of new factory buildings at Canley grew rapidly during 1916, what became affectionately known as 'Ivy Cottage' was established close to the railway halt as the company's new administrative HQ, all private car production had long ended, and by 1917 Canley had become a military powerhouse.

In the meantime, Siegfried Bettman had stood down as chairman during 1916 (he had been in office since 1911), to be replaced by Dick Maudslay (who, therefore, had two massive jobs to do): Bettman returned to his first love, the Triumph motorcycle business, which would eventually go on to sell thousands of motorcycles to the British army.

Standard, like other booming British engineering concerns of that period, turned its hand to making as many, and as varied, weapons of war as were required, and soon discovered that even 'the new Canley' was not big enough to construct all of them. Not only did the company make thousands of BE-12 aircraft, but it would also go on to produce RAE RE-8 reconnaissance biplanes, Sopwith Pups, and Bristol fighter machines as well. No fewer than 1600 aircraft were built at Canley before the War was won; yet the entire operation was abruptly closed down in 1918/1919 when contracts were abruptly terminated. In addition, there were the aeroplane engine components, components for trucks and other commercial vehicles, the Stokes trench mortar, and much more, all built in the same period.

Not only that, but the company also took on the management of a massive, seemingly endless, artillery shell-filling contract that necessitated the requisitioning of four small existing factories in nearby Leamington Spa (one of which had been a skating rink in peacetime!), and utilising a mainly female workforce.

Things did not always go smoothly. By 1917, with more and more aircraft beginning to emerge from the Canley assembly halls, the company found it increasingly irritating to build aircraft, then to have to remove their wings, have the machines transported to a nearby airfield (which would eventually became Coventry's airport) a few miles away to have them re-assembled, and flown off for testing, and delivery!

Surely, the directors thought, a smooth grass runway could be cleared and laid along the north side of the Canley complex for the completed fighters to be delivered? Yes, of course, it could have been done (and there was ample undeveloped ground space at Canley at that time to make this possible), but the local authorities refused permission, not once, but on several occasions.

It was at the height of this military activity that Standard sought to buy another large area of ground immediately to the west of its still-evolving Canley site, and truly underpinned its future. Without this purchase, indeed, the company would not have been able to expand in the way that it finally did.

In mid-1918, negotiations were opened with Lord Leigh to buy a further 99 acres of land. Lord Leigh asked for £10,000. Standard originally offered £9000, but the deal changed a little in the weeks which followed, so that in August 1918 a total of 112 acres was acquired for £10,000: the deal was finalised in 1919. If and when Standard was ready (and could afford) to expand, it now had lots of space to do so, all backed up by planning approval from the local authorities.

Immediately after this, therefore, Standard owned so much land that it could find space for a golf course to be laid out, would eventually add several more factory blocks, and would still have space to give up land (reluctantly, it has to be said) for the construction of the A45 by-pass road, and two large Government-financed 'shadow factories' in the late 1930s.

This is the only known survivor of a Standard-built Sopwith Pup single-seater. Restoration is in progress.

But it wasn't all good news. With the War won in 1918, suddenly there were no more fighter and reconnaissance aircraft to be built – and Standard had to plan to revert to building cars as soon as possible. Even when the shell-filling plants in Leamington Spa had been closed down, there were no fewer than 2600 Standard workers in Coventry who needed employment. Not only that, but the late payment of some government contracts meant that the bank overdraft once reached £130,000.

The next few years, it seemed, were going to be tough.

This was the anatomy of the 1914-1918-type Sopwith Pup single-seater, as built by Standard in big numbers. It would be years before Standard's private cars even approached this level of sophistication.

CHAPTER 3

Vintage Standards 1919-1927

With the Armistice officially in force from 11am on 11 November 1918 (the eleventh hour, on the eleventh day, in the eleventh month ...), Standard could once again begin to think about its future as a motor car manufacturer. The last 'prewar' Standard had been built in May 1915 – more than three years earlier – and, for a time, very little thought seems to have gone into producing a successor to it.

Dick Maudslay, however, had not been completely idle. Maybe it was not totally patriotic to work on private-enterprise engineering while Standard was meant to be absorbed in war work, but in 1917 and 1918 he had commissioned work on a much-improved engine for the little 'S' (the Rhyl model), and had personally done the development driving. As he reported to the Board in April 1918:

"Mr Maudslay took this opportunity of pointing out to the Board that the postwar experimental overhead-valve engine, fitted to his two-seater car, which he was using, and which had already covered some hundreds of miles, required extended testing before a definite opinion could be formed ..."

So, work was at least under way, though at the moment Standard did not know when it would officially be allowed to turn a 'why don't we ...?' proposal into reality. In the meantime, the company had also pulled out of its distribution agreement with the Pytchley Autocar Co in London, for it wished to set up its own West End showrooms in the capital. In due course this was achieved in 1919, at 49 Pall Mall, where Delaunay Belleville had recently been selling its own French-manufactured products, the arrangement lasting until 1929, when the lease expired.

Although Maudslay was by no means the visionary his successor, John Black, later proved to be, he certainly had big plans for the Canley site. To quote from a note made, for the archives (way back in the 1950s, but referring to events which unfolded immediately after the War):

"Ample provision ... could be made for facilities for recreation of the employees ... a testing track for the cars could be made around the boundary of the land.

"With regard to the facilities for recreation, a golf course was constructed and football, cricket, tennis and bowls grounds completed [It is close to these areas that the Standard-Triumph Memorial was set up in the early 2000s]. The testing track was also commenced and partly made. This track would ultimately have been over two miles in length ..."

Early in the 1920s, *The Autocar* visited the burgeoning test track, and commented:

"The track and hills are now principally used for the

testing of brakes and clutches, and enable this work to be carried out better than on a test hill some miles from the factory. The gradients on the hills are not long, but are accurately measured to be 1-in-4, 1-in-5 and 1-in-6 ..."

Unhappily, Maudslay's master-plan was never to be completed – the test track, for instance, was never put into use – because his carefully-assembled property was later savaged by the same Coventry local authority which had encouraged him to expand in the first place ...

In the 1920s, however, this could not be forecast by company planners, which explains why a further ten acres of land – a strip along the northern edge of the site, and adjoining the Tile Hill Road – was bought in 1923 for £1850 and speedily allocated for the building of company-owned houses. Standard, in fact, eventually developed a policy of buying houses in and close to Coventry, in which to install its senior directors and managers (which made them beholden to the company's generosity, in a way, but avoided attention from the tax man) – as Leyland were only to discover after it took over the financially ailing company in 1961.

Although the company was still not financially stable in the first few months of 1919, following the end of hostilities, work went on as rapidly as possible at Canley, to convert the big assembly halls from building aircraft, to producing private cars, especially as there an existing workforce of more than 2600 people looking for machines to build. With that in mind, and frankly, as a commercial stop-gap, as an interim measure, early in the year Standard put together just 198 of the 1915-type Model S.

Then, as its first major postwar project, the company launched the new SLS model in April 1919. This was still a compromise while true postwar projects came to fruition. Based on the layout of the original S, but bigger, better and more completely developed in all respects, it had a 1328cc derivative of the side-valve power unit, which had been 1087cc in the S. The upgrade had been made, rather simply, by increasing the stroke from 90mm to 110mm, the bore, and, therefore, the two-bearing cylinder block, was changed only in detail, and the 'L' of the SLS title clearly stood for Long stroke ...

Clearly, the overhead-valve engine that Dick Maudslay had been testing since 1918 was still not yet ready, so to keep the pedigree fresh and to give its dealers and potential customers something to talk about, the SLS also found itself with a 7ft 8.5in wheelbase – 2.5 inches longer than that of the S – but with the same 4ft 0in wheel tracks. This allowed both two and four-seater tourer bodies to be offered. The front-end had been re-styled in detail, electric lighting and starting was standard, as was a 'dickey seat' in the tourer body (which, as ever, was manufactured and assembled by Standard itself).

Still a light and simple car, it was claimed to have a chassis weight of just 8cwt (896lb/406kg), and went on sale at £275. Prices, of course, had shot up due to the inflationary effects of the war, but the SLS price compared unfavourably with the 1914 price of the S, which was £195. Nevertheless, a temporary boom in demand for new cars ensured that the SLS would succeeded, for more than 200 cars as month were being built by 1920, and profits were being made.

That car, however, was clearly just another interim model, for in mid-1920 yet another new model, the first true postwar Standard, the 11.6hp type SLO model, went on

This extremely smart and well-preserved 'Stratford' derivative of the SLO4 emphasises that Standard was expanding to satisfy middle-class demand in the 1920s.

sale. At first glance, it all looked rather the same as the cars it displaced, but technical analysts saw it for what it was – a very clever and thoughtful up-date of the existing range, a prototype of which Dick Maudslay had been driving for some considerable time.

This latest car not only had a further-enlarged four-cylinder engine (68 x 110mm, 1598cc), but now had an overhead-valve layout, which must have given the company's big rivals, Austin and Morris, cause for concern, as both were still wedded to old-style side-valve power units.

This smart SLO two-seater Tourer, complete with the shoulder-shaped radiator, which currently appeared on all such Standards, was typical of so many 'vintage' cars coming out of Canley in the 1920s.

The Autocar described this new car very aptly as: "... not entirely new, but is a further evolution of that original type which commenced with the prewar S, was followed by the SLS (long stroke), and now enters upon Series SLO (long-stroke, overhead valves). Between this last and the earlier type chassis, the chief difference lies in the larger-sized engine, which just falls within the 1600cc class ..."

Not only was it larger and more completely equipped than any previous 'small' Standard had been, (the wheelbase had been lengthened to 9ft 0in, though the original 4ft 0in tracks were retained), but it ushered in the first of what would be a string of overhead-valve-engined Standards. The design itself was simple and rugged enough, and like several of the units which would be developed from it, there was a cast iron cylinder block and cylinder heads.

Let us not get too excited about the 1920s engineering, however, for Standard revealed that it developed only 13bhp at 1000rpm, while boasting that it could exceed 45mph. All of which came at the very ambitious price of £595 for a two-seater tourer derivative, or £645 for the four-seater.

Ambitious expansion

Even so, this new model was a great success, and Standard expanded swiftly to deal with the demand. Gone were the days when the company might produce a handful of very costly six-cylinder cars – here was an attempt to get in to what passed for a 'mass market' in the first of what we now know as the 'vintage' years. In 1920, indeed, the Board agreed that it needed to increase its authorised capital, raising the limit from £50,000 to a very substantial £300,000.

At corporate level, Coventry solicitor Charles Band, whose company had already done much work for Maudslay in establishing and expanding Standard (not least in finalising the purchase of the Canley estate), joined the board of directors, setting up a personal link which would last for well over thirty years, for Band would eventually become the company's chairman, and not retire (in favour of war hero Lord Tedder) until the 1950s.

The company was already working up a proposal to make it possible to manufacture 100 cars every week. Perhaps sales to back this output would not be made with the SLO, even though the car was a best-seller by any previous Standard levels. The nomination for that task rested with a new range of 'small' Standards, for in October 1921 a new car called the 8hp V1 model was launched, one with an overhead-valve engine, and priced at £325.

Immediately after this occasion, incidentally, the company announced its profits for the 11-month period ending August 1921, which stood at a very creditable £96,240, with £80,697 carried forward to the reserves. Financial stability, it seemed, had been achieved – but, though the company rarely admitted to it at the time, much of this must have been achieved as a result of the recent vast government-financed building and expansion at Canley.

Introduced in 1921, the 8hp V1 type, complete with 1087cc engine (the same size as the original S), was only in production for a short time. It was really too big for an 'Eight,' so only 500 such cars were produced.

As it happened this new car, which keen-eyed observers could see was evolved from the SLO, and juggled with a whole range of already-developed components, was not a success. Although it was very keenly priced by comparison with the SLO, it faced increasingly strong competition in the market place, not only from Morris's all-conquering 'bullnose' Cowley, but shortly from Austin's tiny little Austin Seven as well.

It was, perhaps, too large for an 8hp car, especially when the dimensions of the Austin Seven were considered. Although meant to drop into place in the range as an effective replacement for the SLS, the new 8hp car had an 8ft 6in wheelbase (which was only six inches less than that of the SLO), and retained the same 4ft 0in axles and wheel tracks.

Although the engine itself measured only 1088cc (62 x 90mm), which was exactly the same as that of the original S/Rhyl, it was rated at 9.5hp by the new-fangled Treasury Rating (which meant that its title as a 'new 8hp' car was less than honest), and had overhead valves. By any standards, it was a cut-price effort, as an earlier Standard historian John Davy once described so succinctly:

"... although it looked very modern at the time, and lingered in the catalogues for a year or two, few were made, and it must go down on record as a failure. The engine had overhead valves, the rocker gear was exposed, and required lubricating with an oil can, while the crankshaft ran on two ball bearings. Other innovations included tubular connecting rods, aluminium pistons, coil ignition and, as a supplement to the crank handle, a hand starter was fitted near the driver's seat, consisting of a cable connected to a rack-and-pinion mechanism on the front of the crankshaft ..."

Looked at in retrospect it looks amazingly crude, and even at the time, the exposed pushrods and rocker gear must have vulnerable to dust contamination from the roads of Britain, which were still not all totally sealed.

At the time, the point made by several observers was not only that this car was quite overshadowed in the market place by the SLO, but suffered from a lack of development – indeed, a lack of thought about details in its specification. This, perhaps, explained why Standard made haste to replace it with a different model, called the V2, in April 1923, which was different in many respects. Not only did it use an enlarged overhead-valve engine of 1307cc, but it ran on an 8ft 9in wheelbase.

No doubt prompted by Standard's publicists, *The Autocar* described the new model as: "In the main a revised edition of the recent 8hp car [which, as I have already pointed out, was really a 9.5hp model], the new 11hp vehicle is equipped with an engine of larger bore, namely 68mm, has an improved worm and segment steering gear ..."

The 'Horsepower Tax'

Throughout this book, there are many references to the horsepower 'rating' (or 'Treasury rating') of a particular car, and in Britain in the 1920s, 1930s and 1940s, many models were badged and advertised using that rating – Standard Little Nine, Flying Twelve and Flying Twenty all being perfect cases in point.

What became known as the 'horsepower tax' was introduced in Britain in 1921, being a crude (and, some say, quite unfair) way of charging every car an annual Road Fund Licence. With the tax originally set at £1-per-'horsepower,' this meant that smallest-engined cars paid the least annual duty, which meant that in many ways it encouraged the design of small-engined cars.

After consulting the industry, and motorists' organisations including the Royal Automobile Club (the RAC) as early as 1906, the Government introduced this annual levy in 1921. From that moment on, the engine of every car had what was known as a 'Treasury Rating' (it was sometimes called the 'RAC Rating').

That horsepower rating was calculated using the following mathematical formula:

$$\text{HP} = \frac{d^2 \times n}{2.5}$$

In this equation d is the diameter of the engine cylinder in inches, squared, and n is the number of cylinders. The sum of these, divided by 2.5, gives the horsepower rating – HP.

This means that an engine with a small cylinder bore was automatically rated lower than one with a large bore, which explains why almost all British engines of the period had small bores and long strokes. Standard's Flying Eight engine of 1938, as an example, had a bore and stroke of 57 x 100mm (2.244 x 3.94in), which was grotesque, as it inhibited the breathing and the developed horsepower of the unit.

Manufacturers, however (and Standard was no exception), sometimes 'fudged' the issue by advertising a new model – say – as an 'Eleven or a 'Twelve,' when the official treasuring rating was Fourteen (14). There are many examples of this.

For much of the 1920s, Standard cars used overhead-valve engines (like this 1.3-litre V3 type) in which the valve-gear pushrods and rockers – were totally exposed to dust, water and general debris from the surroundings. Regular – daily, even – cleaning and maintenance was necessary.

In addition, the chassis frame was stiffened, the tourer bodyshell was higher and wider to provide more interior space, the equipment in general was modernised – yet the prices were set to start from a bargain £200. This was less than previously asked of the '8hp' model, and partly explains why demand was brisk from the start.

Amazingly, although the V1 had been designed as a cheaper car, Standard was also working on an upmarket version. Sensationally, this was a V8 based on two identical SLO cylinder cases, mounted in a 60-degree vee layout, on a common crankcase. The pistons drove a flat-plane crankshaft, and the enclosed valves were driven by a 16-lobed camshaft sitting in the vee itself. All this, in a chassis very similar to the SLO, was called the Model AS. Though such a car was shown at the Olympia Show in 1922, it does not seem to have progressed any further than the prototype. Perhaps there were many reasons for this, but one technical point is that flat-plane V8s are notoriously difficult to balance, yet counter-rotating balancer shafts were not incorporated in the Standard design.

At the same time, during 1922, the Standard range was becoming more complex, for the SLO was developed into the SLO4, with an enlarged engine (a 75mm bore instead of 68mm), of 1944cc. This engine was then mounted in a chassis with a 110in wheelbase, and with new wider wheel tracks of 54in: for 1923 that wheelbase was enlarged even further, to 116in.

For Standard, its output, and its prospects were now improving steadily. More than 4000 SLO4 models were produced in 1923. For the next season, the 68 x 90mm/11.4hp engine was fitted into an improved chassis design, still using a 105in wheelbase, but with 51in tracks. This replacement model became the V3, and would be the most successful of the entire 'V-range.' Prices ranged from £200 to £275, depending on the chosen body, and by the time production ended in 1926, no fewer than 15,450 examples had been produced.

More than 10,000 cars were produced in calendar year 1924 – truly this was a boom time for the still young Standard company – for by the end of 1923 the company had settled down with an established model range for the next two years, which pleased the dealer chain (and the customers) very well indeed. 'Count them on the Road' was one of the company's current advertising slogans, which made a simple, truthful, and telling point.

This was a time when the Board directors awarded themselves increased salaries, and at the same time Charles Band was encouraged to keep on looking for extra land, which Lord Leigh might be willing to sell off, so that Standard's Canley 'estate' could be further enlarged.

This was also a period in which the 'footprint' of the Canley factory increased dramatically – it more than doubled in three years, for it had been 188,339ft^2 in 1922, and became 420,042ft^2 by the end of 1925. Even though it was not yet fashionable to talk about such things, Standard (led by Dick Maudslay and ably backed up by General Manager John Budge), was clearly adept at 'product planning,' for at this time the entire private-car range centred around two basic chassis/engine/transmission layouts (the now-familiar 11.4hp four-cylinder engine, complete with its exposed push rods and valve gear, and the new and more conventional 13.9hp engine which had been launched in 1922), all clad in a variety of tourer (mostly) and saloon (some) coachwork, which was manufactured, painted and entirely trimmed 'in house' at Canley.

Standard, however, was not yet a one-site operation, for Cash's Lane (machine shops), Bishopgate Green (mainly sheet metal fabrications), and Widdrington Road (repairs and spare parts operations) were all still in use close to the centre of Coventry. Further rationalisation, of course, was desirable (and undeveloped land was certainly available at Canley), but this further expansion would have to wait for several years (see chapter 4), when the 'new man' – Captain John Black – got his teeth into the re-jigging of the business.

At the Olympia Motor Show in October 1924, there was surprisingly little advance publicity, for the latest models, though cable-operated four-wheel brakes were finally available on a Standard car – not standard, but optional for the add-on cost of a mere £10. Prices started at £345, rising to £475, for the SLO4 model, which compared with the £200 to £275 asked for the contemporary V3 model range.

The engine, too, was improved. Standard, in fact, needed a new engine, not only because the S-derived 'four' had reached the limits of its enlargement (the original of 1913 had been a 1088cc unit, the ultimate mid-1920s version was only 1598cc), but because this was looking rather old-fashioned by modern standards, and could be improved no further unless major redesign took place.

This was the 'Kenilworth' version of open coachwork applied to the V3 chassis in the 1920s.

This was the period in which many such Standards became more familiarly known by the title of their body styles, rather than merely V3 or SLO4 types. By 1924 the smaller-engined V3s were variously known as Canley, Coleshill, Kineton, Kenilworth or Piccadilly types – all but the last of those being the names of towns and villages in Warwickshire, while the larger SLO4 models were also known as Leamington, Warwick, Portland and Pall Mall. In all, it was a complex time for Standard's planners to cope with, for at this time there were eleven different body styles all being built up, and fitted out, at Canley – five of them on V3, and six of them on SLO4 chassis.

[A comparison with Sir John Black's decision to produce the Vanguard in a single saloon body-style in the late 1940s is startling ...]

Even so, although Standard had clearly put a great deal of time, effort and investment capital into developing the new range, because of its relatively high horsepower rating (and taxation!) it was not a car which took the British market by storm, where it had to compete, head on, with cars such as the Austin Twelve at £355, and the wildly-popular Morris Bullnose Oxford at £285. It was, on the other hand, very popular in what were now becoming Standard's strongest overseas markets – notably Australia, India, South Africa, and even parts of the South American continent.

Unhappily (and none of Standard's top people were to discover this until it was almost too late), the V4 range did not sell as well as the company had originally hoped, and the overhead-valve four-cylinder engine, so expensively developed, would only have a life of about four years. Standard, indeed, would eventually realise that its buying public was not very interested in the 'advances' brought by overhead valves (not as much, for sure, as they were in mechanical simplicity and reduced running costs), for when

In the late 1920s, it was cars like this 'Selby' model, which did so much to make the Standard car successful with middle-class motorists. Nothing flashy, nothing technically advanced – just solid, reliable, Coventry engineering.

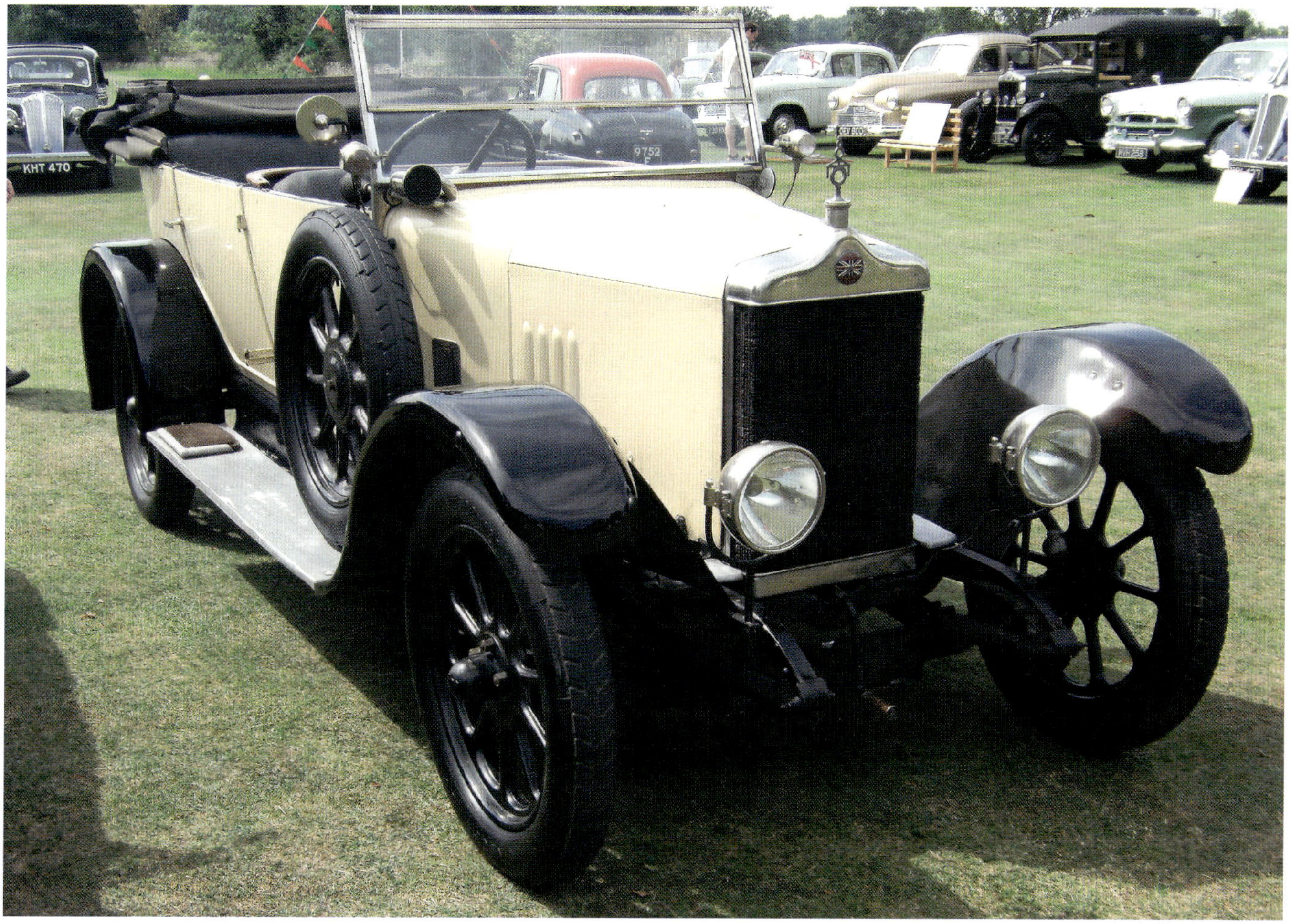

This charming 1924 'Warwick' model was so typical of the mid-vintage Standard period. Note the artillery-style wheels.

In the mid-1920s, Standard's styling was simple, but practical. This was a 1925 'Pall Mall' 14hp model. Four wheel brakes became available as an optional extra on Standards at about this time.

a new engineering regime was unveiled in the late 1920s, new ranges of completely new, simple, and cheap-to-build side-valve engines would be announced, these being good enough to take the company smoothly through the 1930s.

This, perhaps, was one factor in the rather modest launch of the 1926 model range (in September 1925), when the accent seemed to be on detail improvements, rather than massive innovation. Mechanically, the V3 and SLO4 types continued virtually as before, though on the V4, not only did four-wheel brakes become standard, but shock absorbers were also part of the specification, too. A number of new body styles appeared (some of them replacing existing names), which explains the launch of Knowle and Coventry types on the smaller V3, along with Stratford and Charlecote types on the SLO4.

In 1924, the removal of import duties on foreign cars (this was called 'the removal of the McKenna duties ...') had a predictable result: the selling price of foreign cars in the UK decreased considerably, and sales of domestic products were hit hard. Standard, however, survived this (it was, after all Britain's third-biggest carmaker at the time, behind Austin and Morris), but there were more shocks to follow.

At the end of 1926, with the nation's economy still reeling from the economic and sociological impact of the General Strike, Standard seemed to lose its presence of mind by launching, not a new, small-engined car which common sense dictated, but the company's first six-cylinder-engined car since the prewar period.

This beautifully maintained Kenilworth tourer, on the V3 chassis, so typical of the Standards being built in small numbers just before Captain John Black arrived on the managerial scene.

The 11.4hp V3 and the 13.9hp SLO4 models were both dropped, to be replaced by an even larger 4-cylinder model, The 75 x 110mm/1944cc SLO4 engine was much modified, and matched to a new three-speed gearbox fitted to a new 116in wheelbase chassis with generously dimensioned 56in tracks. This was initially described as a 12/24hp, and later changed to a 14/28hp, to become known as the V4.

Madness? Not, according to Standard, if export possibilities were taken into account. One can, however, point out that it was the collapse of a potentially large export contract (for sending V4s and V6s to Australia) which brought on a real financial crisis, when turnover suddenly dropped by a quarter.

But, of what followed, there is no doub: Standard's major financial troubles led its bankers, Barclays, to threaten to send in the Receiver, which led to the appointment of a new chief engineer [as far as I can see, this was the very first time such an official position had been nominated at Standard]. It is also known that William Morris (later, of course, to become Lord Nuffield) intervened on Standard's behalf, threatening to withdraw his substantial accounts from Barclay if it fore-closed on Standard: this, apparently, ensured that Standard was not made bankrupt there and then. This then led to the hurried design of a new small car in 1927 (as described in the next chapter), which all stemmed from this period.

It is easy to see why and how Standard went wrong (the company was moving resolutely up-market, making and developing larger-engined/higher-tax models at precisely the time when British car buyers were demanding small, cheaper and more economical products) but, at this range, it is difficult to see how and why this happened. We know, for sure, that founder Dick Maudslay was no longer young and therefore (to use modern parlance) could not be considered 'trendy,' but it is still a mystery to see how he could not have read the signs.

Though Standard output figures for this period are no longer available, one example (from the dominant rival, Austin) makes a strong point. From 1923, when the little Austin Seven went on sale, its production rocketed to 14,000 in 1926, and to 26,447 in 1929: in the same period, production of the Austin 12/4 (a similar car, in so many ways, to the SLO4 model) fell from 10,000 to 8759 and continued to fall in the years which followed.

All of which is a great pity, for the new car, the V6 (dubbed 18-36 at first, and 18-42 as a follow-up) was a technically interesting car which deserved to succeed more than it actually did. Unhappily, it was not a car with any previous Standard pedigree (there had been no six-cylinder Standard in the range since 1914, and none at all after the Great War was over ...), and accordingly it needed to be reliable from the very start to establish its reputation – which unfortunately it was not.

The new V6 was introduced in October 1926, when it received a positively reverential reception from the specialist media. Almost all the attention went to the new six-cylinder engine, the related gearbox (still a three-speeder) – and the remarkably ambitious price for the tourer of just £345. Several other body derivatives were also available, the most expensive being the £435 asked for the coach-built four-door saloon.

Innovative chassis design at Standard was clearly not a priority at this time, for there were virtually no novelties on the V6. It was, of course, a substantially larger car than anything else which had been produced at Canley since

This metal-panelled 'Teignmouth' saloon of the late 1920s shows off the 'shouldered-radiator' front-end style which was so typical of cars built at Canley during this period.

1919, for it ran on a 10ft 2in wheelbase, with 4ft 8in wheel tracks, yet the half-elliptic leaf springs, the worm-and-wheel steering, the right-hand gear change, and the four-wheel braking installations were no more than updates of what was already available on the V4. This time, though, there was a Dewandre vacuum servo for the brakes.

The engine, however, was big, well-designed, and looking much more modern than could ever have been expected. Although it shared neither the same bore, nor the same stroke as the V4's 1.9-litre 'four,' and had a sturdy seven-bearing crankshaft, it shared a number of common structural features – both in what they did, and how they looked – with that 'four.'

As with the V4 engine, the overhead-valve combustion chamber layout was so laid out as to locate the line of sparkplugs to the left side of the cylinder head, and the dynamo and magneto installation was also on the same side of the engine. Interestingly, there was a new multi-plate clutch, running in oil, to deal with the increased torque.

Amazingly, although it was Standard's next generation of six-cylinder engines which make most of the headlines (these being the power units chosen by William Lyons for the early SS1 models ...], they would have side valves, and appear much less pre-possessing than the V6 engine. There is no doubt, however, that the neat visual style of the V6 engine was well regarded in the industry, and the sturdy layout of the bottom end – not many so-called mass-production sixes had seven-bearing crankshafts – also established its own reputation.

Even so, more major changes had to come, and this could only be achieved by changes of thinking, and with the input of new ideas. Maudslay realised that he needed to re-establish Standard near the cheaper/smaller car end of the British market place, though at that time he had no-one on board, with experience, to achieve it for him.

Finally making the big decision. which had been delayed because, one understands, Dick Maudslay did not want to offend John Budge by bringing a specialist of equal technical standing to him, on 1 March 1927 he appointed Alfred H Wilde as his new Chief Engineer.

Wilde, a Midlander who had started his working life designing aero engines, moved across to the motor industry after the Great War, and later became chief engineer of Hotchkiss in France (a company then controlled by William Morris of Morris Motors fame). In more recent times he had returned to work for Morris at its Engines plant (which was, itself, ex-Hotchkiss) in Coventry, so he was already well-known to the 'motor industry mafia' which operated so efficiently in the city at that time ...)

Clearly Maudslay had thought long and hard about this appointment, certainly enough to record it in the Board minutes, where Wilde was appointed: "... originally for a six-month trial period, at a salary of £800, plus 1 per cent commission on company profits. The commission to be a guaranteed minimum of £400 in a year ..."

Even so, by 1927, as noted, Standard was in financial trouble – big trouble. Major investments in plant, machinery and new models had not yet paid off, and the business was losing money. Realising that it would have to take bold action, or go under, the Board resolved to take further measures. With a new chief engineer now appointed, and already slaving away on the design of a new small Standard, the next move was to bolster up the balance sheet.

First of all, a massive £200,000 Rights issue was proposed (the directors, mainly Dick Maudslay of course, would have to take up those Rights by injecting more money ...), and at the same time Barclays Bank was persuaded to increase the company's overdraft facility to no less than £250,000. No doubt it was because Barclays already had one representative on the Board that this facility was granted, the effect on the company's confidence was soon apparent, and the Rights issue proposal (which might have been difficult to complete) was abandoned.

Deep breath time – all that Standard could now do was to continue selling the existing overhead-valve-engined cars as strongly as it could, hope that Wilde's new small-car design could do the trick in 1928, and pray for better times just around the corner.

CHAPTER 4

The First of the Nines 1927-1935

Starting with its new-for-1928 models, it seemed almost as if Standard had taken a deep breath, given thanks (especially to its bankers!) for continued survival, and was determined to modernise, and get away from what were looking to be increasingly old-fashioned products. All in all, this was to be a turbulent time for the company.

It is easy to say this in hindsight, but all the signs were that Dick Maudslay (already in his mid-fifties) was beginning to tire of business, needed help and inspiration to keep it fresh, yet decided to do something about the product range before that help arrived.

As we have already seen, Standard's 1927 selling season concentrated on two mechanically-related model ranges – the 1944cc 14-28 (four-cylinder) and the 2223cc 18-36 (six-cylinder cars). Both had overhead valves, and both were gradually easing the brand up-market, away from the big competition from Austin and Morris. As has already been noted, with the benefit of hindsight, that strategy now appears to have been misguided.

As *The Autocar* made clear when the new Nine was announced:

"As time progressed, evolution caused the models to grow in size, until the latter years have found these makers with a gap in their programme where the small car used to be. For the future, this gap will be filled by an entirely new model, an 8.9hp four-cylinder car ..."

This big change became clear in September 1927, when Standard astonished the industry by launching the first of the Nine models, prices for which would start at £190 (£215 for the 'Filey' four-door saloon). Although this could not match Morris' amazingly successful Cowley (£170), it was a step in the right direction, and made Standard competitive once again. That price, in fact, would be a Godsend to Britain's Standard dealers, for the previous (and continuing) entry level model, the V4 (also known as the 14-32), cost £260 and was a much more substantial car.

Although legend has it that design and development of the new Nine took only six months (and was initiated by sketching out the full-size chassis on the floor of the Directors' Board Room), that only two hard-working prototypes were ever constructed – and that the new car was supposedly based on the design of the existing French Mathis, this rumour is probably somewhat exaggerated, in view of the large amount of new engineering that went into the new model. Agreed, Standard had purchased a Mathis car (a French design) from Strasbourg for study, but the biggest and most novel influences were certainly those brought by the newly-appointed Chief Engineer, Alfred Wilde, himself.

The fact of the matter is that, although it was a very simple (and what, in hindsight, one might call a typical 'vintage') car, it would still have needed a substantial design staff (which Standard only barely possessed) to design, test, detail and prepare for production a family car which had a brand-new engine, a brand-new three-speed gearbox, and a brand-new worm-drive rear axle.

Canley, let it be made very clear, was extensively reworked, and expanded at this time, to make way for what Dick Maudslay was convinced would be a big seller (he was right), and the first examples were not truly ready for delivery until the start of 1928.

Even before describing the new Nine (it would later be re-engineered, improved, and become known as the Little Nine when a larger-engined Big Nine eventually went on sale), I must now break off to pay homage to its power unit:

A COMPLETELY NEW GENERATION OF ENGINES

Perhaps the pundits did not see it at the time, but the all-new 1153cc engine introduced in late 1927 for the Nine (and inspired by Wilde) was one of the most important 'building blocks' which Standard would ever evolve. Although the original was a modest little power unit at the time – after all, it only had a two-main-bearing crankshaft, a side-valve cylinder head, and powered a sweet, but distinctly underwhelming Standard Nine – it would eventually develop to become larger, more powerful, and would go on to much greater things.

Even before describing its origins, I should, therefore, note than it was the first side-valve engine which Standard had designed since the end of World War One (the immediate postwar SLS and 8hp models had used prewar engine designs). As we now know, it was an astonishingly long-lived engine family, for evolutions and derivatives would be built up to 1948, it would eventually grow to no less than 1776cc, would take on a three-bearing crankshaft, and would even spawn an overhead-valve cylinder head derivative, too. Total production would be in hundreds of thousands – so, by any standard, it has to rank as one of the shrewdest investments ever made by the original management team.

The original engine was at once simple and robust, with a bore and stroke of 60 x 101.6mm, and a capacity of just 1153cc. That suspiciously precise stroke dimension, incidentally, translates to exactly 4.0 inches in Imperial measure, and the cylinder bore was chosen to allow the new car to slip in under the 'Nine Treasury Horsepower' fiscal licensing barrier.

[At this moment – and to repeat the information listed in the panel on page 47 – I should note that the stroke would eventually be lengthened to 106mm, and the cylinder bore would be enlarged to 76mm, all without changing the basic dimensions of the original power unit ...]

Here was a simple engine, with a cast iron cylinder block, and a cast iron head. The casting of the block/crankcase extended down below the centre line of the two-bearing crankshaft, the dynamo and magneto (which provided HT electricity for the sparking plugs) were fitted on the left side of the engine, and the starter motor was on the right side. The single Solex carburettor fed through a passage in the cylinder block, to a gallery below the valves.

This is what *The Autocar* noted about the general layout:

"It is distinctly interesting to see that side valves are used. In this connection it seems that when all modern ideas are incorporated in an up-to-date side-valve design with the best shape combustion chamber, there is little to choose between side valves and overhead valves so far as the efficiency of an ordinary touring engine is concerned ..."

All of which proved, no doubt, that this was what Standard's publicists urged it to understand – as the principal reason for choosing a side-valve layout was to ensure simplicity, and to reduce costs.

To match it there was a new type of three-speed gearbox, still without synchromesh (such refinements were still in the future, and then originally only in North America), but now with a centre gear change (that on the larger models was on the right side of the driver's seat), and for the first time on Standards, with that gearbox mounted in unit with the engine itself. As with the larger Standards, too, there were semi-elliptic leaf springs at front and rear, along with worm drive for the rear axle, this being an under-slung worm, which helped keep the line of the propeller shaft as low as possible. Cable-operated four-wheel brakes were standard equipment.

It soon became evident, by the way, that Standard had clearly worked out a long-term master plan for the use of this engine, as a straight-six derivative, which would use many of the same basic dimensions and machining facilities, would soon follow – and that, too, would have a long and distinguished history in Standard, SS and SS-Jaguar models, too.

Introduced at the end of the 1920s, the Little Nine engine/gearbox assembly was one of the most important 'building blocks' yet to be commissioned by Standard. The Little Nine (and the Big Nine, which soon joined it) were both hugely successful best-sellers, which enabled the new boss, John Black, to expand Standard mightily in the 1930s.

All this, of course, confirms to the author that original project work, maybe even some testing, had already taken place before Alfred Wilde joined the company.

As well as the engine, the rest of the Nine chassis itself was all-new. Although there was little obvious innovation – by almost any measure, this looked like a typical mid/late-20s British family car – the dimensions in general tell us that it was all fresh, and had clearly required a lot of investment to make it so. If only Standard had known at the time this was going to cause some financial heartache in the future.

The whole car, especially the chassis frame itself, was considerably smaller than anything else in the existing Standard range, yet the ever-diplomatic specialist media of the period insisted that the body styles were roomy enough to accommodate 'six foot passengers.' Even so, the new car was only 128in long (remember that 30 years later Alec Issigonis's Mini was 120in long, only eight inches shorter), only had a 92in wheelbase, with channel section chassis sidemembers, and 45in wheel tracks (these were actually three inches narrower than those of the Edwardian S of 15 years earlier), and was simplicity itself. This barely comparing with the 116in and 56in (respectively) dimensions under the existing 14-28 model.

Standard proposed to build most of its own coachwork at Canley, still using the traditional methods of a wooden frame with steel or fabric covering panels, which meant that three models – two-seater and four-seater tourers, and the four-door fabric-covered saloon – were immediately available.

Added to this momentous announcement, both the existing ranges – what we know as the V4 and V6 types – were continued, and improved. Pushing the 'product planning' possibilities to their limits (though that phrase was not yet familiar in the British industry), the 14-28 was continued, with its three-speed gearbox, while a new derivative, the 14-32, had a four-speed gearbox, no transmission brake, and a much stiffer chassis frame, along with a revised front axle, and braking system. Similar changes to the V6 saw the 18-36 continued, but now accompanied by a 28-42, which had the new four-speed gearbox and all the related mechanical updates of the 14-32.

Clearly, Standard was confident about the new Nine and its reputation, for, immediately after the Scottish Motor Show in November, it lent a saloon for *The Autocar* magazine staff to return from Glasgow to Leamington Spa (where the staff writer lived). To quote the publication:

"We were met ... in Glasgow, by a four-seater fabric saloon with some 18,000 miles (28,968km) already to its credit. Being desirous of getting home without waste of time, we arranged with the driver, who had brought the car up from Coventry, to attempt to cover the journey in a single run – 350 miles (563km) without a break, except for meals.

"It was a long trip, but not a wearisome one by any means ... According to the mileage recorder the distance [by way of Scotch Corner] was 347 miles (558km). From end-to-end the Standard ran without a falter ... most of the time we cruised at a good round pace, even though it is not claimed that the car can do more than an honest 45mph ...

"Altogether, the new 9hp Standard saloon appears to be a thoroughly sound taut car, an engineering job without afterthoughts ..."

Because Standard realised that, commercially, the Nine held the future of the business in its hand, it made great efforts to publicise the car, and the business. By March, a whole range of different body styles had been made available on the new small chassis, including 'fabric' saloons, sliding roof saloons, two, and four-seater types, all varying in price between £198.50 and £245. Within a year, too, a longer-wheelbase version, the Teignmouth, complete with an enlarged (1287cc) version of the engine, would also be announced.

The problem, however, was that the new cars were neither ultra-stylish, nor relatively fast movers. Independent road tests showed that a Nine saloon could do no more than 51mph flat out (and just 33mph in second gear), while recording up to 40mpg.

Even so, although Maudslay was already looking around for a 'live-wire' to help him rejuvenate the operation (the live-wire, John Black, was not yet available to him ...), he wanted the media to see how much he had invested in the business. When Maurice Sampson of *The Autocar* visited Standard's Coventry factories in the high-summer of 1928, he found them busy, and well-equipped, but by no means wholly modern. This, no doubt, was one reason why Captain John Black would shortly join the company and revolutionise its methods, and its products.

Although Canley was expanding all the time, car production was still on two major sites. The old Cash's Lane site – just to the north of Coventry's city centre – was devoted to machining, sub-assembly of engines and gearboxes, and related work on components, while Canley – to the west of the city centre, but still separated from it by the green expanse of Hearsall Common – looked after the construction of coachwork, and final assembly of all the cars.

Site plans still exist that show the way Canley evolved over the years (it was still years before the first of the Government-financed factory blocks would be erected, and a full 30 years before work would began on a new assembly hall (which would be nicknamed the 'Rocket Range'), but even by the end of the 1920s there was a complicated number of different departments behind the impressive front façade.

As to the façade itself, visitors to Canley would gain access through gates close to Canley Halt railway station, turning immediately right to the 'Ivy Cottage' administration block, or immediately left to the palatial offices erected in front of the assembly hall itself. All, of course, was hustle and bustle, for these were the days when a car-making factory still relied more on people, and muscle power, than it did on machinery – the days of robots being some years into the future:

"The chassis are erected at Canley on the conveyor system," Sampson wrote, "but instead of being propelled forward as radiators, engines, gearboxes, back axles and

By the late 1920s, Standard was building cars in considerable quantities. This was the chassis build line at Canley – next stop, the body shop!

wheels go on, they are pushed along on little separate trolleys, one close behind the other. The last things to be mounted are the wheels, these coming, complete with tyres, down a ramp from a gallery just above the spot where the chassis, complete save for wheels and tyres, arrives.

"Then the chassis goes on test. The road test reports are so arranged that, as far as possible, human errors are avoided. All being well, the chassis goes to receive its coachwork. This, today, is practically all of the closed type, the sliding roof, fabric panelled, saloon predominating.

"A final road test ensues, and then the car, after it has had, as it were, its face polished and a wash and brush up, is ready for its future owner ..."

The side-valve six-cylinder, which came to maturity in the 1930s, powered not only Standards like this, but was also supplied in big numbers to SS.

A LEGENDARY NEW 'SIX'

Looking back now, it is easy to see that two calendar years, 1927 and 1928, were pivotal times for Standard's business. Not only did the Nine find its feet (and soon begin to expand its scope), but the launch of a new side-valve, seven-bearing six-cylinder engine finally cut Standard's last

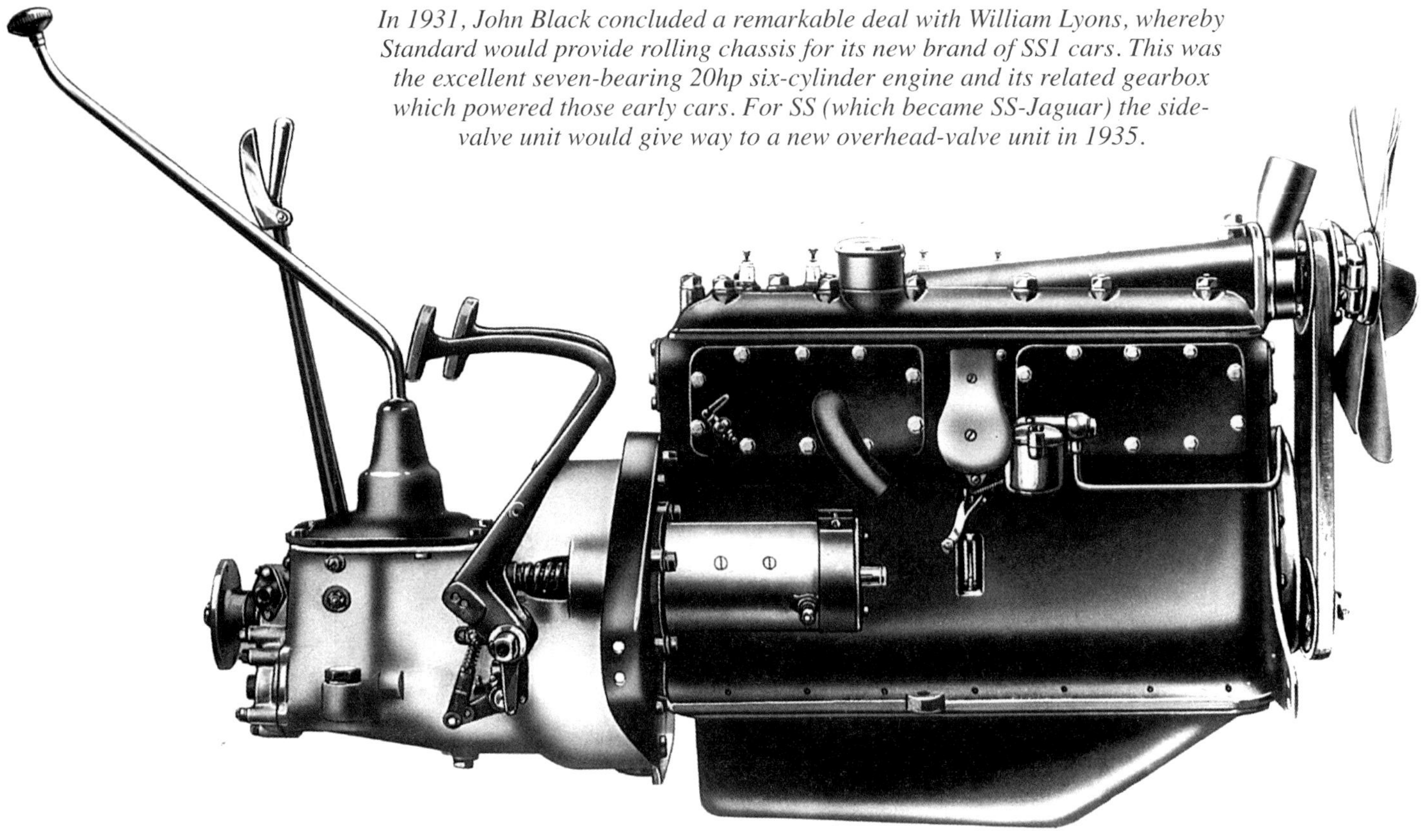

In 1931, John Black concluded a remarkable deal with William Lyons, whereby Standard would provide rolling chassis for its new brand of SS1 cars. This was the excellent seven-bearing 20hp six-cylinder engine and its related gearbox which powered those early cars. For SS (which became SS-Jaguar) the side-valve unit would give way to a new overhead-valve unit in 1935.

ties with the 'overhead-valve' period of the 1920s.

The new 'six,' with a bore of 63.5mm, a stroke of 101.6mm, and a swept volume of 1930cc, was the first of a family which would eventually spread its wings, be developed into a whole variety of sizes, take on overhead valves, power a whole number of Standard (and SS) models, and live on for the next twenty years. It was, in other words, one of the most important 'building blocks' Standard followers would ever see.

Although the brand-new six, launched in September 1928, had a rock-solid seven-main-bearing crankshaft, and featured a styled cover for the cylinder head which gave the impression that it had overhead valves, it was in fact a simply but robustly engineered side-valve engine which was neither no more and no less than a 'big relation' to the side-valve 'four' which had been introduced in the Nine of 1927.

Careful in its pre-planning, Standard had clearly set out to develop a whole new family of engines for the 1930s. Investing as much as it could possibly afford in machinery for the ever-expanding Canley complex (and, arguably, more, when the company's sagging sales performance was noted), Wilde's team had made four-cylinder and six-cylinder versions of the same basic design available, complete with similar valve gear, carburation, accessory drive, and transmission connections, for the layout of the front and rear ends of the cylinder blocks were the same, as was every detail of the valve gear.

The initial 'stats' tell their own story:

'Six'	63.5mm bore x 101.6mm stroke, giving 1930cc
'Four'	60mm bore x 101.6mm stroke, giving 1153cc
	63.5mm bore x 101.6mm stroke, giving 1287cc

As we now know, and as the tables published on page 198 make clear, this range was to carry on, in further and yet further developed form, in sizes up to 1776cc (four-cylinder) and no less than 3485cc (six-cylinder).

In its original manifestation (but this would change in future years), the inlet 'manifold'/passageway of the six was included actually inside the cylinder block itself, with the Zenith carburettor therefore bolted up direct to the right side (offside) of the block casting itself.

The new car, which accepted this engine, had a conventional, but ambitiously detailed chassis, being the basis in the next few years for models labelled Envoy, Exmouth and Ensign. A study of the design (*The Autocar* printed a particularly fine cutaway drawing in September 1928) showed where all the investment had been directed for, compared with the V6, there was a four-speed gearbox (not three), a centre gear change (not right-hand change), and an underslung worm-drive rear axle. Four-wheel brakes, lever-arm dampers, and half-elliptic leaf spring suspension were all as expected, and the price of the standard 'fabric' four-door saloon was set at £325.

Even so, having recently invested so heavily in its future, Standard found itself struggling financially. By 1929, losses of more than £120,000 had built up, and the company was effectively only being kept afloat by its bankers, Barclays, who eventually allowed the company's overdraft to grow to £160,000: an enormous sum by the standards of the day.

Captain John Black arrives – the revolution begins

Captain John Black joined Standard, from Hillman, in 1929, and soon stamped his authority on the company.

In 1929, 'Dick' Maudslay finally moved to restore the fortunes of the company, which he had founded more than twenty-five years earlier. Maudslay was now ageing, no longer found himself at the cutting edge of business, motor car technology, or its publicity methods, and was searching round for an eventual successor. His company, frankly, was tottering, which explains the need for the £200,000 rights issue made in 1927, and an increase in overdraft facilities. By this time, indeed, Standard was so much in debt to Barclay's Bank that the bank was apparently fearful for its survival. Technically moribund except for its modern range of engines, it was producing very mundane cars for which the demand was seen to be slipping.

Something would have to be done, and fast. Maudslay was tired, his business mind was beginning to slow down, and he acknowledged this. He had to find new brains, and new energy, to help Standard stay alive. Not only that, but he realised that he had to find someone who could take over from him. He already knew that this could not be his long-time General Manager, John Budge, who soon retired with failing health.

It was not long before he found that successor close by – he being Captain John Paul Black, a dynamic 34-year-old character who was then serving as a top executive in the newly formed Hillman-Humber-Commer combine at the other side of Coventry. If Standard could be described as the most important employer in the western outskirts of the city, then Hillman-Humber was the most important on the eastern side.

Was it fate, happenstance, or pure naked ambition, that caused John Black to defect from Humber-Hillman to Standard? At Humber-Hillman, did John Black jump, or was he pushed? Whichever it was, there were immediate family complications to be dealt with, for John Black had been with Hillman since 1919, and had married one of the founder's (William Hillman's) six daughters, Margaret Verena, in 1921. By 1928 he had risen to become joint managing director of Hillman, alongside one Spencer Wilks (who had married another Hillman daughter), who would himself shortly move across Coventry in a different direction to join Rover. In November 1928, however, both of them were perturbed by the news that Hillman was to merge with Humber.

Captain (later Sir John) John Black

Born in Kingston-upon-Thames in 1895, John Paul Black studied law at the University of London, served during World War One, first in the Royal Navy Volunteer Reserve, then in the Royal Tank Regiment, where he attained the rank of Captain. After the War, he joined the Hillman Motor Co, of Humber Road, Coventry, as a sales manager.

The founder/owner of Hillman, William Hillman, had six daughters, and in 1921 Capt Black married one of them – Margaret Verena. Before the end of the 1920s, he not only joined the board of directors of Hillman (and Commer, a closely-related truck company), he also became Joint Managing Director.

Upheaval then followed, not only because Hillman and Humber merged, but in a related move the ambitious and thrusting Rootes family took a controlling interest of the new group and began imposing their will upon it. William ('Billy') Rootes and Capt Black were temperamentally too similar ever to cooperate, the result being that Black resigned from Hillman, to join Standard, shortly becoming general manager.

His career with Standard is covered fully in these pages. After becoming sole managing director in 1934, he reigned unchallenged at Standard until the very beginning of 1954. Not only was he knighted in 1943, for his amazingly dynamic work as chairman of the Aero Engine Shadow Committee, but after Charles Band retired from the company in the autumn of 1953, he also became Standard's chairman, too.

It is worth repeating, at this point, that Sir John was not a man to be ignored. The vast majority of his workforce admired him as a businessman, and for what he achieved, but many of his staff suffered the sharp end of his tongue and his abrasive and dictatorial management style. By many he was feared, and by some he was disliked (his sacking was hardly unexpected, although the timing was), though a few – those who relied totally for their position on his attitude to them – insisted that he was kind, loveable, and considerate: they were in a minority.

The events leading up to the boardroom coup, which led to his abrupt, and immediate, loss of office, are reported in detail on pages 139 and 140. After his resignation in January 1954, he virtually retired from business, and lived for the next decade in Wales, near Harlech, where he died at the end of 1965.

This 'Teignmouth,' on the late 1920s Nine, had a fabric body, four passenger doors, and a remarkably roomy cabin. Several of these rugged cars, like this one, are still giving good service today.

Even though they were both now related by marriage to William Hillman, once the founder had merged his company with Humber (which was in an adjoining factory in Coventry), and John Black had found this new combine to be partly financed by the thrusting Rootes family and their powerful backers, the Prudential Assurance Co, both Black and Wilks seem to have made haste to move on. Since W E ('Billy') Rootes was making it clear that he would soon be making all the decisions at Humber-Hillman, neither John Black nor Spencer Wilks was content with that.

John Black's arrival at Standard came abruptly, and as far as the other directors were concerned, they first learned about it at a Board meeting where, on 1 October 1929, he was hired, officially, as 'Assistant to Mr R W Maudslay,' for six months at a flat fee of £500. Well before that six months was up, in February 1930, his position was made permanent, at £1200/annum, with a generous profit-related commission deal on top, and he joined the Board of directors.

Almost at once it seems, his influence in Standard's current position, and its future, became overwhelming, for he instantly became the company's planning and production overlord. Like Leonard Lord (whose career at Wolseley, Morris, then Austin, paralleled his in so many ways), John Black was the compulsive designer, planner and decision-maker who really only needed the staff to take his orders, not to consult him on most matters. Officially appointed General Manager in July 1930, it had taken him only ten months to effectively turn Maudslay's company into his own.

A pamphlet produced many years later by publicity consultants to Standard stated that: "From insolvency and thirty-four cars a week in 1929, he has brought it to a £47 million turnover, and an output of 135,000 cars and tractors in 1951..." This must, surely, have been over-egging the pudding a little (was Standard really only making the equivalent of 1700 cars a year when John Black arrived?), but the bald truth is that he certainly revitalised the entire operation, and the fact is that in 1929 the company's total turnover was a mere £5 million a year.

However, not even John Black could work miracles in no-time at all, for in those early months the battle was for survival, rather than to innovate. [If it was not thought irreverent, I would describe 1929, 1930 and 1931 as the 'sticking plaster' years, when the best was made of what already existed, for it was not until the launch of the 1932 Model Year machines that a definite move to widen the product range, with a new engine family and a wider spread, became evident].

The 1930 programme was announced early, in August 1929, when it was clear that for the moment the company would stand fast with what it had. According to the company's publicists, there were to be no changes in definite types, and the product range would concentrate on the 9hp and the 15hp six-cylinder cars.

However, one piece of product planning juggling was the launch of an enlarged six-cylinder engine (this being the 65.5mm bore/2054cc type), in a car to be badged as an Envoy. This car also had a longer wheelbase, a more spacious cabin, a spiral bevel rear axle by ENV of Willesden, in London (instead of the worm drives which had been a normal fitment on so many vintage Standards) and a whole variety of detail improvements, which would be adopted on future Standard models. The price? £340.

A year later, also announced in August, just as the Canley-based business came back from its annual summer break, the 1931 Model Year offerings broke cover. Although there was much reshuffling of names, engine sizes, and details, the fact is that the Nine – now to be known as the Big Nine – was still the stalwart of the line up, with variously incestuously-related cars powered by the modern six-cylinder engine making up the balance of the line-up.

John Black had clearly studied the way in which American firms got the most out of its 'building blocks.' For 1931, each and every car in the Standard range was to be powered by the same family of basic side-valve engine, all of them sharing the same stroke, and cylinder block height, as follows:

Big Nine	4-cyl, 1287cc (63.5 x 101.6mm)
Light Six (Ensign)	6-cyl, 2054cc (65.5 x 101.6mm)
Envoy	6-cyl, 2552cc (73 x 101.6mm)

– there would be other derivatives to follow in future years, and at this point it is worth noting that William Lyons had already homed in those six-cylinder power units as being ideal for his still-secret SS cars, which would be launched in the autumn of 1931 (see page 192).

Although the body style of all these cars – the cheaper ones panelled in fabric, the more costly in pressed steel – was conventional enough, all now had a new style of rounded radiator grille (the traditional shoulder-shaped radiator had finally been laid to rest), and all – even the Big Nine – featured bodies in which the windscreen was rather daringly raked.

In the early 1930s, Standard styling was simple, but the cars offered great value, and were widely seen as reliable and trustworthy. This was one of the many Nines which left Canley at this time.

Compared with 1930, the 1931-model Nine (the Big Nine, in other words) was a more elegant and significantly larger machine, for the wheel tracks had been widened by three inches (45 to 48 inches). There was a brand-new type of spiral-bevel rear axle (which replaced the old-fashioned worm), along with three, or four-speed gearboxes. Six different body styles encompassed an entry level fabric saloon (£195) all the way to a steel-panelled coach-built saloon for £255.

Higher up the range, at prices ranging from £245 for a fabric saloon to no less than £385 for the latest Envoy saloon, were the six-cylinder cars, with a complex choice of engine sizes, three- or four-speed gearboxes, spiral bevel

Standard did not abandon the 'Weymann' construction of coachwork until the early 1930s – this, in fact, being a transitional model with some Weymann, some conventional steel construction. Seen in 1931, with an exposed spare wheel, and a long and graceful nose, this was the very elegant 20hp saloon of the period.

axles, fabric or coach-built styles, and very closely-related four-door shapes.

This, though, was only the beginning. As early as 1931, and in great secrecy except for his Board members, John Black then presented a plan based on producing 12,500 cars, or alternatively 15,000 cars, in a full year – which was many more than the company had ever previously achieved. By this time, much of the Canley factory's plant had been modernised or replaced, and the company was gradually withdrawing from the old Cash's Lane factory in the centre of Coventry.

[Even so, that plant would not finally be auctioned off until 1937, raising a mere £12,250].

He also wanted to push on with the design of a new 'small car' – which would eventually emerge as the Little Nine. Only months later, he presented 'Programme B' – 8000 small saloons, 5000 Big Nines, 2500 Light Sixes and 500 Envoys (16,000 cars in all) – which was perhaps over-ambitious, but only by a year or so.

One of John Black's key appointments came earlier than expected in January 1931. Unhappily, he had apparently not got on well with Chief Engineer A H Wilde, who decided to leave the company, but Wilde had then died quite unexpectedly at the end of the previous year. A replacement was urgently needed. Instead of making an internal promotion (the Engineering department was, in any case, very small), Black moved swiftly, called up a previous colleague from Hillman, one Edward George Grinham, and appointed him Standard's Chief Engineer.

Except for a four-year period during the Second World War Ted Grinham (Mr Grinham – never Ted – to all his colleagues) then became an important cornerstone of Standard's management team for the next twenty-five years. He joined the Board of Directors in 1936, spending time away from the company during World War Two, before returning in 1945, and then staying until his retirement loomed at the end of 1956.

Not a Standard, you might think – but this, indeed, is an early 1930s 16hp, clothed in a Swan style by Avon – pictured at a modern event in India.

In many ways, Grinham's character was reflected in the type of cars he inspired at the time – for there never seemed to be much gaiety in his existence. Although the author has previously been criticised for quoting the negative part of his character, it seems to be generally agreed by Standard colleagues that he was a hard man, a dour man, with an imposing and forbidding presence, but no apparent sense of humour. Colleagues soon learnt not to be flippant and light-hearted while Ted Grinham was around, as he might abruptly snarl at them, and demand that they got back to business.

As John Lloyd, who later took the same position as Technical Director, which Grinham had held, once commented: "He could not see any fun in working, and I don't think he had much of a home life either ..."

Avon Standard – a special deal developing

As already noted, a number of independent coachbuilders were encouraged to develop their own special-body interpretations on Standard chassis, which continued to use absolutely standard mechanical components. In most cases, such arrangements were conducted in a strictly commercial, or 'arm's length' fashion. There seems, however, to have been one special case, that of the evolution of a range of Avon-bodied cars, which were produced in several phases, from 1929 to 1937.

Avon had originally been set up in 1919, and for the first years of its existence it had produced bodyshells for Lea Francis (another Coventry carmaker). By the late 1920s, however, Alan Jensen (who would eventually become a car maker in his own right), had encountered Standard's Chief Engineer A H Wilde, who loved the lines of a special sports car (based on the Austin Seven), which he had just handcrafted. Wilde then asked him to produce a similar job on the new Standard Nine chassis.

"The chap jumped out," Alan Jensen recalled about their first road-side encounter, "came over and started to ask me all about the car. I was terribly thrilled when he introduced himself as Alfred Wilde, Chief Engineer of the Standard Motor Company, and I became even more excited when he asked me whether Dick [Jensen] and I would like to have a look around the Standard works one day ..."

After seeing the first Jensen-bodied Little Nine, Wilde introduced Jensen to *The Autocar's* Montague Tombs, who introduced him to Avon Bodies of Warwick, where he started to style a series of sports, tourer and DHC body styles. Because much of Avon's capital, at that time, came from the Maudslay family, there was already a 'family connection' with Standard, and after Capt John Black's arrival those links were intensified.

From 1929 to 1932, Avon produced a series of smart Standard-based cars with Jensen-inspired styles, mostly characterised by long bonnets, cycle-type wings and lowered radiators, and we see from the lists that they used 1006cc,

Avon Coachwork might sometimes have had chaotic business finances during the 1930s, but habitually produced some very elegant cars based on Standard chassis. Built in 1932, this was a Little Twelve Tourer.

Because of the Maudslay family connection, Avon of Warwick was a favoured user of Standard chassis. This was an early type of two-seater Coupé on the Little Nine chassis.

Yet another fine example of Avon coachwork on an otherwise Standard chassis, this being a 1935 'Waymaker II' model.

1287cc, or 2054cc four- or six-cylinder engines. Unhappily, all styles were handicapped by having to use unmodified Standard chassis, for although special lowered versions were developed by 1931, for contractural reasons these were confined solely to the Standard-engined SS models of the day. Prices started at £215 for the Little Nine Coupé in 1932, which made them competitive in what was a restricted market.

By that time, the Jensens then jumped ship (to join J A Patrick at Edgbaston Garages in Birmingham), Avon had become New Avon, and styling inspiration now came from one C F Beauvais, a consultant body engineer who had already worked for Star, and for Singer. For the next three years, under Beauvais's guidance (and until the Flying Standard range, and its different chassis came along), a series of elegant-looking cars (some pundits rated them as high as the latest from SS, but there was always controversy over this) they were variously equipped with aluminium-headed 1343cc, 1337cc, and 2143cc four-cylinder and six-cylinder engines.

This, though, was the height of their success, as the events related in the next chapter will confirm.

Canley – the attack of the road-builders

Barely had John Black set out his plans for Standard's long-term future (for which, read 'expansion') when these were hard-hit by the Coventry city council. In its wisdom, and (according to it) looking 'to the future,' it proposed to build a Coventry by-pass road, which would cut a swathe through a part of Standard's Canley estate that was still undeveloped.

That by-pass, later to become an integral part of the A45 road through and around the southern and western parts of Coventry, was intended to provide relief to the existing main London – Birmingham main road, which cut through the very heart of the old city at that time. In that respect, it was a laudable project (and, in fairness, searches for an alternative route showed only that longer, and more costly alignments would have been needed).

As 1950s-era company documents reveal:

"In 1930 the Coventry corporation decided to promote a by-pass road, which cut through the Company's land from Tile Hill Lane to the LMS railway. The new road would divide the Company's land into two parts. The construction of the testing track had to be abandoned, and the golf course seriously curtailed ... After careful consideration, it was decided to dispose of the land beyond the west side of the new by-pass road. Several sites for factories were disposed of ... along with many small areas for housing.

"When the land was purchased, it was never intended to dispose of any part of it, and had it not been for the by-pass road, the company would still be the owners and occupiers of the whole of it ..."

By 1932, the route of the by-pass road scheme had been approved, and was seen to run through the Canley site, so the Board directed company solicitor Charles Band to find ways of selling off no less than 83½ acres of land to the west of the line of the new road (the section, in fact, which would be cut off from the central area where much factory building already existed). This was done on a piecemeal basis – a small plot here, a small plot there – and resulted in several small independent factories being set up by entrepreneurs, some of whom became suppliers to Standard, a large number of housing projects, and finally (in 1936) the sale of a corner site for the building of a cinema, which stands to this day.

Little Nine – and a brand-new range of engines

What was arguably Standard's greatest leap forward (so far) then came in July 1931, with the launch of a new car rather unimaginatively titled 'Little Nine.' If only this car could have been given a new and startling title, we would all have seen just how important it actually was – and how many innovations were brought forward at the same time.

Not only was this the smallest Standard put on sale for some time – priced at £155, with a wheelbase of only 90in, and wheel tracks of just 44in, under an overall length of 130in – it was certainly that, but it was also the cheapest Standard ever. Even so, the body was steel panelled and coach-built (as an act of policy, Standard was dumping the old fabric type, which might have been cheap, and light, but was also liable to speedy deterioration), and looked like a rather shrunken clone of the latest 'Big Nine.'

It was the all-new four-cylinder engine – 60.25 x 88mm, measuring 1006cc, and rated at 8.7 'Treasury Rating' horsepower – which was the vitally interesting feature. Every detail of this simple, rugged, four-cylinder unit was new to Standard and it was not at all related to the considerably larger engine fitted to the 'Big Nine.' The Solex carburettor and both the inlet and exhaust manifolding were positioned on the left (nearside) of the power unit.

Although it only featured two crankshaft main bearings at first, it would eventually be upgraded (for the 1934 range – see below), enlarged, developed, modified, revamped – and even treated to an overhead-valve conversion at one point – but it would last until 1953, when the last of the Standard-produced Triumph Mayflowers would be produced, which equated to a life of 22 years.

Backed by a light-duty three-speed gearbox, a spiral-bevel back axle, simple half-elliptic suspension, controlled at the front by transversely-mounted Andre friction-type dampers, and with Bendix-sourced cable braking, it weighed about 1450lb. It was, in other words, just about as simple a car as could be provided, which is what these badly-hit 'depression' times demanded – so naturally the ever-expanding Standard dealer chain loved it.

Road tests showed that it could reach 57mph and that it recorded about 40mpg, which made it very competitive indeed. No wonder that *The Autocar's* testers concluded that: "This car represents a notable advance in small-car design ..."

By comparison with the new Little Nine, the other three cars in the range – Big Nine, Sixteen and Twenty (all basically the same as before, with little change to the styling, but with some juggling of names and equipment, as the Ensign and Envoy names had been dropped) – could only provide a supporting act. Even so they all shared a new type of four-speed gearbox, complete with a constant-mesh 'silent third' (synchromesh had not yet arrived in the British motor industry), revised front-end styling, which matched that given to the Little Nine, and a range of prices bracketing £205 (coach-built Big Nine) to no less than £355 (coach-built Twenty), each and all of these having steel panelled coachwork.

By any standards, the 1932 range proved to be a roaring success, sales boomed, and waiting lists built up. All of this meant that Standard was in acute danger of running out of stock by mid 1932 – because of the 'sanction' approval system which operated, there was no chance of ordering a small, extra, supplementary batch of any model in the range – and one consequence was that the release of 1933 models had to be brought forward to July 1932.

Small sixes – a calamitous diversion

Unhappily, from mid-1932, when the new cars were launched as part of the 1933 range – and for little more than a single Model Year (these Standard engines did not re-appear for 1934) – Standard was sucked into a current motor industry craze, which was for makers to offer small-capacity six-cylinder engines in family cars: several of its rivals made the same mistake, and all used the same penny-pinching methods. The fact that such products were usually unsatisfactory, and relatively expensive, did not deter the makers – for a time at least – though by the mid-1930s the craze was over.

Anyway, why was this done in the first place? Usually because a company's sales department wanted more power and more models in a range – but thought that enlarged four-cylinder engines would be too rough-and-ready; six-cylinder engines, they were persuaded, would be smoother, sexier and more saleable. But it didn't seem to work like that. The author, having driven almost every such contender at the time, and later, the author's contemporary, and noted historian, Michael Sedgwick was consistently scathing about all of them. Although the author does not have Sedgwick's wide knowledge of all these cars, his opinons are confirmed by many other latter-day observers ...

Without exception, it seems, to accommodate bulkier engines, such cars used longer-wheelbase versions of a four-cylinder chassis (rendered less, rather than more, stiff in the process), their engines generally cobbled-up derivatives of existing 'fours,' and they seemed to be almost universally gutless and lacking in torque. Standard, for sure, followed this trend to keep up with cars like the Austin Light 12-6, the Morris Ten-Six, the Triumph Scorpion, and the Wolseley Hornet, but in the process was no more successful than any of them.

Like every rival, the new Standard models evolved from smaller-engined cars. In the Standard's case, the chassis and coachwork were based on those of the sturdy Little Nine/Big Nine models, but used two versions of a new six-cylinder engine – a 'Little Twelve' with 1337cc and a 6.4in longer wheelbase, and a Big Twelve with 1497cc, and the same wheelbase as the Big Nine; both cars having cruciform bracing on the frame itself, and four-speed gearboxes.

Although Standard's contemporary machine shop technology was as advanced as most in the British motor industry, there was little transfer machinery involved, so the engines could evolve in what was now a time-honoured way – to keep the front of the engine like that of the 'four,' the rear like the rear of the 'four,' but provide six cylinders instead of four cylinders between them. In Standard's case, of course, side-valve heads were retained throughout.

In these new six-cylinder Standards, the cylinder stroke was exactly the same as the power unit of the Little Nine (which meant that the cylinder block was the same depth), the cylinder bore of the Big Twelve was that of the Little Nine, while the bore of the Little Twelve (at 57mm) was new, but would eventually re-appear on the Eight of 1938! The crankshaft was only partially counter-balanced, and had just four main bearings (unlike the seven bearings which featured in the large six supplied to SS, and used on bigger Standards), with carburation by a single downdraught Solex unit.

Along with every other existing model in the range, the new-for-1933 Standards had 12-volt electrics, side-valve engines, four-speed gearboxes, slightly longer wheelbases and wider tracks, all topped by body styles that seemed (and were, of course) to have been shaped by the same hands in the company's small design and development department. Standard experts could pick out detail changes to the style of the radiator, the wings, and the finishing off of the saloon shell.

Even though it had only been launched a year earlier, the Little Nine now had the four-speed box/12-volt electrics package, along with hydraulic dampers and a beefed up

In 1932, Standard's 16hp chassis was strictly conventional by contemporary British standards, but the sturdy seven-bearing side-valve six-cylinder engine was about to make a name for itself in the new SS marque, too.

This was, like so many early 1930s Standards, a 12hp model of 1934, with a spacious six-window bodyshell, which proved very popular with the clientele.

rear axle as standard. Big Nine, Big Twelve and Sixteen models all carried the same four-door coachwork on sturdier chassis frames (the longer wheelbase of the Sixteen being accommodated via a longer bonnet and a 'stretch' ahead of the windscreen).

Even though sales of Standard's top-of-the-range car, the Twenty, were very limited, much work had gone into up-grading it. Although it kept the same side-valve 2552cc engine, and the same basic mechanical layout, hidden away there was a new chassis, with cruciform bracing and a 117in wheelbase, Bendix-Perrot braking for the first time on this model. Not only that, but the capacious rear compartment included fold-up occasional seats, all of which Standard thought would justify a price of £325.

Although the UK pricing of this 1933 range was aggressive – £159 for the latest Little Nine, £189 for the Little Twelve, £205 for the Big Nine, and £215 for the Big Twelve, for instance – the public did not take to any of the six-cylinder engined cars, whether of the 'small' or the 'big' variety.

John Black, who was about to take complete control of Standard as Dick Maudslay prepared to retire, picked up these opinions at an early stage, and was ruthless enough to drop both the 'little-six' cars in favour of larger four-cylinder engined cars (Ten and Twelve) which came along for 1934. Even so, by September 1932, monthly deliveries from Standard were already a 100 per cent higher than they had been at the same time in 1931. At the end of the financial year, the company proudly announced a profit of £201,697, and was able to transfer £140,000 to financial reserves to underpin its future.

Diversions, and expansion

Looking back, this was an exciting time for Standard, which was aggressively expanding its operations in defiance of several industrial trends. Although the nation's economy was currently in tatters (in the face of awful financial problems, a Labour administration had given way to a 'National Government' in 1931), and the motor industry in general was suffering badly (one only has to study Austin's and Morris's output figures at this time to see this confirmed), Standard, and John Black, defied the odds and kept pushing on.

Among the many diversions explored was an approach from the industrialist Sir Denniston Burney, who had already developed several bizarre 'streamlined' cars, and was soon to launch the rear-engined Crossley-Burney model. Burney had been interested in producing a small 'stream-line' car based on the Standard Little Nine – but Standard pulled away from that project before any real money had been spent.

Then, in 1933, the little-known Koastergear Co Ltd concern approached Standard, to see if it would be interested in manufacturing and selling a new type of automatic transmission. Whatever was unique about this project (and precious little is known about it, there being no obvious references to it in internet sources), it did not appeal to Standard, who briskly turned it aside.

On the other hand, technical director Ted Grinham was interested enough in the latest type of Dubonnet independent front suspension to approve some work to go ahead, but,

Both 'Dick' Maudslay and Captain Black were proud of the palatial Standard Recreation Club when it was completed on the northern edge of the Canley complex in 1932. The Duke of Gloucester officially opened it, and it eventually became the only original part of the factory which remained when the wrecking balls moved in during the 1990s. In early 2000, not only was the Club still thriving, but an impressive monument to Standard (and Triumph) was erected close by, to remind city dwellers of what had once been a thriving motor manufacturing business.

When this car was built in the 1933-1934 period, we all thought it was a neat, understated, but nicely styled Standard. John Black and his colleagues, however, were already thinking ahead, to the 'Flying' period.

once again, this was an idea which faded away, in favour of the transverse-leaf-spring setup introduced on Flying Standards from late 1935.

Big changes for 1934

In September 1933, however, Standard astonished its competitors by launching what was effectively a completely new product range. Not only did several new model names appear – 'Ten' and 'Twelve' among them – but each and every version of the two families of engines was considerably up-dated, enlarged, and in most cases made more powerful, too. There was also a new corporate four-speed gearbox, which not only featured synchromesh on top, third and second gears, but also (except for the Nine) had a freewheel too: for the time being, this was a 'first' for the British motor industry, and Standard was very proud of what had been achieved.

Incidentally, it was at this time that the Wilson self-changing, pre-selector transmission (newly fashionable at the time, as used on several other cars, usually in the higher price brackets) became optional, but very few were made, and little seems to be known about that installation.

And there was more. New chassis frames had cruciform bracing throughout, engines and transmissions were placed in rubber mountings to give smoother running, body styles were new and more spacious throughout, and except for the Tourers these were now made from all-steel construction.

The six-cylinder engines, which had reached their fifth birthday, were not only larger, torquier and more powerful than before, but had also been modernised, especially to make them more suitable for sale to SS (see the Appendix on pages 190-193). The original engines had a single carburettor bolted direct to the right side of the cylinder block, with internal passages leading to the inlet valves on the other side of the casting. Now, as commonised with the 106mm stroke, there were to be sensibly placed inlet passages entering from the left side of the block, close to the line of valves, and the carburettor thus migrated from one side of the engine to the other.

Compared with 1933 models, the 1934 range was changed so much that it is really necessary to list the year-on-year engine changes:

Engine sizes (4-cylinder unless noted)

1933	1934	Comment
1006	1052	Longer stroke, three crank bearings
1287	1343	Longer stroke, three crank bearings
1337 (6-cyl)	-	Not carried forward
1497 (6-cyl)		No changes (optional on only one new model)
-	1608	New derivative of 1287cc, bigger bore, longer stroke, three crank bearings
2054 (6-cyl)	2143	Longer stroke, new block
2552 (6-cyl)	2664	Longer stroke, new block

With five basic models, with open Tourer options on four of them, with prices now starting at £135 for the two-door re-launched Nine, all topping out at £415 for the Twenty Landaulette, this was a formidable range. Not surprisingly, investment in these new cars had been so high that annual profits dipped to £132,000, but this figure was nevertheless highly encouraging. The horrifying overdraft levels of the late 1920s were now just a bitter memory, and the company seemed set on steady expansion in the rest of the 1930s.

By 1934, John Black's grip on the direction, and forward planning, of Standard was total, and his plans for the company's future were truly visionary. Since his arrival in 1929, as already noted, sales and production had both soared, and the high-profile deal with SS had worked wonders for Standard's image. As an example, in 1934 the directors approved the following ambitious production sanction for the Canley factory, for no fewer than 18,230 Standards, and 1000 SS types, as follows:

9hp models	5500
10hp models	7900
12hp models	3800
16hp models	950
20hp cars	80
SS1 chassis	500
SS2 chassis	500

This was more than had ever before been achieved at Canley, yet if John Black got his way these were target figures which would soon be surpassed. That soon happened, for only two years later sanctions would be approved for the building of up to 30,000 cars in a year, and by 1939 that sanction would be raised to 50,000.

Figures released at the time show just how sweeping, and how ambitious, the vast expansion of Canley actually was. With the decision made to dispose of the old, cramped and quite ancient Cash's Lane premises, it was necessary to replace the 66,249ft^2 which had been available in that old building. At the time, the machine shops at Canley only occupied 52,447ft^2. Accordingly, a massive new building, totalling 117,000ft^2 was built to the north of the ever-expanding site. This, and extra space gained in other parts of the plant, meant that 191,482ft^2 was henceforth available – this being claimed as a 61 per cent overall increase in machine shop floor space.

Canley, in other words, was now on the way to being self-supporting for Standard – even with its ambitious future strategy in mind – for its engines, transmissions, and many other components were all now being made on the premises.

The Duke of Gloucester shaking hands with the delivery driver of his new Standard in the early 1930s. Captain Black is on the left of this group, with Dick Maudslay in the centre.

Canley site

Until Standard started to develop its new factory at Canley, the ground on which it was placed was pure green field. Standard had outgrown its Cash's Lane factory, which was close to the centre of Coventry, and needed more space in 1916, not only to build fighting aircraft for the British government, but also to prepare for the massive expansion which founder Dick Maudslay had in mind. In fact it was under Capt John Black's control in the 1930s and 1940s that the really huge expansion on the site took place.

No other industrial concern in Coventry had ever operated on this big area of land – it was still green fields, and was owned by an important local grandee, Lord Leigh, at the time – and until the lineal descendants of Standard (by that time called the Rover Group, and owned by British Aerospace) began to 'downsize' the business by closing old factories and selling off the premises, no other company would. Two Government-financed new 'shadow' factory premises built (with Standard approval) in the grounds between 1937 and 1940 were speedily integrated into the Standard orbit in postwar years.

Expansion was persistent – headlong, even, in the 1930s, 1940s, 1950s and 1960s – the entire complex being fully occupied, and very productive, until 1980, when complete car assembly (of Triumphs) finally ended. From 1989, a soulless 'property-developing' subsidiary of Standard's then-owner, British Aerospace, called Arlington Securities (it had been founded, originally as an independent business, in 1981), began to demolish, clear and redevelop the entire complex.

First to disappear, in 1994, were the oldest buildings closest to the centre of Coventry. The original aircraft (later car) assembly halls, Ivy Cottage and the famous old directors' suite close to Canley railway station soon followed, and last of all (in 1996) was Fletchamstead South, the old Sales and Parts block close to the A45. The entire complex was finally obliterated, new roads were laid down (some of them carrying famous Standard-Triumph model names) and before long a series of new industrial units (it would puffing up their pride too much to call them 'factories') took their place. Except for the Standard-Triumph Monument on Herald Way, which was financed by a group of Standard and Triumph one-make clubs, and the Recreation Pavilion that had been opened up in 1932, no trace now remains.

Posed? Surely not! In fact, this is a publicity shot not only showing the 1934 Standard 10, but the fact that Standard now had a modern and very popular Recreation Club for its staff, situated on the northern edge of its estate at Canley.

By 1935, the pedigree of the Nine had settled down, but the style was beginning to look old-fashioned. The 'Flying' revolution was only months away.

Chassis frames and all-steel bodyshells for the saloons, however, still came from major outside suppliers, as they always would until the end of Standard private car assembly in the 1960s, for it made more sense – for cost and capital investment reasons, that is – to do it that way.

For Standard, however, the situation was always fluid, as work was not only going ahead on a new range of cars – these would be the first of the Flying Standards – for which the production facilities at Canley would once again have to be re-equipped, but at the same time SS's William Lyons approached John Black to inform him that he was about the launch a new-type of SS-Jaguar, with a chassis finalised by William Heynes (who had once worked for Ted Grinham at Humber – small world!), and that by 1936 he would want to assemble his own chassis, even though much Standard hardware was to be retained. This meant that Standard's deal to supply complete rolling-chassis to SS only covered four full years 1931 to 1935 and this freed up some space at Canley for more 'own-brand' cars to be manufactured.

Not only that, but (as John Black already knew) the new SS-Jaguars were to use overhead-valve six-cylinder engines, the top end of which had been developed for them by Harry Weslake, and Lyons had to persuade John Black to invest in new machinery and assembly facilities for such a piece of kit, which Standard had not designed itself!

In 1934, the style had changed significantly. It was, however, one of the last of the 'pre-Flying' models which would shortly revolutionise the Standard image.

When the 1935 Model Year range was announced in August 1934, casual observers were mildly disappointed to see no startling innovations – the chassis, the choice of engines, and the basic body styles were all the same as before. Not only that, but like the Rootes Group, Standard had embraced the Detroit strategy of mix-and-match, where different models were invented by placing different engines in existing structures, or by lengthening wheelbases without altering basic cabins.

The more thoughtful, however, realised that the company, having extended itself considerably in 1933 and 1934, was now playing 'catch-up,' by refining what had already been in production for a time. Those who were 'in the know,' too, knew that the next leap forward (the first of the 'Flying Standards' in fact) would be unveiled in 1935.

When the new for 1935 range was revealed, Standard took multi-page adverts in the specialist press to make much of the 'business-as-usual policy). *The Autocar* of 17 August 1934 carried an eight-page gatefold ad, in colour, which started with these ringing claims:

"TESTED – AND FOUND GOOD ... the 1935 Standards are advanced, up-to-date editions of the Standards of 1934 ... Standards which have been proved good by more than 20,000 motorists like yourself ..."

The line-up, therefore, comprised:

Nine (2-door)	£145
Nine (4-door)	£165
Ten	£185
Speed 10-12	£245
Speed 10-12 Coupé (two door)	£265
Twelve	£219
Sixteen	£285
Twenty	£395

As before, there were five different chassis, two different families of four-cylinder engine, along with six-cylinder engines, which were themselves derivatives of one of the

This cute little 'Gordon England' sporty style was added to one of the late 1920s Little Nines. Gordon England was a very fashionable little coachbuilder at the time.

'fours.' No matter what the chassis and engine fitted, all-steel body styles looked very similar (Fisher & Ludlow was now a major supplier), and all closed cars except the entry-level Nine, and the 'Speed' coupé had four passenger doors.

The four-door Nine was effectively the same car as the Ten, but with the smaller/less-powerful 'Nine' engine and a four inch shorter wheelbase. The Speed 10-12 was an interesting, potentially limited-production, model, complete with a twin-carburettor/aluminium head/43bhp

In an attempt to compete against cars like the Wolseley Hornet and coupé versions of the MG Midget, Standard produced this Speed Coupé in the early 1930s.

The 1934 Standard Ten was one of the company's best sellers of that period. Unexciting, conventional in every way, but good value for money.

version of the 1608cc engine, a remote-control gear change and centre-lock wire spoke wheels, all these being closely related to those currently being supplied to SS for its SSII range, and which had been available for some months. Not only was there a four-door saloon style, but also the choice of the Tickford tourer, or the further novelty of a smart, fastback, two-door coupé as well.

Sixteen and Twenty models carried on virtually as in 1934, though Mulliners of Birmingham now provided a long-wheelbase version of the Twenty, a seven-seater costing £495, and therefore destined to sell in very limited numbers. Another novelty was the smart little tourer bodyshell supplied by Tickford, available on the Ten or 10-12 chassis.

In the meantime, the company had to report the death of the its founder, Mr R W Maudslay, who had been ailing for some time, and who never recovered from an operation that had had to be carried out towards the end of 1934. This was not only a sad occasion for traditionalists, but it also meant that a new chairman of the Board had to be appointed. At this stage, John Black was presumably not ready to take on this role as well as being managing director, so instead the accolade went to Charles Band, the legal specialist who had already been a Standard director throughout the 1920s and 1930s.

This appointment was announced formally at the very start of 1935, and at the same time Commander G Herbert was appointed as the company's Sales Director. Mr Herbert was a brother-in-law of the late R W Maudslay. Although this ensured a continued 'Maudslay family connection' at the head of the company, it was to be a short-lived appointment. Herbert apparently found it difficult to get on with John Black, the result being that he would leave the company during 1936.

Even so, as 1935 opened, the business now appeared to be set fair for the future – and the first of the Flying Standards was on the way.

Although the six-cylinder engine was very sound – good enough for use by SS – models like this Standard 16 sold slowly.

CHAPTER 5

FLYING STANDARDS FOR ALL 1935-1940

By the middle of the 1930s, Standard seemed to be covering every possible corner of [what I will call] the 'lower-middle-class' market for family cars. Urged on by John Black, who noted how his major rivals, the Rootes Group (using several different brand names), was seeking to cover all bases, his management team set out to do the same. When fully developed, starting with the Eight, topping out with the Twenty (adding in all manner of permutations in between, and giving great support to Avon in the bespoke market), it was the sort of range which gave the dealers plenty to sell – and the service managers a problem in stocking enough parts!

As the 1930s opened, however, Standard's problem was that all this was being achieved in a very inefficient way. Before John Black arrived at Canley, almost every model – certainly every mainstream model – was equipped with a bodyshell produced, from the ground up, at Canley itself. The framing of each shell was in wood, the body skins were either steel, or fabric, and the labour involved in erecting every shell was intensive. This is how it had always been done in the past, and the old management saw no need to make changes.

Appalled by all this, Black (who had encountered the same attitude at Hillman, and was just about to deal with it when he made the move to Standard in 1929) proposed a long-term strategy, which would deal with the problem. He had a vision, of vastly increasing car production, which would mean that more space would have to be allocated to final assembly: accordingly, this meant that the manufacture of bodyshells – all-steel bodyshells at that – would have to be contracted out. This was one of the truly massive decisions, which the dynamic John Black had to make in his first years with the company.

His views, in fairness, were not unique, nor entirely visionary (Morris and Hillman both beat Standard to the start line with their all-steel bodies, while Austin, Ford and Vauxhall would all join in soon), but it was an exemplary way of planning for the company's future.

Nothing could be done in the short-term, of course (even in those technically simpler days, it took well over a year to tool up for manufacture of welded-up all-steel bodies), and there was also the need to work up a new policy – of which independent body-manufacturing concern should get the first contracts. Although Standard made little of this at the time, we now know that the three largest independent body-building concerns – Briggs Motor Bodies, Fisher & Ludlow, and Pressed Steel Co – were each awarded one major contract to start with, and up to the very outbreak of war this

This was the forerunner of the entire Flying Standard range, the first prototype mounted in a 1934/1935 chassis. Some experts point out resemblances to the Chrysler Airflow style of the period.

situation persisted. Certainly Standard would not make its own bodyshells again until Mulliners (see chapter 8) became a wholly owned subsidiary in the late 1950s.

In any case there were even more pressing decisions to be taken. In some ways, in any case, there were still too many Standard models on the market – so perhaps it is not surprising that the celebrated historian Michael Sedgwick later described the range as 'prolix' (Dictionary definition: "lengthy, tediously wordy ...") in the extreme. Worse, the problem was that the existing cars were beginning to look old-fashioned and upright: in some ways, they felt old-fashioned, too.

In 1933/1934, therefore, John Black had clearly taken a 'brave pill,' committed a great deal of his company's investment capital to his vision, particularly of new engine ranges, and set out a policy which would see the entire range renewed in the next three or four years. This, of course, was the start of a revolution, which led to the progressive appearance of the smart Flying Standards from the end of 1935, and the elimination of all the old types.

Financially, of course, this could only be done by spending huge amounts on new tooling and assembly facilities, both with the bodyshell suppliers, and within the Canley factory itself. Accordingly, and immediately after the launch of the first of the Flying Standards, the company formally increased its Share Capital from £300,000 to £500,000 (in early 21st century terms – for the value of British currency has plummeted in the meantime – these amounts need to be increased by a factor of at least fifty – which means that Standard was asking for a capital injection of £10 million ...).

Two years later, incidentally (and with the increased scale not only of production, but with all the financial implications of 'shadow' factory operations also building up, the issued capital was doubled, to £1 million, which well and truly put Standard in the 'Big League,' definitely and most proudly into the British 'Big Six' of carmakers. When all this was considered, it is easy to see how John Black came to be seen as Standard's miracle worker, as the 'Man of Vision,' and whose foibles could therefore be accepted just so long as he carried on delivering the goods for his shareholders, and for his workforce.

[The fact that Black was also well on the way to making himself a very rich man – one who effectively set his own salary, his own bonuses, and his own perks of office – was glossed over at this time, even by his critics. It was only later, much later, that the excesses were seen to be just that – excessive.]

Edward ('Ted') Grinham became Standard's Technical Chief in 1931, left during the Second World War, but returned in 1945, before retiring as deputy managing director in 1956.

At this time Frank Begg was Chief Body Engineer, and Arthur Ballard was his senior draughtsman, though neither was a dedicated stylist at the time. Even so, the shaping of the new 'Flying' models – sleek and with swooping lines, quite remarkably different from Standard's previous offerings – was nevertheless inspired at Canley itself, which explains why there was such a strong visual resemblance between

This is the same prototype shown on the previous page, but viewed from the other side. Note that this side has no mouldings or bonnet louvres; the two sides were styled differently to each other – and to the result, shown below.

The first of the Flying Standards, introduced in October 1935, was also the largest, this being the Flying Twenty, which made every previous and existing Standard look old-fashioned.

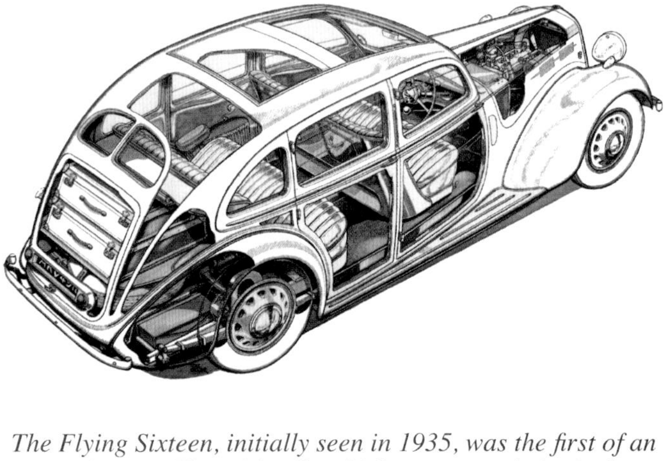

The Flying Sixteen, initially seen in 1935, was the first of an entirely new 'Flying' family which went on sale in the late 1930s. Most were four door saloons, with smooth, sloping back rear body shaping. In this case the engine was a side-valve six-cylinder unit.

First-generation Flying Standards, introduced in 1935, 1936 and 1937: all had similar smoothly sloping tail-end treatment.

Most of Standard's 'Flying' range were two and four-door saloons, but coachbuilt machinery like this very smart Twelve drophead coupé, was also very popular.

each and every car in the new ranges, even though three different bodyshell builders were involved. All of them had a sweeping fast back tail, and each used the shape of what were known as 'helmet'-type front wings. Visually, though, the difference between the old-type cars still being sold in 1935 and 1936, and the range, which was on offer by 1938, was startling. Both Austin and Morris, whose offerings were still very conservative, were known to be jealous of this.

This, in fact, was the period in which the celebrated 'Flying Standards' made their appearance, in a whirlwind series of launches, a process which stretched Standard's finances to their practical limits, but one which offered astounding promise for the future. First to arrive in October 1935 were the Flying Twelve, Flying Sixteen and Flying Twenty types (all of them sharing the same basic new six-window bodyshell provided by Briggs Motor Bodies), next were the Ten and the Light Twelve (which enjoyed a new type of wasp-waisted chassis frame, and a body by Pressed Steel), and finally in September 1936 came the Flying Nine, with bodyshell by Fisher & Ludlow. Those three bodyshell suppliers were vital to Standard's supply chain in the later 1930s.

Standard – and Pressed Steel

The Pressed Steel company was originally set up at Cowley, in Oxford, to be an independent supplier of body panels and complete bodyshells to the motor industry. William Morris (later Lord Nuffield), along with the American Budd Corporation, was a major shareholder at first, but this arrangement was soon un-scrambled when it showed that Morris Motors was thought to have effective control of the new business, which was enough to deter other, rival, car makers from doing business with Pressed Steel.

As motor industry fashion turned away from the use of bodyshells assembled around wooden frames, to shells made entirely from pressed steel panels, welded together, Pressed Steel's business grew rapidly. By the mid-1930s it counted four of Britain's 'Big Six' – Austin, the Nuffield Organisation (Morris, Wolseley), Rootes (Hillman and Humber) and Standard – among its clients, along with Rover and several smaller concerns. Pressed Steel, for instance, provided examples of the sloping-tail Flying Standard shells from 1936.

Steady expansion in the 1930s led Standard to look for outside suppliers to provide complete bodyshells. One of them was Fisher & Ludlow (see the Panel on page 58), another was Briggs Motor Bodies of Essex, the other being Pressed Steel.

As far as can be seen (and Standard were somewhat secretive about this), the very first complete welded-up shell to be provided to Standard, by Pressed Steel, was for the mainstream (four-door/six-light saloon) version of the Twelve, which was announced in the autumn of 1933. But that was just the start. Once the Flying Standard theme was adopted from 1935, the company tended to place much of its business for medium-sized cars with Pressed Steel, while the smaller car shells continued to be manufactured by Fisher & Ludlow, the large ones by Briggs Motor Bodies.

Pressed Steel and Standard then remained as partners for many years – the unit-construction Vanguard III shell of 1955 – 1963, for instance, being produced by Pressed Steel – and in later years, of course, the Vanguards were supplanted by the Triumph 2000, which also came from the same source.

It was not until Pressed Steel was absorbed by Standard-Triumph's deadly rival, the British Motor Corporation, in 1965, that potential commercial problems were seen. This, though, was mainly for Leyland to solve, as it had controlled Standard (and Triumph) since 1961.

Flights of Flying Standards

Under the skin of all these Flying models, their familiar side-valve engines and the old-style beam front axles remained, but there were already plans to do something about that in future years. By 1938, more and more of the original Flying models would inherit independent front suspension, and if World War Two had not intervened, overhead-valve engines (developed from those being designed for Morgan and SS-Jaguar respectively) might have followed.

However, although John Black did not have much spare time on his hands, he could still find space for an adventure or two. One diversion, which involved Standard in the spring of 1935, was that the ailing Lagonda company offered itself for takeover (for which, read 'rescue'), though this was soon rebuffed when the state of that Staines-based company's finances became clear.

Lagonda had been in business since 1906, had begun building sports cars in the mid-1920s, and by the start of the 1930s had achieved fame and prestige on the racetrack. In 1933 and 1934, the company not only had the latest splendid version of its 4½-litre car, the M45, but also previewed an exquisitely-engineered 1.1-litre car with a twin-overhead-camshaft engine, the Rapier.

All this was difficult to finance for a company with an authorised share capital of only £50,000, and as sales faded away at the end of each buying summer, there was usually a cash flow crisis at autumn Motor Show time. Accordingly, though the Lagonda company had welcomed a new chairman and managing director (Sir Edgar Holberton) in 1934, and had delivered about 500 cars during that year, in February 1935 the Lagonda company began to collapse.

Within weeks, Sir Edgar had approached John Black, offering Lagonda for rescue, as a prestige company, which fancied Standard as a comfort blanket. This was briskly turned down at Canley. Sir Edgar therefore returned to Staines, where there were fine cars to sell, but few customers, and in mid-April the Receiver was called in. Almost immediately that Receiver (W Basil Holden) made a further approach to Standard (the financial terms are not known) but was again stalled.

In May, however, John Black decided to make an offer for the wreckage (once again, the actions, but not the financial details, are mentioned in the Board minutes), Standard being one of four companies to express an interest. This, however, was turned down, and as far as Standard was concerned that was the end of the matter. Lagonda, in fact, was later rescued by other interests (that included W O Bentley as Chief Engineer), and survived until 1947, after which it was bought by David Brown (of David Brown Industries who, as we shall see in the next chapter, had been linked to Harry Ferguson in the 1930s), and shortly merged with Aston Martin, where it exists to this day.

In the meantime, the original Flying Standards – the Twelve, Sixteen and Twenty models – were launched in October 1935. John Black had formally introduced them to his Board in January 1935, asking for approval to commit £32,000 to pay for completion of the bodyshell tooling which was already taking shape at Briggs Motor Bodies at Dagenham. Although the details are not spelt out in surviving company records, we know that Standard was unhappy about the original standards of shells received, and was prepared to sue Briggs for breach of contract, was originally prepared to settle the whole matter for a payment of £50,000, but eventually settled for £20,000 – that money to be paid by Briggs, reducing the price of the first 800 bodies by £25 each!

These three new cars all shared what was basically the same, new, six-window body style, though because the Flying Twelve only had to accommodate a four-cylinder 1608cc engine, it could have a shorter (108in) wheelbase, while the Flying Sixteen (2143cc/six cylinders) ran on a 116in wheelbase instead: the cabins were the same throughout, only the front-end pressings being different. Standard, like the Rootes Group, had clearly been studying General Motors in the USA, where juggling with shells and badges (we cynically know this as 'badge-engineering') was already well developed.

Then, as later, the new Flying Twenty (2664cc/six cylinders) was a limited production machine, also on the 116in chassis, which sold only slowly and replaced

Standard in the 1930s – a Coventry car-making giant

When Britain's motor industry was booming in the 1930s, Coventry was still at the centre of the industry. By 1937/1938, with Flying Standards available across the price range, Standard was a positive industrial colossus.

Standard and the Rootes Group (Hillman-Humber) were by far the largest car makers in the city, but purely as an example, in the late 1930s, these were the makes of car being produced in Coventry:

Alvis
Armstrong Siddeley
Autovia (linked to Riley)
BSA (part of Daimler)
Daimler
Hillman (part of Rootes)
Humber (part of Rootes)
Lanchester (part of Daimler)
Lea Francis
Riley
Rover
Singer
SS-Jaguar
Standard
Triumph

– and of course the city also accommodated major body plants such as Carbodies and Morris Bodies, along with a major Morris Engines plant, and other components manufacturers.

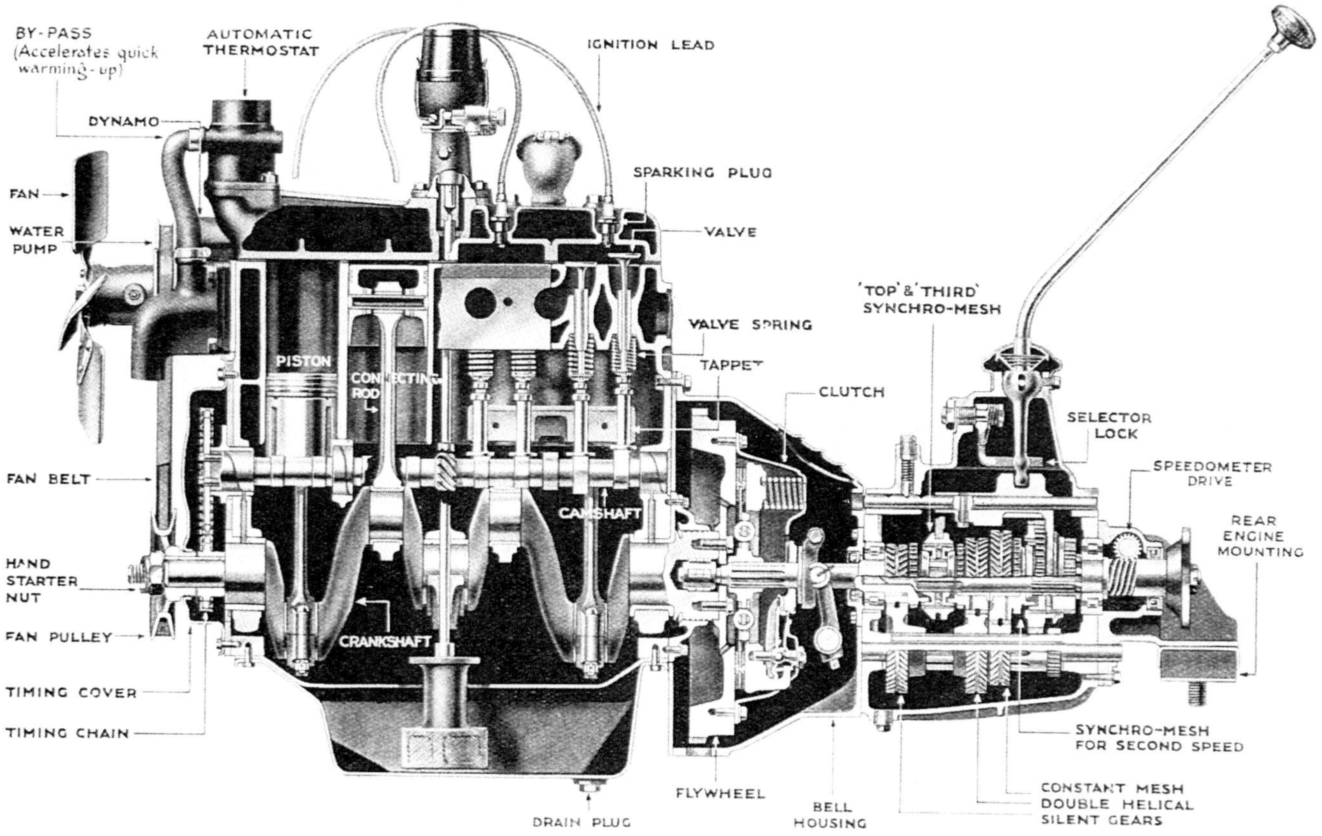

The Flying Fourteen used this side-valve engine and associated four-speed gearbox in the 1930s; other Ten and Twelve models used the same basic engine, but with smaller cylinder bores and reduced capacity.

an ancient upright-style model (originally called Envoy) that had been on sale since 1931: that market sector was very small in any case, and Standard surely cannot have made any money from those cars. Even so, some careful product planning had allowed three new cars to be put on sale with effectively the same four-door cabin, packaging, and equipment. By setting very keen prices (£259 for the Twelve, £299 for the Sixteen, and £315 for the Twenty), Standard got the customers' attention straightaway. Display adverts mentioned 'Streamlined for Speed and Beauty,' along with 'Powerful and Silent in Performance,' and sales were encouraging as soon as deliveries began during the winter.

Even so, these models were later seen to be heavy and underpowered, for the subsequent lighter cars had better performance. Within a year there would be further permutations on the theme, when the Flying 14 was added, this effectively being a Flying Twelve, but fitted with the 1776cc instead of the 1608cc side-valve engine.

Next to arrive were the new Flying Light Twelve (£205) and Flying Ten (£199), which shared their four-cylinder engines and four-speed gearboxes with older models (the Light Twelve also used the Flying Twelve's engine and gearbox), but were different in almost every other mechanical respect. Not only did they share a six-window bodyshell from Pressed Steel, which looked remarkably like that of the big Flying models, but were unique, for the wheelbase was shroter, at a mere 100in. Engines were 1343cc and 1608cc versions of the very well-known side-valve unit, which had now been in production in progressively-developed form since 1933.

In this case, though, the most novel feature was the new chassis frame, which was 'wasp waisted,' did not have longitudinal sidemembers as such, but had the sills of the shell themselves doubling as longitudinal members. This provided extra strength, and also a substantial weight saving, with a consequent improvement in performance and economy. Interestingly enough, this type of construction would be used under the (Standard)-Triumph Spitfire sports car, but it did not appear until 1962!

It is worth noting that, at this stage, Standard split its contracts for chassis suppliers, between The Projectile and Engineering Co, John Thompson, and Sankey. A further link, with Rubery Owen, would follow in the future.

Flying Nine and Flying Ten

Then came the third major launch in just eleven months – the arrival of the Flying Nine and Flying Ten models in September 1936. This type of Flying Ten, incidentally, was

Embellished in more modern times with twin horns, turn indicators, and extra driving lamps, this is a 1343cc-engined Flying Ten of the original 1936 variety.

totally different from that based on the 'Light Twelve,' which had arrived only months earlier: some authorities call it the 'MkII,' but Standard called it the Model 10AL.

By almost any British motor industry standards of the day, this was an astonishing achievement, one currently unmatched by any of Standard's obvious rivals. It was no wonder that Standard had needed to expand its capital base so much, and the miracle was that all this had been done with such a limited pool of engineers and tooling experts. It was no wonder that in its display advertising, the company pointed out that: "Flying Standard. ALL OVER BRITAIN this flag is flying ..."

The Fisher and Ludlow connection

Way back in 1849, a certain Mr Fisher set up in business, in Birmingham, in a small way – a business which shaped metal (kettle necks, lids, spouts, and other domestic items). Over the years he not only survived, but also was joined by a Mr Ludlow, and began producing metal pressings for the motor industry.

By 1920 the company had expanded so far that it was reorganised as Fisher & Ludlow (1920) Ltd. By the end of the 1920s, the company was not only able to supply large numbers of steel pressings, but was ready to begin supplying complete, all-steel, bodyshells.

Standard, like other medium-sized car makers of the day, soon took an interest, and when the time came to progress from using bodies built up around wooden skeletons, to those made entirely of steel, in the early 1930s, the first of a number of contracts was placed with the Birmingham-based concern. At this time, its cramped factory was at Rea Street, close to the centre of the city, but after 1945 it took out a lease on the ex-Nuffield/ex-government Spitfire-manufacturing plant at Castle Bromwich.

These links would then remain strong until the late 1950s when, after the British Motor Corporation had taken over Fisher and Ludlow, Standard found itself frozen out of doing any further business with the company.

Announced in 1936, the Flying Nine was a best-seller for four years up to the outbreak of World War Two.

The arrival of the Flying Nine and Flying Ten models marked the complete takeover of the range by 'Flying' models, for all the old types with stodgy styling – particularly the Nines and Tens which dated from 1933, had been swept aside, and from this time every engine, in every model, now had an aluminium cylinder head. This was the moment at which the third of Standard's major bodyshell suppliers, Fisher & Ludlow, was swept into the net. Those shells came from F&L's downtown Birmingham address, which was now beginning to look distinctly crowded.

Although the new Flying Nine and Flying Ten types had been engineered together, and there were many common components under the skin, they were different enough – and looked different enough, as the Nine was a two-door, while the Ten was a four-door – for the sales force to have much to talk about. Both used the same basic design of chassis frame – still conventional and rather 'whippy,' slung under the line of the rear axle, with exactly the same beam axles at front and rear – steering, brakes and four-speed transmission (with synchromesh on top, third and second gears), though the

Captain John Black (right) congratulates Technical Chief Ted Grinham on the launch of the Standard Flying Nine in 1936.

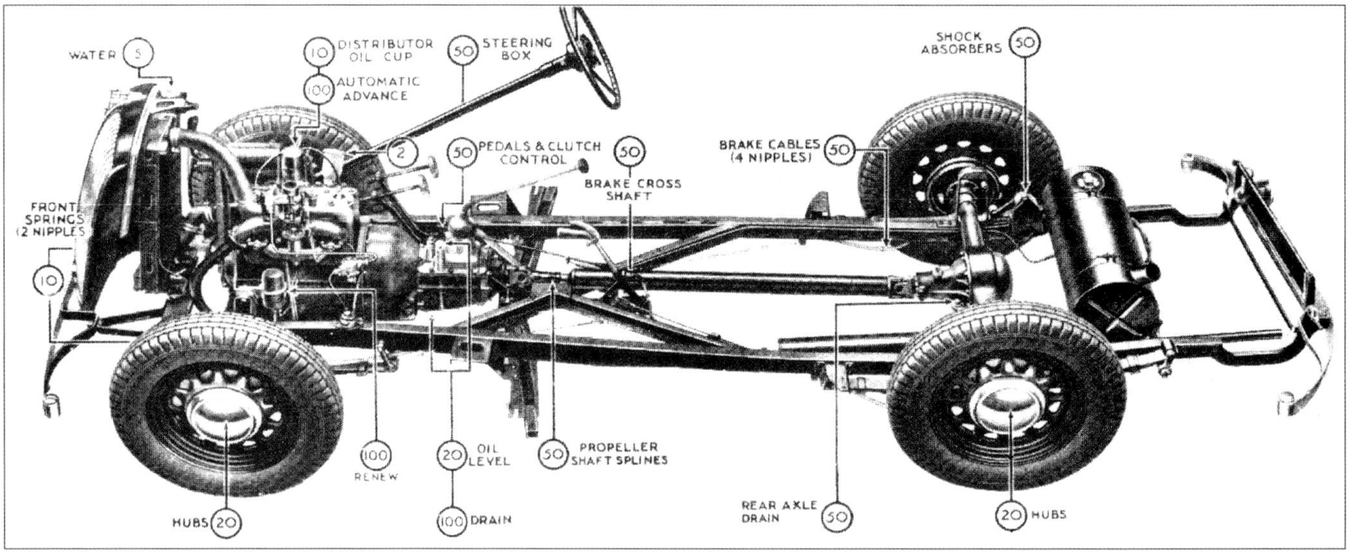

The chassis of the Flying Nine, introduced in 1936, was typical of the range of Standard 'Flying' models produced in the late 1930s

By the late 1930s, simple side-valve engines like this would be used to power almost every Standard on the market. This is one of the legendary series which spanned 1.0-litre to 1.27-litres, and was fitted to a wide range of products.

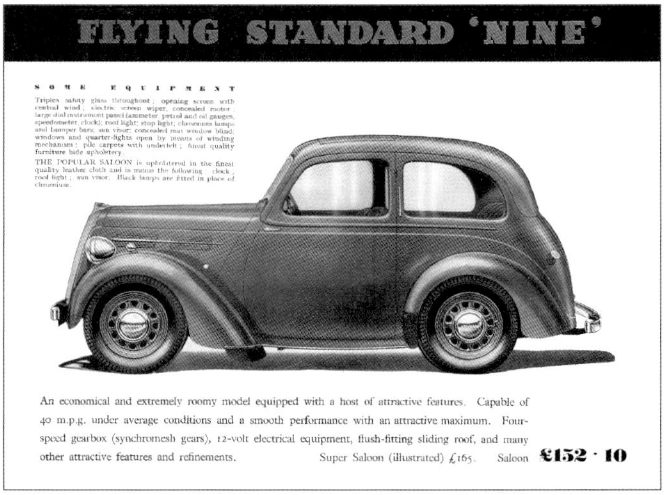

This is how the Flying Nine was advertised in the brochure at the time.

Flying Ten had a five-inch longer wheelbase than the Flying Nine, and a roomier cabin.

The big difference was in the engines, for although both shared the faithful little side-valve power unit, which was now approaching its fourth birthday, it had been upgraded in many respects. The Nine was now 1131cc/30bhp power unit (the old Nine had used a 1052cc version), while the Ten was a 1267cc/33bhp unit (the old Ten had used a 1343cc version of the larger corporate power unit).

Added to this flourish, Standard also rationalised some of its other models, making the 1608cc '12hp' engine available in the Flying Fourteen, and the 2143cc '16hp engine available in the Twenty. Like its main rivals – particularly Humber/Hillman, and Morris, it now seemed to have most bases covered.

Announced in the autumn of 1936, the Flying Nine was a great success. The two door saloon's bodyshell was provided by Fisher & Ludlow.

To summarise, for 1937, the complete range would be:

Model	Saloon bodyshell	Price
Flying Nine	Fisher and Ludlow	£145
Flying Ten	Fisher and Ludlow	£169
Flying Twelve	Pressed Steel	£199
Flying Fourteen (12hp engine optional)	Briggs Motor Bodies	£249
Flying V-Eight	Pressed Steel	£349
Flying Twenty (16hp engine optional)	Briggs Motor Bodies	£299

In view of the feverish, and successful, development work which must have been carried out to make all this possible, it seemed fitting that Ted Grinham was formally invited to join the Board of Directors in September 1936.

Overhead-valve engines for SS Jaguar

Although the world of motoring enthusiasts now knows the heritage of the overhead-valve engines which Standard began supplying to SS-Jaguar (this was the new model name for what had been the original SS brand), it was not always clear: I have described that sequence of events in Appendix A.

Although Standard continued to machine, assemble, test, and deliver such six-cylinder engines to SS-Jaguar, it was not proud of the fact that it was not allowed to use them on Standard models, for contractual details forbade it. Standard apologists would like people to think that these engines were designed by Standard, but the facts are more prosaic. Stuck with Standard's side-valve 2.7-litre, which produced only 68bhp, and delivered a top speed of just 81mph in the SS1 range, William Lyons wanted more. Standard, it seemed, would not, and could not, deliver more.

At this point that ardent self-publicist, Harry Weslake, enters the story. Inviting himself to see Lyons, he apparently greeted his host with the remark:

"Your car reminds me of an overdressed lady with no brains – there's nothing under the bonnet!"

Having recovered from this, Lyons challenged Weslake to come up with a solution, based on the Standard engine, which he duly did, in short order. This time, and for the very first time on this family of six-cylinder engines, he devised a brand new overhead-valve cylinder head to sit on a modified version of the side-valve cylinder block. The new head was of a 'crossflow' design, which, with twin SU carburettors, produced a remarkable 102bhp at 4600rpm. At a stroke this allowed the newly styled SS-Jaguar saloon to reach 86mph, which was considerably better than anything Standard could achieve with the side-valve uniton its own cars.

By this time SS (soon to be SS-Jaguar) had gained a chief engineer for the very first time, this being William Heynes. It was fortunate for all concerned that Heynes had until recently been working for Humber Ltd, that Standard's Ted Grinham was also an ex-Humber man who knew him well, and that, of course, Standard's Captain Black had once been on the Board of that concern as well – for it was they who recommended him to William Lyons in the first place. Each already knew something about the other, and much respect was in evidence from the very beginning.

For William Lyons, the real triumph was that he persuaded John Black to buy the necessary new machinery – plant, jigs and tools – so that this 'foreign' new version of a Standard engine could be manufactured at Canley. This was done in time for the new-generation SS-Jaguars to be launched before the end of the year, and the engines would be in series production until 1939/1940, when the outbreak of war caused Standard to close down all its civilian facilities.

Before long, too, Weslake was asked to transform the four-cylinder version of this engine in the same way, and this was duly done, in time for launch in a small SS-Jaguar (the latest 1½-litre) in 1937. On this occasion, however, this was not an expensive-to-build crossflow design, but one with a more conventional layout. Although this engine was supplied to SS-Jaguar in some numbers up until the start of World War Two, it was never fitted to a Standard. In postwar years, however, from 1946 it would be used on the first-ever 'Standard-Triumphs' – the 1800 saloon and the 1800 Roadster.

Standard Avons – worthy and elegant, but not factory owned

As already noted in the previous chapter, for several years Avon had enjoyed a close and outwardly amicable business arrangement with Standard, whereby its special coachwork

Special bodies for Flying Standards

Although Standard marketed a variety of different body styles on the Flying chassis, the company never built its own bodyshells. As already noted in the text, the mass-production saloons came from Briggs Motor Bodies, Fisher & Ludlow, and Pressed Steel. In additional, several individual coachbuilders provided contracted quantities of the Tourer and Drophead Coupé types, which brought some stardust to the range.

By the mid-1930s, indeed, this is how all of Britain's 'Big Six' carmakers bulked up their range. Having spent its investment capital on tooling-up for new saloon shells (shortly, though not in Standard's case, monocoque shells at that) it then arranged with favoured specialist coachbuilders to produce drop-tops, stripped down tourers, or other derivatives.

To rationalise this, the coachbuilders would usually be supplied with part-complete saloon shells – most often the front-end, complete with bulkhead and instrument panel – after which the rest of the new shell would take shape on the basis of a traditional wooden-skeleton structure. For the motor industry, this was a thriving business: purely as an example, at the Olympia (London) Motor Show of October 1936, there were no fewer than 39 different coachbuilders.

Standard had its own favourite suppliers – those that could be relied upon, and could deliver the goods at the right price. With my grateful thanks to John Carlton, for his advice in compiling this section, here is a listing of different suppliers:

Avon, based in Warwick. Provided a whole range of styles, these being taken under the wing of Standard, though the company finally collapsed at the end of 1936.

Carbodies, based in Coventry, just two miles away from Canley. This company was absorbed by Daimler in the 1950s, and the renamed rump of the company was still building the world-famous London taxicab as the 2010s opened.

Mulliners, of Birmingham (not to be confused with Arthur Mulliner of Northampton, or H J Mulliner of London!). This concern would move closer and closer to Standard in the 1950s, eventually becoming a wholly owned subsidiary in 1958.

Ranalah, of London SW19. This was a well-thought-of 'second division' concern, with many clients, and a versatile product range (which included hearse conversions for other manufacturers). This company does not seem to have survived the Second World War.

Salmons Tickford, of Newport Pagnell. This long-established concern produced shells, including its own patented wind-up soft top, in numbers, for many clients, and by the mid-1930s it was building up to 30 bodies a week. David Brown (who already owned Aston Martin and Lagonda) bought the company in 1955, soon moved car final assembly into the ancient premises, which meant that bespoke bodyshells were no longer available to rival concerned.

(especially drophead coupes) could be applied to otherwise unaltered Standard chassis, and were then sold with considerable factory support and marketing approval.

This deal had lasted for several seasons, but by mid-1936 Avon's business was tottering, such that its failure to pay bills on time to Standard was causing real concern. The fact that its factory was only a few miles from Canley made it easy enough for John Black and his cohorts to keep an eye on it. The third-generation of Standard-based Avons had 1052cc, 1608cc, 2143cc and 2664cc four-cylinder or six-cylinder engines.

By this time, it had moved up-market, to supplying cars which had to compete in the same price sectors as William Lyons's SS-Jaguars, and as other rivals discovered, this was never going to be easy. Pretty and well equipped they might have been, but once SS-Jaguar weighed in with much more powerful overhead-valve engines the writing was on the wall.

By September Avon had 62 Standard chassis in stock which had not yet been invoiced to it, and it already owed the company more than £3000. This was alarming, but because there was still something of a 'family connection' at Avon (John Maudslay, Dick Maudslay's son, was Avon's managing director), Standard proposed to keep it going with a loan of £15,000.

The ruthless Black, however, was not about to squander Standard's money, and concluded that the situation could not be stabilised until Maudslay stepped down (he was thought to be taking too high a salary, and excessive expenses), which he promised to do, but then promptly reneged. Once the Avon company's 1935-1936 results were published – a

This was one of the very last coachbuilt Avon models, constructed on the Flying 20 chassis. Avon had been on life support for some time, and soon collapsed into receivership.

loss of £14,000 was reported – Standard pulled the plug, and the company immediately collapsed. The remnants, of existing stock, were sold off in 1937 – the last of the line being the Flying Twenty-based 'Waymaker.'

Although a rescue was eventually cobbled together (as tended to happen with so many struggling motor concerns in the 1930s), it never again involved the production of bodyshells for Standard.

Flying V-Eight – an aberration

Looking back over the decades, a historian must look at the Flying V-Eight of 1936-1938 and wonder whose capricious idea this had been? As an imaginative punt at entering a new market sector, it was probably outside Ted Grinham's interests, while on the other hand it was the sort of car which John Black would promote as a way to stealing a march on his rivals.

Why was it done, and to whom was it meant to appeal? Whatever, it does not seem to have worked. The fact of the matter is that it was a marketing failure, it fell between too many stools, and it is now a car virtually forgotten by all but the keenest of Standard enthusiasts.

Launched in October 1936, on the eve of the opening of the Olympia Motor Show, the Flying V-Eight (or the '20AV,' as it was known, internally, by a project code) was the last of a flurry of new Flying Standards already lined up for 1937. As already noted, the most important launch was that of the Flying Nine, while other Flying models had all been improved. The old-type Standards had finally been cast off, which meant that the new range looked both smart and totally rational.

The Flying V-Eight, though, always seemed to be an aberration. The engine itself – a side-valve V8 – was never used on any other Standard production car, the style and structure of the car was undistinguished, these being shared with the same basic chassis and four-door bodyshell of the Flying Twelve (though the wheelbase was two inches longer, and the tracks four inches wider), though the 'fencer's mask' type of grille was unique at first and the price, at £349, was the highest in the current range, higher even than the Flying Twenty. Obvious competition came from the new 22hp Ford V8 (priced at just £210), and from Riley (the Eight-Ninety, at £450), with several other rivals from marques such as Rover, SS-Jaguar, Triumph and Wolseley all looking for sales in the same bracket.

Even so, this was a cut above the usual Flying Standard. With 75bhp from 2686cc, in a car which was only 13ft 9in long, and weighing no more than 2950lb, it was good for more than 80mph. Unhappily, the chassis itself was basically that of the wasp-waisted Flying Twelve – though anti-roll torsion bars were specified at front and rear – which meant that the handling wasn't up to much, and the brakes, frankly, were inadequate.

It was the engine, of course, which caused such a stir, for there had never previously been a Standard power unit like it. One look at the engine showed that someone at Canley had certainly taken a good look at Ford's own vee-8 before starting drawing board work, for the general layout was very similar. Ford didn't like that very much, but as no patents were infringed it could do nothing about it ...

Some previous authors have described Standard's new engine as being "in effect two Ten blocks on a common crankcase ..." – which is really quite wrong, and over-simplifies the engineering completely, for a lot of extra work and refinement was involved. Although the cylinder dimensions – a bore of 63.5mm, and a stroke of 106mm – were shared with those of the Ten, on the Flying V-Eight a single cast iron monoblock, with a 90 degree angle between cylinder banks was used. One aluminium cylinder head was the same as that used on the Ten, but the other was a mirror image of it. There was a single twin-choke carburettor, allied to complex inlet manifolding. The four-speed gearbox was that of the Flying Twenty, this box also being supplied to SS-Jaguar at the time.

Although it was never revealed at the time, we now know that it was Coventry-Climax Engines, which produced the components for this engine (and also carried out other unspecified machining operations too). Originally, Coventry Climax was asked to build 500 car sets – 50 sets a week for ten weeks – which it set to do with its accustomed efficiency,

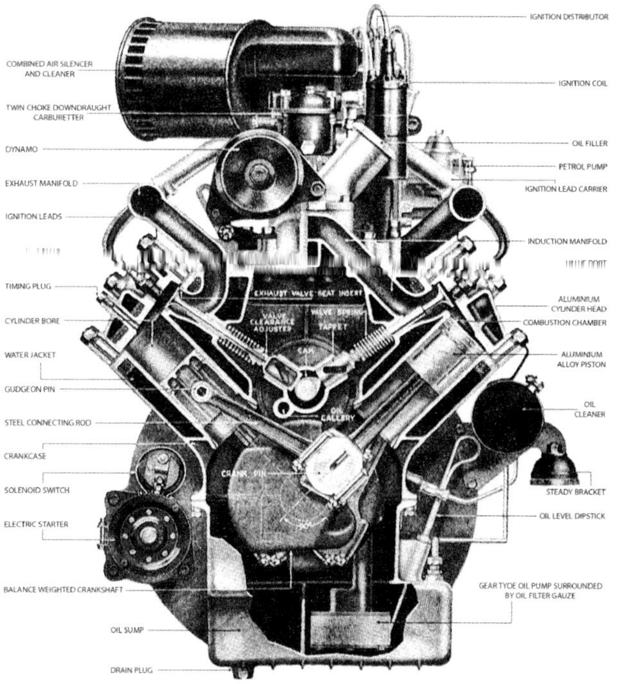

John Black thought that a vee-8 engined Flying Standard could out-run the latest Ford V8s in the late 1930s, but he could not match Ford on price, and the car was a marketing failure. The engine, though, was a real tour de force, as this cutaway drawing confirms.

but that order was briskly curtailed by Standard, which finally took only 250 sets.

Coventry Climax complained, could get no satisfaction, sued Standard, and finally settled for receiving a final cash payment if £7000 to end the dispute. According to this, and to the recurring list of 'sanctions' for new chassis, Flying V-Eight production was all over by the summer of 1937 (though it was still listed until 1938, with a price reduction to £325 to provide a much-needed stimulus), and a few unsold rolling chassis went into store 'just in case.' The 'case' arose in 1939, when Raymond Mays, backed by ERA, took a short-lived interest ...

As was normal, from the ever-diplomatic motoring magazines of the day, this car was given a warm reception. In February 1937 *The Autocar* road test described it as: "New Model Gives an Outstanding Performance, and is Quiet, Comfortable and Docile." Testers positively gushed over its characteristics, describing the acceleration as "exceptional," the maximum speed as "ample and creditable." The top speed was measured at almost exactly 80mph, with 0-60mph in 18.1 seconds, which was indeed brisk by the standards of the late 1930s.

And yet, and yet ... In spite of eulogies like this (other publications certainly followed suit) Standard customers did not seem to take to it, preferring the larger, more roomy and significantly cheaper Flying Twenty instead.

Railton 'Little Chobham' and 'Little Fairmile' – Flying Standards in party frocks

During the 1930s, Noel Macklin produced a variety of high-priced American-engined cars at his tiny factory in Surrey – then in December 1937 astonished everyone by introducing the 'Little Chobham' and 'Little Fairmile' models. These Flying Standard-based machines, which looked like their larger Railton cousins, but were priced at £298.

Although they carried smart two-door two-seater (or, strictly, a 2+1, for there was a tiny rear seat, mounted sideways) drophead-coupé or coupé styles, which came complete with rear-hinged doors, and wind-up windows, these hid a little-modified Flying Nine chassis, though this came complete with a Flying Ten 1267cc side-valve engine, normal four-speed gearbox, Bendix brakes, along with front and rear beam axles with half-elliptic leaf springs at front and rear.

The fact that these models were never mentioned in Standard Board minutes, nor do any 'Railton' chassis find a place in the chassis sanctions of 1938 and 1939, must mean that this was a pure private venture on Railton's behalf. I believe that only 54 such cars were ever built, these starting life as bespoke Flying Nine/Flying Ten chassis, which Standard then delivered to Cobham, where Railton's own bodies – by Carbodies – were fitted.

Commercially, this model was a relative failure, for it was too expensive in its class, and as Railton as a car-making company also effectively closed down when World War Two broke out, very little was later heard of it.

1937-1938: More product action

By this time, business at Canley was positively booming, especially as Aero 1 (the first 'Shadow Factory,' producing Bristol aircraft engine parts) was also about to come on stream. The British motor industry in general had recovered completely from the trade depression of the early 1930s, and the economic future appeared to be bright.

And so it was. However, the developing re-armament programme, and the unsavoury likelihood of another war beginning to look possible, meant that this would soon be seen to be the prewar peak. The fact is that private car production, which had been a mere 169,669 in 1930, rose to 325,192 in 1935, and would peak at 379,310 in 1937, after which it plunged to 341,028 in 1938, and sank even further during 1939.

During 1936 total Board sanctions for the year rose to 33,575, and would rise again in 1937 and 1938. Standard, in fact, boasted that it had completed 4309 cars in March 1937 – more than 1000 a week, and that in the first seven months of the 1936-1937 Model Year it had produced more cars than in the whole of 1934-1935.

Another measure of how well the company was progressing, was that profits for the year ending 31 August 1937 were announced at £300,746. Incidentally, in round figures, that still equated to a profit of less than £10/car, which reflects two factors – one being that Standard was still investing money on new-generation cars rather than simply boosting the profit column, and that it was clearly keeping tight control on all its costs (except for John Black's personal expenses!) and margins at this time.

Even so, after the whirlwind activity of recent years, there had to be something of a pause, which was exemplified by the appearance of the 1937/1938 programme as early as July 1937. The result was that each and every shape now looked familiar, though a great deal of detail improvement had taken place, with much of the work concentrated on the interior, the seating, the fascia/instrument panel and the equipment, while on the more powerful cars there was now a front anti-roll bar.

As in 1936/1937, careful rationalisation under the skin meant that although six distinct model ranges were listed, these were produced with only five bodyshells, three engines (two really, as the V8 was already taking a back seat, and would soon be abandoned), two four-speed gearboxes and two rear axles. All except the 'entry-level' Nine had four

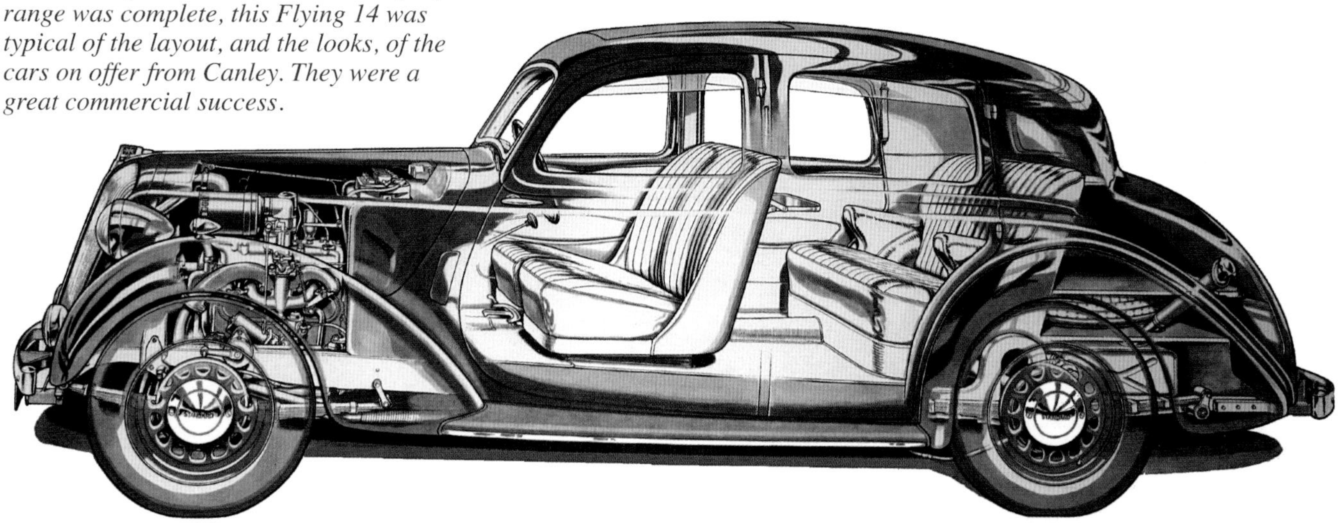

At the end of the 1930s, when the 'Flying' range was complete, this Flying 14 was typical of the layout, and the looks, of the cars on offer from Canley. They were a great commercial success.

passenger doors, and on only one car (at this stage, more would follow) – the Flying Twelve – was there a drophead-coupé option (with bodyshell by Mulliner of Birmingham). Prices spanned £149 to £325, which made the range extremely competitive.

While boasting that it had spent no less than £350,000 on factory extensions and re-organisations to cater for the Flying Standard range, the only visual changes made to the cars were to introduce what enthusiasts like to call the 'fencer's mask' front grille, and to introduce an alternative 'Touring Saloon' style on Fourteen and Twenty models: both those cars, of course, shared the Briggs bodyshell, the company which also provided the new shape.

The Touring style caused the biggest talking point, for it featured a short-lived four-side-window notch-back, rather than a fast-back, passenger cabin, though was still based on the tooling of the fast back machine. Clearly this car was not yet quite ready for series production, as little was said about it in July 1937 when the rest of the Flying range was refreshed, but it soon took centre stage.

Almost every bodyshell to be seen in this picture of the Canley process in 1939 is of an Eight. As the Flying Eight, this model was introduced in 1938, and immediately became the company's best-selling private car.

3XA – THE BIRTH OF THE FLYING EIGHT

It was not until the autumn of 1938 that the general public realised why things had seemed to go so quiet at Canley in recent months. Those were the days when the motoring press might know what was brewing, but would never dream of spilling the beans before an embargo was lifted. The fact is that from the start of 1937, Ted Grinham's small engineering team had been working away on a new project – the '3XA' as they knew it, or the 'Flying Eight' as it would be badged for the general public.

In every way, this was the biggest single project Standard had yet undertaken. Not only would it be the company's first-ever 'Eight,' but it was the first new model to have independent front suspension, and would be the first to have bodyshells produced in a brand-new factory not far from Canley. At this time, too, it would have the smallest engine Standard had ever put on to the market. It was, in every way, the most ambitious project that the company had ever started.

John Black, more than any of his subordinates, was clearly thinking long-term at this stage – both financially, and in terms of what, where, when and how. The 3XA/Flying Eight would complete an ambitious range, but it was a monumental decision to do so. After the launch, of course, it was easy for pundits to look around the current British motor industry, and point out that it was 'obvious' that Standard had to develop a car like this. Ford and Morris already had 8hp cars on the market, and insiders already knew that Austin was rushing to complete its own new Eight. Neither Hillman

The Flying Eight, introduced in 1938, was the largest single investment, with a new chassis, a new bodyshell, and a substantially new engine. The body was built in a new Fisher & Ludlow factory at Tile Hill, Coventry. John Ferguson of The Autocar, who made this drawing, was a much-respected cutaway artist at this time.

nor Vauxhall was interested in going so far down the engine size scale – so this left Standard as the only member of the Big Six, which needed to make its intentions clear.

Statistics proving the need for such a car are readily available. Throughout the 1930s, more than a quarter of all cars sold in Britain were in the RAC '8hp or less' category, and from 1934 cars in the 'RAC 9 and 10hp' category accounted for 32-34 per cent of sales. Standard, therefore, had been wise to produce a brand-new and up-to-the-minute 9hp car (the Flying Nine) in 1936, and now it intended to fill its only remaining gap with a brand-new Eight.

To do this, and to do it well, not only did John Black commit Standard to building a fresh model, but also one that would be new in almost every respect. It was typical of the man that he always thought big – not only by taking a deep breath and asking his backers to provide another big chunk of investment capital to extend and re-equip Canley (again!), but to persuade one of his favourite bodyshell suppliers – Fisher & Ludlow – to build a new plant solely for the benefit of Standard.

Right from the start, Black's ambition was to make and sell up to 800 Flying Eights every week (between 36,000 and 40,000 a year, making allowances for holiday shut down periods ...). In October 1937, to ensure this, he got Board approval to spend up to £350,000 (more than the after-tax profit the company was making in a full year) on new tooling and equipment, though after Fisher & Ludlow agreed to build a new body-manufacturing plant close to Canley, that figure was reduced to £200,000.

Developing the new car took a long time by 1930's standards, because John Black wanted to get it right. In hindsight, in fact, the key to all this activity was the building of Fisher & Ludlow's new factory. Up to that time, F&L had been building bodyshells in an increasingly overcrowded factory in the centre of Birmingham, in Digbeth, not far from Birmingham New Street railway station.

Expansion had to come, and with a guarantee of a new long-term commitment from Standard (other new models, including a revised Flying Nine, were already being discussed), Fisher & Ludlow cast around for a new green-field site. To the great satisfaction of all concerned, this was found in Tile Hill, Coventry, just two-and-a-half miles due west of the Canley site, and close to Tile Hill railway station, one stop down the line from Canley Halt. When completely developed, the new building occupied 221,000ft^2 of factory space.

[That site, incidentally, was just one mile due south of the Banner Lane site where Standard would eventually build aircraft engines, then Ferguson tractors ... but that coincidence was still years down the road ...]

Delivery of complete saloon shells from Tile Hill would always be by transporter lorry, though for a short time there was a startling proposal to build a single-purpose, all-weather, covered and powered delivery track between the two factories, this to run absolutely parallel to the railway line! This did not come to fruition, but it proved just how serious both F&L and Standard were about expanding the business.

Although most Flying Eights were sold as saloons, in 1939 there was also a cute Tourer derivative, which was a very successful rival to existing Ford and Morris open-top models.

Along with other models for 1939, the new Flying Eight was introduced with a real flourish in September 1938, when production had already got under way, which meant that deliveries could begin almost at once. Three versions – the saloon at £129, the De Luxe saloon at £139, and an open Tourer version (with bodyshell by Carbodies) at £125 – were launched at once. A Drophead Coupé with wind-up windows came slightly later.

For Standard, this could not have happened at a better time, with military re-armament going ahead at a rate, and storm clouds gathering over Europe. Only months earlier, the British government had needed to raise money by increasing taxation: one such impost was the hike in the 'horsepower tax' of annual licence fees, which naturally favoured small-engined cars.

Standard's publicists made much of this in their display advertising at the time:

"When the Chancellor spoke, the Flying Standard 'budget cars' were already being made."

"Five months ago a Chancellor spoke – decreeing still more burdens on an already heavily taxed population. An era of THRIFT began! But the Standard Motor Company, ever alert to future trends in public demand, were already building a new series of cars dedicated to ECONOMY!"

[All the capital letters, and the use of underlining emphasis, were used in the original adverts ...]

Standard, in fact, had been incredibly lucky in its timing, and made the most of it. The fact that the new-for-1939 Tens and Twelves were neither more fuel-efficient nor any lighter than before, meant nothing, for it was the new Flying Eight that got all the attention.

All in all, it was a neat, and tiny, little machine, based on a brand new chassis frame (totally unrelated to that of the Flying Nine) wheelbase of only 6ft 11in, with 3ft 9in wheel tracks, and a choice of two-door saloon, or two-door tourer body styles.

Choosing the type of engine had been easy enough, for Standard wanted to use a evolution – a way-down-the-track derivative – of the sturdy, if unexciting, side-valve 'four' which was already in large-scale production at Canley, as

Sweet, nicely built, but too heavy and too specialised to make its mark in the late 1930s, this was the Railton Little Fairmile, hiding its Flying Standard origins under a very smart skin.

used in the existing Flying Nine and Flying Ten models. To get down to the much-hated '8hp' category of annual licence/taxation, the piston area of the existing Nine had to be reduced. Accordingly, and without changing the cylinder stroke (of 100mm), the bore was reduced from 60mm to 57mm, the swept volume came down from 1131cc to 1021cc, and the '8hp' engine was achieved. Peak power, with an aluminium head (like all Flying Standards at this time) might only be 31bhp at 4000rpm, but that was quite enough for the little Flying Eight to reach a credible, if not earth-shattering, 62mph.

Even though, Standard authorities point out that there were very significant basic dimensional differences between the new Eight and the existing Nine/Ten engines. A side-by-side comparison shows that the Eight block was smaller in all dimensions than the Nine/Ten, ensuring that all the major components – block, crankshaft, and camshaft – were new, as were the spacings between cylinder centres.

This, and the fact that the Twelve/Fourteen power unit was yet another entirely different side-valve engine, meant that Canley's spacious machine shops had become incredibly busy. Different machining operations were essential, and this must have accounted for the enormous investment in castings and machine tools already mentioned.

Standard's range of small side-valve four-cylinder engines, which had evolved persistently and successfully through the 1930s, was now almost fully developed, with no fewer than five different capacities – 1021cc to 1776cc – now on sale (and, of course, there had been two short-lived six-cylinder derivatives from 1932 to 1934). By making two tiny reductions in cylinder bore dimensions to match the latest taxation 'barriers', a further two sizes – 1009cc and 1247cc – would appear in the late 1940s, and the last of all would not be produced until 1953.

The new engine, and the matching three-speed gearbox – a cost-conscious derivative of the four-speed box used in the Flying Nine and Flying Ten types – were conventional enough, but the use of independent front suspension was a real breakthrough. [I use that word advisedly, because all of the obvious British competitors – Ford 8hp, Austin 8 (still to come) or newly-launched Morris 8 – retained a beam front-end].

The marketing inspiration, no doubt, came from Europe, where independent front-ends were becoming much more common, but the engineering inspiration, for sure, came from the latest Rootes Group Hillmans and Humbers designed at the other side of the city of Coventry. Introduced in 1935, the Rootes 'Evenkeel' suspension featured a low-mounted transverse leaf spring that also doubled as a locating 'wishbone' for the kingpin at each side of the car.

In 1938, several Flying models were face-lifted, or perhaps one should say 'tail-lifted,' with a notch-back style instead of the originally smoothly sloping tail.

After a great deal of work at Canley, which also included dabbling with the Dubonnet system later adapted by Vauxhall, Standard settled on a system identical in concept, and very similar in detail.

Alford & Alder supplied all the components of this new front suspension, which was not only good business for it, but also cemented a relationship with Standard that would – many years hence – result in it becoming a wholly-owned subsidiary of the company!

Amazingly, at this time Standard also found time to upgrade its Flying Ten/Flying Twelve models, giving them new conventional chassis frames (instead of the early-type wasp-waisted layout), and transverse-leaf spring independent suspensions, though the old-type beam-axle chassis' version was listed for a time [I suspect to help move old stock, both of cars in dealerships, and in the factory itself].

All cars, from the Flying Eight to the Flying Twenty, now came with a modified 'Touring' notchback type of rear end body style as standard (and with six side windows on the four-door cars). No major mechanical changes were made to the Nine, Fourteen and Twenty models. We now know that Standard was already planning a new-generation Flying Nine, and was considering dropping the Twenty completely (for sales were very restricted).

Even so, and in spite of the major expense incurred in launching the Flying Eight, at the end of 1938 the company was able to announce post-tax profits of £167,154.

ENTERPRISE

It was at about this time, in 1938, that a young man called David Eley came to work with Lewis Dawtrey in Standard's Technical Office, and his later reminiscences tell us a lot about the company's enterprise at this time and during the War years:

"He was really very bright, and a nice man, too. He was a very good mentor, who taught us a lot ... He was a gentleman ..."

In later years, when technical director Ted Grinham retired, there were those who thought that Dawtrey should have got that job – but as he was much more at home as an engineer, a 'boffin' even, than in running a department, Harry Webster was preferred instead. It was under Harry that the last Standards, and many of Triumph's most famous cars were designed in the 1950s and 1960s, though Lewis Dawtrey remained as his valued 'behind the scenes' advisor and friend for many years.

"There were no computers," Eley recalls, "or adding

machines, then of course – Lewis Dawtrey had a 20-inch slide rule, but we impecunious young men could only afford a 10-inch rule. There were three of us – Harry Webster, Philip Dunne and myself – Harry, who had once been Apprentice of the Year, stood out, even then, there was no doubt that he was going places ..."

David then flipped through a series of slides showing the sheer variety of work that was being tackled at Canley in the late 1930s:

"That's the coachbuilders' chassis arrangement for the Standard Flying 14 ... there's a Flying Nine ... a Flying 10/ Light 12 ... that's the 20hp V8 in the chassis of the Flying 10/12 ... that's an Avon-bodied Flying 10 ... that's a prewar Flying 8 engine, with its three-speed gearbox ... that's the Flying 10/Light 12 which had a cruciform frame, the chassis sidemembers being incorporated in the body sills ... and that's the Jungle Bug!"

This, indeed, confirms the vibrant atmosphere that existed at Canley at the time, where there is no doubt that John Black's ebullient character had inspired the company to great things. All this new-car activity, together with the building of two new 'shadow' factories on the Canley site, meant that the company was looking forward to exciting times in the 1940s. They would be exciting, of course, but perhaps not in a way that could have been forecast in 1938.

The ERA connection

In mid-1938, British racing driver Raymond Mays was casting around for ways to expand his motor racing business at Bourne, partly to finance continuing development of ERA (English Racing Automobiles) racing cars, and to design a brand-new type of single-seater. Having projected an all-new 4-litre engined road car (two ERA-designed engines were built, but a complete car was never finished), for which he could not find any financial backing, he turned instead to the idea of developing a range of 'Raymond Mays Specials' based on Flying Standard chassis and running gear.

With permission from the author's very experienced historian colleague Doug Nye, I now quote his words, as to what happened:

"Still the dauntless Raymond Mays, Peter Berthon and Philip Merton devised alternative road car schemes to generate some revenue; one for a Standard-based road car to carry the charismatic Raymond Mays name, the other for a whole range of small-engined ERA-Standard road cars ...

"In July 1938 Raymond Mays and Peter Berthon, in partnership with LGO, Prideaux-Brune and Philip Merton, founded 'Shelsley Motors Ltd,' to build a hastily cobbled-up high-performance 'Raymond Mays Special' car, based upon Standard Flying V-Eight parts. The cars were to be assembled at Bourne [in Lincolnshire, where ERA was then based] ...

"Ken Richardson [who was working for Raymond Mays, at this time] recalled that Shelsley Motors simply took delivery of four complete new Standard V-Eights purchased by Prideaux-Brune, and whose bodies were removed at Bourne. Their chassis were therefore stiffened and revamped with new IFS (independent front suspension) front-ends designed by Frankie May, of ERA, and after the specialist Gray Brothers (visiting coachbuilders) had dragged its feet, the cars were ultimately re-bodied by REAL Coachworks in Ealing, West London. Only these four Raymond Mays cars were completed ..."

Chassis supply to AC

AC was one of those prestigious little companies which produced desirable, elegantly styled, cars in small numbers, at premium prices, but always struggled to sell enough to stay financially afloat. Based at Thames Ditton (south west of London), put into voluntary liquidation in 1929, then revived in 1930 by the Hurlock family, AC started building cars again, from a new design, in 1933/1934.

Until 1939 there was always a Standard connection, one which was ever-so-diplomatically suppressed at the time, but which is confirmed by Standard company records, and by modern AC historians. Standard, in fact, supplied chassis frames, and later Moss-type gearboxes, to AC in small numbers – both of which were closely related to SS and SS-Jaguar components of the period, but different in detail!

To quote an authoritative AC historian:

"Although the engine was AC's own, all other mechanical parts, including the chassis frame, were now bought in from specialist makers of good reputation ..."

The SS/SS-Jaguar connection with AC was both tenuous, and not at all publicised by any of the parties. When SS came into existence in 1931, it used specially designed chassis in which Standard installed all the running gear (see page 192), which John Black agreed would be 'exclusive' to that company.

Within two years, however, the waters seem to have been muddied enough, so that modified versions of the frames (the wheelbases were different) could also be relocated under 1934-1939 AC motor cars. And [how can I put this diplomatically?] they were 'remarkably similar' to those of the recently obsolete SSs. Jaguar authorities suggest that SS's William Lyons would certainly have known about this, and made remarkably little public fuss about the situation, happy in the knowledge that what became the first of the new-type Heynes-designed SS-Jaguar frames was already being developed for his own use.

This situation, therefore, trundled on quite amiably until 1939, when AC closed down its car-making activities to concentrate on its wartime efforts: the postwar AC 2-litre also used an update of the same chassis.

Is this the rarest of all Standard-engined 'specials'? This is thought to be one of the few surviving Raymond Mays Specials of the handful built in 1939.

Strangely enough, the archives, and the claimed time schedule, do not quite tie up with Ken Richardson's memories and reminiscences, for the first official news of a 'Raymond Mays' road car was not revealed in the specialist motoring press until April 1939, though its chassis was equally as special as Richardson claimed, and Standard records suggest that seven rolling chassis were provided. At this time Raymond Mays was making much of its potential as a rally car, and (as usual with any project with which he was connected) there was much hype surrounding it.

In 1939 *The Autocar*'s technical analysis, which included an excellent chassis cutaway drawing by F Gordon Crosby, confirmed that this new project was mainly based on the running gear of a Standard Flying V-Eight, but with a special and much stiffened derivative of the chassis, along with a longer wheelbase and a handsome new body style, which Mays promised would be built in saloon, drophead coupé, and open touring guise.

The independent suspension on this car was certainly novel – the Flying V-Eight was a first-generation 'Flying Standard' and had never had IFS – and seemed to be a modified version of the familiar transverse leaf spring front-end which other Flying Standards of the 1939 were adopting – and even the Flying V-Eight's right-hand-side handbrake position was retained. On the Raymond Mays, the Standard gearbox and axle were also retained, the final drive ratio being 4.75:1 (which was the same as the Flying V-Eight). The wheelbase was 9ft 3in, the wheel tracks were 4ft 4in, and top speed was claimed to be 90mph.

As the Standard V-Eight's wheelbase was 8ft 6in, it is difficult to believe that there was much left of the original

Raymond Mays, arguably a better salesman than a racing driver, was sure that he could make a success of sports tourers which used Flying V8 running gear. He was misguided, for the cars were too costly. This was the Carlton-bodied 'Raymond Mays' which made its debut in 1939.

chassis under the Raymond Mays car. It is also difficult to understand why Mays wanted to lengthen the car, for this made it heavier and slower. Not a good start for a competition machine ...

Although this model was provisionally priced at £495, this was clearly not a project which got very far, though enthusiasm ran high at first, and public launch came some months after the two companies had first made contact. Earlier, Mays and Berthon had visited John Black in Coventry on 5 September 1938, when they also laid out their ideas for a series of ERA-Standard (or Standard-ERA, depending on who was talking ...) cars. Not only was the Raymond Mays Special mentioned, but also much of the discussion centred on the development of a proposed less expensive, higher volume, co-production sporting car. According to them, Black received the ideas with great enthusiasm, and production and marketing plans began to move ahead. But not for long ...

The letter which Peter Berthon wrote to John Black on 6 September 1938 tells us as much as is known about this short-lived project, as extracts confirm:

"We feel that it is essential that the car, besides bearing the frontal appearance of an ERA racing car, is assembled here at Bourne ... the car [should be] produced and marketed through the Standard distributing organisation, if possible, and by ERA Motors Ltd, of which the directors would be yourself, Philip Merton, Raymond Mays and myself ... The Standard Motor Company would supply components in assembled sets ..."

There was much more, concerning everything from body styling to a plea for exceptionally generous financing, and the letter also made a guarantee that the cars would do at least 90mph ...

What is most interesting about all this is the implication that Black was already talking about Standard producing a sporting car of its own – "we discussed in connection with your 10hp ERA Sports Car ... the car is the ideal type to sell under the ERA name ..."

By definition, if ERA was thinking in terms of 50bhp from the 10hp (presumably the existing 1267cc Standard engine) it must have been considering the still-secret overhead valve unit, which Standard arranged to begin delivering to the Morgan sports car concern in 1939.

Not only that, but coincident with the ERA approach to Standard, the very latest Flying Ten family car (which was just going on sale as a 1939 model) was newly-equipped with transverse-leaf-spring independent front suspension, which might have been cost-effective, but was not ultimately the sort of thing which Mays and Berthon might like to see on their up-market products.

Like other ERA projects of the day, however, this was only a short-lived craze. Less than two months later, on 5 November 1938, John Black killed it off, with this devastating letter:

"It is with personal regret that I am compelled to write this letter. From the beginning of our negotiations, concerning the proposed small ERA car, I have informed you on many occasions of my understanding with Mr Lyons ... and I now confirm what that arrangement is, viz: that if for any reason either Mr Lyons or myself consider the action of the other to be a breach of our obligations ... then either of us should be free to go our own way ...

"On further consultation with Mr Lyons, he has left no doubt in mind as to his views ... I am, therefore, compelled to give you formal notice that I cannot proceed any further in this matter ..."

Overhead-valve engines for supply to Morgan

In 1939, Standard began supplying engines to the Morgan sports car company, which was based in Malvern Link, not far from Worcester. But not just any old engines – these were specialised overhead-valve 1267cc power units of a type never before fitted to a Standard, or a Triumph model.

Throughout the 1930s, Standard's celebrated little side-valve four-cylinder engines had powered Eights, Nine and Tens in profusion, and in several different sizes (this being brought about by the judicious juggling of bore and stroke dimensions within the same basic type of cast iron block). The smallest of all was of 1006cc (60.3 x 88mm), the largest being 1267cc (63.5 x 100mm). The largest of these engines, incidentally, was fitted to the Flying Ten (1936-1939).

In the late 1930s Standard then developed a new overhead-valve version of this 1267cc engine, using many of the same methods and layout as had already been used in the overhead-valve engines produced, by Standard, for the latest SS-Jaguar units. The difference, in this case, was that whereas the 'SS-Jaguar' engine had been inspired by engineering consultant Harry Weslake, the small Standard conversion seems to have been totally engineered in-house. This engine was then supplied exclusively to Morgan.

The Standard-engined Morgan 4/4 was launched in 1939, and produced a very creditable 40bhp, but very few such engines were delivered before the outbreak of war.

Production restarted in 1945/1946, and went on to 1950, (after which the Morgan 4/4 was replaced by the much more powerful Vanguard-engined Plus 4). According to Morgan, no fewer than 539 Standard-engined 4/4s were built.

Briefly, in the early 1950s, an overhead-valve engine of this genre was considered for use in the still-secret SC (Small Car), but in the end an all-new engine was chosen instead.

May we assume that this letter was written in good faith? Or was the Lyons/Jaguar connection merely raised as a good excuse to wriggle out of a potential deal, that no longer attracted the abrasive John Black?

If it was entirely for real, once again William Lyons had squared up to John Black, face-to-face, and got his own way. Accordingly, it is easy to see why these two powerful Coventry-based tycoons gradually drifted apart, and why William Lyons soon made it clear that he wanted the two companies to become ever more remote.

No new models for 1940

If times had been normal, Standard would have been ready to launch its programme for the following year (1940) in, or around, August or September of 1939. On this occasion, however, the outbreak of war made this usual strategy quite impossible, as military orders had started to flood in to the company, and the government made it clear that all material supplies for civilian car production would soon be cut off.

Even so, notes in company records, and a bit of after-the-event deduction tell us what truly might have been arranged for 1940, if the Nazi party had not got in the way. This, for instance, was the current range of Standard car, which was still selling so well up to the summer/autumn of 1939:

Flying Eight: introduced 1938, 1021cc, with IFS (independent front suspension).

Flying Nine: introduced 1936, 1131cc, with beam front axle.

Flying Ten: introduced 1936, 1267cc, with IFS from late 1938.

Flying Twelve: introduced 1936, 1608cc, with IFS from late 1938.

Flying Fourteen: introduced 1936, 1776cc, still with beam axle front suspension.

Flying Twenty: introduced 1935, 2664cc, still with beam axle front suspension.

One model's future was already in doubt. Although accurate production records no longer exist, from the

This was the third of four versions of the Flying Ten (c1938), complete with an external spare wheel.

Standard car production in the 1930s

Unhappily, I have not discovered any accurate list of Standard car production for the 1930s, the period in which John Black stamped his authority on the company. Such records as once existed have been destroyed or mislaid, and at that time the company Board minutes did not list annual achievements (though 'sanctions' – ie approvals – for a given period were sometimes listed).

During my research, however, a mysterious and unattributable chart turned up, this stating the 'approximate' number of cars built in the calendar years in question. I can offer no proof of authenticity, but offer it as an opening for discussion:

Calendar year	Cars produced (approx)
1930	7000
1931	9000
1932	18,000
1933	20,500
1934	21,000
1935	22,500
1936	24,000
1937	34,000
1938	42,500
1939	53,500

(However, we do know, for certain, that in the 1938/1939 financial year, which ended on 31 August 1939, exactly 50,729 cars were produced ...)

Now you see it, now you don't. This late-1930s Flying Nine, complete with its standard two-door style, features a rear quarter window which could be retracted, by a winding mechanism, to improve ventilation.

Front-wheel drive – an oddity

Many years ago, in 1989, when researching a Classic Cars feature about Pressed Steel, I stumbled across a series of mysterious pictures in the Pressed Steel archive (These were published in the Classic Cars issue of July 1989). In 1938 and 1939, it appeared, Standard and Pressed Steel had cooperated in designing a small front-wheel drive car, one based on the new Flying Eight bodyshell (but with a new flat-floorpan, and a different nose) and its independently-sprung chassis frame, with a side-valve engine and modified front-end styling.

Fifty years on, little seemed to be known about this intriguing project (and there was nothing on record), which raised more questions than could be answered. The engine size was not stated, the origins of the front-wheel drive were a mystery – and why was Pressed Steel involved when the original bodyshell had come from Fisher & Ludlow?

It was only when the author began to research this book that more emerged. This was, it seems, an official (but highly-secret) Standard project, which had been evolved by Bernard Raven and Charlie Phillips, and apparently it was never completed. Not only that, but the size of the little side-valve engine had not been finalised, which explains why it was variously identified in the PSCo archive as a 'Nine,' or even as a '6hp.' A 'Nine' would have been easy enough to produce, but (bearing in mind the exigencies of the Treasury Rating), a cylinder bore of no more than 1.95in/49.5mm would have been needed to produce a 'Six,' which would have made the well-known side-valve engine ludicrously dimensioned and under-powered ...

What happened to it? Although it still existed in 1960, I am now confident that it was scrapped, and that no trace now remains.

chassis sanctions issued by management, it seems that the Twenty was then selling only in the low hundreds, not thousands, of cars in a year, and was certainly considered ripe to be abandoned. Certainly, there were no signs of an up-dated model being engineered. This, incidentally, was not a problem peculiar to Standard, for both Austin and Morris were also having similar problems in selling their own largest-engined private cars: the major reason for this was that the British 'horsepower tax' (the annual licence fee charged for a car to be used) was based broadly on the piston area of an engine – the larger the engine, the higher the tax imposed – and this fee had been increased very markedly in the spring of 1938. Sales figures show that by 1939, only 2 per cent of UK sales went to cars in the 'RAC 15 and 16hp' class.

One of life's little mysteries is that in February 1940, five months after the outbreak of war, and after all normal series-production of civilian-market cars had ceased, Standard unexpectedly launched a four-door notchback Flying Eight. With a longer, 7ft 4in wheelbase, and independent front suspension, it was priced at £159, and given a vibrant reception by specialist media and the motor trade in general.

Even so, no such four-door cars seem to have been delivered during the war years, and when Standard's postwar range was announced in 1945, it was no longer even mentioned. This, however, was almost certainly the forerunner of a new-type Flying Nine that would have followed up if war had not persisted.

There is one important statistic which should prove how market-wise John Black and his sales colleagues actually were – that during the 1930s Standard pushed up its share of British car production from 4 per cent in 1930, to no less than 17 per cent in 1938/1939. No wonder the company was so profitable, and so ready to consider the sort of expansion and investment, which characterised the company at the time.

The Nine and Ten, on the other hand, found themselves in the best-selling market sector, were very successful (and therefore profitable), but ageing. As already mentioned, work, it seems, was going ahead to 'grow' a new Nine out of the recently-introduced Eight (the still-born four-door Flying Eight of February 1940 almost certainly shared the chassis and body style) – and work was certainly advanced on a new Ten. If war had not broken out, and paralysed Standard's forward planning, a new Flying Nine (with independent front suspension), in league with a new Flying Ten (with a different chassis from the Nine), would have been introduced in the next few months.

By 1939 a style of the new Ten had already been settled, the up-dated chassis introduced in late 1938 was fixed for this new model, and the contract for the bodyshell tooling had been let to Briggs Motor Bodies of Dagenham. Unhappily, all work was frozen after September 1939, and in mid 1942 the Briggs contract was cancelled, with a suitable pay-off for work already completed.

Standard, even so, carried on working at full blast as war clouds gathered. To quote *The Autocar* in its first war-time issue of September 1939:

"On August 31st, to mark the conclusion of their financial year, Captain J P Black, Managing Director of the Standard Motor Co, personally delivered to Major R Maude, of Standard Cars, London, largest Standard distributor, the last car to be sold during the financial year. This was the 50,729th Standard car produced since September 1 1938 ..."

In October 1939, therefore, the company announced profits for the year of no less than £322,492.

But that was the height of it, for Standard's private-car activities were about to go into a deep sleep, as the next chapter spells out in great detail.

CHAPTER 6

World War Two – Aero Engines and Aircraft 1939-1945

Far too many books about cars try to ignore their companies' involvement in the Second World War period – in which trucks, guns, bombs, tanks, and aircraft replaced them on assembly lines within existing or even brand-new factories. This is not one of them. Simply, the Standard company that emerged from the Second World War was bigger, financially stronger, more capable, and more prestigious than it was when it entered that War, six years earlier. Much of this was due to the huge effort put behind various military programmes and, therefore, (no excuse is needed for this) to the Government finance that ensured that it would happen. In other words, this was almost entirely due to the vast government-aided expansion brought about by its work on making aircraft, aircraft engines, and much more military hardware.

When Adolf Hitler's army invaded Poland on 1 September 1939, the world changed – forever. Nations which had been reluctant to confront the Führer and the Nazi war machine finally decided that they could no longer stand idly by, and belatedly set about the long, painful, and bloody process of stopping him.

Even so, although Great Britain (and the Empire nations) became the first nation to declare war on Germany on 3 September 1939, at that time it was one of the least prepared to wage it. Its army and the Royal Air Force were still too small, it was short of every possible item of military hardware, and it lacked the infrastructure to change that situation overnight. More factories, more men, and more weapons of war were needed – and Britain's motor industry was soon earmarked to make up that deficit.

Standard and 'shadow' factories

Even by the mid-1930s, a few far-sighted individuals (with the single, honourable, exception of Winston Churchill, it is significant that few of them were politicians, but most were businessmen) realised that the British forces must be rearmed, and rapidly at that, if we were ever to match the aggressive Nazi menace. Before this, however, there were major obstacles to be faced – mostly connected with finance, industrial capacity, and political will.

This story, therefore, really started in 1934 (with a government under Prime Minster Ramsay McDonald, who was rapidly ageing, though it was effectively under the leadership of his éminence grise Stanley Baldwin). Although the government did not want to start any war, it felt that it needed to defend itself, and to match its potential enemies, and therefore to match them gun for gun, ship for ship, tank for tank, and aircraft for aircraft. The problem was that the existing British armaments industry was not large enough to meet the new demand.

In general, although Britain's military technology could still match that of Germany, there was a distinct lack of capacity to do the job. Neither tanks nor aircraft, ships nor aeroplane engines, and guns nor airfields, were yet available in numbers. If this huge gap was ever to be reduced, mountains of money would have to be spent, and more factories would have to be built to manufacture the hardware.

Winston Churchill, an eminent but currently unemployed politician, marooned on the back benches at the time, had been nagging away for years about a need to rearm, yet it was not until March 1934 that Stanley Baldwin finally made this statement in the House of Commons:

"Any government of this country – a National Government more than any, and this Government – will see to it that in air strength and air power this country shall no longer by in a position inferior to any country within striking distance of its shores ..."

Which was, at least, a statement of intent, rather devoid of content. Even so, by the time the government, now under Stanley Baldwin as its Prime Minister since 1935, set about rearmament, Britain's defence industry was far too small to satisfy the demand. Fortunately Lord Weir, a successful Scottish industrialist, who had served as Air Minister in 1918 (the last year of the First World War), had never lost his links with the aircraft industry, and began lobbying for a new 'shadow' armaments industry to be set up, basically to tap in to the mass-production expertise of the British motor industry.

By 'shadow,' incidentally, he did not mean that the factories should be camouflaged, but he envisaged the setting up of a secondary source of supply of every possible item of military hardware, which would operate 'in the shadow' of the original manufacturers. At least 250-300 major manufacturing firms should be involved, he proposed, with the British motor industry's 'Big Six' (including Standard) at the apex of this new system.

Some firms were initially reluctant to get involved (it was typical of the irascible and narrow-minded Lord Nuffield that he refused to let Morris and Wolseley get involved at first, because one of his pet projects, a Wolseley aircraft engine, was not chosen!), but Capt Black (and Standard) was always in favour. By 1936 he had signed up Standard to be one of the most important members of this scheme – and, in doing so (one has a sneaking suspicion that he always hoped that it might be so) arranged that new factories would be built on Standard's land at Canley, factories which he might hopefully annex when the fighting or the crisis was over.

What became known as the 'Group 1' shadow factories included one section devoted to the expansion of Bristol aircraft engine production, the companies involved being the Rootes Group (Hillman and Humber), Austin, Daimler, Rover and Standard. In each case, new factories would be built close to the parent companies' car plants, the deal being that the government would pay for the building and equipment of the plants – the motor companies would produce the engines, manage their operation, and would receive handsome fees in recompense.

[Why were Ford and Vauxhall not involved? Originally because they were correctly seen as USA-owned concerns, which could not be swept into the British rearmament programme, since, the USA was still ostensibly neutral. That view would change in the near future.]

For this ambitious initial scheme, the air-cooled Bristol Mercury VIII engine, a supercharged 25-litre power unit producing 825bhp from a radial layout, was chosen. This would go on to power more than forty different types of aircraft. Standard was to be responsible for what became known as the 'cylinder group' of these engines, while final assembly of the power units would be at the Austin plant at Longbridge, or at Bristol itself.

The original Standard 'shadow' factory, therefore, was built, kitted out and 'worked up' within a year, on the Canley site in 1936 and 1937. Situated at the south-western corner of the Canley estate, it was placed on what, up to that point, had been the company's own golf course – but as Capt Black (who was the most enthusiastic golfer on the staff) ceremonially cut the first sod, no one was likely to argue with that decision. All in all, it covered four acres of land, was originally expected to produce 50 sets of Mercury parts a week, and the annual management fee was £20,000.

Eventually known as Fletchamstead South ('North' was a different building, which would eventually house the Standard-Triumph design, engineering and motorsport operation, as will become clear in chapter 10), this building

A factory is just a factory, right? Not in this case, because it was the original, massive, new 'shadow factory' erected by Standard to face the A45 trunk road in 1937. This plant turned out thousands of Bristol Mercury aero engine components during World War Two, and for a time in the 1950s was the centre of Avon turbojet military engine building. Many years later it was the last of the buildings to be razed by what had become the Rover Group, having been the Group's styling and engineering centre.

Standard's first 'shadow factory,' facing the A45 Coventry by-pass, was completed in 1937, to produce components for Bristol Mercury military aero engines. After the Second World War, and now carrying 'Standard Triumph' identification, it became Standard's Spare Parts division – but there was also a time when it housed manufacture of the massive Avon turbojet engine contract, too.

had an impressive, but typically 'government factory' frontage, which faced on to the A45 Coventry by-pass. In the fullness of time it would take on the manufacture of Rolls-Royce Avon jet engines in the 1950s, would then become one of Standard's major component manufacturing buildings, would be the last building on the Canley site to be retained by what had become Austin-Rover (the rump of British Leyland in the 1980s), for design, development and styling purposes, and was therefore the last to be demolished by the much hated Arlington Securities development operation in the 1990s.

The second new 'shadow' factory was eventually built close to the original, and also faced on to the new A45 Coventry by-pass road. In June 1938, Standard was invited to erect a new building, originally meant to produce AVT 95MB Claudel Hobson carburettors, which could be used on Bristol aircraft engines. This time, 7.22 acres of land was involved (the government could been seen to be chipping away at Standard's 'real estate,' though there was still much undeveloped land in the centre of the estate); the first carburettors were to be produced by mid-1939, with full production of 200 carburettors a month to be produced from mid-1940.

Starting in 1937, at its original shadow factory, Standard built the 'cylinder group' components for thousands of Bristol Mercury aircraft engines.

These targets, as we shall see, were not only achieved, but surpassed, and Standard certainly earned the £10,000 annual fee it was granted for running this new factory block. Before the middle of the war, a further factory would be taken over in Nottingham, in order to make yet more carburettors, and there would also be other 'dispersal' plants for aircraft engine component manufacture in Malvern and at Kendal, too.

This aerial shot of Canley, taken in 1939, is very significant, for it shows how far the main factory had already spread in the 'John Black' era. The Canley Halt railway station is closest to the camera, and in the top left of the shot one can see the second 'shadow' factory, which had just been completed for the manufacture of Claudel Hobson carburettors.

After the war this plant at Fletchamstead North would become the managerial, technical, and development headquarters of the tractor concern Harry Ferguson Ltd, whose machines were being produced by Standard, after which, from 1959, it became Standard's engineering, design, development and motorsport base.

It was an extremely useful and capable building, even into the 1980s, and was still an important part of what had become the 'Rover-Triumph' engineering operation. However, it was finally abandoned in mid-decade, speedily earmarked for demolition, and was soon replaced by a tacky video store.

But, why 'shadow' for shadow factories? To quote the learned paper published, many years later, by S E Little and M S Grieco of Oxford University:

"The term came into widespread use to describe duplicated facilities under the direct control of the parent company, as well as distributed facilities managed by other companies with appropriate skills.

"In the aircraft industry these plants represented a government-sponsored attempt at technology transfer from the automobile industry. Initially, the government constructed a series of co-ordinated aircraft manufacturing facilities to be managed by the motor industry. These were followed by a number of integrated plants, which eventually devolved to the established aircraft industry. They produced 22 per cent of this industry's total output during World War Two, including 45 per cent of heavy bombers."

The use of the phrase 'shadow factory' does not mean that such buildings were hidden (they could not be – though they were, eventually, camouflaged), but that their operation ran in parallel – really 'in the shadow' of established production and assembly lines already set up by Britain's aircraft industry.

Banner Lane – the Big One

By the end of 1937, the motor industry's first phase of shadow-factory construction was already complete. Amazingly enough, Standard took well under a year to get its new building up, equipped, filled with new machinery, and manufacturing the first sets of components for the Bristol Mercury aircraft engines: in fairness, the architectural design had already been completed by government before the deal was initiated. The companies, gathered together as a cohesive group, had all impressed the government with decisive action – which meant that repeat orders were likely in due course.

These arrived much earlier than originally envisaged. Faced with further aggression from Germany – which included its army marching back into the Rhineland in 1936 (which had been de-militarised in 1919), allocating aircraft to take part in the Spanish Civil War to aid General Franco, annexing Austria in early 1938, precipitating what became known as the 'Munich crisis' in September 1938, and finally occupying Czechoslovakia in March 1939 – the British government decided on full-scale rearmament, and set about building new factories, with expanded facilities, in a big way.

Major contracts for all manner of military machinery were placed in 1938 and 1939 – for Britain's motor industry these eventually covering projects as varied: as the 'Midlands Group' producing aircraft engines; Vauxhall producing tanks; Ford producing Rolls-Royce Merlin engines near Glasgow; and the Rootes Group producing four-engined heavy bombers on Merseyside.

Delighted with the response that the motor industry had given to building Bristol Mercury engines, the government now set out on an even more ambitious task – to commission the mass production of the much larger, more complex, and more powerful Bristol Hercules radial engine. Bristol, of course, was already building this engine in series, but not

The Banner Lane factory was completed in 1940, and for the next five years would be dedicated to the assembly of Bristol Hercules aero engines. Later it would be turned over to Ferguson tractor manufacture. By the 21st century it had been demolished, replaced by housing!

Banner Lane

As the demand for military aircraft and aero-engines continued to increase, the second wave of Government-financed 'shadow' factories had to be built all over the UK in 1938, 1939 and 1940. One of the very largest was at Banner Lane, to the west of Coventry, where (for a considerable management fee – eventually set at £40,000/annum) Standard was persuaded to manage a huge establishment.

This covered at 80-acre site, the floor area was in excess of one million square feet, and it cost £1.7 million to build, at a time when the price of – say – a Standard Flying Eight was just £129. In Coventry, only the very similar new Rootes Group plant at Ryton-on-Dunsmore was comparable in size. Architectural students have pointed out that the facades of Banner Lane and the two other Standard shadow factories in the grounds of the Canley estate looked very similar indeed, as well they might, for government had a certain, settled, way of shaping its own new factories at the time.

By the early 1940s, Banner Lane was heavily involved in producing Bristol Hercules aero engines (many thousands were eventually completed), and it was as a direct result of his efforts with this factory, and as chairman of the Aero Engine Shadow Committee, that John Black became Sir John in 1943.

From mid-1945, when the European war was over, Banner Lane became surplus to government and military requirements, the Bristol company was not interested in taking it over, and it was about to become empty. As detailed in chapters 6 and 8, Standard then took over the lease, settled on a cooperative deal with Harry Ferguson Ltd, and from mid-1946 set about building Ferguson tractors in huge numbers.

The original ten-year deal to build tractors ran to 1955, but was extended by Sir John Black to 1965 just before he was ousted from office. In the meantime, Ferguson had sold itself to Massey Harris of Canada, and by 1958 what had become Massey-Harris-Ferguson made it aggressively clear, that it wanted a split from Standard as soon as possible, and Standard made haste to vacate the site.

Early in 1959, Standard achieved the divorce from M-H-F, securing a great deal of ready cash (£11.8 million) and reclaiming its shareholding from M-H-F into the bargain. Although Standard thought it should have got more money, and M-H-F thought it had been charged too much, the deal eventually went through.

After disentangling itself from Massey-Ferguson, Standard lost no time in relocating all its managerial, design and development functions to the Canley site, this being done remarkably smoothly in 1959. Harry Ferguson Ltd moved its technical and administrative HQ out of Fletchamstead North (one of the original shadow factories, which had built Claudel Hobson carburettors), and almost at once Standard moved its design, engineering, styling and (soon) its motorsport departments into that building.

Thereafter Banner lane was owned and operated by Massey-Ferguson, and in later years, after a complex pattern of takeovers and mergers, the parent company changed its name to AGCO.

Tractor assembly continued until 2002, after which assembly of tractors was closed down, and all the manufacturing facilities were moved to overseas plants. As with other old Standard plants in Coventry, demolition eventually commenced, this being virtually completed in 2005. By 2010, only the modern (post-Standard) business tower block remained (though ring-fenced and empty), while much of the site had been redeveloped with private housing.

in sufficient numbers. To improve on this, there seemed to be no question of splitting the effort between various companies, but of awarding one major contract – which went to Standard, who would assembly and deliver complete power plants.

If you will excuse the pun, to produce the new Hercules was always going to be a herculean task. Whereas the Mercury had been a 25-litre single-row nine-cylinder air-cooled radial, the more modern Hercules (which had first flown in 1936), was a 38.7-litre twin-row, fourteen-cylinder radial with sleeve-valves instead of conventional poppet valves. It was nearly twice as heavy, and it must have been three to four times more complex, and costly to produce, than the Mercury had ever been, which was a daunting prospect for a company like Standard, a company far more used to making relatively simple side-valve-engined cars with about 40 or 50bhp!

The Banner Lane factory, later taken over by Standard to build tractors, was originally set up to make this massive twin-row 14-cylinder Bristol Hercules aircraft engine.

This engine, depending on its application, could produce up to 1800bhp, and was demonstrably vital to Britain's war effort. It would eventually be used in many thousands of Beaufighter fighter-bombers, along with Lancaster, Halifax, Stirling and Wellington bombers. A typical Hercules engine weighed about 1900lb (as much as a complete Flying Standard car), and was 52 inches in diameter, complete with cowling.

It was as late as May 1939 that John Black reported to his Board that there had been an approach from the Air Ministry, for Standard to erect and run a 'No 2 shadow factory' at Banner Lane, Coventry, where Bristol Hercules engines were to produced in big numbers. There would, of course, be no problem over planning permission, or of finding and purchasing a suitable location, for the government had already done this, by requisitioning an 83-acre site.

In 1939, Banner Lane was a green-field site, just outside the western boundary of Coventry itself – though in postwar years city housing would grow out to meet it! Three miles from Canley, and two miles from the A45 by-pass road (the completion of which was never announced in case the Luftwaffe decided to give it special attention – it never did), Banner Lane was ideally placed, and escaped the mass onslaught of the two major bombing raids which were made on Coventry in 1940.

At a cost of £2,775,000. which included factory construction, and equipment, it was made available to Standard, first of all at a management fee of £4000/month, which settled down to a flat payment of £40,000/annum when the factory was in full and regular production. All in all, Standard was taking a bigger and bigger part in the production of military material, with the dynamic and increasingly well-respected John Black inevitably in the headlines.

When the government set up a Joint Aero Engine Committee in July 1941, it was almost inevitable that Black should be asked to become its chairman. Along with his overall control of the Standard complex, this was so impressively done that he was rightly knighted in July 1943. Thereafter he was Sir John Black, relished the title, and insisted on being called that by every single one of his staff and employees.

When it was first built, the Banner Lane factory dwarfed any other building in Standard's 'empire.' Two massive office blocks faced the main road itself, behind them being four impressive rows of inter-connected factory buildings. Separate from them, and even further away from the city centre itself, was a long row of test bed facilities.

Once up and running (this being achieved before the end of 1940) Banner Lane was virtually a self-governing factory within the Standard group, for it concentrated solely on the building of Hercules engines, with some components for the production lines arriving from other factories in the city, including (from the winter of 1942/1943) Standard's original shadow factory in Canley itself, and from satellite plants in Malvern, and in the Kendal area.

This cutaway display example of the massive Hercules engine shows just what a complicated job Standard had to tackle at Banner Lane between 1940 and 1945, but it produced many thousands of the unit to a very high standard.

All in all, the Banner Lane project became a fantastically successful operation, and by the time the last massive Hercules engines were built in 1945, no fewer than 20,000 had been produced.

It was this factory, and this project, incidentally, which gave Alick Dick his first introduction to management. Having joined Standard, as a pupil apprentice in 1934, he then graduated to the Purchase department, and was subsequently drafted into Banner Lane as Chief Buyer, with a staff of no fewer than 250 people reporting to him. Then, from 1943, he took over production control in the Mosquito project, before becoming Sir John Black's personal assistant in 1945.

Banner Lane's significance to the Standard story, however, was only just beginning during the war years, for from 1945 it was progressively re-equipped to manufacture Ferguson tractors, which was itself a fascinating project, which is described fully in chapter 8.

Do you want style or utility? In this case the government decided that it needed plain but reliable light vans/pick-ups – this being a Flying 12 on a Flying 14 chassis.

Canley at war

Although Standard was just as reluctant to turn itself into a military provider in 1939, as it had been in 1914, preparations at Canley began in a much more organised manner in the late 1930s. Not only did the commissioning of three shadow factories provide a hefty kickstart to this transformation, but also government and other engineering concerns began to offer other contracts during 1939, while the peace still persisted.

As already described, the massive contract to build and run the Banner Lane plant had been awarded in mid-1939, and at the same time Standard also received an approach from Birmingham Small Arms (BSA) of Birmingham, inviting it to take on the manufacture of parts for the 0.303 Browning machine guns which were to be fitted to aircraft.

No caption needed really, for the sign writing tells us just what the simple van conversion of the Flying Eight was meant to do in 1940!

This, though, was only the beginning for, as a flood of other orders of enquiries arrived, Standard promoted Chief Engineer Ted Grinham to be Deputy Managing Director. This, in theory was to let Grinham run Canley, and to allow John Black to concentrate on the development of Banner Lane. As a temporary appointment (this, at least, is what the Board minutes noted) it was a good idea, but it soon became permanent – yet John Black still continued to rule over anything to which the word of 'Standard' applied.

Could Standard build De Havilland Gypsy Major engines for training aircraft? It could, and made ready – but that contract finally went elsewhere. Would it manufacture Bomb Release Slips to equip the RAF's bombers? No problem – and 250,000 eventually left the factory. Could it also build constant speed airscrew units for aero-engines? Yes, of course – and in the end there would be 65,000 of those. Would it please build a great number of tea vans, vans, pick-ups and ambulances for military and civil defence purposes, based on existing Flying Eight, Twelve and Fourteen chassis? Of course. And what about producing

Like others of Britain's 'Big Six' carmakers, Standard produced thousands of military versions of its late 1930s private cars during World War Two, this being a van version of the Flying Twelve. Note the Hawker Hurricane fighter plane in the background.

Somewhere under all that camouflage, and very basic bodywork in the early 1940s, is the chassis of a Flying Twelve, with a Flying Fourteen engine.

complete gearboxes for Guy Motors, for use in heavy-duty trucks? Easy.

Not only that, but in the early part of the war, a batch of Flying Tens were built as Air Ministry staff cars. Not only that, but some thousands of a rather fragile-looking 'Light Armoured Car' called the Beaverette were introduced in 1940, its main armament being the Bren (British Enfield) machine gun. These were mainly allocated to the Home Guard, but were also used for defence of UK military establishments, all of them being based on the underpinnings of the Flying Fourteen chassis. The Fourteen was chosen as being less complex than the Flying Twelve, which had independent front suspension.

Although the Beaverette could never be described as formidable, and especially not bomb or gun proof (a German tank, or anti-tank gun, would have pulverised a Beaverette with a single shot ...), they were cheap to build and simple to maintain. There were 852 original-type MkIs, which weighed about two tons, MkIIs looked similar but had more comprehensive armoured plate. While the later MkIIIs and MkIVs (1935 of both types were made) looked even more like mobile armoured block-houses than original.

All this, no doubt, should have been enough to give both John Black and Ted Grinham ulcers, but those were the days in which no one seemed to complain, and the slogan was KBO (Keep B*******g On ...) to the end.

Looks like a toy, right? But no, this was a serious, though cheap and cheerful, attempt to provide a lightly-armoured vehicle for purposes such as airfield defence. During World War Two, the RAF took delivery of hundreds of these Standard Beaverette MkIIIs.

An armoured car? Well, sort of, this being the simple plating applied to the chassis of a Flying Twelve to produce the Beaverette MkI. The armour was lined with oak to make it even more effective, but such machines would only have been effective against enemy infantry equipped with light weapons.

Aircraft projects

If the contracts already mentioned sound big and prestigious, the production and part assembly of training and fighter aircraft, which was to follow, was both mighty and profitable – plus extremely praiseworthy. In five years, not only did Standard build magnificent twin-engined fighter-bombers like the Bristol Beaufighter and the De Havilland Mosquito, it was also involved, at the very early stage, in the development of the UK's very first jet-powered fighter, the Gloster Meteor. In all three cases, these were 'shadow' assembly operations for the particular manufacturers, but in all cases it was Standard's mass-production expertise which made such programmes viable.

First of all, Standard was asked to assemble Airspeed Oxford training aircraft, these having been designed by Airspeed of Portsmouth. These were low wing monoplanes, with two 355hp Armstrong-Siddeley Cheetah engines: semi-monocoque construction was a feature of the fuselage, while there was much wood in the build-up of the wings themselves.

Standard completed its first Oxford in October 1940, and subsequently built up to a completion rate of 45 planes every month. All in all, more than 8000 Oxfords would be built during the war, of which Standard would produce 750 by the time the contract was completed in 1943. The Oxford then smoothly made way for the very important Beaufighter and Mosquito projects instead. Airspeed, incidentally, was absorbed by de Havilland in 1940, this being a concern with which Standard forged closer and closer links as the war years progressed.

As in the First World War Standard, incidentally, did not have its own airfield, and could not, therefore, fly out the completed aircraft for delivery. At this time, however, the government sponsored the completion of a new airfield at Ansty, on the outskirts of the city (which also doubled as part of the defences of this important city), where all of these, and subsequent Standard planes, would be finally assembled and flown. The Ansty site was five miles northeast of the city centre (close to the future junction of the M6 motorway and A46 highway) and, almost from the start, had a concrete runway. Incidentally, Standard had no further use for Ansty

When World War Two broke out, Standard was originally asked to build Airspeed Oxford training aircraft, which it did with considerable success.

Standard built the first few centre sections for the famous jet-powered Meteor fighter, after which the production contract was awarded to SS.

after the war, after which Rolls-Royce took over the lease, and it closed down well before the end of the century.

Knowing the growing importance of Coventry as a centre of military production, Germany's Luftwaffe gave it special attention in two air raids; one in September 1940, the second on the devastating night of 14 November. Although damage to the city was brutal and widespread, Standard was lucky, for only the Canley factory was hit by bombs, and not too severely at that. The first raid cost £51,440 to set right, the second a mere £4528 – and in both cases the repairs were completed very quickly indeed.

By mid-1941 Standard had not only repaired this damage, but had also increased the factory space available for manufacturing aircraft – or, at least, manufacturing major parts of aircraft, sometimes with many other sub-assemblies being supplied by other companies.

The company was currently jockeying for a major contract to produce Beaufighters (which were powered by two Rolls-Royce Merlin engines – or, on later Marks by twin Bristol Hercules engines), and for producing the radically different twin-Merlin-engined Mosquito (affectionately known as the 'wooden wonder' because of its reliance on wood for most of its structure).

There was also the prospect of building the still very mysterious Gloster F9/40 twin-engined fighter, a machine cautiously described by John Black to his colleagues in the Board minutes as an: "... entirely new aircraft of novel design, and highly secret ..." At first, Standard was asked to manufacture ten prototype sets of the centre section, then hold itself ready to tool up to produce 80 sets of centre sections every month.

At this time, it seems, Standard was given very few more details of this machine, and certainly not any details about the 'revolutionary engines' – but we now know that this was the company's first contact with Britain's first-ever jet-powered fighter, the Gloster Meteor, which would have

When Standard built the first centre sections for the Gloster Meteor project in the early 1940s, the new Rolls-Royce jet engine was so secret that it was not even allowed to see one!

Rolls-Royce Derwent engines, with production beginning in 1943/1944.

In the event, Gloster suffered delays in completing the design, so Standard only had to build four prototype centre sections for the Meteor. The production contract was then allocated elsewhere – in fact to SS Cars, also in Coventry. SS/Jaguar historian Andrew Whyte made much of this in his books about the company, suggesting that the company 'took this contract from under Standard's nose,' but conspiracy theorists might like to know that the truth was simpler than that. By 1942/1943, Standard was fully committed to its Beaufighter and Mosquito programmes, whereas SS (which had just seen another aircraft programme cancelled as its new 'shadow' factory in Swallow Road was completed) was actively looking for work ...

In the meantime, in April 1941, Deputy Managing Director Ted Grinham abruptly left Standard, to run the De Havilland production and engineering facilities at Hatfield in Hertfordshire. This came as a shock to John Black, who had

Although the Beaufighter was a totally different type of product from family cars, Standard coped admirably, and produced hundreds for the war effort.

little warning of the move, but it seems that the government was closely involved, and since Standard was already hoping to work on the Mosquito project, there seemed to be little point in complaining.

Even so, since 'elephants' (and John Black) never seemed to forget, some rancour would be stored away, and used in the early 1950s. Incidentally, when Ted Grinham returned to Standard in October 1945, to be re-appointed as Technical Director, the Board meeting noted that he was: "... entering into the undertaking that he will immediately resign from this office if called upon to do so ..." This gives an idea of how 'Stalinist' the company became when Sir John Black was at the height if his powers.

Meantime, the Bristol Beaufighter aircraft assembly contract was finally secured, and would come to dominate the halls at Canley. Standard would eventually build 3000 fuselages (of the total global production of 5928), along with the making of much of the rest of the aircraft, before the kits were sent off to Ansty airfield for final assembly, flight-test and delivery. This aeroplane was a formidable piece of engineering. Designed in Bristol in 1938, effectively as a lineal descendant of the Beaufort, and the even earlier Blenheim, this twin-Hercules-engined craft first flew in July 1939.

First as a night fighter, then as a rugged, multi-purpose, fighter-bomber, then as a torpedo carrier and a ground attack machine, and with some Marks produced with Merlin engines, this 320mph craft proved to be utterly vital to Allied operations in Africa, Italy and the Far East. Built to conventional (by current aircraft technology, that is) design standards, it featured an all-monocoque fuselage, and a smooth light-alloy skin, with large amounts of tubing used in mounting and supporting the under-carriage and engine assemblies.

Standard, need I point out, revelled in making the most of this new technology, and would use both the expertise, and the tooling acquired, when designing the original postwar Triumphs which followed (see chapter 7). The very first Standard-built Beaufighter was built even before the Oxford contract came to end, but as the trainer programme ended, Beaufighter assembly built up smoothly and would continue until 1945. At it's peak, at least 20 fuselages were being completed every working week.

Then came the excitement of participation in the Mosquito programme. Every aviation enthusiast, I am sure, knows that this was technically a very different machine from almost everything else in the world at the time, for its structure, and much of the skin surfaces, was mainly built

Mosquito aircraft

Although Standard had no influence on the actual design of the world-famous De Havilland Mosquito aircraft, during World War Two it assembled no fewer than 800 examples at Canley (and Ansty, an airfield near to Coventry), and 266 at a factory in Luton nominally owned by Percival Aircraft.

Often nicknamed, affectionately, as 'The Wooden Wonder,' the structure of the Mosquito was built mainly from wood, which made it very light. Power was by two Rolls-Royce Merlin V12 engines, originally of 1460hp, but later models had up to 1635hp.

Mosquitos were produced on several sites from 1941, and a grand total of 7781 were completed before assembly closed down in 1950. At Standard, Mosquito assembly covered 1943 to 1945 and covered the Mk VI fighter-bomber variety, which eventually proved to be the most numerous Mosquito of all.

Standard built the last of its Mosquitos in 1946 – with final assembly taking place at Ansty airfield near Coventry. This nostalgic study shows the last Mosquito of all, with a line-up of immediate postwar Standard cars in front of it.

The fitters involved in building Mosquitos in the early 1940s soon returned to building Standard private cars instead.

from wood instead of metal, in order to save weight, and to make it quicker to manufacture. Designed at De Havilland in 1938, it entered service in 1941, soon proving to be amazingly versatile and (with a top speed of around 400mph) could also fly higher than Lancaster bombers, which made it almost uncatchable by enemy fighters.

Although De Havilland sourced many of the structural wood sections from companies in the Thames Valley (where the long-established furniture makers proved to be ideal to meet this sort of challenge), it found that it could not build enough aircraft at its HQ in Hatfield. To rectify this, not only was assembly also inaugurated in Australia and in Canada, but in 1943 Standard also set up a subsidiary assembly line in which many sections were provided by outside concerns. Ted Grinham, then ensconced at De Havilland, certainly had much influence over this decision.

All the Mosquitos assembled at Canley (and Ansty, of course) were Mk VI derivatives with twin Merlin engines (some engine types had up to 1640hp each), not only armed with guns, but able to carry up to 2000lb of bombs, either in the bomb bay, or on external pylons. These were magnificently successful aircraft, which could not only outfight almost any Axis plane, but could bomb targets with pinpoint accuracy, all while able to fly faster and higher than their opponents.

Records show that, whereas the Beaufighters were in continuous production at Canley, the 'Standard' Mosquitos were produced in two batches – 500 during the latter half of 1943, then a further 566 from the very end of 1944 to the end of 1945. 266 of that final batch were then completed at Percival Aircraft at Luton instead of Ansty: total assembly, therefore, was of 1066 invaluable machines.

The author's distinguished colleague Robin Penrice, once employed as a junior Public Relations staffer with the company, struck up a friendship with Sir John's butler, Tom Thorne, who recounted one unintended consequence of this programme. It seems that at one time the chief test pilot of newly-built Mosquitos had endured a massive disagreement with Sir John Black, which led to Sir John insisting that he should 'see' every plane completed at Ansty.

A compromise, rather gleefully reached by the pilot, was that Sir John would be warned in advance, then each and every plane would overfly Canley later in the day:

"Black had coffee in the morning, served at his desk at 10.00am, and tea in the afternoon at 3.00pm: the faithful Thorne placing the drinks before his master precisely on time. While ensuring that every Mosquito flew over Canley as instructed, Pilot 'X' learnt of the times that Sir John took his tea and coffee ... Timing his take-off to coincide with the daily ritual, and dropping down to rooftop height, he set his course for Canley, and when 350 knots was registered on the airspeed indicator ... exploded over the factory, spot on time. The blast of noise and vibration was such that cups, saucers, glasses and other utensils vibrated off the shelves in Tom's pantry. Sir John's cup, wherever it was, emptied of its own accord, plaster flakes fell from the ceiling, and a dust storm was created ...

"Tom said the bombardment lasted for about a week before Sir John decided to call a truce ..."

The Merlin-engined Mosquito, of which Standard built hundreds, was a formidable 400mph fighter bomber which was almost invulnerable to attack from the Luftwaffe. Much of the structure was made of wood.

No time to play with cars

While all this was going on, Standard had little time to devote to preparing new cars for a postwar market. Indeed, for years the government made it clear that no design and development work should be done if it meant interfering with war-machine activities. Even so, it is now known that almost every British company managed to get round these rules, either by blatantly ignoring them, or by persuading key staff to work on postwar projects out of official hours.

This explains, of course, how Standard was ready to start designing new Triumphs just as soon as the rescue was formalised at the end of 1944 (this process is described in chapter 7), and how substantial improvements were launched, and made available, on Standard Flying Eights and Flying Twelves in the summer of 1945.

[Standard was not alone in this, of course. Austin previewed its new 16hp car in 1944, Jaguar schemed up the famous twin-cam XK engine during 'fire-watching' sessions at its factory, while we now know that Alec Issigonis designed the original Morris Minor in the 1943-1945 period, that Armstrong Siddeley and Riley were both ready to launch substantially new models in 1945, and that Donald Healey laid plans for his very first own-brand sports car while working at the Rootes Group during the war.]

Standard, for its part, worked up the design for a 'mechanised hand cart' (as it was unkindly described) – which really belongs to the convoluted Ferguson tractor saga, and is therefore described in chapter 8, while its military projects included the Flying Eight powered 'Jungle Bug' prototype (this was a tiny, almost square, machine designed for air-dropping, and for use by parachute troops – but it never came close to the production stage.

The author's distinguished predecessor as a Standard historian, John Davy, sums up this project so well, and so succinctly, that I quote his very words:

"The first of these austere vehicles had conventional drive, and the second four-wheel-drive, and two men could easily manhandle it out of difficult terrain. It was originally intended that the vehicle would draw a small trailer, into which it could be placed for ferrying across rivers. At a trial in the factory static water tank the vehicle and trailer immediately sank to the bottom, and the designer and his staff [not Standard engineers, one might add] were left contemplating the rising bubbles ..."

Davy later confirmed that the Jungle Bug, which had motorcycle saddles instead of car-type seats, was extremely uncomfortable to ride in/on. Later fitted with a Mayflower-type 10hp engine, it was taken over by the Army, coming out on various publicity occasions, but never finding any sensible use.

By 1945, however, Standard staff – Sir John Black in particular – were all looking forward avidly to the future, when peace would return and when, they hoped, a normal market would be re-established. Not that the Standard of 1945 was going to be like the Standard of 1939. Not only did Sir John have big plans for the use of the Banner Lane factory – but he also now had an extra brand to nurture – Triumph.

One of the 'why-don't-we? ...' projects tackled by Standard during World War Two was to produce this tiny, go-anywhere 'Jungle Bug,' which had only two very uncomfortable seats, aircraft-type tyres, and power courtesy of a small Standard Eight/Nine side-valve engine. Only one prototype was built.

CHAPTER 7

The takeover of Triumph, and after 1944-1946

When World War Two was at its height, Triumph, as a motor car manufacturer, was defunct. The name existed, the reputation lived on, but there seemed to be no way back from the bankruptcy, and the devastation, which had hit the company in recent years.

Up to this moment, there had never been any technical or financial links between the two Coventry car makers, Standard and Triumph. Triumph, as a brand, had been set up in Coventry in the 1880s, first to sell sewing machines, then bicycles and (from the early 1900s) motorcycles. The very first Triumph car was launched in 1923, and thereafter expansion steadily followed.

In the 1930s, with Col Claude Holbrook at the helm, Triumph not only developed a series of sporting cars, but also built a great reputation for the elegant style of its machines. That famous sportsman, Donald Healey, joined the company in 1933, soon became its technical director, and always encouraged the sporting activities of the concern. Even so, throughout the 1930s, there were no engineering and technical links with Standard, for Triumph wanted to stay independent (and nearly succeeded).

At this time however, finance – the lack of it, especially – was always a problem at Triumph, and not even the selling off its thriving motorcycle subsidiary could solve the problem. Perhaps it is ironic that Triumph, the motorcycle, then survived strongly into the 1970s (and has been reborn in the 21st century), whereas the car concern did not.

By 1944 Triumph was moribund – the assets being owned by a Yorkshire-based steel company – and comprised little more than the brand name, the intellectual naming rights, and some bombed-out buildings. It was at this time that Standard (or, rather, Sir John Black) pounced. This, though, was not a sudden inspiration, for there had already been a decade of financial trauma to set the scene, which had been well recorded in Coventry at the time.

What follows is a summary of the way that Standard eventually came to own Triumph. The reason that so much historical detail is included is to demonstrate that the Standard-Triumph union came about after at least a decade in which the Triumph business, and Triumph brand, staggered from crisis to crisis. The merger of Standard with Triumph, it seems, was by no means pre-ordained – and might even be described as a chance encounter ...

Mergers and manoeuvres

When Standard eventually moved to buy Triumph, it was just

one of many such manoeuvres which the motor industry had seen in the late 1930s and early 1940s. The cosy British motor industry of the late 1930s had been shaken up by the slump in car sales, which followed tax increases in 1937 and 1938. The 'Big Six' survived well, as everyone thought they would, but it was the 'second division' which suffered most of all.

First of all, in Coventry, by 1938 Riley had finally encountered one crisis too many, and had somewhat gratefully been bought up by Lord Nuffield, who immediately sold it on to his own Nuffield Organisation (where it joined Morris, MG and Wolseley). A year later, in 1939, at about the same time as Triumph went into receivership, SS-Jaguar bought up Motor Panels Ltd (pressed-steel panel supply specialist) – both of those concerns being geographically 'cheek-by-jowl' with the still-independent Triumph concern.

John Black, however, got on with making Standard much larger, not only by running shadow factories in the grounds at Canley, but by also running the vast new Banner Lane complex. Although race-driver Raymond Mays had recently set up a small company to build road cars (and was proposing to use much-modified Standard Flying V-Eight chassis and engines for that job), Sir John had refused an offer to join the board of his company.

There was more – for the famous Staines-based manufacturer, Lagonda, had twice offered itself to Standard. The first approach had come in 1935, when Lagonda's money ran out for the first time, and the second came in approx 1943, when Lagonda was not only busy with war work, but had also set its technical director, W O Bentley, to design a new-generation of twin-overhead camshaft engines. Neither approach appealed to Standard, for Lagonda was perhaps a little bit too far up-market to appeal to the practical-minded Coventry engineer.

The biggest rebuff, however, came from SS-Jaguar, with whom Sir John would have loved to merge. In retrospect, it was never likely that two towering industrialists like Sir John Black and SS's William Lyons could ever have co-habited – yet the approach was indeed made. As we now know, Sir John Black was a man of moods, a man whose emotions often ruled his business decisions, and this is nowhere more obvious than in the purchase of Triumph.

However, and as already noted, Sir John was jealous of the high-profile success gained by William Lyons with his stylish SS, later SS-Jaguar, cars – particularly if much of the hidden engineering features were directly borrowed from Standard.

If Standard had not provided complete rolling chassis for the first-generation SS models – frames, engines, transmissions and suspensions – would SS even have become established? Black thought not. If Standard had ceased manufacturing engines for SS in the late 1930s, could SS have afforded to do it itself? Again, Sir John thought not.

This rumbling discontent originated in the early 1930s. As already noted, Standard had begun supplying complete rolling chassis, with six-cylinder engines and Standard four-speed transmissions, to SS, which then completed its own bodyshells and began marketing the smart SSI and SSII range. From 1935, SS became SS-Jaguar, the new Technical Chief Bill Heynes designed a new chassis, and Standard began making a series of overhead-valve six-cylinder engines, which would never be used in any Standard model. Throughout this period, SS made no attempt to build up Standard's invaluable part in this enterprise.

By the end of the 1930s, it seems, Sir John Black was so jealous of SS-Jaguar's own success that he set out to build a more sporting image for his company. Not only that, but he decided to encourage his engineers to evolve a completely new engine, transmission and chassis for his postwar cars. With this in mind, he decided that there was really no logical place for the manufacture of the existing six-cylinder engines.

No sooner had he advised Jaguar's William Lyons of this, than Mr Lyons offered to buy the machinery and manufacturing plant connected with these engines, to take over the manufacture for his own purposes, and to reinstall everything at his burgeoning factory in the Whitmore Park estate in Foleshill.

In October 1942 that deal was speedily done and (knowing that John Black could be both perverse and capricious in his dealings), Mr Lyons made sure that a cheque for payment arrived post-haste on Black's desk, speedily followed by the arrival of trucks, and machinery specialists, to uplift the engine-manufacturing machinery from Canley, and move it a few miles to Jaguar's own buildings in Foleshill! The story goes that when this job had been completed, only then did Standard comprehend that it would no longer be able to build six-cylinder engines of any type at Canley ...

To quote Sir William Lyons in his 1969 Lord Wakefield Gold Medal Paper:

"Sir John Black told me that he would no longer be able to make our engine, and after some discussion offered to sell us the special plant he had put down for its production ... I had a great admiration for John Black in many respects, but I quickly grasped the opportunity to obtain security ... It turned out that I had been right to do so for it was not long before Black proposed that we should revert to the previous arrangement, and return the plant to Standard. He pressed me very hard, even to the extent of suggesting that we should form a separate company together ..."

According to that celebrated Jaguar historian, Andrew Whyte: 'When Black wanted to change his mind a little later, of course, Lyons was not interested. A suggestion that SS and Standard should join forces was met with a similar rebuff. If Black believed that 15 years of cooperation between the two companies would soften William Lyons, he was soon disillusioned ...'

The implications were obvious. By any commercial standards, Standard was much larger than SS-Jaguar, there seemed to be no chance of such a union being a merger of equals, and Mr Lyons was not likely to enjoy becoming a junior partner in any enterprise where John Black was the king-pin. But was William Lyons justified in refusing a merger bid from Standard at the end of the 1930s? Sir John thought not.

By the middle of the war years, therefore, Sir John Black seemed to be suffering from split priorities, or split intentions. How, for instance, could he justify going for a more sporting image, if he was also set on following a single-model policy with his postwar range of cars. And, let's be honest, there was never anything remotely sporting about the Standard Vanguard, which was the result of these deliberations ...

But, was a plan to providing Standard with a more sporting image feasible, or advisable? In fairness, it seemed to be quite justified, for even the latest Flying Standards might be good looking, but were not at all exciting to own or to drive. Naturally he wanted his new cars' image to be the best – and, by definition, he wanted to out-do Jaguar, the company which had refused to join hands with him. All this, no doubt, influenced him when the chance to buy up Triumph arose.

Dead, or merely dormant?

The first big losses had been recorded at Triumph in 1932, further losses followed in the next three years, yet an incredibly complex (and expensive!) Dolomite Straight-eight project had been revealed in 1934, and a new factory had been acquired (at Holbrooks Lane, in Coventry) in 1935, this partly being financed by the sale of the motorcycle business. Even so, by the end of 1936 Triumph owed nearly £500,000 (mainly to the Midland Bank) and had no reserves, so a serious write-down of existing share stock was made, and new capital was pumped in by new investors, to stabilise the business.

For a time this strategy seemed to work, there was even talk of a merger with the loss-making Riley concern (this, on reflection, looks like the classic case of two drunks propping each other up on a lamp-post, in case one of them should fall down!), but nothing came of it, and by 1939 the losses were once again mounting up. SS-Jaguar (whose cars were powered by Standard engines) was partly to blame, for its cars were faster, smarter, sold for lower prices and were hitting several of what I might call Britain's 'middle-class' car makers.

The end came abruptly on 7 June 1939, when a Receiver was appointed to safeguard the interests of the bank (today we would talk about the company going in to 'Administration' ...), and from that moment Triumph, as an independent car maker, ceased to exist.

So, what were the assets at that time? Cars were currently being manufactured in two factories – the more modern one in Holbrooks Lane, Foleshill, to the north of the city centre, where all final assembly took place, with some component work (and all the body manufacture) being carried out at the original, historic, site at Clay Lane/Briton Road, to the east of the city centre (known locally as the 'Stoke Works'). Holbrooks Lane, incidentally, was quite literally 'next door' to the thriving SS-Jaguar concern.

Modern overhead-valve four-cylinder and six-cylinder engines (1.5-litre, 1.7-litre and 2.0-litre) and transmissions, all announced in 1936, were all made on machinery in one or other of these factories. By 1939 there was an existing range of rather conventionally engineered cars – everything from the Twelve (priced at £285) to the Dolomite Roadster Coupé (£450) – and a long-suffering line-up of dealers who were not selling many cars at all!

Within weeks the Receiver advertised the business, the Triumph factory and all its equipment, as a 'going concern' – and it was shortly purchased by Thos W Ward Ltd, which was a well-respected engineering and steel-making group, based in Sheffield, Yorkshire.

Then, and later, it was clear that if war had not intervened, this would have developed as a classic asset-stripping opportunity, as this quote from Thos W Ward's joint managing director Ashley Ward – made at a Board Meeting – tells us:

"He ... had established contact with the Receiver, and after certain preliminaries an inspection had been made of the two works in Coventry, the Gloria works [Holbrooks Lane – GR] comprising 10¾ acres, the Stoke Works [Clay Lane/Briton Road – GR] comprising 3½ acres, and after taking a full inventory and discussions of the matter with his chairman, it had been decided to make an offer for the concern ...'

This offer was made in August 1939, Thos W Ward told the world it had purchased Triumph on 1 September 1939 – and World War Two broke out just two days later! Although Thos W Ward might indeed have wanted to revive Triumph as a car-manufacturing business, Adolf Hitler's ambitions clearly changed everything, and no serious attempt was ever made to start again.

Much, however, happened in the next few weeks. First of all, Donald Healey was installed as general manager, some time went into negotiating with Armstrong-Siddeley (also of Coventry) with a view to making aeroplane engines, then after some weeks the Holbrooks Lane site was hived off to the long-established H M Hobson (Aircraft and Motor) Components Ltd business, for the manufacture of Claudel-Hobson military aircraft carburettors. Thos W Ward was well into the negotiations over price when it discovered that Hobson was actually being backed by the British government, who soon applied its powers of compulsory purchase.

What happened next certainly qualifies for inclusion in the 'Fortunes of War' category. Although Thos W Ward's avowed public intention was to revive Triumph when peace followed war, it was either not very serious about this, or not capable of working out the space and facilities, which might be needed. With the 10¾-acre Gloria works now sold out to H M Hobson/the British government, it was left only with the 3½-acre Stoke Works – which Triumph had already concluded was too small, several years earlier, and which was, in any case, now carrying out aircraft sub-contract work for Armstrong-Whitworth of Coventry.

Adolf Hitler now intervened decisively, for on the night of 14/15 November 1940, much of the centre of Coventry was bombed out of existence by a fleet of Luftwaffe aircraft. Clay Lane/Briton Road (the Stoke Works) was very badly damaged, and was no longer of any use to Thos W Ward, or indeed to the war effort. As the author once commented in another place:

Historic Triumph factory sites

Although this has little to do with the development of postwar Triumphs under the Standard banner, the story will become neat and tidy if the location of original Triumph factory premises is made clear:

The original Triumph motorcycle engineering and assembly plant was in Priory Street, Coventry, in the very centre of the city. The first Triumph cars were designed there, but never built there. This factory then concentrated solely on motorcycle production (which had been hived off from Triumph's motor car operation in the 1930s), and was completely bombed out in November 1940, which meant that it was never a part of the original Standard purchase in 1944. Its precise location is actually under the foundations of the modern Coventry cathedral, which was built in the 1950s.

The first Triumph cars, announced in 1923, were built in a factory in Clay Lane, Coventry, which is attached to the main A4660 Walsgrave Road, to the east of the city centre. This factory also had access from Briton Road, a parallel road to Clay Lane – and these buildings have carried both names during their lives! Car assembly was moved out to Foleshill in 1935, but bodyshell manufacture carried on there until 1940. This factory was badly damaged by bombing in November 1940, and it was this damaged, patched-up, site, which Standard bought in October 1944. As related in the main text, the patched-up building itself (but not the rights to the Triumph name) was eventually sold off to the B O Morris concern for £42,000.

Triumph car assembly began in an ex-government shell-filling plant off Holbrooks Lane in 1935. This was located in an industrial estate in Foleshill to the north of the city centre, and was actually next door to the SS-Jaguar business, those two companies sharing a boundary wall. After the Triumph business went bankrupt in 1939, the Receiver hived it off to the British government, which installed H M Hobson (Aircraft and Motor) Components Ltd, there to build aircraft Claudel Hobson carburettors.

This complex, once known as the 'New Gloria Works,' had no further contact with Triumph, and none with Standard – even though at this time there was already another Hobson 'cuckoo' operation within the spacious grounds at Canley!

"... Although enough of the old factory was left standing for Walter Belgrove [Triumph's Chief Stylist and Body Engineer] to be able to pay a visit to collect what drawing-office schemes and details remained, it was really the end of the Triumphs of the 1930s as enthusiasts knew them. No attempt was ever made to rescue and repair the spare parts, most of which were bulldozed into the ground, or sold off as scrap."

All the remaining vitality then drained out of Triumph, which became moribund, and remained so for almost four years, for Thos W Ward seemed to lose all heart in its Coventry purchase. Walter Belgrove joined Standard on the other side of the city, to become involved in the Process Planning departments, and what remained of the workforce also dispersed to other concerns in and around Coventry.

Although Donald Healey joined the Rootes Group during the war years, he spent most of his spare time (and some of that of his employers' time, we now know ...) scheming up ways of reviving a personal sports car project. This was a quite independent idea, and although initially he wanted it to have it taken up by Triumph, the brand's owners, Thos W Ward, turned him away at a meeting in early 1944. As we now know, Healey then turned to his old friends in the city, the Riley family, secured a supply promise of engines and transmissions from them, and set up the Healey Motor Company, where the first Healeys, manufactured in Warwick, went on sale in 1946.

Standard strikes

It was at about this time that the Coventry grapevine began to buzz with rumours about 'The Triumph.' Every businessman in the city knew that the business had been badly hit by bombing in 1940, and that though some restitution work had been done at the Stoke Works, no forward-thinking planning seemed to have been made. Thos W Ward then let it be known that it might after all be interesting in shedding its unsuccessful investment (with which, frankly, it had done nothing since completing the purchase), and sat back to await developments.

There was no immediate rush. No-one with any financial acumen was about to make rash offers for a business, which had little more than a brand reputation, and a few trademarks to offer. The factories had gone, the tooling had been destroyed, the management and the workforce had all been dispersed so – what was left?

Let us, for the moment, discount the pressures of the war – which was well on its way to being won, but much more remained to be done. It would not be until May 1945 (the Germans) and August 1945 (the Japanese) that both surrendered unconditionally to the Allies.

Who, then, might be interested? Apart from one of Britain's 'Big Six' carmakers (of which Standard was undoubtedly one), the only sizeable Coventry-based carmakers who might, just might, be interested were Alvis, Armstrong-Siddeley, Daimler, and Jaguar. Riley had already been subsumed into the Nuffield organisation, and no other enterprise seemed to be large enough to cope with the challenge.

All of those companies had their own postwar reconstruction to worry about (in Coventry the bombing had been heavy, and wide-spread), so that list soon shrank. Alvis and Armstrong-Siddeley were heavily involved in aircraft engine, and air-frame, manufacture, Daimler not only built cars, but military vehicles and buses, and Jaguar found itself with other rationalisation problems (it had recently taken over Motor Panels, a body-building business) which took precedence.

So, what about one of the 'Big Six?' Not Austin, who were only interested in its own brand, and not Nuffield (who, with Morris, MG, Riley and Wolseley on its books, had quite enough to digest). Vauxhall was owned by General Motors, who also owned Opel of Germany, a subsidiary that had been shattered by Allied bombing, Ford was also American-owned (and also had German interests to repair), while the Rootes Group (Hillman, Humber and Sunbeam-Talbot) was also heavily committed to its own business.

Which, by a combination of fate and happenstance, left only Standard as likely saviours, who just happened to have a Managing Director, Sir John Black, for whom the limits of ambition had not yet been reached. Sir John, as we now know, had enjoyed what the business fraternity called 'A Good War,' and was much admired by the British government. Knighted for his efforts in 1943, respected and admired (if not actually loved) by his colleagues and workforce, he could be expected to look around for new challenges.

By 1945 Britain's war machine was winding down rapidly. Government orders for aircraft, and for aero engines, were being scaled down (even so, many costly pieces of machinery built in that year would never even be uncrated for military use, and would be sold off for scrap ...), and it was going to take time for companies like Standard to get back into full-scale peace-time car production.

Alick Dick, who would become Standard's Managing Director in 1954, was Sir John's personal assistant at this time, and once granted the author a fascinating interview about the events, which then unfolded. This is what happened after the Coventry 'grapevine' got to know that Thos W Ward was ready to sell off the remains of Triumph:

"Just before the end of the war in 1944, Triumph itself was effectively still bust. John Black wanted another name alongside Standard – just that. As far as I can remember, Sir John sent me out to the Stoke Works with Charles Band, Standard's chairman. We looked at the place, which wasn't worth a farthing. But we went ahead and bought the place ..."

Sir John, coincidentally, was still irked by William Lyons attitude. Standard, as a concern, had had a very profitable war, the factories had not suffered much bomb damage, and there was money in the bank. Accordingly, this was what Standard's Board minutes, dated 20 October 1944, had to say:

"Resolved that the action of the managing director [Sir John Black] in paying a deposit of £7500 for the purchase by the company of the freehold property known as the Triumph works, Briton Road, Coventry, subject to and with the benefit of the lease of a portion of such works to Armstrong-Whitworth Aircraft Ltd, together with all plant, stock, office furniture, fittings and effects, in and around such premises, including all finished and unfinished parts, together with the drawings and jigs and tools necessary for the manufacture of Triumph cars, including working drawings of engines, gearboxes and other parts, and together with the goodwill of the business, with the right to use the name Triumph in conjunction with any company to be registered by the Standard Motor Co Ltd be approved ...

"It was further resolved that the aforementioned premises ... be purchased by the company at a cost of £75,000."

Clearly there was to be absolutely no doubt in anyone's mind about the Triumph purchase, for this was a typical lawyer's 'business-speak' entry in the company's official minute book, so that everything would be clear now, and in the future.

In many ways, however, this entry was misleading, for it implied that the purchase was a prelude to getting the Briton Road work-place back into action when soon-to-be-realised peacetime conditions were realised. However, as Alick Dick made crystal clear in the same interview:

"We sold the factory to the B O Morris group for about the same amount, and all we got was the name – for nothing – plus, I suppose, an obligation to supply spares for Triumph cars. But as there were hardly any of them, we really didn't feel any obligation to the old customers ..."

[In fact, and as Board minutes from a meeting held on 21 March 1946 confirmed, B O Morris paid £42,000.]

At this point, therefore, Briton Road and the possibilities of renewed manufacture on those premises, immediately fades out of the overall Standard picture. Little is known, or needs to be known, about 'B O Morris,' except that it was one of the hundreds of small/medium-sized engineering concerns, based in Coventry, which needed new and or more promising premises in which to rebuild its postwar enterprise. We may, however, thank it for allowing Sir John Black to get his hands on a fine Coventry brand of car, at very low net cost.

Although the general public was not to know this for some time, this little manoeuvre fitted in perfectly with Sir John Black's master plan. By buying, then selling, the Clay Lane/Briton road factory, but not the trade mark rights to Triumph, Standard had ended up with ownership of a much-respected brand of motor car, which had built itself a fine reputation in the 1930s, for cars which looked elegant, and which had a sporting character.

There was obfuscation, of course, about Standard's plans for the revival of the brand, but none of the previous directors – especially Donald Healey – was still connected with it, and there seemed to be no way that the existing Triumph engines or running gear could ever be revived.

Neither Sir John, nor Standard, had any interest in retaining either, as Alick Dick confirms:

"Not one tiny little bit. We never even gave it a thought. But what you have to remember is that before the War, Standard had been supplying parts to SS. Standard had special tooling for the six-cylinder engines, and for the overhead valve version of the four-cylinder, of which Lyons took all supplies. Bill Lyons wanted to buy the tooling – he wanted to make all of his Jaguars in the future and John Black was willing to let him have that, so that we could build a competitive car. We kept the four-cylinder tooling, but it wasn't viable without a new chassis and a new name. So that's why we bought Triumph. Just because Bill Lyons made a sporting saloon, or a sports car, John Black was not going to let him get away with it!"

The deal was formally revealed to the public on 9 November 1944, when Standard's publicists made this announcement:

"The Standard Motor Co Ltd have purchased the Triumph Co Ltd. Sir John Black, Managing Director of the Standard Co, states that after the war [it did not know it at the time, but it was still six months away ...] the experience and technique gained in the production of aircraft will be applied to the production of Triumph cars of character and distinction."

Thos W Ward, it seemed, was delighted to get its unsuccessful investment off its hands, so negotiations for the sale went ahead very rapidly. Neither Ward nor Standard had any major points to be settled, so the formal conveyance of Triumph to Standard took place on 24 November 1944 – just one calendar month after the deal was first floated at a Standard board meeting.

For legal reasons, a new company then had to be set up, even though this was never going to affect the way that Standard carried out its postwar activities. Accordingly, the Triumph Motor Company (1945) Ltd was set up and held its first formal Board meeting on 17 April 1945. As expected, Sir John Black was elected chairman and managing director (though, of course, he was still only deputy chairman of the parent company at Standard).

Sir John, who was his own product planner, of course, already seemed to know what he intended to do with his two brands: In February 1945 Standard revealed that its immediate postwar programme would soon involve four models – from Standard an Eight and a Twelve, and from Triumph a 10hp type (of '1300cc') and a 15hp type (of '1800cc'). The pundits thought they knew what the Standards would be like, but they had no idea about the new Triumphs. Neither, it seemed, did Sir John Black, for at that moment, no detail engineering work had even been carried out ...

The first postwar Standards

As the end of the Second World War approached, Standard could look around, see what premises it controlled (or might control), and decide what strategy to adopt for its future. On the one hand, it now had a new brand to play with, but on the other it had not been able to spend much time on up-dating its cars during the frenetic war years.

On the other hand, there were some up-beat factors. The tooling for existing Standard models (including the body press tools at the suppliers) had been in store throughout the fighting, and had survived the bombing raids. With the connivance of the government, some limited work on private car development began at the end of 1944. The Canley factory had been modernised during the 1939-1945 period, and was now better-equipped than it had ever been.

Finally – and this would take on great importance in the immediate postwar period – war-timc activity in building aircraft meant that Standard now found itself in possession of two important aids to the limited production of new cars – one was the ability to shape, form, and weld a whole variety of tubular sections, the other was that it now had press-shop facilities which had never before featured at Canley.

The results were encouraging. On Friday, 18 May 1945 – little over a week after VE Day (Victory in Europe Day) had been celebrated, Standard announced its postwar programme. Clearly, management had been planning its private-car future for some time. They were so far ahead of the game, in fact, that the first new cars were actually assembled in June 1945, and production was going ahead with a swing by the autumn of the year.

Only two models were re-introduced – one of them the Flying Eight, the other the Flying Twelve (with a Fourteen engine option into the bargain, at no extra cost, though originally only for export). The 'Flying' part of the titles was quietly dropped from company literature almost at once. This was in quite startling contrast with the 1939/1940 programme, which had encompassed no fewer than seven different 'Flying' models. There was nothing rushed about these decisions. As already pointed out, even in 1939/1940 Standard had concluded that it would not replace the Flying Twenty, the Flying Nine was technically obsolete, and body tooling (at Briggs Motor Bodies) for what is believed to be a

Immediately after World War Two, Standard filled its production lines once again by concentrating on just two saloon styles – the Twelve (just dropping off the assembly line), and the Eight.

To get the show back on the road as soon as possible in 1945, Standard reintroduced the Twelve, unchanged in almost every respect from the Flying Twelve of 1939/1940 model. The backdrop is the Saxon Mill hotel, near Warwick.

This was the stripped out Tourer version of the Eight which appeared in 1945 and ran through to 1948. Compared with the prewar (1938-1940) Flying Eight, the latest car had a four-speed gearbox.

This nostalgic shot links Standard's rebirth after the Second World War with the Ferguson tractor project, which was to bring so much well-earned profit to the company. The van was based on a Standard Fourteen of the late 1940s.

new-generation Flying Ten had been cancelled and scrapped during the War.

None of those 'missing' models would ever re-appear. Even as early as 1941, in fact, the company had decided that it would re-enter the civil market with just two of its existing cars – the Eight and the Twelve. A year later, in the summer of 1942, engineers had visited Fisher & Ludlow and Pressed Steel to survey the state of the existing body tooling for these cars (which had been put into 'safe storage' for the duration. There had been 'certain losses due to enemy action' at F&L, a report concluded, while Twelve tooling was in satisfactory condition – which was encouraging. This meant that production of postwar cars could re start as soon as supplies were available. Not only that, but such a postwar range could make do with a mere two chassis, two side-valve engine families – and would share a single gearbox.

With a huge pent-up demand for new cars, Standard could not be labelled complacent about this limited range, as it seemed that it really could sell just as many cars as it

Before the end of 1945, Standard had put the Flying Twelve/Fourteen models back into production, though without the 'Flying' title – this one being a Fourteen.

The Twelve had been on sale before the Second World War, and went back on sale as soon as possible after 1945. It would remain in the showrooms until 1948.

If one wanted to buy an Eight Tourer like this in 1945, one had to stand in line, for waiting lists were enormous, and growing all the time.

From 1945 to 1948, the drophead coupé version of the Fourteen was rare, but surprisingly neat and elegantly detailed.

Although Standard never marketed an estate version of the Flying models, an enterprising coachbuilder produced a 'Woody' version of the postwar Twelve (or is it a Fourteen?) model in the late 1940s.

built. A major decision, however, must have been made, to abandon so many sectors of the market place, which it had served in the late 1930s. As we now know, there were still some stocks of chassis, which could have been used to make other models – for as late as 1952 the stocks of redundant Flying Nine chassis (which lacked independent front suspension), might have been used as the basis of new Triumph sports car frames ...

In its description of the revived cars, *The Autocar* was as kind to the company as could be expected, pointing out that it was going to take time to return Canley's assembly halls to peace-time normality:

"Again, although the whole Standard resources were turned over rapidly to the production of war equipment and aircraft, and several vast new enterprises were brought into virile activity, all through those weary years an output of Standard vehicles consisting of vans, ambulances, light armoured cars, fire pumps and other types for war purposes has been kept going ..."

The postwar cars, in truth, were little changed from those which might have been built in 1939/1940, but were distinguished by the removal of bonnet-side louvres. The larger model – the Twelve or the Fourteen, depending on which of the well-known four-cylinder side valve units was fitted – looked much the same as before. The Pressed Steel saloon shell was claimed to be three inches wider than before, and the rear axle track had been enlarged to 4ft 6.5in. There appeared to be no changes of any type to the four-seater drophead coupé derivative, which was the only alternative. With just 44bhp claimed for the Twelve's 1608cc engine, this was all set to be a successful, middle-of-the-market, conventional family car.

Although the Eight saloons and drophead coupes looked much the same as in 1939/1940 (though there was no re-emergence of the longer-wheelbase four-door variety which had been previewed, briefly, in February 1940), there had been a tiny change to the engine, and a massive one to the transmission. Compared with the 1939/1940 model – at least, according to the official figures – the cylinder bore had been reduced to 56.7mm (from 57mm), which brought the engine neatly under the official 'Treasury' 8hp rating, instead of 8.05 as it had been in 1939. The swept volume, accordingly, came down from 1021cc to 1009cc.

According to Standard's publicists, the four-speed gearbox fitted to the latest Eight was 'new' – whereas, in fact, it was much the same assembly as had already fitted to Flying Twelves and Flying Fourteens for some years: all that was needed to mate it to the little Flying Eight engine was a new clutch bell housing and a few details. Prompted, no doubt, by the publicists, *The Autocar* described the new box as "sturdy," whereas *The Motor* described it as "unusually robust," and "remarkably substantial."

Since this 'box' only had to deal with the 28bhp of the Flying Eight's 1009cc engine, it was going to have an easy time of it in that car. The reason for the change? It cannot have been on engineering, or even on cost grounds, except that it obviously made production scheduling easier than before. In fact, although we did not know it at the time, it allowed one part of Canley's machine shops to be cleared at an early stage, to allow for machinery to build an all-new gearbox for the forthcoming Vanguard to be installed on the factory floor instead: when it came, that gearbox, or lineal descendants of it, would be used on many Standard and Triumph models built up until 1980 – more than 30 years later.

Three versions of the postwar Flying Eight were to be manufactured – the two door saloon coming from Fisher & Ludlow's Tile Hill premises, the drophead coupé and a new two-door/four-seater tourer from Carbodies: these were clearly intended to compete with similar offerings from Ford, Austin and Morris: the Tourer gained full-size doors, like those on the DHC (drop-head coupé).

Rare when new, and even rarer sixty years later, this is a drophead coupé version of the Eight of 1945-1948.

The two-door Eight Tourer was built in small numbers from 1945 to 1948.

The majority of all 1945-1948 Standards were two-door Eights, though few can ever have been as carefully preserved as this example.

By the autumn of 1945, a Purchase Tax (this had been invented to stifle consumption in the early months of the war, and as a revenue-raiser became a permanent feature of the fiscal landscape) was being applied to the sale of many British goods, which meant that the price of these new Standards was considerably more than that asked of the very similar 1939/1940 models:

Model	Basic price	Purchase tax	Total price	1939 price
Flying Eight saloon	£245	£68.80	£313.80	£129
Flying Eight Tourer	£235	£66.03	£301.03	£129
Flying Eight DHC	£275	£77.14	£352.14	£159
Flying Twelve saloon	£375	£104.82	£479.82	£219
Flying Twelve DHC	£395	£110.47	£505.47	£268

Except that prices inexorably rose in the three years which followed, these Standards still on sale in 1948 when the all-new Vanguard finally elbowed them out of the assembly halls at Canley, and were identical to the 1945 models.

In October 1945, the company announced profits, after tax, of £263,056, and in the years, which followed, these built up steadily. In round figures, although only about 2500 of the prewar-type Standards were built in 1945, nearly 27,000 followed in 1946, more than 34,000 in 1947 then, in 1948 when the new-generation Vanguard went on sale at last, a final 21,600 followed. By any reckoning, this was a speedy and enterprising recovery from the war years, and it gave Standard a sturdy spring-board for the future.

Triumph – reinventing a pedigree

In 1945, as far as private cars were concerned, Sir John Black's priorities were:

- To start design work on a brand-new Standard car – this would eventually become known as the Vanguard.

• In order to re-establish the Triumph brand, to rush through a pair of 'interim' Triumph models, using existing Flying Standard components.

• To begin work on a new small/medium car, which might once have been a Standard, but which would ultimately become the Triumph Mayflower.

As we now know, it was the new Triumphs, that broke cover first, and the Vanguard, which followed. The Triumphs must be analysed in some detail, as, without Standard, and all the existing componentry, these models would never have come into existence.

As Alick Dick has already pointed out, Standard did not buy the 'Triumph' company for what could be made of its existing models (the tooling for which no longer existed), but so that Sir John Black's dream of providing more sporting models with which to fight back at William Lyons and Jaguar could go ahead. Although he was not about to produce a series of 'badge-engineered' Standards (Sir John might have been hard-hitting, but he was by no means as cynical as the Rootes family), he also knew that Standard could not afford the time or the capital cost of developing entirely new Triumphs.

New Triumphs, therefore, would have to use Standard mechanical equipment, which could be more or less disguised under body styles, which would at least look distinctive. Sir John really had no choice. Although the drawings for Triumph engines and transmissions still existed, in almost every case the tooling did not. Austin's Leonard Lord had also made it clear that he would no longer be willing to supply the gearbox internals, which he had habitually supplied to Triumph at the independent Triumph company in the late 1930s.

Because several of Sir John's top executives – notably Ted Grinham, who had been his prewar technical director, but who was still seconded to De Havilland Aircraft until 1943, then moved to the Rootes Group – were still unavailable, he had to act as his own product planner, and his own technical chief. He wanted to use as many of Standard's existing components, facilities and expertise as possible.

In particular, revised arrangements with Jaguar meant that the overhead-valve 1776cc engine, which had previously been exclusive to it, was now also available for Standard's own purposes. Sir John had no plans to use this in the revived Flying Standards, but with tooling already available to manufacture far more of the OHV engines than Jaguar could possibly absorb (eventually it would take just 5761 engines, for its '1½-litre' models between 1945 to 1949) there was an opportunity to use them in the first Standard-Triumphs.

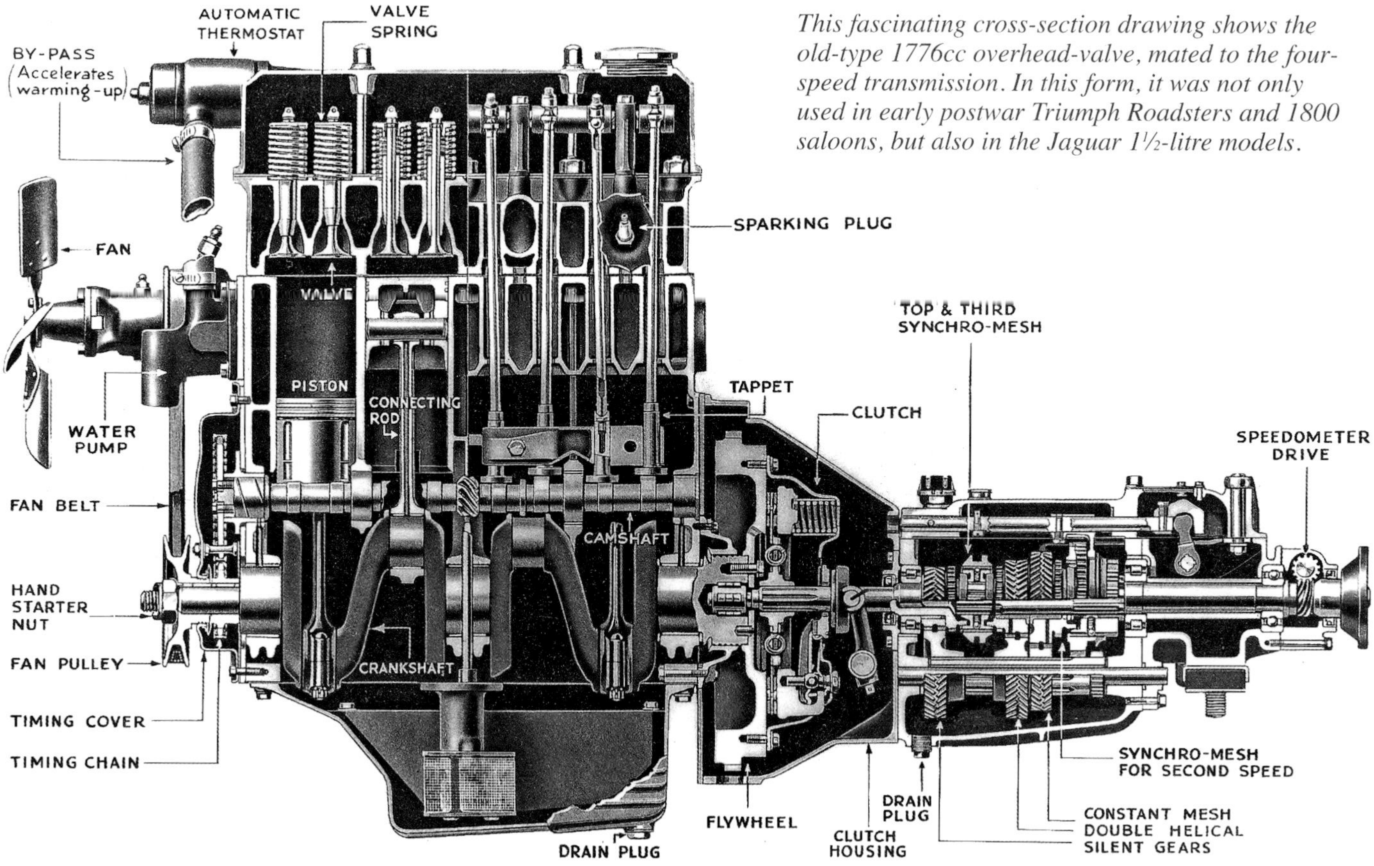

This fascinating cross-section drawing shows the old-type 1776cc overhead-valve, mated to the four-speed transmission. In this form, it was not only used in early postwar Triumph Roadsters and 1800 saloons, but also in the Jaguar 1½-litre models.

Even so, it is important to note that 1776cc engines supplied to Jaguar at this time, and engines used in the early postwar Triumphs, differed in detail. The Standard-Triumph engine was rated at 63bhp (net) at 4500rpm, with a 6.7:1 compression ratio and a single downdraught Solex carburettor, while the Jaguar engine developed 65bhp (net) at 4600rpm, with a 7.6:1 compression ratio, and a single horizontal SU carburettor.

As David Eley, that long-standing engineering stalwart from Canley and Banner Lane, once told the author:

"Well before VE Day I was back at Canley, installed in the Advanced Drawing Office, working on new models. I was asked to do the induction manifolding, with a single downdraught carburettor, on the postwar version of the 1776cc engine. We needed more power, but we didn't want to use SU carburettors, as fitted to the Jaguar versions, because they were expensive, and SU was owned by Nuffield ..."

[Was motor car engineering ever free of corporate politics ...?]

Decisive action saw a 'new Triumph' policy rapidly take shape in 1945 – which was to develop an all new chassis in two wheelbase lengths; one for a sporting tourer and one for a smart, up-market, saloon. Ray Turner, who was Ted Grinham's Chief Designer for some years, got the job of refining, installing and finalising all the running gear.

As this is basically a corporate history of Standard, and details of all such Triumphs have been related in suitable Triumph histories, I need only sketch in the details of its design, which was led by Ray Turner before he left the company to join Ford in Dagenham. Basically, the two cars had similar mechanical engineering, the 1800 Roadster with a 100in wheelbase, the 1800 Town and Country Saloon [what a snobbish name!] with 108in.

Those chassis frames did not require much capital spending on tooling facilities, and could take shape rapidly – constructed mainly of tubular steel sidemembers and welded-up crossmembers, using manufacturing techniques refined through building aircraft during the war (in particular the Bristol Beaufighter fighter-bombers). The basic design was very simple, for the difference in wheelbase was found merely by using different length main sidemembers, and the tubes were fed underneath the line of the beam rear axle.

After Standard bought the corporate remains of Triumph, its first new models were the Triumph Roadster, and (longer-wheelbase) Triumph 1800 saloons, which had Flying Fourteen side-valve engines. Later cars (this being the prototype example) used the Vanguard engine instead.

One important advance (an installation that Sir John wanted to 'blood' on these cars before he applied it to the Vanguard) was that these new cars would continue to use the existing corporate four-speed gearbox (as seen under Flying Standards in the 1930s, and in all the revived cars reintroduced in 1945), but would have a complex linkage to allow for a steering column gear change. Maybe such an installation was never likely to be as precise as a centre floor change, but it was at once fashionable (Standard had exports to North America in mind, though it had never broken in to that market in the 1930s), and would liberate floor space ahead of the centre of the bench front seat to allow a third passenger to be carried.

The rest of the chassis was familiar, mainly coming from the Twelve/Fourteen, using the transverse leaf spring independent front suspension, with lever arm shock absorbers. At the rear there were conventional half-elliptic leaf springs, with the beam axle being a widened version of the existing spiral bevel unit from the Twelve.

Now it was time to find suppliers for two entirely different types of bodyshell – a razor-edge-styled four/five-seater saloon, and a special type of sports roadster, which would not only accommodate three abreast in the front seat, but another two occupants in an occasional 'dickey seat' above and behind the line of the rear axle.

Except to describe, very briefly, the process by which each style was reached, the rest of this story belongs to Triumph. As it happens, whereas the Roadster was erected by Standard, at Canley, the saloon would have a style by Mulliners Ltd, the body batch-production specialists of Birmingham.

No doubt it was because Sir John Black had commissioned an extremely elegant razor-edge style on an SS-Jaguar chassis from Mulliners Ltd in 1939, and had struck up a warm relationship with managing director Louis Antweiller, that he awarded the saloon contract to that concern. Although Standard's Frank Callaby produced an early sketch, based on the packaging of the existing Twelve, and Walter Belgrove later was involved, it was Mulliners' Chief Body Engineer Leslie Moore who did most of the styling work on this body; this was to be built on traditional wooden frame/alloy panel lines at Bordesley Green, in Birmingham, then painted and trimmed before being transported to Canley for completion.

Although the Roadster was styled completely 'in house,' there were obvious packaging connections with the Triumph Dolomite Roadster of 1938/1939, a car in which three abreast front-seating had been linked to occasional rear seating in fold-away 'dickey' seats (known in America as 'rumble seats'), which were normally covered by a panel in the tail. Although there was no mechanical link between the two types of car (not even Walter Belgrove, who was about to become Standard's chief body engineer, did any work on the new Triumph), there could be no doubting the heritage.

In 1945, Sir John Black was still in love with razor-edge styling, which explains why the very first 'Standard-Triumph' saloon – the 1800 – looked the way it did.

In this case it was a young Standard designer called Frank Callaby who conceived the agreed shape, while it was he and Arthur Ballard who did much of the detailed engineering. The bodyshell was based on a traditional-style ash frame, while the majority of the aluminium body panels were shaped on rubber presses, which had been installed at Canley for the production of aircraft panels a few years earlier. These press tools were only suitable for limited-production runs, of panels in considerably more workable light-alloy rather than pressed steel (for the squeezing force was considerably less), as one side of the formers used was made of hard, but not impenetrable rubber.

Both cars were launched on the same day in March 1946, with deliveries beginning in the weeks that followed, and until the new Vanguard appeared (in prototype form) in 1947, they took most of the media's attention. As far as Standard was concerned, however, they were merely stop-gap models, as much attention had already turned to two massive new projects – that of the all-new Vanguard, and to the production of the Ferguson tractor.

Not only was the Triumph Roadster of 1946 one of the first pair of 'Standard Triumphs,' it was also the world's last car to have a 'dickey' (or, as the American would say: 'rumble') seat over the back axle.

CHAPTER 8

Tractors, Banner Lane, and jet engines ... 1940-1959

Standard's continuing and sometimes turbulent involvement in the factory in Banner Lane, Coventry, and the tractors which it produced, deserves a complete chapter of its own – and spanned from 1940 to 1958, which was a commercially eventful period in the life of the marque.

As has already been noted, in chapter 6, long before the end of the Second World War Standard, its directors were faced with a dilemma – and an opportunity. Drawn in to the government's 'Shadow Factory' scheme in the 1930s, and having profited considerably from the work carried out on aircraft engine and airframe construction, they realised that when the war was won, their business might soon be faced with a sudden cessation of military work. Sir John Black, a visionary in so many ways, began to think about this at an early stage. Not only was he happy to integrate 'Shadow Factory 1' (Fletchamstead South, as we later began to know it) into the rest of the Canley complex, but he also hoped to find a use for Banner Lane.

We now know that, soon after he was appointed Deputy Chairman of Standard (to the long-serving Charles Band) in October 1944, he approached the Air Ministry about taking over the lease at Banner Lane. Government officials, [I understand], were delighted, so Sir John was provisionally quoted a lease of £37,000/annum. In order to secure the Ferguson tractor deal, discussed below, in mid-1945 he eventually recommended a ten-year lease, at a fixed rate of £36,500/annum, though from 1948 this figure would be further reduced to £33,000/annum.

[The lease of Shadow Factory 1, on the other hand – the original plant, which was close to the main Canley complex, took time to settle, for at one point Fisher & Ludlow, which already had the modern body plant in Tile Hill, also expressed an interest in the same 'Shadow' building. This must have confused the government civil servants for a time – but they were soon persuaded to 'back off.' That lease finally went to Standard, and cost £19,500/annum ...]

Now, it seemed, the planning for postwar expansion could begin.

Tractors – the turbulent partnership

This is the moment at which that restless, sometimes irascible, but always ambitious Irish businessman, Harry Ferguson, enters the story. Ferguson, who had already made a fortune in the design of tractors and (equally important) the

Ferguson and Ford

Well before Irish-born Harry Ferguson signed a deal with Sir John Black for Standard to manufacture Ferguson tractors, he had endured a turbulent partnership with Ford-USA. Born of farming stock in 1884, Henry George Ferguson (he was always known as Harry) took an interest in engineering as soon as he began tinkering with farm machinery.

First of all by selling ploughs, new linkages for tractor machinery, and by selling other makes of tractor, and eventually branching out on his own design, Ferguson finally became a big name in Britain's motor industry. His first 'own-brand' tractor was built for him by the David Brown engineering business in Huddersfield from 1936 to 1939, but as David Brown then made it clear that it wanted to make its own tractors, he looked across the Atlantic Ocean for a new opportunity. His first truly big break came shortly afterwards, when he struck a deal with Henry Ford, in the USA, for his tractors to be produced by Ford-USA in Detroit.

This arrangement was always commercially turbulent (neither Ferguson nor Henry Ford were soft-hearted or easy-going men), and the troubled American finally foundered end in 1947, by which time Ferguson had already started working with Sir John Black and the Standard Motor Co in England. Not that Ferguson was ready to wash his hands of Ford-USA, but in addition he sued it for loss of business, patent infringements, and whatever else his lawyers could dredge up – and finally won a multi-million Dollar battle in 1952.

original 'Ferguson system' of attaching implements to the rear of his machines, was looking for new opportunities. In the late 1930s David Brown Industries in Huddersfield had built his tractors, but that venture was quite short lived, and since 1939 new-type (but technically similar) machines had been built, for him, by Ford-USA in Detroit.

By 1945, Ferguson wanted to get re-established in the UK, was perfectly happy to have his tractors built for him by another concern (that way, he reasoned, he would not have to commit millions to erect factory buildings, or to lay down production tooling), and set about finding a partner.

This was never going to be easy – if only because the Irishman's turbulent character, and his desire to dominate any partnership which was set up, was already well known in the motoring and engineering industry. First of all, therefore, he stood back from the search, and the first face-to-face negotiations, and set his UK sales manager, Trevor Knox, to do the job for him.

Colin Fraser, whose book *Harry Ferguson, Inventor & Pioneer* tells us much about the volatile character of the man himself, and tells us much about this period. Knox had originally been an apprentice for Ferguson, and always stayed in Britain even when the Ferguson tractor-building project emigrated to North America. In 1945, therefore, it was logical that he should be charged with finding a client/partner for the new British enterprise.

Accordingly, Knox was installed at the Farmers Club in London, where he let it be known that 'Ferguson was back,' sending out feelers to his many contacts at the top of the motor industry. We know that Knox contacted Leonard Lord of Austin and Lord Nuffield of the Nuffield Organisation at an early stage, but both of whom turned him down (there was certainly a 'personal' element here, for each of them had strong characters which were not likely to blend easily together).

The definitive approach to Standard occurred almost purely by chance. It just so happened that a director of the Distillers Company was also staying semi-permanently in the Farmers' Club at this time, and he soon struck up an acquaintanceship with Knox, who was beginning to feel like a forgotten spare part at this time. According to Fraser:

"During their conversations, the Distillers' director learned of the reason for Knox's presence ... It happened that the Distillers man travelled regularly to Brighton at weekends, and a frequent companion on the journey was an advertising executive from a company that handled publicity affairs for the Standard Motor Co ... During the course of one train journey to Brighton, the Distillers' director told the advertising executive about Knox, and his quest for a manufacturer for the Ferguson System tractor.

"The advertising man remarked that Standards were thinking of developing a motorised farm cart for postwar production, and that if Sir John Black ... knew of Knox's quest he might be interested. From that point the message sped further along the grapevine until it reached Sir John's office ..."

Standard, in fact, had already built a prototype 'farm cart' (a development of one of the military machines already described), and photographs and a brief technical description were released in March 1945. This one-off machine, strictly a two-seater with very little space for stowage, was registered FDU 143, and was tiny, with a wheelbase of a mere 5ft 0in and an overall length of just 7ft 10in. It seems certain that the chassis of this machine was an evolution of the 'Jungle Bug' (see chapter 6), for it had the same squat dimensions, and the same grossly fat tyres.

To quote from *The Autocar's* preview:

"It is as useful for running about a farm as for driving to market. Four-wheel transmission is available at will [this was a 'Jungle Bug' feature too], giving six-speeds forward and two reverse. The frame is tubular and the body of pressed steel. Independent suspension is employed, and the engine is a four-cylinder Standard Eight of 1009cc. A petrol consumption of 30mpg is quoted for road use, and a maximum speed of 50mph. The price is expected to be between £100 and £140. Rough ground can be traversed in this vehicle; grass or loose-surfaced 'trials'-type gradients up to 1-in-3 are said to be within its capacity ..."

The style was utilitarian in the extreme – like the (eventually) more famous Land Rover there appeared to be not a single pressed or shaped panel in sight, though the windscreen was a generous size. Headlamps were of the freestanding variety, and there was a rudimentary canvas 'tilt.' Accommodation? Like that of the 'Jungle Bug,' it was small – two passengers and one pig, is how one cynic described it – but it would certainly have had its uses.

In fairness, it was more promising than the BMC Mini-Moke, which followed fifteen years later, for it had more ground clearance, better traction, and might have been a relatively short-lived and limited success. As a business proposition, too, it might have made good sense, for tooling costs for the body would have been very limited indeed.

Although this project, in itself, was fascinating enough, it does not seem to have progressed any further, and was certainly killed off after the Ferguson deal had been was established.

Way back in the early 1950s, a biography of Sir John, published by the Standard Motor Co, told the world that:

"As the end of the war approached, Sir John foresaw that once again the aftermath of war would bring a shortage of food, and the mechanisation of the land would obviously be our most urgent need. He had gone as far as to start on the design of a light 'Jeep' tractor [amazingly, Rover would shortly come to similar conclusions – the Land Rover of 1948 being the result of their deliberations], and because of it, decided to have a look at what others had done. The tractor that impressed him was the Ferguson-designed tractor produced by the Ford Motor Co of America. He heard that Mr Harry Ferguson was over here, looking for someone to manufacture his tractors for the Eastern Hemisphere."

Was this a case of Great Minds thinking alike, or was some of this statement a classic case of after-the-event PR-supposition? No matter. Knox, for sure, wanted Harry Ferguson to see all the possibilities, so by the time that the Irishman arrived back in the UK in mid-1945, and established himself in luxury, in a suite at Claridges Hotel in London, he found that a great deal of ground work had already been completed. Not only had Knox and an associate arranged to inspect plants in Cardiff, Newcastle and Sheffield, but they had already been to see Standard's rapidly emptying, and increasingly forlorn, shadow factory at Banner Lane, in Coventry.

Although Ferguson himself had wanted to establish a tractor plant in his native Northern Ireland, there was no suitable factory building available over there: Shorts, of Belfast, presumably had such premises, but were busy enough with its own maritime and aerospace projects not to need a partner. Before long it became clear that some sort of partnership with Standard might make sense – for not only was the Banner Lane factory likely to be available almost at once, but both Standard and Ferguson wanted to set up a new industrial project for which steel supplies in impoverished postwar Britain were going to be limited.

Eventually, the British government, in the shape of Sir Stafford Cripps (President of the Board of Trade), was persuaded, steel and other metal supplies (particularly sheet steel, which was in very short supply) were allocated and re-equipment of the Banner Lane premises went rapidly ahead. As landlords of the Banner Lane factory (it had financed the building of the plant in 1939/1940, of course), the government was delighted to see Banner Lane put to such good use, and speedily agreed to a plan for Standard to build up to 200 Ferguson tractors every day (which equates to about 50,000 a year). Standard, for its part, took on a ten-year lease of the huge premises.

Getting Sir John Black and Harry Ferguson to meet, let alone to agree on a plan of action, was like arranging to have two rather unwilling porcupines start mating – it had to be done very carefully, and after a great deal of thought. In the end, the first face-to-face encounter, it seems, took place in London's Claridges hotel on 5 September 1945, where the two tycoons seemed to get on surprisingly well (they both had a common aim, it seemed ...), and the original deal was scribbled on the back of a menu card over dinner.

As Alick Dick later confirmed, in an unpublished memoir:

Alick Dick

By almost any standards, at Standard Alick Dick was a 'gilded youth' who found himself in the right place, at the right time. Family connections with John Black led to him securing work at Standard, in 1934, as an apprentice, at the end of World War Two he became Sir John Black's personal assistant, and then his official deputy in 1951. Whether reluctantly or not (he never spelt this out to interviewers), he found himself leading the boardroom coup in January 1954, which deposed Sir John, and installed him in his place.

Born in Norfolk, the son of a country doctor, and with an uncle (Major Dick) who had married one of William Hillman's six daughters, the family connection to John Black was obvious. Apprenticed to Standard in the 1930s, he became Head Buyer at Standard's Banner Lane plant during World War Two, became Sir John Black's personal assistant in 1945, and was unexpectedly appointed to the Board of directors in 1947: this, it seemed, was a classic study in nepotism, but when he then became Sir John's deputy in 1951, his destined path to the top job became clear.

After 1954, Alick Dick was then managing director of Standard until September 1961, when he was equally imperiously swept out of office by Leyland Motors' management, and replaced by Stanley Markland of Leyland. He left the company immediately, had no further connection with Leyland, Standard or Triumph, and eventually set up his own management consultancy in Coventry. He was only 70 years old when he died in 1986.

"The only business people present were John Black, Harry Ferguson, Oliver Lucas (who, of course, was head of the Lucas organisation), and Henry Tiarks, who was a director of Schroders in London, a merchant bank, along with four wives or relatives.

[Tiarks was also a director of Pressed Steel, and later also of Joseph Lucas]

"The signatures are recorded on the back of a Claridges menu, and it read: 'Dedicated to Oliver the parson who wed Harry and John.' The text is in Maureen Ferguson's handwriting."

There is no written agreement on the menu. Although there is evidence that Ferguson himself soon regretted what he had signed away (that becomes clear in Colin Fraser's published biography), the deal was that Standard would set up Banner Lane to manufacture Ferguson tractors (they would be known as TE-20 – where TE stood for Tractor England – and were significantly different from the US-built 9N and 2N types), and would sell them to the Ferguson organisation at an agreed internal inter-company price. Standard was to have the manufacturing rights everywhere in the world, except for North, South and Central America, and the Philippines.

If ever there was what appeared to be a moneymaking project for Standard, this was it. If the product was good enough (and Ferguson himself had no doubts about this), the tractors would virtually sell themselves. Standard would make money on every tractor it built, and would be able to minimise the aggravation of selling, servicing, and supporting them in the wide world.

At the same time, there was space, and to spare, for Standard to move its entire engineering, design and development departments from Canley to Banner Lane. Ferguson, for its part, would occupy the modern ex-shadow factory plant at Fletchamstead North (on the north-west corner of the Canley site). Amazingly, in 1959, when the final Standard-Ferguson links were dissolved, that arrangement would be completely, and very efficiently, reversed.

Standard's first problem – financial and practical – was to sort out the equipping of the plant, but this was eased when Sir Stafford Cripps agreed to authorise tightly-controlled Dollar loans, so that Standard could order special machine tools and – equally important for the first two or three years – complete Continental engines from the USA.

Sir John Black (right) and tractor tycoon Harry Ferguson were both ruthless businessmen who found it difficult to co-exist, but did so in order to make the Standard-Ferguson tractor project work. More than half-a-million of the original TE20 tractors would be built in ten years, making this venture extremely profitable for both concerns.

Originally built as the second of Standard's shadow factories, what became known as 'Fletchamstead North' first built aircraft carburettors. It was then taken over by Harry Ferguson as corporate HQ/design/development premises for the tractor project. From 1959 it became the home of Standard's engineering, design, development and styling departments. Following closure in the 1980s, it was the first Canley building to be demolished.

Tractor design and engineering

The original tractors, which Ferguson wanted Standard to produce, were basically similar to those that had been built, in enormous numbers (more than 300,000 would eventually be produced), by Ford-USA in Detroit, during the Second World War, and were still to make, in an increasingly fractious relationship, until 1947. Time, experience, and European manufacturing realities, however, meant that there would be many different details, especially in regard to the engine and a new four-speed transmission.

The Ferguson-Standard deal, and the implications of what might follow, were announced in stages, first in August 1945, and in more detail a few weeks later. Sir John Black originally leaked his intention to take Standard into the tractor market at a relatively obscure National Farmers Union meeting in Leamington Spa in August, but at the time the media thought this meant that Standard's own mini-farm vehicle, just described, was to be the subject. It was not.

Only seven weeks after that, Standard and Ferguson were finally ready to tell the world about their new enterprise, it was announced:

"One of Coventry's shadow factories, taken over from the Government by the Standard Motor Co, is to go into production of farm tractors of a new type. Sir John Black, Managing Director of the company, has entered into partnership with Mr Harry Ferguson, inventor of the Ferguson Tractor and System of Implements, and manufacture of the tractor in great volume is to be undertaken forthwith."

The point was made that the first deliveries would be made in 1946, and that three-quarters of them were to be available for export. The Banner Lane factory, it was pointed out to those who did not know, covered 1 million square feet of floor space, and would employ more than 6000 people.

Although there were many detail differences between the 2N Ferguson tractor as still being built by Ford-USA, and the new TE-20 model, engineering work progressed rapidly. Both machines, of course, shared the same type of massive engine/transmission/rear axle layout – there was no separate chassis as such – so all stresses and strains, both in bending and in torsion, had to be taken by the major castings.

Although the first TE-20s would use an interim supply of proprietary engine – USA-built Fergusons had always employed a Ford-USA power unit, but the first British Banner Lane-built tractors would use an American Continental power unit – the regular use of a brand-new petrol engine, one of a family which would also find a home in postwar Standards (and Triumphs), initially the Standard Vanguard, was always a 'given' to the entire project. Because this engine, and all its derivations (which is affectionately known as the 'wet-liner' engine), is integral to the Standard company's fortunes, its genesis is described in much more detail in the next chapter.

At this point, however, it is important to emphasise that the tractor version of the engine was really quite radically different from that fitted to cars. In the Ferguson tractor, the engine was the only structural member connecting the front axle to the rear of the machine, by way of an equally massive combined gearbox/rear axle assembly. Accordingly, the only direct dimensional connection between the cylinder block of the tractor, and that of private cars like the Vanguard, and the closely related postwar Triumphs, was that the bore centres and the choice of cylinder bore dimensions were the same (which was, of course, a 'given' for mass-production machining purposes) though it now seems that the two similar-but-different engines each had their own dedicated assembly lines at Canley!

There was so much bending stress on engines used in this way, that on Continental-engined Ferguson tractors there were additional ¾-inch diameter tie bars running alongside the bottom of that engine's pressed steel sump, to help provide the necessary beam strength. Standard's engine designers knew this, and made sure that their cylinder blocks were (and always were) far more massive than those specified for Vanguard private cars.

The original Standard engines fitted to Ferguson tractors from January 1948 measured 1850cc (80 x 92mm bore and stroke) and produced 25bhp at a regulated 2000rpm: an increase to 2088cc (a well-known 'Vanguard' dimension) followed in 1949, and was further increased to 2188cc (with an 87mm cylinder bore) for a bigger and heavier Ferguson tractor in 1956.

Another major problem was that Standard soon discovered that the level of the technical details handed over to it by Ferguson was by no means good enough, or complete enough, for major tooling, and manufacturing, to start. Although it has often been pointed out that Ferguson handed over engineering drawings, and that Standard then had to redraw all of them 'for its own purposes,' it has not always been clear as to why.

In fact, Standard had to develop many of its own material specifications (which were not provided), and that major items such as the gearbox, back axle and power take-off had to be completely redesigned by Standard: all the evidence is that Ferguson never thanked it for this, though undoubtedly it saved the project from disaster.

As Alick Dick later told the author:

"When the drawings arrived at Banner Lane for us to make the tractor, there was no drawing of any engine, there was no gearbox and there was no differential. Henry Ford, of course, had made all these, in America, and they were part of the Ford truck programme. We had no drawings or process sheets so we didn't have any idea of what materials were that the tractor was made of ...

"So we had to start, and engineer the tractor from scratch ..."

To quote from one of Sir John Black's coruscating notes preserved in the company archives: "without exaggeration, 75 per cent of the engineering that we believed had been completed and proved in the USA has been completed by us ..."

This was the original Ferguson TE20 tractor of 1946, as substantially re-engineered and completed by Standard. Production at Banner Lane began in that year – that is the front office block of Banner Lane in the background – and eventually more than 500,000 of these machines would be built.

He then put the cost of revision/completion at £450,000 (which, at 1946 currency values, was a vast sum of money, but which presumably had been 'talked up' in Sir John's usual ruthless business manner), and managed to get Ferguson to foot the bill over a period of time. This extra workload, of course, significantly delayed work on the brand-new Vanguard, for Standard certainly did not have enough engineers, nor a big enough management team, to work on both projects at once.

Problems, problems

Even while thousands of man-hours were already being expended on engineering design, and on the re-equipment of Banner Lane to produce tractors in big numbers, major disagreements then erupted between the two dominant personalities involved – Sir John Black and Harry Ferguson. The seeds of these volcanic arguments were

Sir John Black (right) and tractor tycoon Harry Ferguson, early in their tempestuous tractor manufacturing project.

really sewn from the very first day, for Ferguson wanted a 'Gentleman's Agreement' with Sir John, rather than a written contract – which effectively gave both of them the scope to act as anything but gentlemen, and to disagree over many matters.

According to Fraser:

"It did not take long for Sir John Black and Harry Ferguson to have their first serious differences of opinion. The fact that such arguments arose was as unavoidable as a crash between two express trains hurtling towards each other down the same length of track. Both men were inflexible and aggressively certain that their opinions were invariably right. Their basic attitudes were therefore incompatible, unless they happened to agree entirely on a given topic.

"They did agree in principle that they could derive mutual benefit from an arrangement to manufacture and market Ferguson System tractors. However, working out the details of that arrangement, equipping the Banner Lane factory with plant, and finalising design matters gave rise to an abundance of minor controversies that the two men's characters fanned into major issues."

At one point the arguments reached such a level in 1946, that Sir John threatened to withdraw from the whole deal – even after much money had already been spent, and when Banner Lane had already been partially re-equipped, preparatory to making tractors – and it was only after a great deal of hard talking between Ferguson's top executives and Ferguson himself that this particular problem was resolved.

Many of the early problems, for sure, could have been avoided, if some sort of formal agreement had been drawn up, and approved, before either party began to spend money on the project. According to Standard's own Board Minutes, the two tycoons made their 'Gentleman's Agreement' on 28 August 1945 (a week before the Claridges meeting – the mystery continues to this day), yet a formal agreement was not signed until the summer of 1946, by which time series production was just beginning!

It was at that point that Black's friend Oliver Lucas stepped in to mediate between the two industrialists. He chaired and minuted a formal meeting where every pertinent issue was exposed and perhaps surprisingly, resolved. There can be no doubt that the successful outcome of this encounter was instrumental in putting the project back on track.

The gravy train begins to roll

Although it had cost Standard a great deal of money to prepare Banner Lane to build tractors – £3 million was one figure bandied around, which must equate to at least £100 million at early-21st century currency values – for Standard the financial rewards would be enormous.

Not for nothing did Standard (which really meant Sir John Black, with the usual supine agreement of his fellow directors) once consider converting itself into a dedicated

This was the main front office of Banner Lane, in all its postwar pomp, having been converted from building Hercules military aircraft engines to manufacturing Ferguson tractors in big numbers.

Standard spent lavishly to enable up to 300 Ferguson tractors to be built every day at Banner Lane.

Master and pupil – Sir John Black (seated) and Alick Dick, who would replace him in 1954. Dick forged his reputation as buyer at the Banner Lane factory during the Second World War.

tractor manufacturer, while dropping car manufacture altogether.

One result was that Harry Ferguson regularly complained about the inter-company prices he had to pay Standard before marketing the tractors, which bore his name [But then, he spent his whole working life railing against the business methods, motives, and policies of others, especially when it might harm him ...]. This, therefore, was not unexpected to anyone who knew Ferguson, as in these years he also floated an impossible project with the British government, which was what he called a 'Price Reducing Scheme:' this, he proposed, would force every British enterprise to first freeze, than start reducing its prices – though he never seems to have worked out, or concerned himself, it has to be said, with the long-term effect that it would have had on corporate profits!

Series production of TE-20 tractors, in fact, started very slowly at Banner Lane, with the first machine being delivered personally to Harry Ferguson in July 1946, the second going to Sir John Black shortly afterwards, and a mere 314 machines being completed before the end of the year. Thereafter the trickle became a flood, more than 20,000 were produced in 1947, and with the Vanguard-based 'wet-liner' engine becoming available, well over 50,000 followed in 1948.

It was at this point that Sir John Black considered, however briefly, turning Standard into a tractor-producing company, and abandoning cars completely – though this whim soon passed. In March 1947 he told his board that "serious consideration should be given to converting Canley completely to tractor production, and stopping building cars altogether. There was an acute international shortage of tractors, and Sir John Black's proposed production rate of 150,000 cars a year was simply not attainable because of supplies problems."

Clearly there was resistance to this proposal for:

"It was eventually agreed that complete conversion was not practical, as it depended so much on the Ferguson selling operation, so it was decided to plan on a restricted (50,000 cars a year) car output, and expanded tractor output ..."

In the end, not even this plan was pushed forward.

In the years which followed, Ferguson derivatives multiplied, special versions appeared for many applications, and overseas assembly began in several locations. As far as Ferguson was concerned, his engineering team at what we now know as the Fletchamstead North building on the Canley complex (along with their development colleagues, who did much testing on Ferguson's own private estate in the Cotswolds), Standard's on-going involvement with these amazing machines was now to collaborate in producing special or new-type engines (one running on Tractor Vaporising Oil – TVO – and a specialised diesel power unit being the most significant), and in keeping those modern assembly lines rolling, and rolling, and rolling ...

Even so, before describing how Harry Ferguson's business came to be sold to Massey Harris, and how a 'divorce' with Standard became inevitable, I should therefore state a few bald facts:

Standard completed the 500,000th Standard-produced Ferguson tractor at Banner Lane in 1956. Managing Director Alick Dick, and his Sales Director Mike Whitfield pose happily with that significant machine.

• As far as the TE-20-generation Ferguson tractor was concerned, Banner Lane eventually produced 517,651 machines, the last of all being built in October 1956.

• An all-new 2.1-litre diesel engine option (designed by Standard as a private venture, then sold to Ferguson after a brisk comparison with rival power units – described in detail below) became available in 1951.

• The famous TE-20 'Grey Fergie' was replaced by the bigger, more powerful, 2188cc-engined FE-35 in 1956, which carried on until the last days of 1957, after which it was replaced by a modified model rebadged as the 'Massey Ferguson 35.' Under the contract initiated by Sir John Black in 1953, Standard carried on building Massey Fergusons until 1959, after which was the divorce was completed, and the two businesses were speedily split asunder. This was the moment at which Standard withdrew its design, engineering and development departments from Banner Lane, and re-located them at Canley's Fletchamstead North plant.

Standard's first diesel

Jumping ahead a little – but in view of its importance to the Ferguson tractor, and to Standard's automotive business too, this is justified – it is now time to analyse the diesel engine project. This, although finally launched in the Standard Vanguard saloon in 1954, was already in use in Standard-built Ferguson tractors, where it had first been seen in 1951.

Even when the Ferguson agreement was in its formative years, the idea of producing a diesel-engined version of the TE20 had been considered, but there was neither time, nor available capital, for this to be done. We now know that work on an all-new tractor-type diesel engine did not even begin until 1947 – which was after design work on the entirely different Ferguson/Vanguard wet-liner petrol engine had been completed – and the first prototype ran in January 1948. The design team was delighted to note that the diesel's fuel consumption was approximately half of that of the equivalent petrol engine.

Yet at this moment in history, for Standard to develop an all-new diesel engine was going to be a real challenge. Small diesels already existed of course – in the UK, Perkins (based in Peterborough) were already in that market – but at this time the only cars to use such engines were all European – Borgward, Fiat and Mercedes-Benz. At this time existing technology allowed diesel engines to be very torquey, but they were still woefully underpowered. Those of us who use modern-day cars with turbo diesel power units, where outputs of more than 100bhp/litre are normal, may find it difficult to accept that in the late 1940s, figures of no more than 20bhp/litre were still quite normal.

Just as he had done on the original 'wet-liner' Vanguard engine, Charlie Phillips took charge of design work at Banner Lane, this time with David Eley doing much of the pencil work, and with important consultancy advice from Arthur Freeman Sanders, who had been an important UK diesel engineer since the 1920s.

Although the engine was always intended to fit into the same 'space' as the new Vanguard wet-liner' engine, it also had to go into the same area under the fuel tank of the Ferguson tractor, and the wheelbase of the tractor had to stay the same length, and used the same layout of engine mountings and (in the case of the tractor) the same pick-up facilities for the front axle forging, though it could be different in every other detail.

It is important, indeed, to emphasise that the Vanguard 'wet-liner' engine, and this new diesel, shared absolutely no common parts – castings, crankshaft, camshafts, details or whatever. This simple little table proves the point:

Feature	New diesel	Wet-liner
Year first fitted to tractors	1951	1946
Year first fitted to cars	1954	1948
Capacity	2092cc	2088cc
Bore x Stroke (mm)	80.96 x 101.6	85 x 92
Cylinder block	Conventional 'barrel crankcase'	Wet-liner
Fuel supply	CAV fuel-injection system	Single Solex carburettor
Peak power	40bhp at 3000rpm	68bhp at 4200rpm
Peak torque	85lbft at 1500rpm	108lbft at 2000rpm

Note that, when it was announced, Standard called this a 'high-speed' diesel' – yet it peaked at only 3000rpm! The very precisely stated bore and stroke dimensions of the diesel, incidentally, translate more prosaically to 3³⁄₁₆ x 4.00 inches in Imperial measure. Traditionalism lived on in Coventry ...

Standard pronounced the new engine ready to go into production in mid-1949, noting that production could begin in mid-1950, that 153 new machine tools would be needed to produce 110 engines every week, and that the tooling/investment costs would be £250,000. Even so, crankshafts, cylinder liners, pistons and valve gear would be bought in from outside suppliers.

This was, by any standard, a sturdy power unit, and so it should have been, for we now know that it weighed almost 100lb more than the Vanguard unit. When the extra weight of heavy-duty batteries, a reinforced chassis, and other details were all added, it meant that the diesel-engined Vanguard private car was more than 200lb heavier than the equivalent petrol-engined machine.

Ferguson announced a diesel-engined tractor in 1951, while Standard did not put the diesel-engined Vanguard on sale until 1954, still with its three-speed gearbox, and still with optional Laycock overdrive. At £1063.66, it cost a substantial £437.62 more than the petrol powered equivalent model.

Although diesel-engined tractors were undoubtedly a success, the diesel-engined Vanguard was, quite simply, a commercial failure. When *The Autocar* tested a car in July 1954, it recorded a pathetic top speed of 60mph in direct top (64.5mph in overdrive top). Even more depressing was the fact that it took 47.5 seconds (and that is no misprint) for the car to reach 60mph from rest. Overall fuel economy of 44mpg, on the other hand, was extremely impressive, and although there was some 'fleet' business, this car clearly did not attract many private customers.

We now know that only 1973 were sold, and that when the Phase II Vanguard died at the end of 1955, the diesel-option died with it. This, therefore, was the first and last of diesel-engined Standards of any type. Even so, it is worth emphasising that it was also the first British production car of all time to be offered with a diesel engine, and that the first rival to respond was BMC, who did not offer diesel-engined Morris Oxfords until the early 1960s.

Standard, Ferguson and Massey-Harris – commercial battles

For tractor enthusiasts, the evolution of the original TE-20 into the Massey Ferguson 35 is fascinating, but for automotive historians, the twisting, turning and eventual untangling of the web which linked Standard to Ferguson, and on to Massey Harris, is even more enthralling.

All was well, at first, it seemed, until 1952, when the ageing Harry Ferguson, perpetually worried about the financial fortunes of his North American factory, and doubly aware that he had no family members to whom he could eventually hand on the business, began to considered selling out or, ideally, shaping a merger with another tractor concern.

Even so, because the world of business now knew how difficult it was going to be to cooperate with this irascible self-made millionaire, there was no bidding frenzy. Standard, for sure, was not interested, but Ferguson eventually attracted another tractor manufacturer, Massey-Harris (M-H) of Canada, with whom exploratory talks had already begun about sharing engine supplies from Standard, and which later progressed to the thought of merging its interests in North America.

Amazingly, these talks advanced so far, and so smoothly, that in June 1953 M-H's President, James Duncan, flew to the UK to meet Harry Ferguson himself. After much convoluted (and, at times, comical) negotiation, Ferguson agreed to sell all his shareholding to M-H (a deal which netted him $16 million, about £5.7 million), he becoming chairman of the merged enterprise. That arrangement, incidentally, lasted for only a year, after which Ferguson walked away from the merged company, lost all remaining contact with Standard, and now fades out of our story.

This initially left Standard out on a limb (Harry Ferguson had not consulted Standard's management about the deal until it was ready to be publicly announced), but as the company retained a share-holding, and still held a tractor production contract which was valid until the end of 1955, there seemed to be no immediate panic.

Or was there? Sir John Black, who thought 'long' rather than 'short,' considered otherwise, as he was still keen to retain the munificent cash flow (and profits), which came from making tractors on behalf of another company, for a number of years to come.

As we now know, without even consulting the other Standard directors in advance, in October 1953 Sir John made an immediate visit to the top bosses at Massey-Harris-Ferguson, almost immediately signing up a new deal which, for a further 12 years, would commit Standard to continue producing Ferguson tractors (or whatever the name might become in the future) at Banner Lane.

When Sir John announced this to his Board colleagues at a meeting dated 24 November 1953, there was consternation but, in the end, what seems to have been rather reluctant acceptance of the realities of the situation. From that moment, however, the two companies – Standard and Massey Ferguson – gradually seemed to have drifted apart.

Although Standard continued to build large number of tractors, there were several underlying problems – mainly connected with Massey's belief that Standard was charging it too much money (and therefore making excessive profits), and Standard's fear that it was continuing to be altogether too reliant on the tractor operations.

Extracts from a personal interview of Alick Dick, given to the author many years ago, make this clear:

"To give us greater strength, the first thing I had to do [as managing director ...] was to get rid of the tractor business ... but the company really wasn't viable without it, as we would be selling more than half of the profits, and keeping more than half the overheads ..."

Then there was what many Standard people called 'the Perkins' problem.' Frank Perkins had been building diesel engines in Peterborough since the 1930s, started offering a 32bhp three-cylinder P3 (TA) diesel conversion for Ferguson TE-20 tractors in the early 1950s, and rapidly found that this was being compared favourably with the diesel engine provided by Standard at the time.

Relations became more glacial in 1958, as by this time Standard had not only begun to expand by buying up other concerns (Beans Industries, for instance) but in addition to discussing a full-blooded merger with Massey Ferguson, had also engaged in fruitless merger talks with companies as varied as Rover and the Rootes Group. Not only did Massey Ferguson see the possibility of its own substantial shareholding in Standard being diluted if such moves intensified, but it sensed that it would be sidelined in the process. All this is explained in more detail in chapter 11.

Matters came to a head in 1958 when Standard mounted an agreed takeover bid for Mulliners Ltd, its major Birmingham-based bodyshell suppliers. When Massey offered to buy every one of those new shares from the Mulliners' shareholders who were about to receive them! It was a stratagem which failed, but it meant that all trust had been destroyed, and a divorce from Standard was now seen as inevitable, especially after Massey also secured control of the Perkins diesel engine business, which meant that it would no longer be reliant on supplies of diesels from Standard.

In the summer of 1959, the fourteen-year marriage with Ferguson, and with its tractors, finally came to an end, Standard speedily pulled out of Banner Lane, and quickly centred all its operations on the Canley-Fletchamstead complex instead.

Not that this was Standard's final connection with tractor engineering, for no sooner had the divorce been finalised, than the company began working on a tractor of its own.

A sad end to a fine building – in early 2000 the Banner Lane factory was emptied of all its remaining machinery, and demolished by developers. Not a trace remains.

By the 1960s, and after Standard had sold out its interests to Massey Ferguson, Banner Land had become one of the very largest factories in Coventry. In this serial shot, the multi-storey office block, and the white-roofed extension on the right (north, actually) were recent additions. By 2010, almost the entire site had been razed, and redeveloped for housing.

In the 1950s, incidentally, a four-wheel-drive vehicle had already been designed, and partly developed, but little is now known about this, and no trace now remains.

Tucked away in a modest workshop to the rear of the newly-converted Engineering block (Fletchamstead North), a team managed by John Chambers and Trevor Knox (Graham Stanley ran the workshops) rapidly produced two new diesel-engined machines, which carried the Experimental Register Code of 'Zero 1,' and were numbered X671 and X672. These were ready soon after the divorce (although the Register dates them as in 1961 models), and had the latest 23C (2.3-litre) 'high-speed' diesel engine.

Soon after this, a second pair of re-designed machines,(Zero 2, being X677 and X678) followed up, but the project was speedily cancelled by Leyland Motors in the wake of that company's rescue of the Standard business. The prototypes were sold off, the workshops were taken over by the newly re-opened Motorsport Department (which the author then managed from 1962 to 1965) and all links with agricultural engineering were then concluded.

Jet engines for Rolls-Royce

In the 1950s, Standard showed just how versatile it was – and what vaunting ambitions Sir John Black held for 'his' company – when it spent several years producing ultra-powerful military gas turbine jet engines. The initial approach came from the Ministry of Supply (MoS), who no doubt retained fond memories of the sterling work carried out by Standard in its various shadow factories during the Second World War.

Early in the 1950s Britain's government had started to rearm at an ambitious rate, but soon found that its military infrastructure had been run down extremely rapidly after

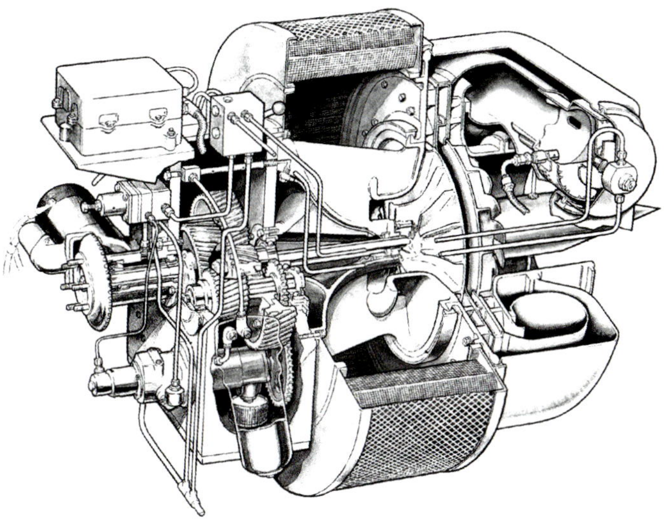

In the 1950s, Standard also dabbled with the development of a small gas turbine/power generator of its own, the IS/250, but it was never more than a sideline. The low profile project went public in March 1957, but was then sold off to Auto Diesels Ltd in mid-1958.

World War Two. This, no doubt, explains why Rolls-Royce developed the B40, B60 and B80 petrol engines in the late 1940s (these were four-, six- and eight-cylinder versions of the same basic design), for use in trucks, 4x4s and personnel carriers, and noting that the B60 was a 'blood relative' of the engine fitted to current Rolls-Royce and Bentley cars. Even so, Rolls-Royce had no spare capacity to build this engine, which may explain why the MoS spent time negotiating with Sir John Black, though nothing, in the end, came of it.

But as one door closed, another opened ...

Once the Germans had been defeated in 1945, the UK and USA had become world leaders in gas turbine ('jet engine') technology. Unhappily, the west's research and knowledge was then shared with the USSR, which rapidly adapted it to its own military purposes.

Then, in 1950, the Korean War broke out, in which the Soviets sided with North Korea against the western powers. When Soviet MIG 15 jet fighters then appeared over South Korea, the authorities were thoroughly alarmed, and rearmament went ahead as rapidly as possible (though British civil service sloth made this look like a very leisurely business for a time ...).

Britain's most advanced jet engine of the period was the modern axial-flow Rolls-Royce Avon, for not only did this power the Canberra bomber, it was later fitted to the De Havilland Comet civil airliner, and to the very important (but still not ready for mass production) Hawker Hunter single-seater fighter. Spurred on by the crisis, the UK government sought to increase Avon output, and because Rolls-Royce was already working at full capacity, decided to involve several other trusted contractors.

Following informal exchanges, which began before the end of 1950, Standard received a formal invitation to sign a contract to build Avons in August 1951, when a total output of 650 engines was mentioned. This was accepted in October, when the type of Avon – Mk109 – was laid down, these to be for use in twin-engined Canberras, which were already in production at the English Electric factories near Preston.

Standard's own gas turbine engine

No sooner had the government cancelled the Avon jet engine contract in 1955, it seems, than Standard began work on its own much less ambitious gas turbine project. This surely, counts as a 'vanity' programme, for Standard (-Triumph) had no immediate use for such a machine. Gas turbines, however, were fashionable for not only had Rover, but Austin, started work on gas turbines, too.

IS/250, as it was coded, was always intended as a constant-speed industrial engine, which might have found favour as an auxiliary power unit in big passenger aircraft, or as a stationary engine. It was designed to run at 24,000rpm (these figures might have been mind-boggling to automotive enthusiasts, but were normal for rotary engines of the period), and was rated at 250bhp. This is not the place to go into a detailed analysis of the design, but, to summarise, it featured a single-stage centrifugal compressor, two combustion chambers, a single inward-flowing (centripetal) power turbine, and a drive shaft protruding through the starter gearing.

The complete engine was just 30.5in long and 39in wide, weighing in at 350lb. One interesting feature was that the compressor was totally surrounded by a massive intake air filter.

The IS/250 was revealed in March 1957 when, in *The Autocar*, Technical Editor Harry Mundy expertly pointed out that as a constant-speed design it was quite unsuitable for automotive use. It was, in any case, very specialised, for some of the components would be running at temperatures of 1500 degrees centigrade. Not only that, but overall thermal efficiency was low, there was no heat exchanger in the airflow system so, (to quote Mundy): "an automobile turbine without this important component is not worthy of serious consideration ..."

Not only that but: "... they [Standard] will be able to assess future possibilities without being committed to an expensive research programme, which might take many years to recover if the work were directed towards automobile use alone ..."

This, in effect, was a coded message from a true engine expert saying "Forget it," and by mid-1958 Standard's design team came to agree with this analysis, when (except for car use) the project was sold off to Auto Diesels Ltd.

When Standard was asked to manufacture Rolls-Royce Avon jet engines in 1951, this was by far the most complex project ever tackled by the company. Hundreds were built before the contract was ended in 1954.

In the next two years progress now appears to have been glacial, such that by mid-1953 Standard had only produced 15 complete engines, though the government had paid the company £8 million to tool up for series production. In the meantime, the military and political crisis had already eased, a Korean cease-fire was in the offing, and the contract had been reduced to just 250 (later 300) engines.

Avon assembly was concentrated on the Fletchamstead South complex (this, of course, had originally been Standard's first 'Shadow 1' factory) where more than 300,000ft^2 was allocated, along with another 56,000ft^2 at Banner Lane (this mainly involving test bed facilities behind the main tractor plant, and remote from the public highway). This need for factory space 'at headquarters' was a major influence on Standard's search for a new 'satellite' factory, to build spare parts and other components, which went ahead in Lancashire in the early 1950s.

In 1953 and 1954, Avon production activity at Standard was frenetic, to say the least. Not only were contract numbers raised, then lowered, then converted to a different type of Avon (Mk113s were mentioned), but there was a constant wrangle over costs and profits. Sir John seems to have been hard-nosed as ever, but met his match with the Ministry, who finally agreed to a fixed profit of £250,000 to cover the first 100 engines to be completed.

Standard pointed out that the first 100 engines would be completed by March 1954 (this date slipped, later), by which time it would be capable of building up to 15 engines every month. The government then agreed to place orders for 150 new Mk113s to be built before December 1955 – until suddenly, in mid-1954, the entire programme was culled, to a grand total of 300 engines.

The Kirkby (Liverpool) project – stillborn

When Standard won the massive contract to build Rolls-Royce Avon gas turbine engines in 1951, this made the acquisition of more factory space imperative. However, because Government policy banned Standard from expanding its own operations in Coventry, the search began for a major new 'satellite' operation.

With the object of producing spare parts and other components in a new factory, Standard then settled on a 400,000ft^2 site in Kirkby, a north-eastern suburb of Liverpool, ideally placed near the A580 East Lancs Road (and, coincidentally, close to the world-famous Aintree race course). The Liverpool development corporation offered a 999-year lease at a 'peppercorn' rent, and all seemed promising at first.

Delay then followed delay, building never started, and after nearly £300,000 had been spent on the project, the likely demise of the Rolls-Royce contract saw Standard lose all interest in Kirkby. Finally, Standard sold its interests to Kraft Foods, who set up a massive food production plant on the same site.

Standard's stillborn 'Kirkby' project should never be confused with the buildings and operations the company later developed at Speke (also a suburb of Liverpool), which was not in the same district, and not connected.

Standard's contract to manufacture Avon turbojet engines was offered in 1951, with several hundred units being scheduled for fitment to twin-engined Canberra bombers. In the main, the engines were assembled at Fletchamstead South, Canley, with much testing being carried out at Banner Lane.

Standard's official announcement, to the workforce, told only part of the story:

"Owing to the suspension of the Comet flying programmes [this followed two tragic crashes of Comet airliners, which was subsequently found to be due to airframe fatigue], and new aircraft manufacture, it has been necessary for reductions to be made in the manufacturing programme for jet engines. This has resulted in the cancellation of 145 engines, and in view of our present uncompetitive manufacturing costs, both in man-hours and rates-per-hour, the Company find it difficult to resist these cancellations. At our scheduled and present rate of production, our remaining contracts will operate until June 1955 ..."

Even so, at this time the company calculated that the jet engine business was adding about £200,000/annum charges to fixed costs, though the net profit was about £250,000/annum.

Suddenly, and equally unexpected though, there was a further contraction, when the contract was wound up. On 18 November 1954, a headline in the *Coventry Evening Telegraph* screamed: "Minister confirms decision over jets ... ," with further comment stressing that nationwide demand for Avons was now only one third of that which had been estimated in 1952, that Bristol and Napier (of London) had already ceased building Avons, and that Standard was the last business, apart from Rolls-Royce itself, still to be building them.

Although it then took months for every piece of government 'red tape' to be tied off, Standard's involvement in jet engine production was over, and would never be revived. Except that there appears to have been a financial benefit at the end of the period (and Standard, for sure, kept some of the production machines, purchasing them as used items at very advantageous prices) there seems to be have been general relief at a return to the building of wheeled vehicles.

Massive expansion in the 1950s

Although Standard did not admit it freely at the time, the abandonment of the gas turbine programme, and a gradual withdrawal from the tractor business in the mid-1950s, made it easier for management to concentrate on its core activity – which was that of making cars and light commercial vehicles. By that time, not only had the Standard Vanguard, but small cars and Triumph sports cars, all become vitally important to the company and its future.

THE BRM PROJECT – DABBLING WITH FORMULA ONE

Raymond Mays might not have been the world's best racing driver, but he was certainly a world-class scrounger. In the 1920s and 1930s he had often begged, borrowed, or been given money and hardware to enable him to go motor racing – the ERA project of the 1930s was his crowning glory – but in postwar years he then set out on his biggest-ever quest. This was to develop a sensational new Grand Prix car – which, when it finally appeared in 1949, was to be known as the BRM (British Racing Motor).

Not only did Mays not have much money of his own, but his little 'factory,' at Bourne, in Lincolnshire, had little equipment and few facilities. Accordingly, when the time came to design the new 'world-beater,' he spent months touring the motor industry, begging for money, for technical assistance, and for sub-contracting help in making parts of the cars. The original BRMs, by the way, were to be extraordinary machines, with 1½-litre supercharged V16 engines intended to produce more than 500bhp.

In 1945 one of his first calls was on Sir John Black – though, of course, this was not the first time Mays had met the Standard boss. Way back in 1938, Mays had conceived the idea of a 4-litre (it had a six-cylinder overhead camshaft) engined ERA road car that he thought Standard might build – that engine being designed for him by Murray Jamieson and a then-young Harry Mundy (who later became Coventry-Climax's chief designer in the 1950s) – but William Lyons, sensing a business conflict with his own dealings with Standard, persuaded Sir John to turn him down.

After designer Murray Jamieson was killed in a crash (as a spectator) at the Brooklands race circuit, that project died in any case, and was soon replaced in Mays's fertile mind, first by a Standard-based sports car (with the Flying V-Eight engine and chassis – see page 70), and later by a Flying 10-based design instead. As we now know, neither came to fruition, so, as World War Two raged, Mays and Sir John Black lost touch with each other for the next seven years.

Then came 1944/1945, when Mays finally dragged himself out from under his wartime activities (the family business was involved in wool-broking, and there seemed to be limitless demand for wool by the Armed Forces ...) he could once again return to his passion – motor racing.

Determined to get Britain into the forefront of Grand Prix racing, Mays concluded that only he and his close-knit coterie could design and build a car to do the job. There was only one snag – that a great deal of money, equipment and expertise was going to be needed, and he had none.

Standard's contribution to the V16 BRM project was to machine many major castings, and to have Walter Belgrove style the finished product. This was the original car, as unveiled in 1949.

However, he possessed a hide as thick as a rhinoceros, and set out on a lengthy trawl through the British motor industry – to beg, borrow, and solicit, though not to steal – everything that his new project required.

In 1945, this was the foundation of the BRM project, which was to take up mountains of time, piles of money (other peoples' money ...), and to break many hearts in the years that followed. It was at this time that he once again approached Sir John Black for help – and he must have caught him at the right time. To quote BRM authority Doug Nye:

"Black was an extrovert and extravagant character, but as a manic-depressive was entirely victim to mood ... Raymond Mays was organizing a luncheon for his new backers in the Angel Hotel at Bourne, and invited Black to attend. The day before the function, Black telephoned to say he could not attend after all, but he was sending his deputy Alick Dick ... 'and he is going to hand you a cheque for £5000 ...' He also offered Standard's help, to cast and machine many of the V16's major mechanical components, in the tool room, without charge."

In those days £5000 was a considerable amount of money – the pre-tax price of a new Standard Twelve, if you could find one that was not already allocated to 'essential users,' was a mere £375. Clearly, Sir John had been taken in by Raymond Mays' persuasive blarney, so for the next few years Standard would become an active contributor to the BRM project.

First of all, there was Standard's commitment to use the excellent tool room facilities at Banner Lane to machine major castings for the BRM's engine and transmission assemblies. The earlier promise to cast the components too was never practical, as Standard had no such facilities in Coventry or elsewhere, so these were produced by a Standard supplier – Aeroplane & Motor Aluminium Castings. Standard also underpinned the cost, installation and checking out of the new engine test bed at Bourne: in the end this cost an extra £7000.

By 1953, Standard's contribution to the BRM project was over, and the Belgrove-inspired lines of the original car had been spoilt by the addition of various scoops and vents.

This, though, was not the end of Standard's involvement, for when the time came for the BRM's design to be settled, and a shape prepared to wrap over the complex machinery, Raymond Mays persuaded Sir John Black to have his Chief Body Engineer, Walter Belgrove, do that job. Belgrove, the rather 'chippy' artist/engineer who had been with Triumph in the 1930s, enjoyed this task. And so he should, because his previous major task had been to style the first of the Standard Vanguards, and his next would be to shape the unhappy Triumph TRX sports car, and a stillborn proposal for a 'Vanguard Phase II,' which bore a resemblance to it.

The original BRM style, first featured in a small-scale model used in publicity pictures in 1948, looked gorgeous, but there was one major deficiency, which had to be rectified as soon as a car took to the racetrack. Through no fault of Belgrove's – after all, he had never before worked on a powerful single-seater race car – there was no provision for channelling hot air out of the engine bay, and no cooling vents in the bonnet. These duly appeared, on the car, in the first year ...

In the traumatic years that followed, Standard was an active supporter of the BRM project, not only financially, but by loaning the company several Standard Vanguard cars for various transport purposes. Even as late as 1952, new engine castings were still being machined at Standard, but this was almost the end.

Although Standard donated a further £10,000 to BRM in January 1952, at the same time it warned that no new machining work would be carried out when the current engine 'sets' had been completed.

Other suppliers and sponsors obviously felt the same, for shortly the project came close to financial and sporting collapse. At the end of that year, the entire BRM project was sold off to Rubery Owen, and Standard's involvement came to an end.

CHAPTER 9

VANGUARDS, RENOWNS AND MAYFLOWERS 1947-1953

Probably the most important decision of Standard's postwar strategy was to plan for, and introduce, the all-new Vanguard, which did so much for the company's reputation and its balance sheet in the next decade or so. Inside the industry, if not out in the wide world, Sir John Black's policy of embracing the design, development, and proliferation of just one all-new postwar car became well-known – but it was not until mid-1947 that the world got its first view of that new car. The new model, the Vanguard, would dominate Standard's production lines for the next six or seven years.

This was to be one of those occasions, rare in the British motor industry of the period, when a new model was to be planned, and where the product was new from end-to-end. Not only would there be a new chassis, new independent front suspension, a new engine, and a new transmission, but an entirely new pressed steel body style as well. You might say that this was all a colossal gamble – and you would be right – but it was not the first, and would certainly not be the last, successful gamble that John Black had made.

The entire car could be – and would be – engineered 'in house,' mainly at Banner Lane, but, as ever, Standard would be obliged to find a body-manufacturing concern to produce bodyshells, and a Midlands specialist to produce chassis frames. Since it was going to take much longer than anything else – to produce new press tools for steel panels, and assembly jigs to turn them into bodyshells – work on the style had to come first of all.

But who should shape the new car, and how should that style be converted into reality? The sad fact is that in the late 1930s, when the range of Flying Standards evolved, Standard did not appear to have many artistically accomplished body designers on its staff, and that situation did not improve during the war years.

Because Sir John Black does not seem to have been artistically minded (he had needed help to get the styling of the Flying Standard models finalised, his taste in 'razor-edge' styling, encouraged by Mulliners, was already becoming obsolescent, though he would insist on it being incorporated in the Triumph Mayflower of 1949), he had to rely on his staff for ideas.

Fortunately, by this time a successful stylist/body engineer, Walter Belgrove, had already joined the firm. Belgrove, employed at the still-independent Triumph concern in the 1920s and 1930s, had became that company's Chief Body Engineer in 1935, and was responsible for shaping some of the most elegant Triumphs of the period (not for nothing was one of its advertising slogans: "The Smartest Cars in the Land ...").

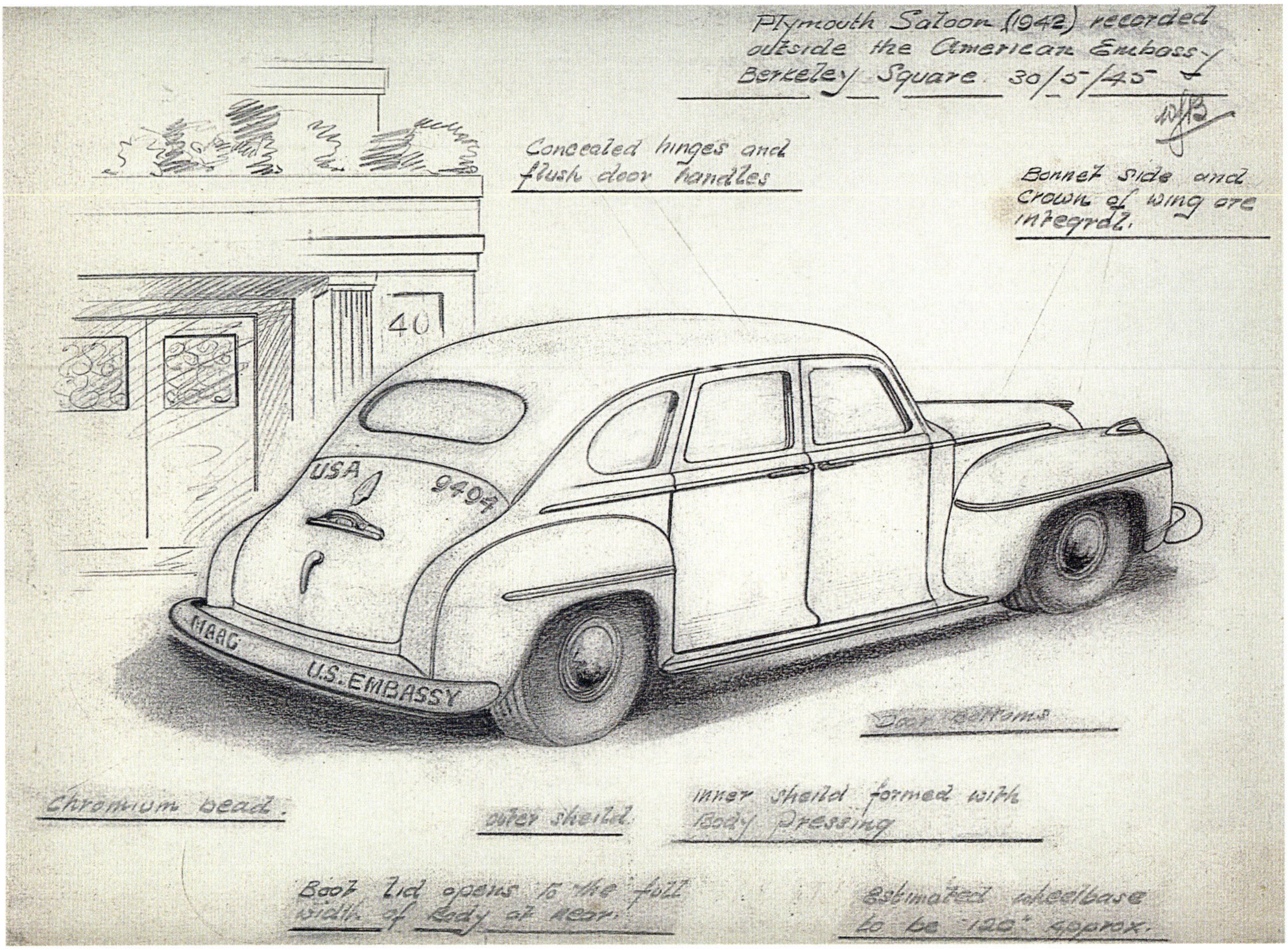

A sketch made by Walter Belgrove, outside the USA's London Embassy, of a late-model Plymouth in May 1945, clearly shows where the inspiration for the Vanguard came from.

Having joined Standard in 1939 ("I found myself engaged on the layout, full scale, of the Airspeed Oxford aircraft ... and spent much of the war-time years on tooling for the Mosquito fighter-bombers ..." Belgrove once told the author), he then spent the first part of 1945 finalising the style of the new Triumph 1800 saloon, a car that had been dreamed up in a matter of days by Sir John, improved but not completed by Mulliners itself (see page 102), and made ready for launch in 1946. Little coherent work, therefore, had yet begun on what would become known as the Vanguard. Sir John Black, however, was known to be impressed by the latest American-car styles, and had an eye on exporting cars in large numbers when the fighting was over.

Suddenly, therefore, the project turned from dream to reality. Belgrove once told the author that, one morning, Sir John Black arrived in his office and announced: "Belgrove, the best-looking Yankee motor car is the Plymouth, and the best place to study one is outside the American embassy in London! I suggest you take yourself off to Grosvenor Square. The place is swarming with embassy vehicles, take whom you like, and whatever you wish, and come back only when you have got all you want – and don't get shot ..."

"I duly toddled off to London by road," Belgrove said, "taking my wife with me, plus a camera and a sketch block ... There appeared to be no parking restrictions ... but I felt that my little Standard Eight must be very conspicuous amongst the American Goliaths."

The rest of the story is simply summarised. Although Belgrove was not at all happy with this assault on his own artistic tendencies (left to his own devices, he would probably not have designed a Vanguard in this way, he said), he took himself off to the capital, acquired all the pictures he needed, sketched many details, and returned triumphantly to Coventry without either being arrested or even questioned. Sir John who "was enamoured of the Plymouth – particularly the rear end," told Belgrove that he would like, as much as was feasible, the main styling features of the Plymouth incorporated into a scale drawing on the shortest possible wheelbase ...

This 1949 Standard Vanguard poses by the riverside in Stoneleigh village, just a few miles from the factory in Coventry.

Although undated, this study certainly dates from 1945/1946, when Standard's own craftsmen were hurrying to complete the bodyshell of the very first Vanguard prototype. Fisher & Ludlow would eventually make the bodies in volume.

Belgrove, need one add, was offended at the idea of having to produce a copy, or even a clone of an American machine, but was so in awe of his managing director that he produced scale drawings on a 120in wheelbase (that of the contemporary Plymouth was 117in), a 108in wheelbase and a 102in wheelbase. None of these, of course, were acceptable to Sir John, who finally settled on a stubby 94in wheelbase.

Belgrove and his colleagues were depressed by this – the new Vanguard, it seemed, would have a much shorter wheelbase than the Triumph 1800 saloon which was just about to be announced, along with what Belgrove always whinged about "the reverse crab-track chassis" (the rear track was significantly wider than the front). This, and Sir John's insistence on specifying a bench front seat and a steering column gearchange – both of them with the aim of providing the possible three-abreast seating up front – made life difficult for the body department.

This is the point at which the controversial figure of Technical Director Ted Grinham re-enters the story, as he had

Nearly there! This colour rendering shows that Walter Belgrove had almost gained approval for the shape of the new Vanguard at the end of 1946, though work was still to be done on the front grille.

just returned from a four-year absence, originally at De Havilland, and latterly with Humber Ltd, (Rootes's design and manufacturing subsidiary, in Coventry). Walter Belgrove recalled being introduced to him on 'neutral ground,' (in Sir John Black's office):

"I was introduced to Grinham in Sir John's office, and I well remember the occasion. The ensuing discussion centred around the new [Vanguard] project, which Sir John pointed out was well forward, and indeed in the main conceived by him. Grinham, not to be outdone in enthusiasm, produced several prints and details of projects, and initial schemes in process of development in his late [Humber] company ...

"At the conclusion of this introductory conference, Sir John suggested that Grinham should visit my office and Department, and acquaint himself with what was in progress. I cannot say that our relationship got off to a very good start. Grinham did not appear to be interested so much in the project, as in his desire to impress on me his theories of inter-departmental discipline and implicit obedience to his authority ..."

Grinham made this sort of impression on almost everyone he encountered at Standard – senior or junior to him, the result being that no esprit de corps ever seemed to build up within Engineering, and quite a number of accomplished engineers hastened to leave (including, in due course, Chief Chassis Designer Ray Turner, who was a real loss). Belgrove summed up his own feelings about this difficult man as: "Quite candidly, he was an arrogant, sadistic, unscrupulous, vain, power lusting, over-ambitious bastard. He was universally disliked and feared throughout the organisation ..."

Laying the foundations

Even so, from 1945 Standard began, inexorably, to turn all its efforts to preparing the new postwar car, the Vanguard. As already noted, the initial effort had gone into developing the first-ever 'Standard-Triumphs' (the 1800 saloon and the 1800 Roadster), but by 1946 these cars were already entering production, and were no longer concerning the design, development and styling teams, which had been located in newly kitted-out offices at the 'tractor' factory at Banner Lane.

As Sir John Black had already emphasised to Ted Grinham (when re-appointing him in 1945) and to stylist Walter Belgrove when sending him off to study the latest model in American Plymouths, he always looked upon the Vanguard as his own invention. It was Sir John who had decided to have the car look like an Anglicised version of

HMS VANGUARD

As most Standard enthusiasts surely know, the Vanguard of 1947 (which went on sale in 1948) was named after Britain's last-ever battleship, which had been commissioned in 1946. It was no coincidence, by the way, that there would also be a Triumph Renown and a Triumph Mayflower, both of which also picked up the names of famous and historic ships of the past, for Sir John Black seemed to love the naval connection.

The ship in question, which was built during the Second World War, launched in 1944, and commissioned in 1946, was the tenth such vessel to carry this famous name (the first was built in 1586). When fully loaded and ready for battle, she weighed no less than 51,820 tons – in fact as large as the German behemoths, the Bismark and the Tirpitz, which she had been designed to counter.

However, because she was not completed until after the end of the war, Vanguard never fired her guns in anger, though she took part in many postwar training exercises. Relegated to the Navy's Reserve Fleet in 1956, she was eventually committed for scrap in 1960. Towed to Faslane, in Scotland (this base became, and still is, the HQ of Britain's nuclear submarine fleet), she was then cut-up, and reduced to scrap steel, finally ceasing to exist, even as a hulk, in 1962.

This, however, was not the end of the Vanguard tradition, for in 1992 this famous name was applied to the very first of Britain's formidable fleet of nuclear-powered Trident submarines.

Pictured here at Banner Lane is probably the very first Vanguard mock-up, which was completed in 1945/1946. Some visual features would change before it was launched in mid-1947.

This, according to the Standard caption applied to the print, shows the very first Vanguard to be shown to the public. This car was previewed in 1947, when it had a 1850cc version of the soon-to-be-legendary 'wet-liner' engine, though when it went on sale in 1948 that engine would already have grown to 2088cc.

the Plymouth, that it would be built on a brand new chassis with a mere 7ft 10in (94-inch) wheelbase, that it would have seating for five (six, if three willing passengers could be persuaded to use the bench front seat together), along with a brand-new four-cylinder engine, a new transmission, and the then-fashionable steering-column-located gear change.

However, not even Sir John could make miracles become reality in a matter of months (there were times, it must be said, when his attitude was that such feats ought to be possible!), so at a very early stage he had to finalise the style, and to award a contract for production of the bodyshell. Standard, of course, was not yet capable of pressing, welding up and assembling complete shells, for in the previous 'Flying Standard' era it had awarded shell production contracts to three independent businesses – Briggs, Fisher & Ludlow, and Pressed Steel.

Here, then, was his first conundrum. If Standard was to go ahead with what was effectively a 'single model' policy in the first years, it would have to choose between the three. That conundrum, it seems, soon solved itself. Briggs (though still independent, and about to produce bodies for the Jowett Javelin) was increasingly becoming beholden to Ford, Pressed Steel was already being inundated with orders from Austin, Morris, Rover, Hillman, Rolls-Royce and others – which left just one possibility – Fisher & Ludlow.

Even this was not going to be quick and easy, for F&L was also undergoing a massive transformation. As noted in the panel on page 136, soon after 1945, Fisher & Ludlow bought a huge shadow factory, which had been set up at Castle Bromwich to manufacture Spitfire fighter aircraft, but this had to be emptied of Spitfires, then re-equipped to build car bodies.

Originally F&L thought this could be done before the end of 1947, but the timetable slipped, and the first 'off-line' Vanguard shells did not appear until early 1948. This was not too difficult for Standard, as the new wet-liner engine for the Vanguard (and also for the Ferguson tractor) project was also running a few months late.

Sir John, therefore, had to be satisfied with previewing the new Vanguard to the media in July 1947, when it only had a prototype 1.85-litre engine (as being used in Ferguson tractors at the time), and when production was

This historic shot, dating from 1946, shows Standard's dynamic MD, Sir John Black, posing on a country road in Wales, with the very first Vanguard prototype.

being forecast for July 1948. *The Motor* magazine, fulsome as ever concerning all things British in the motor industry, commented at the time that:

"The Vanguard is, in fact, a credit to Sir John Black and his engineers, and a worthy example of British automobile engineering and production genius."

Keeping the brand alive

In the meantime, and while the costly and lengthy business of re-equipping Canley went ahead, Standard had to keep its production lines busy, and its dealers (all round the world) satisfied, if only for the time being. Just as soon as possible after the tumultuous events of World War Two came to an end, Canley was cleared of the mass of military hardware, which had occupied it for the previous six years – and prepared to embrace a peaceful future.

There was, of course, no question of picking up exactly where the entire range of 1939/1940 models had left off. For a whole variety of reasons, in fact, this was neither practical, nor even desirable.

[Six years of war had changed every possible commercial reality but, purely for interest, I would like to re-list the seven-car range of Standard cars which was ready to be produced in the 1940 model year]:

Flying Eight	4-cyl, SV, 1021cc
Flying Nine	4-cyl, SV, 1131cc
Flying Ten	4-cyl, SV, 1267cc
Flying Twelve	4-cyl, SV, 1608cc
Flying Fourteen	4-cyl, SV, 1776cc
Flying Sixteen	6-cyl, SV, 2143cc
Flying Twenty	6-cyl, SV, 2664cc

Times (and the markets) had changed in the six years that had passed since then, of course, for Standard had already sold off its six-cylinder engine manufacturing facilities to Jaguar in 1942 – which meant that the Sixteen and Twenty models could not now be revived (Standard could no longer build its own engines for them), even if a restricted market demand for those machines had still seemed to exist: in fairness, Standard was probably relieved to bring an end to their careers, for sales had always been very restricted.

Of the other five models, the Flying Eight and latest Flying Ten had a modern chassis with independent front suspension, as did the Flying Twelve and Fourteen models, which left the old-type Flying Nine out on a limb.

Standard, therefore, took a deep breath, decided that for the time being it would concentrate on the Eight and Twelve (with a Fourteen also available, at first only for export) models, which would mean that for the first two or three years, at least, Canley would have to accommodate two different chassis frames, two types of side-valve engines and – a brave decision, this – only one gearbox (as the Eight got the 'box from the larger cars).

The re-launch of these models has already been described in chapter 7. As far as Standard – and particularly Sir John Black – was concerned, however, they were 'Old News,' for every effort was henceforth to be concentrated on finalising two new products – one was the tractor Standard would make for Ferguson – the other being the new Vanguard.

Vanguard – a new car for a new generation

When the new Vanguard was officially revealed in July 1947, there seemed to be a collective sigh of relief from everyone at Standard, for behind closed doors the previous two years had been hectic for all concerned. First of all, Canley had been cleared of all its military work, then the Ferguson transaction had been announced, next the postwar Triumphs had been introduced, while all the time engineering and development work was going ahead on the Ferguson tractor, and on the new Vanguard car.

This was the period in which Sir John Black confirmed Standard's 'one-model' policy for the immediate future, pointing out that when production sanctions of the existing (prewar type) of cars ended in July 1948, they would not be extended. However, as we shall see, it all depended on what was meant by 'one model' ...

Even so, this encouraged *The Motor* magazine, one of Britain's 'establishment' journals, to comment in an editorial:

"The Standard Vanguard is the result of a bold and fundamentally sound piece of engineering planning, by means of which a great manufacturer voluntarily rationalises his output to the extent of producing a single model for the home as well as the overseas market. To carry out such a

In certain colours – this gold is an excellent example – Walter Belgrove's original Vanguard was an impressive beast.

drastic degree of concentration might be almost impossible in more normal times ...

"As it is [and before the Vanguard goes on sale], the motorist will continue to buy any sound form of modern vehicle ... The fact that the Standard Co are showing a benevolent wisdom by manufacturing large quantities of spare parts for the now out-dated types is another good reason for general confidence in the future."

The Vanguard, indeed, was entirely new, with a style reflecting the most modern of North American shapes, all wrapped around a five-seater interior, with what we would now call a 'fastback.' The wheelbase, at 94in, was six inches shorter than that of the old-type 12hp/14hp range, though at 13ft 9in it was just the same length. Amazingly, and in spite of this, the interior of the cabin was more spacious (considerably wider in fact) than before.

The box-section chassis frame supported a new type of independent front suspension, which featured coil springs and lever arm shock absorbers (the old-type Flying models had used a transverse leaf spring layout), there was a brand-new type of all-synchromesh three speed gearbox, which was operated by a steering column change, in which the change

This was where the rolling chassis of the Vanguard met its partly trimmed bodyshell, at Canley in 1948.

speed lever was placed on the right side of the steering column.

No doubt with an eye to getting the most out of a considerable financial investment, that new gearbox, or derivatives of the same, was always intended to have a long life, as was the hypoid bevel rear axle introduced at the same time. No-one, however, could possibly have guessed just how long that gearbox layout would survive – as spelt out in the panel on the left, direct descendants would still be use on the final models built when Canley closed down 33 years later in 1980!

LONG-LIVED GEARBOX

Maybe it's difficult to believe, at first glance, but there was a definite family connection between the Standard Vanguard gearbox of 1948, and the Triumph Dolomite Sprint of 1980, which brought its career to an end. Even though the original had three forward speeds and a steering column change, whereas the last had four forward speeds and synchromesh on all forward ratios, optional Laycock overdrive, and a centre-floor gear change, the two were closely related.

This is how Standard (and the Triumph brand which followed) achieved so much, over the years, with limited capital and development resources. First of all there was the Vanguard three-speed all-synchromesh box, which, in late 1949, was also being used in the Triumph 2000 Roadster, the Triumph Renown saloon, and the Triumph Mayflower. Optional Laycock overdrive became available (not on the Mayflower) during 1950.

The next big change came in 1952, when the box was modified for use in what became the Triumph TR2 sports car, not only to have four forward speeds (and no synchromesh on first gear), but a modified casing with a remote-control centre gear change. The same gearbox, but with a long central gear lever, was then found in the Vanguard-based Ensign of 1957, and became optional on Vanguards a few months later, and standard on the Vanguard Six of 1960.

From late 1961 the new Triumph TR4 sports car got a modified version, this time with four forward speeds and all-synchromesh, which meant that a new alloy casing, just 0.44in longer than before, was required to accommodate everything: the remote control change was as before. This box was then adopted as the standard piece of kit on all Triumph 2000 family machines, on later TRs, the Stag, and on the Dolomite Sprint saloon, and was used with few major modifications until the late 1970s. It was also used in the Spitfire Le Mans racing coupes of 1964.

Early in the 1970s, Standard-Triumph even developed a five-speed conversion of this gearbox, but only prototypes were made. If the engineers had not been encouraged to design a brand-new five-speed transmission for the Rover SD1 and the Triumph TR7/TR8 (many other companies also bought supplies for their own specialist cars), it might have lasted even longer.

VANGUARD – THE LEGENDARY NEW ENGINE

As already noted, Sir John Black's intentions for Standard's postwar private car range were that only a single all-new family of cars should be developed. Engines, gearboxes and other details designed for that car – which became known as the Standard Vanguard – might eventually be used as 'building blocks' in other models, but that would come later. In the meantime, the existing 1939/1940-type Standards already mentioned – Eight, Twelve and Fourteen – would have to hold the fort until the new car was ready.

The development of a new four-cylinder engine was central to the entire Vanguard project, for none of Standard's existing (and frankly, ageing) engines was thought to be suitable for further development. The engine in the Flying Fourteen – a side-valve 1776cc power unit – had its original

WET-LINER ENGINE SIZES

For the record, these were the different engine sizes, all of which featured, over the years, in the 'wet-liner' range originally seen in Ferguson tractors and the Standard Vanguard:

Capacity (cc)	Bore (mm)	Stroke (mm)
1760	76	92
1849	80	92
1991	83	92
2088	85	92
2138	86	92
2188	87	92

– in addition, in the early 1950s, there was a definite intention to produce an engine with a 90mm bore, to provide more torque for tractors and commercial vehicles, and more power for the Renown. This never went beyond prototype form, as follows:

Capacity (cc)	Bore (mm)	Stroke (mm)
2341	90	92

Finally, in the early 1960s, there was a proposal to produce a 'dry-liner' version of the venerable engine, to allow an even larger cylinder bore to be employed, and fitted to the TR4A sports car. Prototypes were built, but proved to be unacceptably unrefined, and the project was abandoned. Records are sparse, but as far as is known, here were the details:

Capacity (cc)	Bore (mm)	Stroke (mm)
2446	92	92

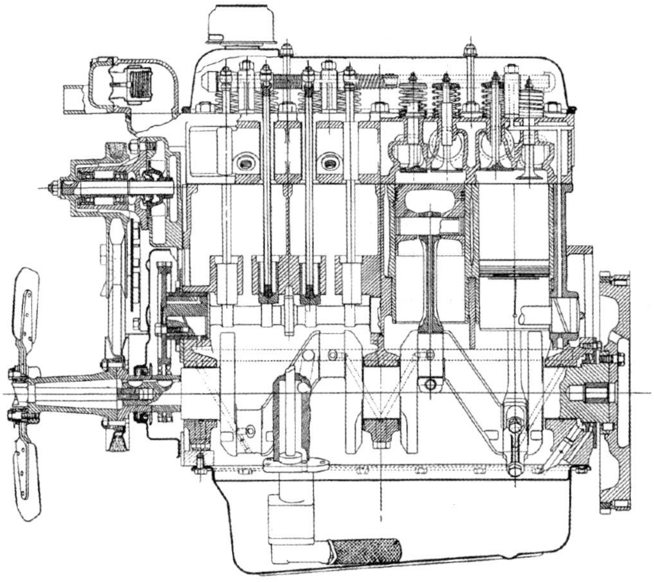

This shows the ultra-sturdy construction of the legendary 'wet-liner' engine that first powered the Standard Vanguard and Ferguson tractor of the 1940s. This derivative, in fact, is the Triumph TR sports car unit of the 1950s.

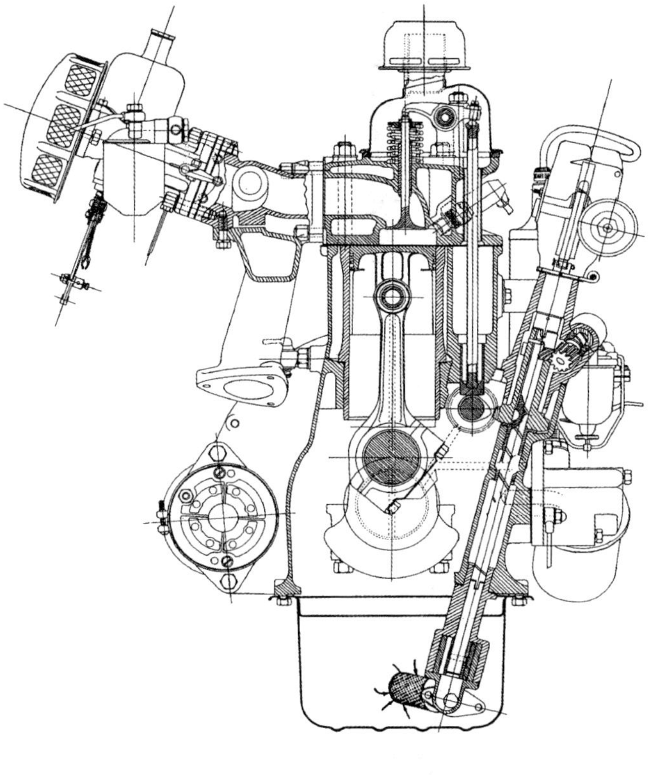

The cross-section of the wet-liner engine (this being the Triumph TR2 derivative, with 83mm cylinder bore dimension), shows the simple construction and layout. If properly maintained, this engine was virtually indestructible.

design roots in the 1920s, and the overhead-valve derivative (as already being supplied to Jaguar for the 1½-litre) was at its limits, and no further capacity or performance 'stretch' was possible.

Even before 1945, such a new project was already assumed, but as soon as the Ferguson project was initiated, the need for a new engine became imperative. Standard's strategy was soon settled – there would be an all-new engine family, one that would immediately have different derivatives; one for Standard and Triumph private cars, the other (much more robust, and with different castings – this must be stressed) for use in Ferguson tractors.

As long-time Standard employee David Eley once reminded the author:

"Ray Turner had been running Engineering throughout the war – Lewis Dawtrey and Jim Parkinson were always there in the Tech Office – but then Ted Grinham came back to us, as Technical Director. Charlie Phillips, an engines/transmissions specialist, also returned, and this was the start of the Vanguard project ..."

Lewis Dawtrey [an unsung hero, if ever I met one ...] provided much of the technological guidance over the new engine:

"Charlie did the original layouts of the new engine – Vanguard and tractor versions – together. The cylinder blocks were very similar, but not the same at front or rear, because there was a 12in clutch on the tractor, and on the front face of the tractor block there were four big bolts to carry the axle: they were entirely different castings. Charlie's wet-liner layout was influenced by the front-wheel drive Citroën, the Traction Avant engine – influenced, but no more than that ..."

As with most engines ever designed, it started out at one size, with a little space for eventually 'stretching' – and the 'stretch' was required almost at once. The various sizes, all of them due to changes made in the cylinder bore, are listed in the panel on page 128. As we now know, at the initial design stage, the 80mm bore/1849cc capacity engine was intended for use in the Ferguson tractor and the Vanguard. This engine made it into the original production Fergusons, but was only ever seen on the prototype Vanguards of 1947. When the Vanguard actually went on sale in 1948, it was equipped with an 85mm bore/2088cc power unit instead.

With Technical Chief Ted Grinham now back from his war-time secondments to De Havilland and the Rootes Group, he soon set his team to evolve the engine, which would be a relatively conventional overhead-valve power unit. Now, as every thinking engineer admits, very few new designs leap out of thin air, fully formed, but are often influenced, if only in detail, by something which has already been seen elsewhere.

In this case, influence came from the Citroën Traction Avant engine, launched in the mid-1930s, that had already been built in several different sizes. To Standard's engineers, the importance of that engine was not that it was in a front-wheel drive car – nothing so technically advanced was ever considered for the Vanguard project – but that it had what was called 'wet-liner' construction. This meant that instead of the cylinder bores being machined out of solid cast iron castings, the cylinder block would feature ready-machined drop-in steel cylinder liners, which would be sealed against water loss by gaskets on ridges towards the bottom of their structure.

Introduced in 1934, the original engine in Citroëns front-wheel drive car measured just 1302cc (72 x 80mm, bore and stroke), but it would soon be expanded to 1911cc (78 x 100mm) and would remain that size into the 1960s: there was even a six-cylinder derivative of the engine, too. Even Standard did not even try to build in as much 'stretch,' or long-life, as that

Even so, the Citroën 'wet-liner' layout was duly adopted for the Standard engine, which saw the 'long-life' possibilities of a removable-wet-liner layout. This theory always worked well in practice too, especially in the tractors, where it was difficult to keep dirt and other abrasive particles out of the engine. Even so, although this was the first time, as it happened it was also the last time that a Standard-Triumph engine ever had such a feature.

If only because the original tractor derivative of the wet-liner engine had to be at least as powerful as the American Continental power unit when it replaced it in 1947/1948, it was almost inevitable that it would be similar in overall dimensions to that existing Continental engine, though there

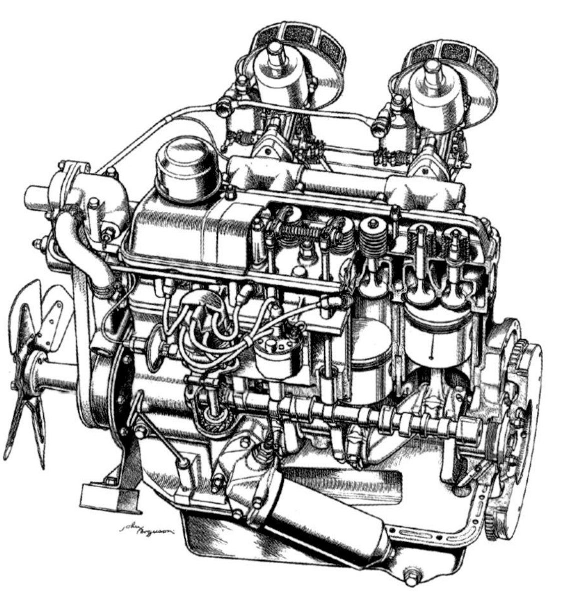

As modified by David Eley's engine design team, the 'wet liner' engine found a home in the TR2 sports car of the 1950s. [The original of this fine cutaway drawing now hangs on the author's study wall!]

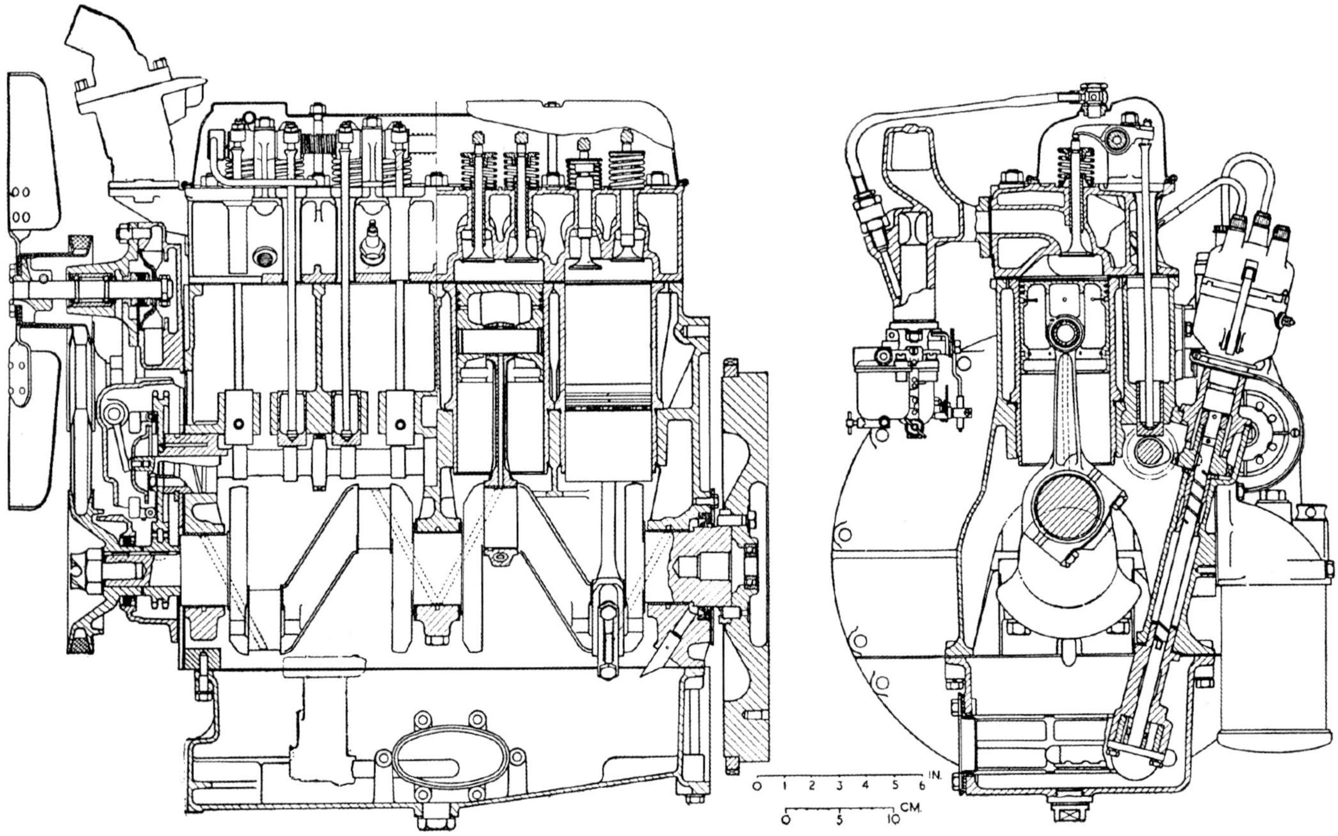

The 'wet-liner' engine – this is the original Vanguard-type – featured drop-in 'wet' cylinder liners, and had a sturdy three bearing crankshaft. As Standard soon found, and as latter-day tuners have also come to recognise, there was very little scope for the cylinder bore to be increased, because the cylinder block casting was very close to the camshaft tunnel.

was absolutely no design connection between the two types. For the record, in Ferguson form, the Z-120 Continental engine was a 1966cc unit that produced 24bhp – or 'belt horsepower,' which denotes the way that tractor engine power was measured in those days.

We must not, however, become too absorbed in the Ferguson application of this engine, for it was even more vitally important to the future of Standard (and, if we paused to think about it, Triumph too). It would be used on Vanguard and Ensign De Luxes to the very end of Standard private car manufacture in 1963, and on Triumph TR sports cars until the last of the TR4As was manufactured in 1967. It achieved, in other words, a production life of almost 20 years. Other engines have lived longer (Standard's forthcoming little SC engine, for instance, would be built for 27 years!), but none did as much to change the image of an entire group of companies.

Standard kept a well-equipped medical team in operation at Canley for many years, and in the 1950s used this Vanguard II-based ambulance where needed.

Corporate expansion

Standard (or, as it increasingly became known in future years, Standard-Triumph), had now embarked on a great period of commercial and financial expansion, which made it the envy of almost every other car-making company in the Midlands. If I am brutally honest about this, however, I should also emphasise that Sir John Black was not only out to make 'his' company bigger, more successful and more prosperous than any of his rivals, but according to all the written and anecdotal evidence we have, he was also determined to make himself personally rich, too. It was this – and, yes, I will describe it as personal greed – which must have contributed to his abrupt dismissal in January 1954.

Financially, both Standard and Sir John Black progressed in parallel in the first ten postwar years. First of all, in 1946 Sir John's personal salary was raised to £12,000/year, plus a whopping £6000 'entertainment allowance,' then the company bought his house in Wales (Mallory-y-Mor, near Lanbedr) from him for £8500, along with £5525 for fixtures, fittings, and boats. Then in 1949 his salary was raised once again, this time to £15,000/year.

The most contentious change, however, also came in June 1949, when he agreed to sign a restrictive covenant, making it clear that he agreed that, no matter what happened, he would never work for another car/tractor/motor industry manufacturer. In consideration for this, he was granted the equivalent of £25,000 in Standard shares.

Not that this benefitted Sir John in the end, for the Labour government of the day, whose Chancellor of the Exchequer was Sir Stafford Cripps, rushed through retrospective legislation which taxed all such gifts at 'Supertax' (19/6d, or 97.5 pence in the Pound) levels. Described by many as "an evil and unjust measure," this rendered the gift worthless. [At the same time, incidentally, Austin chairman, Leonard Lord, was ensnared in the same trap – and, unsurprisingly, both then became life-long enemies of the left-leaning politicians of the day ...].

These were only the major, and obvious manifestations of the way that Sir John was enriching himself (no other executive, not even any Board member, was rewarded on anything like the same scale), with others, such as the employment of a personal butler at Canley (Tom Thorne), who looked after him faithfully and elegantly for many years, and the provision of a fleet of cars, not only Standard and Triumph products, but usually a Bentley, too. It was no surprise, therefore, that the Board 'invited' Sir John to sit for his portrait 'in oils,' so that this could be hung in the Board room as a permanent reminder of how much he had done for the Standard company.

In the same period, and in spite of the big financial burden imposed by capital spending on the Ferguson and Vanguard programmes, annual after-tax company profits increased as year followed year. After 1945 (£263,056), the figure rose to £283,463 (1946), £198,915 (1947), £453,833 (1948), £555,249 (1949), £578,318 (1950) to £853,069 in 1951. By that time, the Standard factory complex (Canley, Fletchamstead and Banner Lane) covered 2,700,000ft^2, and 205 acres of land, and was turning over £4 million every month.

Not only that, but this was the time when Sir John's thirst for even greater corporate glory led him to make a civilised – polite, even – enquiry of the Morgan family, if it would consider being taken over by Standard? One major reason for this approach, which came at the Earls Court Motor Show in October 1950, was that Sir John was becoming increasingly jealous of MG's success in selling sports cars, particularly in North America, and wanted to match, and later to outstrip, it.

Standard, of course, had been supplying engines to Morgan for some years, had recently seen the launch of the new Plus 4 (which used the Vanguard engine), knew that Morgan was only making about ten cars every week, and thought that this drastically under-rated the demand.

Many years later Peter Morgan told the author that:

"Sir John mentioned being impressed by the potential of the Plus 4 and asked my father if he would like to join forces with Standard-Triumph to make the car in larger quantities? ... Sir John assured my father that whatever his answer might be, it would not affect the supply of engine units ... Subsequent to the interview, I am sure my father and I wished to keep Morgan independent ...'

And there the matter was laid to rest, though it must, surely, have been a factor in Standard's rush to develop its own two-seater sports car (which became the TR2) in 1952 and 1953. Was Morgan correct to reject this approach? Probably it was, for being taken over would inevitably have led to Morgan assembly being moved from Malvern to Canley, and to the ancient Morgan factory being closed down. Sixty years on, incidentally, Morgan is still alive, well, profitable and thriving at its Malvern premises ...

Sir John's legacy, it seems, was already written and obvious to one and all. At this time the published minutes of Board meetings made regular, gushing, reference to the advance made by the company under his leadership, and there is no evidence that Sir John was other than delighted by all this, nor thought that it was more than his due reward. Even though he had effectively been in control of Standard since 1930, there were no signs that he had any plans to retire, or even to work less ferociously. Clearly he had eyes on eventually becoming Chairman, but only when the long-serving Charles Band chose to retire, but his only real move to underpin the succession was to make Alick Dick his Assistant Managing Director in June 1947, then officially his Deputy Managing Director in July 1951.

New Triumphs for 1949 and 1950

No sooner had the Vanguard gone into production in 1948 (along with plans being finalised for the launch of estate car, van and pick-up derivatives, all of which followed), than Sir John, Ted Grinham and their staff turned their attention to developing a new Triumph model – it would be called the Mayflower when previewed in 1949 – and in modernising the existing 'interim' 'Triumph' badged cars.

With the old-style Twelve/Fourteen models already abandoned in mid-1948, to make way for concentration on the Vanguard and its derivatives, this meant that supplies of its engines, gearboxes and front suspensions, all of which had been bequeathed for use in the early postwar Triumphs, would cease. Now was the ideal time to 'Standard-ise' the 1800 Roadster and 1800 Saloon models as much as possible, and also to honour Sir John's 1945 promise of evolving a 'one-model' policy.

[This, of course, was a pledge honoured only in the breach, for once the Mayflower came on stream, Standard-Triumph became a two-model company again ...].

Consequently, much Vanguard engineering was skilfully grafted into the two existing Triumphs (though there would be no style changes to make this obvious), 'Standardising' the bigger Triumphs has already been covered in major Triumph marque histories, and need not concern us in detail here.

This, however, was completed in two phases. Firstly, as announced at the first postwar Earls Court Motor Show,

Maybe it wasn't stylish, and certainly not sporty, but the original type of Vanguard Estate, as constructed, in this instance, by Imperia in Belgium, was a very useful and practical machine.

This was the Triumph TRX of 1950. If stylist Walter Belgrove had got his way, the next generation Vanguard would have shared the same type of front-end style.

in October 1948, the '1800 Roadster' became the '2000 Roadster,' by getting the Vanguard engine, transmission and back axle, all grafted on to the existing tubular chassis, but without any styling changes. Only 2000 such machines were ever made, the last of them in October 1949.

Then it was the turn of the saloon. First of all, from February 1949, the same engine/transmission transplant was carried out, though the existing tubular chassis frame was retained. At the end of the year, however, the 2000 Saloon then became the Renown, the big change being that the tubular frame and old-type Flying Standard front suspension was thrown out after the first sanction of 2000 cars had been completed, to be replaced by a long-wheelbase (108in instead of 94in) version of the Vanguard's chassis. As with the Vanguard of the period, Laycock overdrive became optional in 1950.

The Renown story was not, however, complete for (although the strict chronological sequence of this book must now be disturbed) from in the winter of 1951/1952 the wheelbase of the razor-edged model was once again increased – this time to 111 inches – and as a top-of-the-range addition, a limousine version was also introduced. Thus modified/updated, the Renown staggered on until 1954 when, even after a considerable price reduction had been made, no more sales could be expected. Standard later justified the life of these two cars by pointing out that a total of 4501 Roadsters, and no fewer than 15,491 razor-edge saloons were produced in eight years: the old independent Triumph concern, no question, would have been proud of that achievement.

There was one other 'Standard-Triumph' project in this period – badged as Triumph – which gained much publicity, but in the end was abandoned before it went into production. This was the TRX Roadster (also colloquially known as the 'Bullet') which occupied much of Standard stylist Walter Belgrove's time after 1947, was shown at the 1950 Earls Court Motor Show, but was eventually abandoned after just three prototypes had been built.

The 'Bullet'/TRX story has been told many times in Triumph histories, so need only be summarised here. Basically it was intended to replace the postwar Triumph 1800 Roadster, ran on a lightly-modified Standard Vanguard chassis, and was otherwise conceived, styled, and cosseted by Belgrove himself. It was such a 'personal' indulgence that the prototypes carried the letter 'B' on the flanks – which apparently inspired Sir John Black to ask Belgrove if that letter: "stood for Black, Belgrove, or balls ...?"

It was a project always likely to fail – and fail it did. The styling was controversial – Belgrove thought it elegant [but he would, wouldn't he?], but others thought it blowsy and nodding too far towards transatlantic fashions. The body construction (featuring much aluminium, and double-skinned construction) was potentially expensive to replicate, and Helliwells of Walsall in Staffordshire (a Tube Investments subsidiary to whom Sir John owed a favour for help it had given Standard during the war years) took ages to produce the three bodyshells, and drastically over-ran its schedule.

Launched at the 1950 Show, it caused controversy over its looks, and its specification (several features relied on electro-hydraulic controls to make them work – some of which burnt out when demonstrated to HRH Princess Margaret!), so all plans to put the car into production were indefinitely delayed. British body suppliers such as Fisher & Ludlow and Mulliners both turned the job down, while talks with Carrozzeria Touring and Farina of Italy also stalled. By the end of 1951, with Sir John now reluctantly accepting that his, and Belgrove's taste in car styling was not that of the public, the project was allowed to die. Amazingly, two prototypes were sold off, and survive to this day.

Triumph Mayflower – not a real 'Standard,' but very odd, and very endearing

There is much evidence to suggest that the Mayflower was always a particular 'pet' of Sir John Black. Not only did it draw its styling from the razor-edged bodies being produced by Mulliners, but was also a car which Sir John always seemed to have in his personal fleet. When he left the company in 1954, indeed, one of the cars that he took with him into retirement was – a Mayflower.

Once again, and because this was a Triumph-badged car, I must treat it rather briefly, though in many ways the Mayflower was a Standard, in all but name. There was so much of the Standard pedigree in the car, and so much of it that would also be handed down in future. The engine, after all, was pure 1930s-style Flying Standard, the gearbox was cheapened-down Vanguard, and the new front suspension would be bequeathed to the ultra-successful TR2/TR3 and TR4 sports cars of the 1950s, and be intended for the first iteration of the Standard 'Zebu' range.

Standard, in fact, had originally forecast the birth of cars like the Mayflower when it took up the Triumph name in 1945, though in the euphoria which followed the preview of the new Vanguard, and the promise to become a 'one-model' company, its development was quietly and discreetly put on the back-burner for some time. It was not until October 1949, when the 'Standardising' of the bigger Triumphs was completed (and the 'one model' policy was abandoned), that a new car badged as a 'Mayflower' was unveiled – named by Lady Black.

For the moment, however, let us forget the controversy of the name. In postwar years, smaller-engined Standards always outsold larger-engined types – 17,549 Eights against 9322 Twelves/Fourteens in 1946, and 11,037 Eights against 10,611 Twelves/Fourteens in 1948, before assembly of both types was wound up in mid-year, to make space for the Vanguard. And, as Standard publicists so gleefully told everyone on 9 July 1948 when the last Eight of all was produced, no fewer than 83,139 of those cars had been built in no more than four active years (we must not forget that all

Although the razor-edge styling vogue had passed by the time the Triumph Mayflower was developed, this was how it looked when it went on sale in 1950.

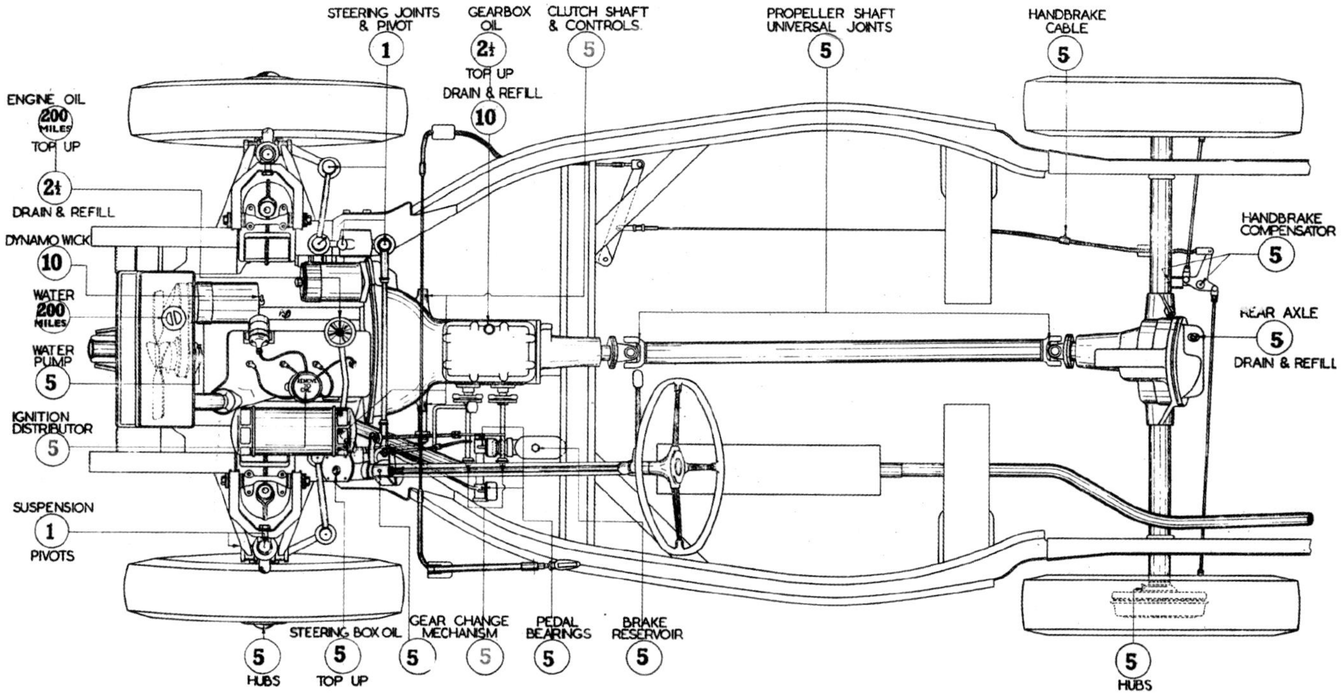

Standard's very first unit-construction bodyshell was that of the Triumph Mayflower, which was designed with Fisher & Ludlow's help in 1947, and launched in 1949. This was the last Standard product to use the legendary small side-valve unit of the 1930s, and the first to use a new type of independent front suspension which would find itself under the TR2 sports car.

private-car production had ended between 1940 and mid-1945).

There was therefore no doubt that a new corporate 'small' car, which was actually coded '1200T' when under development at Banner Lane, was needed. The result, as designed in 1947 and 1948, under development in 1949, and finally on sale from mid-1950, was idiosyncratic in so many ways. Some features – like the structure and the independent front suspension – were forward-looking, while others – the engine, and the styling – were old-fashioned.

Any study of this new car must start with the style, which was influenced by Sir John Black himself, and which also had a definite family resemblance to the 1800/2000/Renown model. At first glance, one might guess that there were panels common with those which clad the Renown, but this was not so. The situation was much more complicated than that, as Walter Belgrove told the author in later years:

"I believe that the model which came to be known as the Mayflower was on the stocks in 1947 or 1948. This motorcar was intended to be a short-wheelbase [84in, compared with 111in] version of the Renown saloon, and also the first volume-produced Triumph. This was continuing 'knife-edged' styling with a vengeance and I believe the policy stemmed from Sir John Black's discussions with Mr Louis Antweiller [who was Managing Director of Mulliners in Birmingham].

"I remember doing some work on the front-end of this vehicle, but the Triumph Mayflower was really styled by Leslie Moore, Chief Body Designer of Mulliners. It was not possible to reproduce the lines of the Renown on a 'shut-up' wheelbase, and in the circumstances I do not think that Leslie Moore's work could have been bettered. The side elevation was very good indeed, and although of contemporary 'slab-sided' style, the swept line from headlamp boss to tail endeavoured to retain some characteristic feature of the bigger model."

Sir John Black with one of the first Triumph Mayflowers. This car was very much a 'personal' pet of his – and when he resigned in 1954 he took one into retirement with him.

This cutaway example of the new Mayflower is pictured in the experimental workshops at Banner Lane in 1949. What is also fascinating is the variety of machines in the background – including a Vanguard estate, an old-type Fourteen, and a Ferguson tractor!

Not everyone was kind about the style, especially some of those supercilious journalists and opinion-formers who had never had to carry out market surveys, or commit a mountain of shareholders' money for new models, but in this case everyone seemed content to defer to the forceful Sir John Black's wishes.

By any measure, though, the structure itself, which was basically a two-door saloon (with the thought that other derivatives such as convertibles might also be developed from it) was novel, and was much admired. This, in fact, was the very first Standard-Triumph model that had a unit-construction bodyshell, though it was by no means the first in the industry, or even in the tight-knit little motor industry 'family' in Coventry.

Company publicists later gave much of the technical credit to Harry Webster who, by this time, was a rising star in the Engineering Department, but one should also admit that he and his senior colleagues took advice from Fisher

Fisher and Ludlow, Standard and Castle Bromwich

There is a romantic connection, however tenuous, between the world-famous Spitfire fighter aircraft of World War Two, and Standard cars, that link being via the Fisher & Ludlow bodybuilding concern.

With the Spitfire ready to go into series production in the late 1930s, but with more factory space required to build up to 60 fighters every week, Lord Nuffield accepted an offer from the British government to set up a massive new aircraft assembly facility. Starting in 1938, Nuffield bought a site in Birmingham (from the Dunlop Rubber Company), and began erecting a huge new plant at Castle Bromwich on the eastern edge of the city.

The build-up of the factory, and of fighter production, was slow, and in 1940 Lord Nuffield complained that if modifications continued to be made to the Spitfire design, then he could not deliver aircraft, and in a fit of pique suggested that the government might like to take over instead! Aircraft production supremo Lord Beaverbrook immediately agreed, took control, handed it over to Vickers (who in any case owned the design rights to the Spitfire) and, as history now relates, we all lived happily ever after. More than 10,000 Spitfires (and several hundred Lancaster bombers) were all produced at Castle Bromwich.

Soon after the war was won, Castle Bromwich was emptied, and almost immediately Fisher & Ludlow took over the lease, installing its entire car body/pressings business from its old premises in the city. It was there that pressings for tens of thousands of postwar Standard saloon shells were produced, the last of all being the Standard Pennant.

& Ludlow, who were about to get the contract to produce production cars, and were fast modernising – and filling up – its ex-Spitfire factory at Castle Bromwich. This new hull, of course, had no connection with earlier Standards (and absolutely none, for sure, with the Vanguard), and at the time was intended to have a long production life.

Running on a compact 84in wheelbase, in which the shell featured old-style 'chassis rails' welded to the floor, and linking the front to the rear of the car, and featuring new-type coil spring independent front suspension, the shell hid several otherwise well-proven Standard 'building blocks.' The engine itself was a 1247cc version of the famous little side-valve unit that had been powering many different Standards since the 1930s, coming complete with an aluminium head, and producing 38bhp, while the three-speed gearbox was a slightly modified version of the Vanguard, complete with a steering column gear change.

Company records indicate that the building, testing and development of the Mayflower had to wait at Banner Lane until the more pressing tractor, Vanguard and 'Standardised' Roadster/Renown models had all been finalised. Then, during 1949, four prototype cars – X485, X486 and X487 and X491 – were completed, one of them with left-hand steering. One of those cars, incidentally (X491), was originally coded 10T, and is thought to have had an Eight engine of 1009cc, though this project was speedily abandoned, that car being re-engined with a 1247cc power unit.

Although Standard launched the new Mayflower in September 1949, it was not yet ready to go on sale. Not only were Fisher & Ludlow not yet ready to deliver bodyshells in quantity, but Standard was busily re-working the final assembly lines at Canley, so that part-complete cars would henceforth be sideways as they travelled down the tracks. Standard claimed that this allowed more cars than usual to be housed in a particular limited space, and in some ways allowed better access to the front, and the rear, of partly-completed machines.

[Standard, later Standard-Triumph, later Leyland-owned Standard-Triumph, would persist with this 'sideways' feature for more than twenty years – even when the new assembly hall was completed in 1961 – but as far as the author is aware, it was rarely taken up by any rival concern in the UK]

Production-line assembly, in fact, did not begin until the late spring of 1950, after which the trickle turned into a flood. 2894 cars were built before the end of August 1950 (the end of the company's financial year), and 13,107 would follow in the next twelve month period.

Sir John always had big plans for the Mayflower, if only because he had seen Standard invest heavily in new equipment to make the car – Alick Dick recalls that it cost more than £1 million in total, a huge sum by 1940s standards, for a great deal of money had also been sunk into the re-equipping of the side-valve engine assembly facilities (which had been taken out of use, and 'mothballed' when the Eight was dropped in the summer of 1948). This was one of the reasons why Sir John pressed Nash of the USA to bring

Standard had high hopes of selling a large number of Mayflowers in the 1950s, but the 'Olde Worlde' style was not to everyone's taste. 34,000 would eventually be built in just three years.

NXI – The Nash small-car project

Most classic car enthusiasts will have seen a flamboyant model built by BMC in the 1950s: this used Austin A40 or A50 running gear, and was usually badged as the Nash Metropolitan (and later, when marketed in the UK, as a 'Metropolitan,' without Austin or Nash badging). Not everyone realises, however, that this American–inspired machine, which was invented by the Nash-Kelvinator Corporation in 1949 as the 'NXI,' might perhaps have had a Standard (-Triumph) connection. The NXI was hawked around Europe's motor industry in 1950 (as a non-running prototype), in the hope of tying down some sort of cooperative design and production agreement, whereby cars would be built in Europe, but sold in the USA.

Fiat, Austin (which became BMC) and Standard were all approached at first. Sir John Black was initially attracted to the idea (as with Ferguson tractors, he was sure that he could cope with cuckoos in his automotive nest), and suggested most strongly to George Mason (the CEO of Nash) that he should use Triumph Mayflower running gear and other chassis items in the finalised design. (Having recently invested heavily in new transfer machine tooling for the Mayflower engine, he was anxious to use it as intensively as possible).

Even though the platform of the Mayflower was almost exactly the same size as that of the NXI – the Mayflower wheelbase was 84in, and that finally chosen for the 'Metropolitan' was 85in – nothing further came of the proposal, and no prototypes were ever built. The project was eventually taken up by Austin/BMC, and reached the market place in 1954.

The Phase II Vanguard was introduced in 1953, and ran through until high summer of 1955.

its own small-car project to the company (see the panel – NXI – the Nash small-car project – on page 136).

Early in the programme, the directors were discussing building coupé, tourer and convertible versions of the Mayflower, and even as early as August 1950 there were thoughts of using the 'Morgan' type of overhead-valve engine in the car as an alternative to the existing side-valve power unit. In the end, the engine up-grade was totally abandoned, and although Mulliners later built just ten convertibles in late 1950 by what might diplomatically be called 'knife-and-fork' methods from original F&L saloon shells, that project bit the dust, too.

Some such upgrades might eventually have filtered through to the market place except for one basic problem – that the Mayflower simply did not sell in the numbers originally envisaged for it. Several reasons were responsible: the style was disliked by a rising proportion of the market place (the car certainly did not succeed in many export markets, especially North America, because of this), and the selling costs were too high. When Standard, faced with acquiring only limited quantities of sheet steel, had to make decisions, it decided to keep pushing the Vanguard, which was a great marketing success.

Early in 1953, a Vanguard Phase II bodyshell meets its rolling chassis in what is often called 'the marriage,' on the assembly line at Canley. Triumph Mayflowers can also be seen in the background.

Suggestions for improving the Mayflower came and went. Not only an overhead valve engine, but a re-styling proposal, and finally the radical (but ultimately unwise) proposal to evolve a brand-new small Standard saloon on the under-pan of the Mayflower bodyshell were all made.

By 1952, however, the Big Decision – to abandon the Mayflower – had to be made. Big changes at Standard were afoot – not only was the Rolls-Royce Avon jet engine production contract gathering place, and a Vanguard Series II project was getting under way, but the company was struggling with the plan to build a massive new component manufacturing factory in Lancashire, and was also 'girding its loins' to build a new small car (which would be ready by mid-1953).

Accordingly, the company decided to wind-up the Mayflower project when the agreed 'sanction' of 34,000 cars was complete in mid-1953. This meant that 10,387 cars were produced in 1952, followed by 7612 cars in 1953.

At which point the 'Standard' name came back into prominence, the 'Triumph' name began to be applied to a new breed of sports car – the TR2 – and (except for use on certain export-market models) it would no longer appear on saloons for the next six years.

In 1953, however, the loss of the Mayflower was not big news – but the arrival of the new Eight most certainly was.

CHAPTER 10

Eights, Tens, Triumph sports cars – and a new Vanguard 1953-1960

No one connected with Standard in the mid-1950s will ever forget the frenetically busy atmosphere at Canley and Banner Lane in 1953 and 1954. For Standard this was a time which included corporate, financial, technical and personal upheavals.

How to summarise it all? Succinctly, I hope, by mentioning the arrival of an all-new Standard Eight family car, that of a much-changed Phase II Vanguard, and the rather stuttering launch of the original Triumph TR2. There was more, for Harry Ferguson also decided to merge his tractor business with Massey Harris of Canada, the diesel engine was finally ready – and Sir John Black's increasingly unpredictable behaviour caused concern at the top levels of the company.

Standard's progress in the early 1950s was meteoric for, apart from introducing the new cars and getting its teeth into the Rolls-Royce jet engine contract, Standard also spent ages working up a new 'satellite' factory proposal for Kirkby (Liverpool – see the panel on page 116), and also took over a smart Art Deco building at Allesley, overlooking the A45 main road to Birmingham. This building, acquired from Peerless & Ericsson Ltd for £227,500, became the company's service department, and for some years was also the home of Ken Richardson's much-respected Standard-Triumph Competitions Department.

In spite of this action, the company reported after-tax profits of £578,318 in 1950, £853,069 in 1951, £530,631 in 1952 and £644,330 in 1953, and felt that it could also justify spending £40,000 on a Percival light aircraft for use as executive transport. By that time the company was making nearly 250 cars, and more than 300 tractors, every day. Such activities clearly generated enough cash flow to underpin new investment, and by 1951 Standard was so confident, that it issued no fewer than 14,650,000 shares (worth 5 shillings/25 pence each), free of charge, as a scrip payment to existing shareholders.

On the other hand, settling on the design of a revised Vanguard – which would eventually become the Phase II model – proved to be much more difficult. Originally, in 1950, Walter Belgrove provided sketches of a new car on a 98in wheelbase, which had totally fresh styling (its shape was clearly inspired by the shape of the controversial new Triumph TRX Roadster), but this was not liked, and it was a full year before Belgrove's team completed a more conventional restyle.

The new Phase II saloon used a notchback shape instead of the original fastback (this time around, Sir John Black had not directed Belgrove to copy something American!), with four-light instead of six-light window styling, and

Walter Belgrove had never wanted the original Vanguard to have such a short wheelbase, and in this study of the Phase II, which retained the same chassis and much of the original body/front-end, one can see why. Even so, a huge number of Vanguards would be sold in the 1940s and 1950s.

Posed outside the factory at Banner Lane in 1953, this shows how the Vanguard Phase II differs from the original, with a notchback rear-end shape. This resulted in a more spacious rear seat, and a greater luggage storage volume.

significantly larger doors. There were two important improvements – one being that there was more leg space and general room in the rear seats, while the boot capacity was up from 14cuft to 21cuft. Leather-faced upholstery was an optional extra. To enlarge the range still further, the existing four-door estate car was now to be joined by a two-door type, this quite clearly developed from the panel van. As before, Fisher & Ludlow manufactured saloon shells, with Mulliners providing all the derivatives.

Mechanical changes? The wheelbase remained at 94in, and apart from a number of minor updates to the engine – where the power output was still pegged at 68bhp at 4200rpm – and with Laycock overdrive becoming an increasingly popular option, the most important update was the fitment of a hydraulically actuated clutch withdrawal system. In conjunction with the restyle to the body, the fuel tank had been moved – though smaller by three gallons, it was now tucked in behind the rear seat squab. In production before the end of 1952, the model was launched early in 1953.

Road tests show that the latest car's top speed was about 77mph, and because the UK retail price was £919 (with a radio, a heater, and Laycock overdrive all frequently ordered

In 1952, Standard's top stylist, Walter Belgrove, produced this rendering of what he hoped a future Vanguard could look like. It was considered carefully, but finally abandoned.

optional extras), customers and dealers now had a big choice of specifications. As this was also the period in postwar Britain when waiting lists finally fell away (yes, it really had been that long ...), the Phase II made an immediate impact.

By corporate standards, of course, this was all a sideshow, for in 1953 the company was launching the Eight, with a brand-new monocoque bodyshell supplied by Fisher & Ludlow, was also shaking down initial production of the new small-car SC four-cylinder engine, and a new-generation of four-speed gearbox, and a new light-duty rear axle. There had been major change, not to say disruption, to the massive machine shops and engine facilities at Canley.

Soon after this, however, the company's corporate structure was shaken to its very core.

This must be one of the last publicity shots ever taken of Sir John Black, for the new Standard 8hp was launched in September 1953, his major accident in the Swallow Doretti prototype followed in November 1953, and he was ousted in January 1954. Incidentally, he always thought the original Eight was too starkly furnished.

The sacking of Sir John Black

Even before beginning to describe the new model launches, and the corporate developments of the mid-1950s that came with them, I must describe the abrupt way that executive power, at Standard, moved from Sir John Black to Alick Dick in 1954, and in which the atmosphere changed so completely. As the world of motoring now knows, Sir John was ousted by his fellow directors on 4 January 1954 – though at the time it was officially put about that he was retiring due to health problems.

Sir John's personal character defects have already been emphasised. This is not merely a personal observation, but a judgement, which has been filled out, and distilled, by a number of colleagues and so-called workmates who had to deal with him on a regular basis. Only a few single-issue fanatics now deny that such flaws were present – every one of his Standard colleagues realised how unpredictable he had become – the remaining deniers usually had a personal or financial reason for needing to stay loyal to him.

There was nothing sudden about all this, for Sir John had become increasingly remote from the feelings of his colleagues. Late in 1953, however, Sir John had become thoroughly upset about the potential problems thrown up by Harry Ferguson's latest plan, which was to merge his tractor operation with that of a rival, Massey-Harris of Canada. Not only did this throw Sir John's own vaguely

This was the aftermath of the Swallow Doretti crash outside Banner Lane in 1953, in which Sir John Black was a passenger. Only weeks later, Sir John 'retired' from the top of the company which he had run for almost twenty-five years.

expressed desire to get Standard together with Ferguson into some disarray, but he now also feared for Banner Lane's future.

Then came a typical piece of John Black behaviour. As already related in chapter 8, not only did he persuade the Board to give Ferguson an ultimatum, namely that Standard would not be willing to carry on making tractors when the existing ten year agreement ran out in 1955 – but only days later, it seemed, Sir John then had a change of plan, approached Massey-Ferguson as soon as it had been formed, and in November 1953 set about making a manufacturing deal, that would cover the next twelve years, up until 1965. This, incidentally, was a personal deal, done without the agreement of the Board, who were apparently infuriated. Nevertheless, when Standard's long-serving chairman, Charles Band, decided to step down before the end of the year (he was 79 years old, and had been chairman since 1934), Sir John took up that position as well. He had therefore become the total dictator of anything and everything that Standard was doing at this time.

All of this added to the corporate turmoil, and I can do no better than to quote Graham Turner's book *The Leyland Papers* about this period:

"Many of the Board were becoming increasingly unhappy with the behaviour of Black himself. He was subject to violent fluctuations of mood, and in the view of one his closest colleagues had become almost schizophrenic: 'He could be the kindest or the cruellest man in the world, the gayest or the most depressed, a heavy drinker or a total abstainer. He lived on a razor's edge, and nobody knew which side he would fall.' ... Black was not only a dictator, but an unpredictable one as well."

This, of course, had been known for some years, and a forensic look through Standard's Board minutes make this quite clear, as from time-to-time his colleagues would feel that praise or even financial largesse had to be lavished on him to keep him on side. Those minutes, which are safely housed, but in the public domain, tell a riveting story.

In 1953, however, the final straw came at the end of the year. Having been badly knocked about in a road accident (when he was passenger in a prototype Swallow Doretti being driven to Banner Lane by test driver Ken Richardson), he must have been feeling below par when he attended the firm's annual pre-Christmas party for his management team. As related to Graham Turner, on these occasions he saw the number of managers who were present, frequently decided that there were too many of them, and would arbitrarily decide to sack a number of them! (Another source, incidentally, puts that occasion at a fully attended Board meeting ...).

On this occasion his basilisk eye apparently settled on Ted Grinham, of all people, who was one of his Board colleagues, and a long-serving one at that. Such a move, of course, was sheer arrogant stupidity. Grinham might never have been the life and soul of any party, and by no means as cavalier in his tastes as Sir John, but for many years he had been an extremely effective and successful technical director and corner-stone of the business, not only of Standard, but of the re-emerging Triumph brand.

For many of his colleagues, this was apparently the final straw, and even before Grinham's sacking could take place, a management coup was immediately mounted:

"Early in the New Year [of 1954]," Graham Turner reminds us, "the Board met at Alick Dick's home at Hill Wootton, near Kenilworth: Black, they decided, must be ousted, though he had only been appointed chairman as recently as 16 December 1953. Black had had a motor accident a couple of months before, however, and this – they agreed – would be sufficient explanation for his precipitate departure. Alick Dick's wife typed up a suitably mealy-mouthed letter of resignation, which Sir John would be asked to sign, and the 'posse' then drove over to Sir John's house to confront him."

Alick Dick's job was to lead the deputation and make the request for resignation – which was a task made doubly difficult because he owed his entire Standard career, and his current position of deputy managing director, to Sir John himself. The job had to be done, however, the confrontation was duly made, and after Sir John had made ritual threats to sack all of those who faced him, he caved in and signed the document.

This, dated 4 January 1954, was a magnificent work of fiction, and stated:

"As a result of consultations with my doctor today, I have been advised that I am not considered fit enough to return to the enormous responsibilities as managing director of our very important company, and I am recommended to go away for an extended period to overcome the effects of the very serious accident which I recently received.

"My wife and closest friends feel, therefore, with me that I should retire from the Board of Directors, and, consequently, from my office as chairman of the Board.

"It is with the greatest regret that I have reluctantly come to this decision, and I wish my very efficient team every success in carrying on where I left off."

And so, almost at a stroke, Sir John's reign at the head of Standard (he had been sole managing director for almost twenty years) came abruptly to an end, and as far as is known his only further connection with the company was to empty his palatial office at Canley, of personal effects, and to disappear from the scene.

By the standards of the day, his pay-off was generous enough – £30,000 in cash, the gift of the Bentley and Triumph Mayflower saloons, which had recently been his company cars, and the use of the company house in Wales for the next five years. Later he took up farming near Harlech in Wales, but apart from brief links with Enfield Cables Ltd, he had no further links with the motor industry, and therefore drops out of our story.

'The King is dead, long live the King'

Within twenty-four hours of the dramatic resignation, Charles Band returned to the Chairmanship on a temporary basis, Ted Grinham was re-confirmed as Deputy Managing Director, while Alick Dick became Standard's Managing Director, – and, as he was only 37 years old, this made him the youngest chief executive in the British motor industry.

His approach to running Standard was totally different from that of Sir John Black (Sir John had always been known as dictator, Alick Dick sometimes being known as the 'Laughing Cavalier' ...). Almost all his colleagues, senior or junior, respected and admired him for that, and for the next seven or eight years the company enjoyed a very exciting ride.

Two important appointments, and two retirements, eventually emerged from this cataclysm. Although Charles Band returned as chairman for some months, this was only meant to be a temporary arrangement, after which the illustrious ex-World War Two hero, Marshal of the Royal Air Force Lord Tedder was appointed in June 1954: he would hold that position for the next six eventful years. Not that he was totally committed to aviation, for within months the company's Percival Prince aircraft was sold off – after all, with the Kirkby factory scheme abandoned, there was little need for a light plane to ferry round the directors any more.

Then, in mid-1955, a new post – that of Director and General Manager – was created to relieve Alick Dick of many routine duties. It was at this point that Martin Tustin was attracted from Ford to fill that job, one which he would then hold down until 1961: after the Leyland rescue he would then be sent off to run the North American distribution network which, cynically, one has to view as a demotion.

Technical Chief Ted Grinham, who had been in charge of all Standard's private-car design and development activities since 1931, finally retired at the end of 1956 (Charles Band

Lord Tedder (Standard chairman, June 1954 to November 1960)

Although Lord Tedder was not a died-in-the-wool motoring industrialist, he was always an extremely respected personality. Before being appointed Standard's chairman in June 1954, he had already built up a formidable record in the Royal Air Force.

Born in Scotland in 1890, Arthur William Tedder joined the army in 1914, transferred to the Royal Flying Corps in 1916, thereafter rising steadily through the ranks, eventually to become Marshal of the Royal Air Force in 1945. Along the way, he sealed his reputation by directing allied air operations in Africa and Italy during the Second World War, became General Eisenhower's Deputy in Operation Overlord (the assault on France in 1944), and ended his military career as Britain's Chief of the Air Staff from 1945 to 1950. Along the way, he was knighted in 1942, and became Baron Tedder in 1946.

After spending some years as Chancellor of the University of Cambridge, and Vice-Chairman of the BBC Board of Governors, he joined Standard, to chair the Board in June 1954. For the next six years, in a prestigious, but non-executive, post, he headed the company's management, until he reached his 70th birthday in 1960, and elected to retire, after which he was the company's Honorary President.

He died in 1967.

A reminder that before he became chairman of Standard in 1954, Lord Tedder had been a Second World War hero, as Air Chief Marshal, and deputy to General Eisenhower in the Overlord project of 1944.

What are they cooking up now? In the late 1950s: left to right – Technical Chief Harry Webster, stylist Giovanni Michelotti, and General Manager Martin Tustin.

Towards the end of Standard's independent corporate existence, c1960, this was the main Board. Lord Tedder (Chairman) is at the head of the table. Alick Dick is to his right, and General Manager Martin Tustin is in the centre on the far side of the table.

also left the board at the same time), and it was to replace him that Harry Webster (who had already been Chief Chassis Engineer in recent years) became Special Director – Director of Engineering in May 1957.

Within three years, therefore, Alick Dick had re-shaped his top management structure, to reflect a younger, more enthusiast, and more vibrant attitude to motorcars and motoring. It showed, in the type of cars that the company produced at that time.

Almost from the beginning of his near-eight year reign at Standard, however, one of Alick Dick's main objectives was to find and inspire a merger with a bigger (and, by unspoken definition, financially more resilient) partner. On thc other side of the coin, he also spent much time absorbing smaller components suppliers who had expertise, which Standard could not otherwise match, in an effort to develop what economists call a 'vertically-integrated' organisation.

There is no doubt about the purpose and evolution of this philosophy for, as Dick once told the author in an interview:

"My mission at Standard-Triumph was to look around for a partner, a partner to secure our future. In the next few years I had flirtations with almost every other independent concern except Chrysler. I never talked to them ..."

The main problem, evidently, was that Standard had to face up to competition from other motor-manufacturing

concerns which were getting bigger, and more threatening as every year passed by. The threat from BMC (Austin and Nuffield got together in 1952) was already obvious, while both Ford-UK and Vauxhall were expanding with the aid of much investment capital from their North American parent companies. The next big threat, however, came from the Rootes Group, who already boasted Hillman, Humber, and Sunbeam-Talbot among the brands: suddenly, at the end of 1955, Rootes also annexed Singer, and became the biggest employer in Coventry.

Dick, the realist, concluded that he would have to match this trend. He knew that it was one thing to preserve the independence of a proud marque, but it was quite another to be complacent about its long-term future. In those eight years, Standard considered an amazing number of merger proposals, some of them logical, some of them appealing, and some now looking to have been bizarre, but it was only in the financial blizzard which hit them so hard in 1960 that a lasting partnership was made with Leyland Motors.

Although such manoeuvres were always held under very secret conditions, they did not affect the day-to-day running of the business. Even though this part of the corporate story now jumps ahead rapidly by several years, the entire series of negotiations must now be analysed to see how Standard might have changed if any one of them had come to fruition:

February/March 1954: Alick Dick contacted Spencer Wilks of Rover. The obvious immediate synergy was in providing diesel engines to Rover (which did not have a diesel of its own), and of somehow getting Land Rover and the Massey-Harris-Ferguson tractor business closer together.

Incidentally, there were family connections, which probably eased the way at first. Although Spencer Wilks was Sir John Black's brother-in-law (both of them had married Hillman daughters in the 1920s), the two did not get on, so Wilks was delighted to see Sir John ousted. However, Alick Dick's uncle (who originally got him his first job at Standard) had married another of Mr Hillman's daughters, and relationships with Dick were much more cordial!

A new holding company was proposed (United Motor Corporation, Consolidated Motors, United Motors and finally, Allied Motors Ltd were all considered), much manoeuvring took place over share swaps and values, and who was to have the top executive position, and even where the corporate HQ might eventually be situated.

All, eventually, might have been well if word had not got out, that Willys-Overland of the USA (who made the astoundingly successful Jeep, of course) was proposing to set up Jeep manufacture in Europe, and was talking to Standard about this. Jeep – versus – Land Rover made no sense, so the atmosphere was soured.

Although there was much potential for links between the two companies (none of the product lines competed directly with each other), the financially-cautious Rover company became nervous about Standard's performance at this time, eventually thought a merger sounded unattractive, so all talks between the two companies were discontinued in July 1954.

January 1955: The next series of talks, with Dennis Bros, of Guildford, also made some industrial sense, but on a more modest scale. Dennis was a company with an illustrious past, and had come to concentrate on commercial vehicles – particularly public service machines such as fire engines

Harry Webster – charismatic engineer

It was a measure of Harry Webster's reputation with his staff that after he retired the 'Standard Triumph Engineering Society' was set up. Harry led this purely social group, which was only for those who worked for him up to 1968 (when he moved on to Austin-Morris at Longbridge) were eligible: it was enormously popular.

Although he only enjoyed real technical influence over Standard and Triumph cars after 1948 (when he was appointed chief chassis engineer), his Standard record stretched from the early 1930s, when he joined as an apprentice. After becoming Apprentice of the Year, he spent the war years on aircraft engine inspection duties, before taking up permanent residence in the Engineering division in 1945.

His first job as Chief Chassis Engineer was to run the team which created the structure of the Triumph Mayflower, then that of the Standard Eight/Ten 'small car,' after which he tackled the Triumph TR2 and a whole host of new Standard and Triumph models. After taking over from Ted Grinham when the latter retired, he became a 'Special Director of Engineering' in 1957, and would be the company's technical supremo for the next decade.

Shrewdly building a team of associates (it would be unfair to call them subordinates), he gleefully took a hand in projects as various as the 'Zobo' (Triumph Herald) and Standard 'Zebu' projects, the Triumph TRS and Spitfire race cars, and the six-cylinder engine which served the company so well after 1960. Along with Alick Dick. Martin Tustin and George Turnbull, he was one of the group of 'Cavaliers' who did so much to change the company's marketing image at this time and, not only that, but he was the first company man to recognise the importance, and the flair, that Giovanni Michelotti offered.

After Leyland took control of Standard in 1961, his star rose even further and faster, so when the British Leyland colossus was born in 1968 it was no surprise to see him rapidly moved across to Longbridge to take control of the Austin-Morris engineering programme.

During many happy years of retirement, he became a real icon of all the Standard and Triumph enthusiasts and one-make clubs, but always made it clear that he was the leader of a dedicated and successful team.

and refuse trucks. In this case it was Dennis, which was the smaller of the two enterprises, though with under-used factory space, trying to underpin its financial future.

Dennis had extensive factory premises in and around Guildford, but no apparent strategy for breaking out of its existing product cycle. Although Standard initially warmed to the idea of opening up in a different geographic area, it eventually quailed at the thought of the financial investment which would be needed, and called off the discussions in March 1955.

December 1956: The next, and the most extensive, series of merger talks were then with the Rootes Group, which was of course controlled by the Rootes family. As already noted, in Coventry the Rootes business was already as large as the Standard-Triumph Group, but the Rootes Group also included coachbuilding concerns in London (Thrupp & Maberly being the most prestigious), and truck manufacturing at Commer and Karrier.

Initial talks, in which Massey-Ferguson was also involved on the fringes, centred around a plan to merge marketing operations overseas, but before long these developed into full-scale merger discussions. Problems arose straightaway, for although Rootes was a public company, the voting capital was controlled by Rootes family members, allied to a series of shadowy trusts in overseas tax havens. They also controlled many Rootes dealerships. The Rootes family made it clear that they wanted to retain hands-on control over the running of a new company, and it was not long before Alick Dick saw that he and his chairman, Lord Tedder, might spend more time battling with Rootes egos than they would with the company and its finances.

By the spring of 1957, there was a proposal to set up a new parent company (R&S Holdings), in which, after a great deal of bickering at the very top level, it looked as Sir William Rootes might become Chairman, while Alick Dick and Geoffrey Rootes (Sir William's son) would become joint managing directors. But it was all very difficult – personal issues, the notional values of each company's shares, and the number of personalities to be allotted posts on the new Holdings board were all argued over – so it all meant that Rootes would effectively have had structural control, and Dick would have lost out.

Massey Ferguson, for its part, was widely seen as a trouble maker here, for in recent months it had been building up its shareholding of Standard stock, and was thought to be eyeing up the possibility of buying the Banner Lane business after Rootes eventually took control. The final stage came in April 1957, when the proposed management structure became impossibly complex (Sir William as President, Lord Tedder as Chairman, Sir Reginald Rootes as Vice-Chairman, and no less than five joint managing directors, of only one – Alick Dick – would be a Standard man).

This was the point at which all attempts to form an agreeable link were abandoned: they would never be resumed.

December 1956: In the meantime, desultory contact, but no actual negotiations, had been made with Chrysler of the USA, which wanted to expand its influence in Europe. Over in Detroit, Chrysler was third in the pecking order, behind General Motors and Ford. General Motors (with Vauxhall and Opel) and Ford (with its own-brand subsidiaries) were all strongly represented in Europe, so Chrysler thought it should follow suit.

Chrysler originally considered setting up its own factory to produce a small car (Small? How small? They never spelled this out ...), and approached Standard with a view to sharing common engines and other chassis components, but later took this a stage further. However, before a stage could be reached where head-to-head meetings, the possibility of sharing factories, and financial injections could be mentioned, the talks were abandoned.

April 1957: With a possible Rootes merger abandoned, and therefore with Massey-Ferguson eliminated along with those discussions, the spotlight turned closer to home. No sooner had Alick Dick returned empty-handed from the last Rootes meeting in the Bahamas, then Massey-Ferguson made a separate, quite independent approach of its own.

The Canadians were quite straightforward about this. What it proposed was a straightforward, agreed, bid for Standard, which would involve a considerable financial injection of £2 million into Standard. Standard would be owned by Massey Ferguson, but would continue to have a separate existence.

That was the outwardly friendly approach, but since Standard discovered, almost at once, that Massey-Ferguson had already accumulated 20 per cent of the Standard share capital, it all began to look rather more suspicious.

Fortunately for Standard, and before negotiations could become frigid, the world's stock market provided a solution. The original takeover proposal would have been carried out on the basis of share swaps, at agreed values for both Standard and Massey-Ferguson shares. Later in 1957 Massey's share values were badly hit when its own financial results disappointed the markets, which gave Standard the excuse that this then under-valued the worth of the company.

In September 1957 Standard's Board decided to withdraw from negotiations with Massey-Ferguson – but a great deal of 'face' was lost by a number of people, on both sides of the argument, so this was not the end of the matter. Massey-Ferguson would be back, in a belligerent mood, and make it very difficult for Alick Dick to plan his company's development. The final 'divorce,' which was finalised in 1959, played a crucial role in what could be done when Standard's fortunes hit the rocks in 1960.

May 1959: The final divorce from Massey-Ferguson came after a traumatic year, in which Massey-Ferguson had tried to interfere with the Standard takeover of Mulliners (see page 167), and it was as a direct result of this that Rover was once again attracted to discuss a merger with Standard.

Once again there were real personal differences to be resolved – neither Alick Dick, nor Rover's Managing Director Maurice Wilks was willing to cede control and seniority to the other – and there was also the fact that Rover was not impressed with what Standard's profit possibilities would be when there was no benefit from tractors to fill up the coffers.

There was also a major clash of interests over new-model plans and possibilities. The author once wrote in an earlier book:

"Before talks broke down ... both engineering groups were astonished to realise they were proposing to build the same sort of 'executive' 2-litre saloon car in the foreseeable future. Rover had already settled on the bare bones of the P6 Rover 2000 project, while Standard-Triumph were still trying to settle the prototype version of an advanced six-cylinder car coded 'Zebu' ..."

The end came soon after the Triumph Herald was launched, and there would be no more talk about mergers until Leyland came on the scene at the end of 1960.

SC – THE BIRTH OF A GREAT LITTLE CAR, AND A GREAT ENGINE

In the meantime, Standard had completed work on a brand new range of cars, and a new small four-cylinder petrol engine to go with it. Always known as the 'SC' (Small-Car') project, the engine and the car – the two being inextricably interlinked – took shape in 1950/1951, was ready for public launch in September 1953 – and the engine and its associated gearbox would be used in the whole variety of Standards, Triumphs and MGs built until 1980.

When SC design work was started, Standard had little experience and knowledge of small-scale modern cars on which to draw. Their previous small engine range (as used in the recently-discontinued Triumph Mayflower), was a side-valve unit which had started life as a 1006cc engine with a two-bearing crankshaft in 1931, which had reached its size and development limits at the end of the 1930s in the Flying Ten, and was thoroughly obsolete.

So, how were Grinham's team to begin? Their brief from John Black was simple enough – now that the political pressures of pursuing a 'single model policy' had eased, he wanted to add a new small Standard to the range, which would fill the marketing gap under the Vanguard range. The Triumph Mayflower, he had to admit, had not been a roaring success – and he was looking for sales of up to 50,000/year from a small Standard. It was to be a four-door saloon, built down to aggressive price targets, and would ignore luxury if such features were to cost money.

The competition was fierce, and likely to get more so. By the spring of 1952, when the design of 'SC' was being settled, this was the British domestic 'small-car' pecking order:

Ford Anglia	£479
Austin A30	£520
Morris Minor	£582

– whereas the Mayflower cost £701, and the Standard Vanguard no less than £919. Even so, Sir John wanted to start selling the new small Standard at rock bottom prices. On the other hand, he was able to commit up to £6 million for new tooling.

All manner of schemes were put forward, though all were constrained by the need to produce a very cheap car. First of all, though, Standard briefly fell in love with the idea of making a car like Renault's latest rear-engined 4CV saloon, which was selling fast in France, but since Banner

Styles changed considerably over the years. At this club meeting in Gloucestershire, not only are there Eights and Tens, but Flying types of the 1930s, and even a Triumph Stag of the 1970s in the line-up.

Birds of a feather (Eights, Tens and a Pennant) at a recent club meeting.

SC – THE STORY OF AN ENGINE

Although the story of Standard's amazing little 'SC' engine is told fully in the main text, this is a brief summary of its production life:

Year announced	Capacity (cc)	Power output (bhp)	First model to use this	Comment
1953	803	28	Standard 8	
1954	948	33	Standard 10	
1961	1147	39	Triumph Herald 1200	
1965	1296	61	Triumph 1300	
1970	1493	61	Triumph 1500	

– also –

1965	1147	109	Triumph Spitfire Le Mans car	Race engine

– the SC being last used in the Triumph Dolomite 1300/1500 range of 1980.

Lane knew nothing at all about engineering rear-engined cars, this idea was speedily dropped.

Even by the summer of 1950 (when the Mayflower had only been in production for months), thoughts were then given to restyling the Mayflower while retaining its expensively tooled platform and suspension, using a three-speed gearbox without synchromesh of any type, and to use a newly designed side-valve engine. The gearbox had already been schemed up when the possibility of building Nash's NXI model (see the panel on page 137) was in the balance. A lot of design work on a new side-valve engine was actually completed, but this, too, was eventually cancelled.

Then there was the influence of BMC's two modern baby cars – the Austin A30 and the Morris Minor, which had both come to the market after complex beginnings. The Morris Minor, finally made famous by the charisma of its designer, Alec Issigonis, was originally meant to have a flat-four engine, and was originally high and narrow – but that engine was dropped in favour of an old-style side-valve unit from the 1930s, while the entire body had to be widened at a late stage of development. The A30 had started out as an advanced car, which was gradually cut down to size and specification by the irascible Austin chairman Len Lord, originally had styling by the Loewy Studio, and might even have had a brand-new side-valve engine. Standard knew all about the troubled beginnings of each car (it was impossible to keep secrets for long in the British motor industry), so was quite prepared to go through a variety of proposals of its own.

As far as the engine was concerned, there was an attempt to look at its own Vanguard engine for inspiration (but there was very little scope, as its wet-liner engine layout was now considered as too expensive to build, and therefore not suitable), and another was to take account of the expensive transfer line machine tools which had only recently been installed to make Mayflower engines: for obvious practical and economic reasons this meant that the same cylinder centre dimensions in the cylinder block would have to be retained). There was also a new kid on the block to be considered – Austin's promising new A-Series power unit, which was also about to be added to the Morris Minor, too.

Although, in later years, Standard engineers have always insisted that the A-Series meant little to them, there is evidence that it was studied carefully at the design stage. It can be no coincidence, surely, that both the A-Series and the original Standard Eight/SC engine shared the same bore and stroke dimensions (58 x 76mm) and swept volume (803cc). We now know, by the way, that alternative cylinder bore dimensions of 60mm, 65mm and 70mm were all considered.

How much notice did Standard take of the new A-Series engine? Some, but maybe not as much as some observers thought. Vic Hammond, who was one of Walter Belgrove's stylist/body engineers in the 1950s (and no friend of some of mechanical engineers with whom he had to liaise), once mistakenly said:

"The new engine in the Standard Eight of 1953 was not an entirely new design of our own, it was actually a 'Chinese' copy of the Austin A30 engine, because I saw our draughtsmen copying and modifying it from the Austin blue-prints ..."

This, no doubt, is partly hyperbole, for except for their similarity in bore and stroke dimensions, the two engines were different in almost every way, notably in the cylinder head and cylinder block designs. On the new Standard, the sparkplugs and the camshaft were on the left side, with the manifolding on the right side, whereas the A30 had its plugs on the right and its manifolding on the left. Not only that, but the Austin engine had siamesed centre exhaust ports (in other words, only three exhaust ports for four cylinders), while the exhaust ports of the Standard engine were completely separate.

That canard, therefore, can surely be laid to rest, especially as I can also quote the fact that the Austin (BMC) engine could not be enlarged to more than 1275cc, whereas the SC unit eventually made it all the way to 1493cc. The

David Eley, whose team designed the Small-Car engine, posing beside a Standard Pennant in early 2000s.

ultimate disgrace for the BMC unit was that, from 1975, it was displaced in the MG Midget by – the Standard-Triumph SC unit!

David Eley led the design team that produced the new SC engine, and once told the author:

"By this time," David recalls, "there were four sections in the mechanical design office – engine, gearbox, axle and chassis – and I was promoted to lead the engine section. For the SC, I had to do all the engine layout drawing, and detail drawings of the cylinder block and head, and specified all the bearing sizes.

"My experience with jig and tool design was invaluable. Even before I put pencil to paper, two people came to see me – one was John Harris, a talented production engineer, the other was Harold Albutt, our pattern shop executive – who were invaluable.

"Sir John Black gave us a very open brief – and we knew we had to design an engine which would last for at least ten years. But he would come to see us at the drop of a hat – he always wanted to know what was going on. We formed a new drawing office to do this work. I tackled the engine (with three or four people), Ron Sydney in charge of the gearbox, Howard Grubb the axle, and Ralph Wigginton the chassis – it was totally new. I was reporting straight up to Harry Webster, and I started with a clean sheet of paper.

"The BMC A-Series engine came along about the same time, but we never looked at it. Later I looked at it, and thought the use of a low-mounted distributor was a major failing ...

"We looked at various options, and soon concluded that a four-cylinder, water-cooled, overhead-valve, pushrod engine was the thing to go for. However, when we started out, John Harris asked us to use the same cylinder centres as the Mayflower engine – Standard had just got a modern suite of cylinder block boring and honing tackle for the Mayflower engine at Canley – so we did. The request came just in time! We worked as quickly as we could, but once the block – for instance – was designed, I reckon it took us four weeks to dimension every detail on the four main drawings of that casting!

"We only ever planned that this engine would be an 803cc or 948cc size, we designed both types together – with the same stroke and different cylinder bores – with water

This display unit shows the results of Standard's huge investment in a new engine (the SC), and a related four-speed gearbox, first seen in the 1953/1954 Standard Eight. By the end of the decade this particular installation had been tailored for the twin-SU-equipped Herald Coupé.

between the bores on the 803cc, but with siamesed bores on the 948cc. Accessibility was considered very important, and Harry Webster insisted that we put all the electrics – distributor, starter, dynamo – on the same, camshaft, side of the block. I thought it was important, too, that the distributor was high, up at the side of the rocker cover. With short HT leads to the plugs, the whole thing was very tidy.

"In the first place, the 803cc engine produced 26bhp at 4500rpm, and the 948cc engine 30bhp at 4500rpm. Quite soon, too, we produced a twin-SU carburettor version which was sold as a kit – and it made the Standard 10 into a useful rally car."

David still smiled at the thought that 'his' 948cc engine was eventually stretched to 1493cc ('We never planned for that, no, certainly not') and that the eight-port 1296cc engine as used in 'Works' rally cars in 1965 produced 117bhp. He is very proud of the fact that this could eventually be done, with great reliability.

By the time the very first 'SC' prototype was put on the road in 1952 – eventually registered MRW900, it carried the experimental chassis number X510 – all the main investment decisions had been taken, Not only would there be a four door saloon, but an estate car and a van derivative, the cars would be badged as 'Triumphs' in certain export markets, and there would be Eights (803cc) and Tens (948cc) in the range. Vic Hammond styled the bodyshell, and Albert Coaley worked out the monocoque, both being forced to reduce costs by deleting the boot lid from the original Eight, and using what Hammond called "Renault-type sliding windows, and spartan trim with a cardboard glove box ..."

The first test car originally ran with an old-type side-valve engine, for the first overhead-valve engines were not fitted until a few weeks later. X513 (MVC 610) ran later in the year, but the third prototype (X518) did not follow until

This was a display model of the Standard Eight/Ten 'SC' overhead-valve engine, as modified for use in the Herald of 1959, showing that all the electrical components – dynamo, starter, distributor and sparkplugs – were on the same side of the engine. So was the camshaft and the valve-gear, but the ports were on the other side of the block.

Originally available as an 'homologation extra,' but as standard on the Herald Coupé of 1959, the twin-SU derivative of the 948cc SC engine was a sturdy little power unit.

Designed in 1951, on sale from 1953, and produced for the next 27 years, the Standard SC engine was used in many applications – even up to and including the Le Mans 24 Hour race. This was the original 1950s type, complete with single downdraught carburettor.

The SC engine started life with 30bhp at 803cc, but eventually produced up to 109bhp from 1147cc for racing purposes. This was Bill Bradley's Works-maintained Spitfire of 1965.

1953. It was only after this, that testing of the up-market derivative, the Ten could begin.

Incidentally, when the new SC was originally, and officially, mentioned at Board level in May 1953, the point was made that they were to be marketed without 'Standard' badges – as the 'Beaver Eight' and 'Beaver Ten' – but this rather bizarre suggestion was speedily abandoned.

The new car would have an entirely new four-door platform – though for cost-saving reasons there would be no separate boot-lid access on the Eight – running on an 84in wheelbase. Two-door types were considered but not produced, while vans and estate cars were held over until the saloons had made their mark. Mechanically, everything, but everything, in the running gear, was new – new engine, new gearbox, new axle, and new suspension.

It was the trim and fittings of the Eight – or, rather, the lack of them, which caused most discussion, and dissension, at first. Because Sir John was determined to put the car on the market at a price undercutting its major rivals, the trim was skeletal, features such as wind-up windows were absent, and equipment was stark, to say the least. Sliding door window panes (as later seen in Minis) were standard, the rear seats had to be somersaulted forward to gain access to

This was the original, very basically equipped, Standard Eight of 1953, with an 803cc engine, but with no separate boot access, no wheel covers, and with sliding window glass to save money. Sir John Black nicknamed it the 'Belsen Line,' which was in poor taste, but everyone could see why ...

This was how Standard sold the original Eight of 1953; very basically equipped, but at a very low price, too. It was a great commercial success. The wheelcaps on this car were added later.

the boot (no boot lid, as already mentioned) , but the general ambience was stark in the extreme. Why else would Sir John Black, in a letter from his convalescent quarters refer to the 'Belsen Line.'

Stripping out specification, and costs, however, seemed to have been justified, for at launch, at the 1953 Earls Motor Show, these were comparative retail prices of four-door saloon cars in the class:

Renault 4CV	£610
Ford Prefect	£561
Morris Minor	£561
Austin A30	£504
Standard Eight	**£481**

– which made the new Eight a price leader by any standards, Only the two-door Austin A30 and Ford's impossibly archaic old two-door Popular could undercut it. It was no wonder that road test reviews were welcoming, and even though there were vocal complaints about the stark level of trim and fittings, sales took off like a rocket. With production still building up, no fewer than 9921 cars were produced before the end of 1953, and more than 50,000 would follow in 1954.

Although a favourable road test report was only to be expected from the patriotic British motoring press of the period, (*The Motor* recorded 61.3mph, and overall fuel economy of 43mpg from its car), the cheerful report of a London-Glasgow-London trek was less predictable. In fact Laurence Pomeroy and Joe Lowrey of *The Motor* did the new Eight proud in November 1953, when they used ODU 826 to reach Glasgow, and the opening of the Scottish Motor Show.

On the way north they aimed at a maximum economy run, while on the return leg they aimed on as fast a transit as possible: in both cases they followed a London-Doncaster-Scotch Corner-Penrith-Carlisle route. Although, at times, the trip must have felt interminable, the result was remarkable. By cruising at no more than 40mph on the 'economy' leg, and taking all of 13 hours for the 397 mile journey, they averaged 46.03mpg, while on the return trip, using every possible rev, they took just 9 hours 8.5 minutes, averaging 43.5mph. Pomeroy's conclusion was that: "We had shown that the Standard Eight is a most unusual and quite possibly a unique, proposition as a combination of large carrying capacity with extremely low fuel consumption when driven gently, to which can be added average speed possibilities hard to beat by any substantial margin by any car of any size ..."

This, of course, was only the beginning, for the new and larger-engined version of the car, the Ten, appeared in the spring of 1954, this having all the features which the

In 1954, only months after the original 'stripped out' Standard Eight had been launched, the company announced the much more up-market Ten, complete with 948cc engine, wind-up windows, and a more styled nose ...

... along with an opening boot lid (which the Eight lacked).

When was a Standard Ten not a Standard Ten? When it was rebadged as a Vanguard Junior in certain expat territories.

market-place really wanted – more power, an opening boot lid, wind-up windows in the doors, and more complete and comfortable trim. It was, of course, more costly – at £580 it cost £100 more than the Eight – but soon began to sell really well.

'Standard' or 'Triumph' – what's in a name?

In the meantime, significant corporate changes were brewing up at Standard. Wasn't it William Shakespeare who penned these immortal words in Romeo & Juliet?:

"What's in a name? That which we call a rose, by any other name would smell as sweet ..."

By the early 1950s this famous quotation (or the questions it asked) had come to haunt Standard. Their own cars, worthy and successful as they might be, were still seen as staid, work-a-day, machines. On the other hand the brand that it had secured as recently as 1944 – Triumph – seemed to be getting more glamorous by the day.

Standard's first attempt at styling a two-seater sports car for the 1950s was not a success, but an evolution of it, the TR2, turned the tide. Not only is this the first, and only, 20TS sports prototype to be completed in 1952, but the photo also shows the Banner Lane experimental department, which includes a Triumph Mayflower, and (tucked away) a still-secret Phase II Vanguard.

The 'Triumph' side of the business, in fact, was a slow burner which had taken time to become important, but this had certainly happened. To a certain class of people the Triumph Renown was a much more desirable car than the Standard on which it was based. The stubby Mayflower might have seemed bizarre to some, but it was certainly interesting to others – and it certainly made a talking point.

Then, in 1953, there came the TR2 sports car, whose story has often been told in dedicated Triumph histories. Conceived in 1952 by Sir John Black, originally to hit hard at MG, whose TD was selling so well in North America, he originally thought it was a car which could be built around redundant 1930s-style Standard Nine chassis, with many Vanguard and Mayflower' building blocks' hidden away under a Belgrove-designed skin.

Soon discovered to be something of a disastrous 'dogs-dinner' of an idea, a new chassis frame, a restyle, and Ken Richardson's undoubted development driving skills were all needed to turn it round, but the job was done. High speeds on the Jabbeke highway in Belgium made a point, so that against all the odds, this cheaply and quickly developed two seater showed how fast it was, and what good value it offered.

The original 20TS chassis frame was cobbled together from a prewar Standard Flying Nine, and was not a success. The second attempt – this one of mid-1952 – was more promising, but still not sturdy enough, and a complete redesign was needed to get the TR2 ready for sale. Standard experts will immediately notice the use of Vanguard-based engine and transmission assemblies, and the front suspension of the Triumph Mayflower.

The TR2, which went on sale in 1953, was really the first 'Triumph' badged model to completely change the face of Standard in the 1950s. Hidden behind a forest of conveyors and stillages is the parallel line of new Standard Eights.

Canley at its busiest, in 1957. In this engine assembly/test department, many of the 'wet-liner' engines in shot are destined for TR3 sports cars.

At Sir John Black's specific request, the Phase III Vanguard shape was worked up by one Carl Otto, an American with his own independent styling house. It was his only contact with Standard.

When the TR2 started winning races and rallies, defeating rivals from MG and Austin-Healey along the way, a reputation was soon established. Image was all and, particularly in North America, the TR2/TR3 became the British sports car to own.

Standard's marketing staff (more particularly after Martin Tustin arrived from Ford-UK) soon took advantage of this, renaming mundane Standard models such as the Ten as Triumph Tens in export markets such as Australia, New Zealand, and North America. Those subscribing to media cuttings services soon realised, too, that 'Triumph' was getting much more attention than 'Standard.'

What followed would probably never have happened if Sir John Black was still at the helm (since 1929 he had been a 'Standard' man, through and through), but eventually the pragmatic Alick Dick realised that a change was almost inevitable, and by the end of the decade the original 'Standard' name would be in decline.

Vanguard III – a major change of direction

In the meantime, Standard had embarked on another major project, which was to develop a new type of Vanguard, the Phase III. It seems to be agreed that the Vanguard Phase II had only ever been a 'stop-gap' project, and that the Phase III would be a mostly-new type, which would eventually take over as soon as possible. The early types, though, had been a commercial success: the statistics tell their own story, for 184,999 original-style Vanguards had been sold, along with 83,047 Phase II types.

Not only was the new car to have a totally fresh look, but a new structure, too. Although it meant another big financial investment, the new car was to have a unit-construction bodyshell (for which Pressed Steel finally got the business), though the engine, transmission and much chassis engineering would be carried forward from existing cars.

In many ways, Standard was unlucky with its timing, for although F&L was still an independent concern when the Vanguard III project got under way (and might have expected to win the contract), the company then sold out to the British Motor Corporation, which put in an agreed bid in the summer of 1953. BMC soon made it clear that it would restrict future F&L activity to its own projects – which obliged Standard to look elsewhere.

To Walter Belgrove's dismay, the contract to style the new Vanguard bodyshell went to the ex-Loewy Studio designer Carl Otto (see the panel on the opposite page), who was currently toting his skills around Europe. Not that this deal was without controversy, for after his initial style was received, and a full-scale mock-up had been readied at Banner Lane, Sir John and his cohorts then rejected it as too large. Walter Belgrove was asked to make it smaller and then – when this process was under way – was asked to revive his earlier 'Vanguard II' shape for consideration, too. In the end, however, the Otto-modified-by-Belgrove style was chosen before the end of 1953, Pressed Steel began making the tooling for the structure, and the launch was fixed for the Earls Court Motor Show of October 1955.

The new car was novel in many ways, for it would run on a 102-inch wheelbase – eight inches longer than before – although the roof line was three and a half inches lower, and the rear wheel track had been reduced by three inches: the new car, too, was almost 200lb lighter than the Vanguard II. That said, much of the rest of the running gear was familiar – the 2088cc 'wet-liner' engine was rated at 62bhp (net), the three-speed gearbox retained its steering column change, and there was an overdrive option. Interestingly enough, there was no diesel engine option (which had been added to the Vanguard as recently as 1954), as sales had been very poor. Deliveries began almost at once, with prices set at £900, more costly than competition from BMC's Austin A90, Ford's Zephyr and Vauxhall's Velox to be sure, but still very competitive.

Incidentally, it didn't take long for Standard to discover that the Vanguard III had no future as a competition car. For the 1956 Monte Carlo rally, where open-top sports cars were still not eligible (which meant that Triumph TR3s could not be used), Ken Richardson's 'Works' team was asked to run Vanguards instead. Except for a remarkable

Carl Otto

Although stylists tend to be flamboyant people, ready and willing to take every possible headline, Carlo Otto was apparently not one of those. Known within the Standard enthusiast's hobby as the man whose business shaped the Vanguard Phase III, he had no earlier connections with the company, nor apparently retained any after that car was launched.

Born in Michigan, he was an industrial designer by profession, Otto originally worked with Auburn-Cord-Duesenberg (ACD), and was responsible for the style of the Cord L29. Associated with Gordon Buehrig, he was also involved in the shaping of the famous Cord 810 of the 1930s.

Later he joined the legendary Raymond Loewy Studio, first of all working on Pennyslvania Railroad designs, and was then sent across the Atlantic to open up Loewy's first studio in London, where his company picked up the lucrative and high profile Rootes Group (Hillman, Humber and Sunbeam-Talbot) styling accounts.

This part of Loewy's development is well documented, in the UK and elsewhere, and it is probable that Otto's reputation spread around Coventry, and the domestic motor industry, at this time.

Nevertheless, while still working for Loewy, Otto returned to the USA after the War, and is known to have managed projects for Coca-Cola, Edison, and even for the Schick electric razor company. In 1951, however, he split from Loewy, and set up his own concern, Carl Otto Associates, in North America.

This was the period when Otto set out to expand his auto-design interests still further, and it is now known that this was also the time when Standard's Sir John Black was looking for new and diverse talent to help him shape Standards of the 1950s. It was not entirely because his own staff (led, of course, by Walter Belgrove) could not do a good job, but that there existed what could be described as some 'creative tension' between Belgrove and Technical Director Ted Grinham. Black, therefore, thought that a shake-up would do everyone a bit of good!

Otto's links with Standard-Triumph, however, seem to have been brief, for once the Vanguard Phase III was finalised, he does not seem to have been connected with the company on any further projects.

Careful artistry made the Vanguard III looked sleeker than it actually was ...

When used in Mediterranean climes such as this, the Canary Islands, Sportman's colour scheme looks appropriate.

Not familiar in the UK, the Vanguard Pickup (commonly called a 'Ute' in 1950s Australia) was a very significant machine.

Vanguards were very popular with the British Armed Forces. This was a Vanguard Phase Ia pick-up, as used by the Royal Air Force.

performance by Maurice Gatsonides (who had previously won the event in 1953 in a Ford Zephyr) it was not a success.

Except for additional 'winter' equipment, the six 'Works' Vanguards were virtually standard – the cars being driven by Gatsonides, Ken Richardson, Peter Bolton, Peter Cooper, Ms Jo Ashfield, and Ms Jo Osborne.

On an event where ice driving skills were at a premium, and where accurate time-keeping paid big dividends, the redoubtable Gatsonides took eighth place, but no other Vanguard finished in the top ninety placings. Gatso then took the same car out to tackle the East African Safari, but was forced to retire, at which point the Vanguard's rally career came to an abrupt halt.

Sportsman and Ensign

Later in the 1950s, two Vanguard III derivatives – the Sportsman and the Ensign – were added to the line-up. The Sportsman, to be frank, was a marketing disaster, while the Ensign was a commercial success. Neither achieved greatness, and neither is preserved today as a laudable example of what Standard could do at the time.

As far as the Sportsman is concerned, we must reel back the years to 1953, when the razor-edge Triumph Renown was still on the market. Launched in 1946, with a style dear to Sir John Black's heart, this car had inherited Vanguard running gear in 1949. Although 15,491 such razor-edge cars would eventually be built, by 1953 only 614 cars were made in a full year. More than 400 unsold cars were in stock, only two cars a day were being completed, and the pressure to drop the model was intense.

Because Sir John still treated the Renown as his baby, no-one in Standard's management dared to do this, so after the selling price was dropped significantly in mid-year, it carried on, something of a lame duck in a more modern-looking Standard-Triumph range. By mid-1954, with Sir John ousted, the directors discussed producing a restyled version, but nothing came of this, and the last car was built at the end of 1954.

Although Standard was quite determined to replace the old Renown with a new model, it would have to make many compromises. Because the likely sales volumes would be restricted, and because the existing Vanguard's separate chassis frame would be killed off during 1955, the development of an entirely new body style was out of the question. Work therefore began on a new model that would be no more, and no less, than a derivative of the still-to-be-launched Vanguard III, but it would retain the well-known name of Triumph Renown.

The immediate result was the evolution of a much more powerful version of the new Vanguard, a four-door saloon with a new nose incorporating a Triumph-like grille, and powered by a 90bhp/twin-SU version of the 2088cc 'wet-liner' engine. Standard publicists described this unit as a 'hybrid development' between the Vanguard III and TR3 power units, which indeed it was, because the new car had

In 1956 Standard mated a modified version of the TR3 sports car engine to the Vanguard III, gave it a new front-end style, and called it the Vanguard Sportsman. Originally, it was to have been called the Triumph Renown. It was a commercial failure.

a massive oil bath air cleaner, a lower compression ratio than the TR3, but more mid-range torque.

This was all well and good, but at a very late stage – reputedly only weeks before the new car was due to be launched in August 1956 – the sales department had a change of mind, and decided to market the car as a Standard – a 'Vanguard Sportsman' – and not as a Triumph. In the fullness of time, this came as a great relief to every Triumph enthusiast, for at a selling price of £1231.35, complete with overdrive as standard equipment, the Sportsman was an unmitigated disaster. The market place, it seems, would have liked to see a four-speed gearbox, and separate front seats, but got neither, so a top speed of 90mph, with 0-60mph acceleration in a rather leisurely 17 or 18 seconds could not really compensate. In the end, only 901 examples were produced (of which just 241 cars were exported) before the programme was cancelled early in 1958.

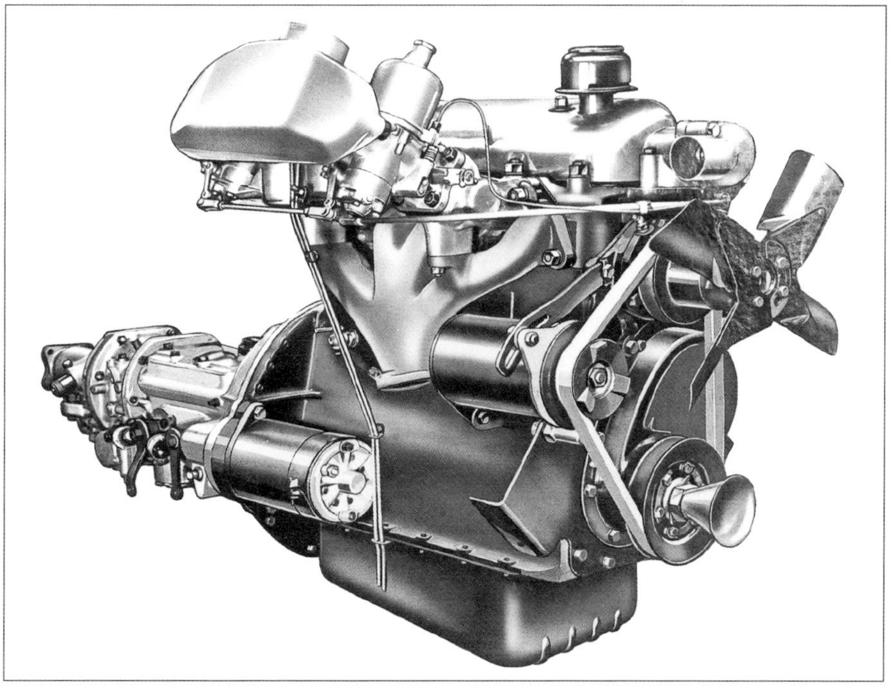

This was the engine/transmission fitted to the Vanguard Sportsman of 1956-1958, the engine being a hybrid evolution of the Vanguard and Triumph TR3.

The original Standard Ensign was seen at the end of the 1920s. The Vanguard-based Ensign, launched in 1957, might have been 'Plain Jane,' but was a low-budget marketing success.

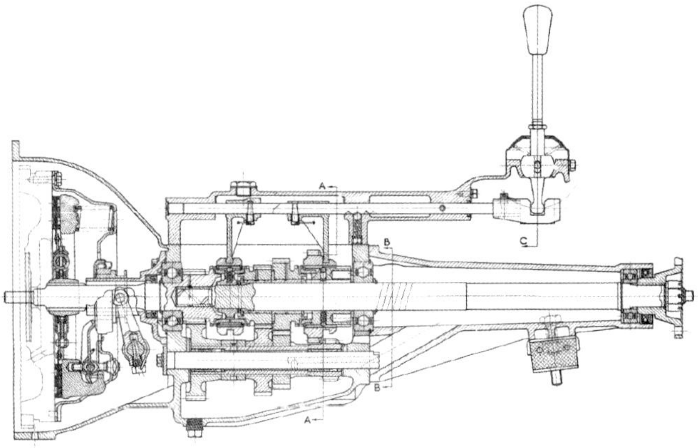

The postwar gearbox, as originally designed for the Vanguard, but in use in many models for more than thirty years, was one of Standard's unsung profit makers. Made in three-speed, four-speed, with or without overdrive, with a column change or central change, it was an amazingly versatile 'building block.' This was the four-speed TR2 unit of the 1950s.

The Vanguard III-based Ensign, on the other hand, revived a famous Standard model name of the 1930s. Announced in October 1957, it was much more successful than the Sportsman. In later years, no doubt, we would describe this either as an 'entry level' or 'fleet market' version of the Vanguard, for it was both of those things, and did a good job for the company. From late 1957 until 1961 (it disappeared soon after the six-cylinder Vanguard Six had appeared and, probably coincidentally, soon after Leyland arrived to rescue Standard from financial disaster), no fewer than 18,852 saloons and estate car types were produced.

Not only was the new Ensign cheaper (it cost only £900 in the UK, compared with £1104 for the contemporary Vanguard III), and was fitted with a 60bhp/1670cc version of the 'wet-liner' engine, but company planners had clearly gone right through the Vanguard's body specification, stripping out some of the existing features and reducing costs even further. The new front grille was a simple mesh fitment, the fascia/instrument panel was both simplified and made clearer to read.

On the other hand, this was the first of the Vanguard-based cars to be equipped with a four-speed gearbox (overdrive was optional), and it was also fitted with a direct-acting central gear change lever. Compared with the Vanguard, these were distinct advances, which made up for much. Unhappily, though, this was only a 75mph car, in which acceleration could best be described as 'ponderous,' though up to 30mpg was sometimes possible in day-to-day running. So, who bought Ensigns? As expected by Standard, company fleet buyers, and the British armed forces seemed to be good customers – and company accountants rubbed their hands in glee.

When the Vanguard III became the Vignale Vanguard for 1959 (Michelotti was credited with the retouching), this car was captured outside Coventry's then-new Telephone Exchange in the still war-torn centre of Coventry.

In comparison with all this flamboyant product action, the addition of an automatic transmission option (by Borg Warner) for the Vanguard III in 1957 came along almost without fanfare – yet this was the very first time that a Standard had received such a system.

Better Eights, better Tens – and Pennants

With work on the new Vanguard III now completed, and with the Eight/Ten range selling well, Standard could now tackle its next project – to face-lift the Ten and extend the range, before deciding how to replace it.

Although the basic style of the small Standards did not change for some years, the sales departments (egged on by General Manager Martin Tustin, who had learned all about year-on-year titivation from his previous employers, Ford) produced change upon change without the company having to spend a fortune in new investment.

To summarise, The Eight De Luxe models featured wind-up door windows from mid-1954, these being adopted for all Eights from May 1955. From late 1955, there was also a Super Eight, with more basic equipment, and from March 1957 Laycock overdrive (operating on top, third and second gears) became optionally extra for £63.75. Weeks later all versions were treated to opening boot lids (with a mesh front grille to match), and with 33bhp as standard.

Tens also went through several upgrades – starting with the four-door Good Companion estate car from October 1954, a Family Ten in March 1956 (Ten running gear, Super Eight trim and fittings, but no external boot lid!), optional 'Standrive' two-pedal transmission control from October 1956, and optional overdrive from March 1957. It was a frenetic period which Standard, and its dealer chain, survived remarkably well.

Eights and Tens were also game little competition cars, which handled well, and was strong into the bargain. By juggling with engine specifications whenever and wherever the event regulations allowed, Ken Richardson encouraged 'Works' Eights and Tens to put up some remarkable performances in International rallies. Using a twin-carburettor engine equipped Ten, Jimmy Ray and Brian Harrocks won the 1955 RAC rally outright, 'Works' Eights and Tens finished second, third and fourth in the 1956 Tulip rally, and there were also several class wins to add to the roll of honour.

By this time, however, BMC had upgraded and up-engined its Austin A30/Morris Minor cars to A35/Minor 1000 levels, which meant that Standard came under pressure to do something to change and improve the Ten. The problem was that, with Walter Belgrove at 'daggers drawn' with Ted Grinham for some time (Belgrove stormed out of the company in October 1955, never to return), there had seemed to be an artistic 'vacuum' in the styling area. Accordingly, when Alick Dick decided to change the Ten, it took time for a suitable style to emerge. The result, launched in October 1957 (on the same day as the Vanguard-based Ensign) was the Pennant.

Was the Standard 8/10 family a success? Just look at this shot, and work it out for yourself.

Once the Standard Ten was established, Standard added a small estate car to the range, originally calling it the Good Companion.

As ever with Standard, one major problem was a shortage of investment capital – so, how to achieve this without spending a fortune on new tools and fixtures? In the end, it was decided to do this in two ways. Although the main platform, cabin and structural members were to be retained unchanged, there would be new front and rear wings, a much changed fascia/instrument panel, and important changes to the SC-type engine and gearbox.

Work began in 1955, and by March 1956 the directors reported that a £50,000/£60,000 investment would be needed at Fisher & Ludlow, and there was a slim possibility that the new car could be launched at the 1956 Motor Show. Unfortunately, that fell into the 'high hopes' category, as the launch duly slipped to late 1957, and the tooling costs for a car that was provisionally (but only briefly) proposed for

Three 'Works' Standards Eights took second, third and fourth overall in the Tulip rally of 1956. Left to right: Johnny Wallwork, Bill Bleakley, Paddy Hopkirk, J Garvey, Denis Taylor, and Lou Tracey.

badging as a new 'Triumph Mayflower' rose to £125,000. There was even talk of producing a two-door saloon derivative, which would cost an extra £100,000 in tooling, but nothing became of this.

Strangely, there is no mention of the Pennant in the Prototype Register, or even of any suitable SC-based car carrying an appropriate Project Code, until the first Pennant-styled Companion (X626) was built up for the crazy Cape Town-Tangier-Coventry proving expedition of late 1958. As far as we know, just one car was mocked up at Banner Lane, and all the development work was carried out on it. Fisher & Ludlow produced the saloon car shells at Tile Hill, while Mulliners eventually produced the estate car bodies after the derivative was launched.

Although the Pennant was clearly based closely on the Ten, the motoring media received it politely enough. Compared with the Ten, there were new front and rear wings, a new front-end treatment (which included hooded headlamps, which were fashionable at the time), and duo-tone paint finish was optional. Inside the car, the fascia was new, and neat, as was the steering wheel (it would also appear on the forthcoming Triumph Herald), and the rear seat squab was arranged to fold forward to give access to the boot from inside the cabin.

Hidden away was a slightly tuned-up 948cc SC engine – 39bhp@5000rpm, compared with 35bhp@4500rpm – and either overdrive, or 'Standrive' two-pedal control were optional extras. The most significant transmission change, however, was that a remote control gear change was provided – and, once again – this was also due to be used in Triumph Heralds, Spitfires and such related models.

All this came at a price – £728.85, which was £75 more than the equivalent Ten – yet even if the £63.75 overdrive option was specified, this was still only a 66mph car. But ... don't knock it, for as *The Autocar's* testers summarised in 1958: "It is extremely useful as a commuting car, its handy size enables it to be tucked away in a confined parking place ... with an exceptionally smooth and sweet engine, which makes no protest even at maximum attainable crankshaft speeds, the Standard Pennant has a long stride and good road manners ..."

The proof of the pudding ... came in the sales figures, which were substantial. According to Standard's own official archive, 42,910 (plus 335 'Triumph Pennants') were produced in two years, before the new-generation Triumph Herald displaced it in 1959. [Incidentally, Standard specialist and enthusiast John Carlton disagrees with this figure, and says that it is too high, but I have to stick by the figures given

To extend the life of the Standard Ten of the 1950s, the styling team topped and tailed the shell, producing the Pennant, which held the line well until the Triumph Herald family was developed.

For a time after the Triumph Herald was announced, Standard also produced this estate car version of the Ten Companion, with the now-obsolete Pennant nose.

During the 1960s, Pennants built in India were known and sold as Standard Tens.

to me by the official historians]. Along the way, it enjoyed one brief moment of motorsport fame, when 'Works' rally cars driven by Ron Goldbourn and Tom Gold finished second and third overall in the 1958 RAC rally.

Big changes ahead

It was in the same period that Standard also introduced a new medium-sized van – the Atlas (coded 'Zany' – and it was ...) – which was drastically under-engined as first designed (fitted with a 948cc Standard Ten engine, it was only just capable of dragging itself along) – and in which Standard's new consultant stylist Giovanni Michelotti was encouraged to retouch the Vanguard III without costing the company a fortune in re-tooling costs with Pressed Steel. This was 'Project Zoic,' the result being the Vanguard Vignale, a model which featured enlarged front and rear screen area, with a new front grille and revised (more subtly-styled) tail lamps, all at a tooling cost of a mere £36,750.

But that was nothing, compared with what lay ahead. Not only did Standard get involved in a blizzard of mergers, takeovers and sales, but the Board began to get to grips with two major new projects – the 'Zobo' (small car) and 'Zebu' (Vanguard-sized range). If all its financial planning came to fruition, the 1960s was going to be a frenetically busy period.

Life wasn't always glamorous – this is the 6cwt van derivative of the Standard Ten, which sold steadily in the late 1950s/early 1960s.

This was the Vignale Vanguard, as launched in 1958 as a retouched Phase III. Two years later the same body structure would accept the first of Standard's new-generation six-cylinder engines, and become the Vanguard Luxury Six.

CHAPTER 11

TRIUMPH TAKES CENTRE STAGE 1959-1960s

WOULD STANDARD SOON GIVE WAY TO TRIUMPH?

Starting in the late 1950s, the 'Triumph' brand began to make most of the headlines at Canley, the 'Standard' brand gradually slipped into the background, and many Standard followers are still bitter about that. However, make no mistake – this did not happen by accident. Quite suddenly, it seemed, 'Triumph' had succeeded in North America where 'Standard' had always failed, and the sales implications were there for all to see.

Businessmen, particularly at Board level, can be cold-hearted and dispassionate people. Under Sir John Black and Ted Grinham this had certainly seemed to be true, but once Alick Dick took over in 1954, the corporate atmosphere changed significantly. Under the Black-Grinham regime, no one ever seemed to be having fun, but under the Dick-Tustin-Webster management which followed, there was often brightness in the air.

It wasn't only that, of course. The new TR2/TR3 sports cars made friends all over the world, the stubby little Standard Eights and Tens sold in huge numbers, and from 1957 the promise of what Giovanni Michelotti's new styles could do for the company's image were quite electrifying.

ZOBO – THE SEARCH FOR A NEW SMALL CAR

By 1957 the SC range – Eight, Ten and (soon) Pennant – was at its peak. Not only did it sell well against direct rivals like the Austin A35, and the Morris Minor 1000, but along the way it was also delivering exceptionally good profits to the company coffers. But with the SC now approaching its fourth birthday, it was time for Standard to start planning a successor.

Because the SC was the company's best-seller (it sold much faster than the Vanguard, which had just been updated into Phase III), the decisions to be faced were as large as any the company had taken in recent years. Straightaway, the company was faced with several dilemmas. How should the new car be badged? How much technical innovation should be included? Most important of all – where should the bodyshells be made?

By the mid-1950s, Standard had to face up to a truly major problem. Starting in the mid-1930s, it had elected not to make its own bodyshells anymore, its policy being to put out its business to major independent suppliers. Fisher & Ludlow, Briggs, and Pressed Steel had got the major

Giovanni Michelotti

When Giovanni Michelotti died in 1980, struck down by a disease connected with his life's work, he was almost a forgotten man. Yet ten years earlier he had been at the height of his fame, a man toasted by every Standard-Triumph enthusiast.

If it hadn't been for Michelotti's links with Standard-Triumph, in fact, we might never have known him well in Britain. It was as a quick-thinking, fast-acting and amazingly productive genius like Michelotti first made his reputation. Standard-Triumph's then Technical Chief, Harry Webster, who also became great friends with Michelotti, once told the author:

"He couldn't speak English, and I couldn't speak Italian, but that didn't matter. We got on well in French!"

Alick Dick, Standard's managing director when Michelotti was first hired, also said:

"Michelotti was always reeling off designs, no matter where he was, you couldn't stop him. If you took him out to dinner he'd get hold of practically every menu in the restaurant, design a car, and hand one out to each waiter ..."

The young Michelotti left school in Turin at 16, and then started as the odd-job man at Stabilimenti Farina. In what was then a tiny coachbuilding house, he learned his craft by seeing it done – and eventually becoming a fully-fledged designer/stylist himself.

After the Second World War, he produced stunning shapes for Farina then in 1949, set out to go it alone. Although he worked for several coachbuilding concerns at first his links with Vignale became particularly strong. Even so, it was not until 1957 that Michelotti's genius started to be used outside Italy, first by Standard-Triumph, and later by BMW.

Early in 1957 Standard Technical Chief Harry Webster had a chance meeting with Raymond Flower, who wanted to buy engines and axles. Flower boasted that he could get a body built in two or three months, which led to the magic of Michelotti becoming known to the company.

Webster speedily signed up the Italian, first to produce a one-off TR3 'dream car,' then to retouch the Vanguard III, following up with a new commission for the 'Zobo,' which became the Herald. Because Michelotti's renderings for the 'Zobo' all looked so sporty – and 'Triumph,' rather than 'Standard' was the sporty brand in Coventry – this was a major factor in ensuring that 'Zobo' became a Triumph, and the Standard brand began to fade away.

Above all, Michelotti was the archetypal 'hands-on' designer who preferred working on full-size drafts than on scale renderings on a drawing board. Clients still speak glowingly of the way he would produce stunning full-scale proposals at high speed, using chalk to sketch up lines, rubbing out vigorously and re-drawing, before he even used a pencil or crayon.

By the early 1970s, with Standard long gone, Michelotti's creative juices seemed to be past their best. In any case, once Triumph disappeared into the maw of British Leyland, his influence waned rapidly, and there was great resistance from the Longbridge (BMC) and Solihull (Rover) design offices to him being used. His proposals for what became the TR7, the SD1, and the stillborn SD2 were all turned down – but then so was Pininfarina in several such British Leyland 'design competitions' ...

When he died in 1980, the heart really went out of his business, and although his son Edgardo carried on the business, very few new styles were produced. The Michelotti business finally closed down in 1991.

contracts, while Mulliners (smaller, but still body specialists) had got most of the rest.

Twenty years on, the industrial scenario had changed – considerably. Unhappily, two of those four concerns were no longer independent. One of them (Mulliners) was still not really large enough to tackle a major tooling job, while Pressed Steel was constantly overworked: not only had Standard become an important customer at Pressed Steel, but so were BMC, the Rootes Group, Rover, Jaguar, Daimler and Rolls-Royce.

Standard, naturally, was always inclined to hire Fisher & Ludlow to do the job, but this was never likely to be easy. Although Fisher & Ludlow had been supplying Standard since the mid-1930s, and had built its factory at Tile Hill, Coventry, specifically to produce shells for the Flying Eight, in 1953 it was taken over by BMC, whose chairman, Leonard Lord, was not known for a cooperative attitude to any of his rivals.

As a reminder, BMC's takeover bid for Fisher & Ludlow came in August 1953, and was speedily formalised on 30 September 1953, just days after series production of SC bodyshells had begun at Tile Hill, and the new Standard Eight had been announced! Because BMC immediately announced that: "the company's future trading policy would be materially unaltered ..." Standard was not too unhappy about this, especially as F&L went on to cooperate freely in supplying incomplete shells to Mulliners for vans and pick-ups to be completed.

For a time, indeed, everything was sweetness and light in the relations between the two companies, but perhaps Standard was wise when it placed the bodyshell contract for the unit-construction Vanguard Phase III with Pressed Steel at Cowley. Even so, in 1956, when Alick Dick then started planning a new car to replace the SC, a routine visit to see Sir Leonard Lord, produced a rude shock:

"When I went to see Len Lord," Alick Dick told the

author, "he turned me down flat. He said something like: 'I'm not going to use the Austin Motor Company's money for the benefit of the Standard company: you can push off and look somewhere else ...'

"Even though he was cutting off his own nose to spite his face – the Tile Hill factory was no good at all to F&L if they weren't making bodies for us – he wouldn't take on the job ..."

Dick was appalled, but tried to deal with the situation by approaching Pressed Steel instead:

"I negotiated with Pressed Steel, but they hadn't the tooling capacity at the time. Joe Edwards would have loved to have the business, but we couldn't wait, the other models were dying, and we had to have it by 1959. That was when it became clear that we had to have our pressing and body-assembly division, and for the next few years all our policy was directed to this ..."

Dick, in fact, did much more than merely build up the body assembly side of the business. By using company reserves, plus the money (and more) released by the 'divorce' from Massey-Ferguson in 1958/1959 [the unsavoury saga is detailed in chapter 8] he set about building up a network of specialist suppliers, which became part of the Standard group of companies.

Because this strategy was, commercially and financially, so vital to Standard's future, I now ought to detail just what businesses Alick Dick, with the approval of his senior colleagues, gathered in from 1954 to 1959:

1954 to 1958 – absorbing Mulliners

Most Standard enthusiasts realise that Standard took over Mulliners in 1958, but the complexities of such a deal are rarely spelt out. In fact, although Standard benefitted greatly from the deal, it took years of patient negotiation to unscramble the independent Mulliners' links with its past.

First of all, I should emphasise that there was no link between other coachbuilders, which bore the Mulliner name at the time. Neither H J Mulliner (which was soon to be absorbed by Rolls-Royce), nor Arthur Mulliner of Northampton, were connected with the Birmingham-based Mulliners Ltd (its factory was in Bordesley Green), with which Standard did an increasing amount of business in the post-1945 era.

Standard's first formal link with Mulliners came in 1939, when Captain Black commissioned it to style and build a magnificent razor-edge saloon on the rolling chassis of a 3½-litre SS-Jaguar. After 1945 Sir John then chose Mulliners to produce all the saloon bodyshells for the Triumph 1800/2000/Renown model, and followed up this deal with other contracts on derivatives of the original Standard Vanguard such as the estate car and panel van.

By the early 1950s, Mulliners had expanded considerably. Not only was it building Triumph TR2 bodies,

It was cars like the TR3A which did so much to change Standard-Triumph's image in the1950s. These sports cars sold in high numbers – and here just one day's output of bare bodyshells is ready for delivery from Mulliners (in Birmingham) to Canley.

and those for the Standard Vanguard estate car, but it was also supplying bodyshells for models as diverse as the Alvis TA14 and TA21 saloons, the Aston Martin DB2/4 coupé, the Daimler Consort and Regency models, and the Sunbeam (Talbot) Alpine sports car.

By 1954, with Standard policy changing rapidly, the company saw (or could see, in its dreams) the need to source more and more shells from Mulliners. Fisher & Ludlow (Standard Eight/Ten, Vanguard II and Triumph Mayflower) and Pressed Steel (soon-to-be-launched Vanguard III) supplied the mass-market saloons, but Standard already needed a source for all its derivatives. Not only that, but Fisher & Ludlow had just been taken over by Standard's deadly rival, BMC, so the future of its links with Standard was already in doubt.

Alick Dick therefore moved decisively in June 1954, sealing an agreement with Mulliners, that although Mulliners should honour its existing contracts with other companies, it would then put the whole of its future capacity at Standard's disposal for the next ten years. This was a brilliant commercial deal, for it not only underpinned Standard's bodyshell strategy, but it also ensured Mulliners' survival in an increasingly competitive business.

Within three years it was clear that this move had worked well. At the 1957 London Motor Show, for instance, every car shown on the Mulliners stand was a Standard-Triumph product, while behind the scenes, Standard had already arranged to put a lot of business towards Mulliners for the forthcoming 'Zobo' (Triumph Herald) project. In the meantime, Mulliners had also acquired a controlling interest in another Birmingham-based body-making concern, Forward Radiator, which made it even more attractive.

Then, in May 1958, Standard made an agreed takeover for the whole of the Mulliners share capital (offering new

Standard shares, rather than cash), but this caused Massey-Harris-Ferguson (with whom Standard was still connected) to take-offence, and to put in a counter bid of its own in July 1958, by offering to buy up those new shares as soon as they were issued!

The Massey-Harris-Ferguson move failed, the Standard-Mulliners deal then went through without a hitch, which meant that Mulliners (along with Forward Radiator) became wholly-owned subsidiaries of Standard. By that time Mulliners had four different plants, totalling 360,000ft^2, producing up to 700 bodies every week: progressively, these would be integrated into Standard (-Triumph) in the 1960s.

January 1956: Standard made a takeover offer for Beans Industries, which was already a Midlands-based major supplier of castings to Standard, and to Ferguson. This company was currently building a big factory extension (in connection with the new and larger Ferguson FE-35 tractor project), and was happy to be taken over on the right terms. Beans accepted the deal in March 1956, the company then becoming a recognised subsidiary and major supplier for the next thirty years.

February 1958: Purely by chance (but happily for Standard), Daimler was looking to divest itself of a one-time 'shadow' factory in Capmartin Road, Coventry (for details see the panel on The Radford Plant on page 169). Standard swooped to take up the long-term government-owned lease of what it always knew as the Radford plant (Radford was the suburb of Coventry in which this factory was situated), formalised it in November 1958, and soon turned it into a major producer of gearboxes, axles, and – later – engines.

May 1958: Massey-Ferguson's failed in an attempt to take over Mulliners. As already noted in chapter 8, Massey-Ferguson took exception to Standard's intention to absorb Mulliners in 1958, for it was clear that this would effectively dilute its own stake in Standard. In an astonishing and quite counter-productive move, it then offered to buy all the newly issued Standard shares, which were going to erstwhile Mulliners shareholders!

This strategy failed completely and humiliatingly, especially as Massey-Ferguson soon followed up by making its own takeover bid for the Perkins engine company of Peterborough, thus endangering the long-term need for Standard diesel engines.

The long-term result was predictable. Not only did Mulliners formally become a part of Standard in July 1958, but Alick Dick and his senior colleagues were so angry that they made haste, forthwith, to make a formal break with Massey-Ferguson. This would follow in 1959.

November 1958: Once it became clear that Fisher & Ludlow would not be supplying bodies for the forthcoming 'Zobo' (which would soon be named 'Triumph Herald'), the future of the F&L Tile Hill, Coventry, factory was in doubt. This plant had specifically built Standard Eight, Ten and Pennant bodies since 1953, and F&L's owners (BMC) made it clear that when that contract came to an end, then it would close it down.

This aerial shot shows the entire Daimler complex in Radford, Coventry, in the 1950s. At the top right of the estate is the 'shadow' factory, of which Standard took over the lease of in 1958. This became what Standard-watchers called 'the Radford plant,' and was used for engine and transmission component manufacture until the business closed down in the 1980s.

Standard, for its part, saw it as an opportunity to rationalise the assembly of Herald bodyshells (Standard called this 'integration') from their major components, which were due to flow in from several outside sources. Accordingly, an approach was made to BMC, which proved to be surprisingly welcome (for there was still no love lost between Alick Dick and the BMC Chairman, Sir Leonard Lord), the result being that Standard bought the Tile Hill complex, fully-equipped, for £725,000.

Once Tile Hill was cleared of SC facilities in 1959, it was speedily converted for Standard's more general use, became an important bodyshell fettling 'feeder' to the Canley assembly halls, old and new, and would remain so until the very end of the British Leyland era in the late 1970s.

1958 and 1959: As already described in chapter 8, the final 'divorce' from Massey-Ferguson, the disentangling of all

The Radford plant

As already explained earlier in this book, the British government financed the building of several important 'shadow factory' complexes in the late 1930s, several of these being concentrated in and close to the city of Coventry.

One of these, which was allied to the Daimler company in the Radford suburb of the city, was built just to the north of Daimler's factory complex, though connected to it. Daimler operated this new plant, at the same time as it operated a factory in Browns Lane, Allesley, Coventry (a factory which was eventually taken over by Jaguar), with access from Capmartin Road. During the Second World War, what Standard later called the 'Radford plant' then went on to manufacture Daimler scout cars, armoured cars, Bristol aircraft engine components, and millions – literally – of other military items.

Despite special attention from German bombers, Daimler's war effort was not destroyed, but by the 1950s the 'shadow' factories were surplus to its requirements. Eventually, in January 1958, Standard took over the lease of the premises, paying £30,000/year from 1959 onwards, rapidly converting it into a specialised transmissions machining and assembly operation, and used it as an important 'feeder' building to the Canley site for the next thirty years.

Radford/Capmartin Road, therefore, which had a total floor area of 296,533ft^2, became important as a provider of pieces for Standards of the 1950s and 1960s, and of Triumphs from the late 1950s until 1980, but was finally emptied when the BAE-owned Rover Group was down-sized at the end of the 1980s. The plant was then demolished, the site has been redeveloped, and no 'Standard' trace now exists: in the meantime, Ford had already demolished the old ex-Daimler plant, and most of this part of Coventry was later covered by modern housing.

the legal and financial niceties, and the relocation of staff and workshop equipment from one factory to another (in particular, the swapping of engineering facilities at Banner Lane with Fletchamstead North, Standard moving one way as Massey-Ferguson moved the other way ...) was a complex business.

In this chapter, however, the important point is to note that the £12.5 million in cash, and the other credits (£5 million in capital profits, £3 million in 'exceptional revenue credits') which Standard gained, all helped to finance the takeovers listed here.

September 1959: Standard first made an offer for a company based at Hemel Hempstead, Hertfordshire, called Alforder Newton Ltd (whose principal business was Alford and Alder), which was a respected supplier to the industry of suspension, steering components and assemblies.

[Purely as an example, although A&A front suspension components were fitted to the Triumph Mayflower and the TR2/TR3 sports cars, similar units were also to be found in the Daimler SP250 and Reliant Sabre/Scimitar/GTE sports cars, too.]

This offer, rated at more than £500,000, was formally made in December 1959, and speedily accepted. Not only did Standard then expand the business, but also involve it in other activities, notably in the development of a new-type Standard-designed carburettor, which was effectively an improved, Patent-free, version of the SU, and would eventually be handed over to Zenith for production as the Zenith-Stromberg design.

December 1959: An agreed bid was made for Hall Engineering (Holdings) Ltd of Liverpool, a pressings company in Speke where Triumph Herald bonnet assemblies were already being produced.

After its acquisition, this plant (which had originally been built in 1936), was considerably expanded, to produce complete Triumph TR4, and other 1300/1500-type bodyshells in the 1960s. Hall also held a controlling interest in Auto Body Dies of Dunstable, which also became part of the deal.

This cost about £2 million in cash but, as Alick Dick later told the author:

"We paid cash for Hall, which was really a mistake. We would have been more liquid in 1960 when the financial tide turned against us, if only we'd paid Hall in shares and a small dollop of cash, but I didn't want to let a company like Massey embarrass us again by bidding for the new shares. I think it was an error, but we really had gone through a lot with Massey, and I wasn't prepared to suffer that sort of thing again."

While all this frenetic corporate activity was going ahead, the company continued to make good after-tax profits. This was fortunate, for most of this money would be needed to finance the 'Zobo' (Herald) and 'Zebu' (Vanguard-replacement) projects.

£419,925 was made in 1957, £1,003,582 in 1958, and no less than £2,223,739 followed in 1959. That was the year in which three major events took place, all of which had major effects on Standard, and what the company would become in the next months and years.

To mark the divorce from Massey-Ferguson, Standard's own corporate and financial structure changed dramatically. The main holding company was re-formulated, as Standard-Triumph International Ltd (which was colloquially known as STI), with the Standard Motor Co Ltd acting as the main manufacturing subsidiary.

According to the official structure, other subsidiaries such as 'Group Services,' 'Sales,' 'Triumph Motor Co 1945,' 'Beans Industries,' and 'Mulliners Ltd' all continued to report to STI, but this was a process honoured more 'in the breach' than in any other meaningful way.

Unhappily for Standard fanatics, it was at this time that 'Triumph' gradually became the dominant brand at Canley. This, therefore, is where the author must strike a balance.

Although the rest of this history must, perforce, make more mention of 'Triumph,' the story of that marque has already been exhaustively researched and published and can merely be summarised here.

By the mid-1950s it was clear that the world-wide success of the Triumph TR2/TR3 sports car had significantly changed the public's perception of the company and its products. Indeed, in several of Standard's overseas markets – Australia, Canada, New Zealand and the USA, for example – the importers asked for some Standard models to be rebadged as Triumphs. These were small, but significant, nails being driven into Standard's coffin, for the trend, when established, seemed to be unstoppable.

Accordingly, in 1956, when thoughts turned to producing a replacement for the SC (Eight/Ten/Pennant), the new machine was known internally by its project code – 'Zobo' – at first. In June 1958 the directors thought it could be badged as the 'Triumph Torch,' but well before its launch that was changed to 'Triumph Herald' – the 'Herald' part of the title apparently coming because that was the name already carried by Alick Dick's pleasure boat.

The traumatic birth, ecstatic reception, troubled development, and exuberant launch of the Herald has been told in great detail in Triumph histories. Basically, though, at the outset in 1956/1957 there were two major problems to be solved – one being to establish a new structure, the other being to set a style.

The two problems were inter-related. Once BMC had made it clear that it was not willing to make a replacement model for the SC, any further restyle of that monocoque was out of the question – and until Giovanni Michelotti came on board as the miracle-working consultant stylist Standard also found it difficult to evolve a new shape either. 'Zobo' – its dictionary definition as a 'Tibetan pack animal of indeterminate sex ...' – began to look singularly significant.

By 1957, though, Alick Dick and his new Technical Chief, Harry Webster, had solved the problem of the structure. At the time, shallow-thinking pundits called it a backward move, but since it was neither their investment funds, nor their knowledge of export and overseas markets which were involved, they can be discounted.

The big decision was to revert to a separate chassis layout, and to arrange to bring in large, but definitely separate, sections of bodyshell from companies as diverse as Pressed Steel (in Oxford), Standard-Triumph (in Liverpool) and Mulliners (in Birmingham), ready for bolting up. To quote Webster:

"We decided to use a separate chassis. We had to provide a good foundation for assembling all those different bits and pieces of bodywork ... and if we sent 'knocked down' cars for assembly in other countries we could use the chassis as a jig if necessary ..."

The striking style which graced the Herald, finally emerged after one high-intensity weekend in Turin in September 1957, when Harry Webster visited Giovanni Michelotti. Current attempts to update the theme of the SC/Pennant had failed, artistically, and Webster was in despair:

Thank goodness this style proposal for a Standard Eight replacement never got beyond the scale model stage. Happily, Giovanni Michelotti waved his magic wand in 1957, and Standard's future was saved.

"Then I said something like: 'We are wasting our bloody time. Look, suppose you could start from scratch here in Italy, based only on this chassis, what would you propose?' Well, to Michelotti, that was like a red rag to a bull. Within three or four minutes he had sketched up the Herald as we know it, and we instantly started transferring this to a full-scale draft on the wall ..."

The rest of the story, too, is well known. The Standard Board gave instant approval to the new schemes, the very first prototype Herald shell arrived at Banner Lane three months later, testing and proving began days later, and the very first production cars were ready to roll early in 1959. According to Alick Dick:

"The first body arrived, on a lorry, as promised, actually on Christmas Eve, we put it straight into the styling studio, on the turntable, and we were so thrilled with that coupé body style that we all downed tools and went out for a pint ..."

It was fabulous coup de main, for Michelotti had asked for (and received) just £10,000 to style, and manufacture, the first three prototype shells – coupé, saloon and estate car. [The convertible, and the van which derived from the estate car, would follow a few months later]. Not a line of that exterior style was changed, or abandoned and, as we now know, that family of new 'Standards' would be in production in Coventry until 1970.

As to the rest of the car – the 'oily bits' – though some of it was a descendant of what was hidden away in the Pennant (the 948cc engine and a four-speed gearbox with remote control change were virtually the same), there was new front suspension with rack-and-pinion steering, which allowed an impressive 25-foot turning circle, along with transverse leaf spring independent rear suspension. Once front-wheel disc brakes became available, this would form the basis of a chassis from which the six-cylinder Vitesse, the Spitfire and

Ready to leave Coventry for the now-famous Cape Town–Tangier proving run for prototype Heralds, a Pennant and a Standard Atlas van in 1958. After several agonising weeks, the intrepid team made it – just!

Yes, that really is Tombouctou (or Timbuctoo, as we also know it) on the southern outskirts of the Sahara desert in the autumn of 1958. Refuelling, repairs and – yes – time for a cup of tea ...

Nearing journey's end, the intrepid Cape Town to Tangier expedition caravan of Atlas van, two Herald prototypes, a Vanguard III estate car, and a Pennant Companion pause for breath. Team leader John Lloyd leans on the Atlas and looks exhausted – which he probably was.

the GT6 sports cars would all evolve. Interestingly enough, after a very short honeymoon with the latest technology, Standard lost interest in its own two-pedal 'Standrive' clutchless transmission, which would never re-appear on any of the company's cars. Overdrive, however, still had an assured future, though not on the Herald.

Zobo gets a name – 'Herald'

Alick Dick's corporate strategy for Standard-Triumph became more obvious to the outside world in 1959 when the new Triumph Herald – a direct replacement for the Standard Eight/Ten/Pennant family – was unveiled in April.

First of all, it was necessary for the Eight and Ten to be killed off, and for the Pennant to come to the end of its natural life. When this was done, Tile Hill, which Standard had purchased from Fisher & Ludlow, became the initial meeting point for many Herald components. For this purpose, Standard had elected to build every Herald derivative around a separate chassis frame, while entire sections of the bodies arrived at Tile Hill from several sources, including Mulliners, Hall Engineering and Pressed Steel, after which they were bolted to the chassis, painted, then delivered to Canley for final assembly. Coupes were first to go into series production, four-seater saloons followed, after which convertibles then (with the enlarged 1147cc engine) the estate car completed the set.

With Standard reaching for record outputs in 1959, the Triumph Herald assembly line was chock-full of partly-built cars proceeding down the assembly line in a sideways fashion. Mayflowers had previously been built in this manner.

Sammy Newsome owned the Standard-Triumph main dealership in Coventry for many years, and is here seen with Standard Managing Director Alick Dick at the launch of the Triumph Herald in 1959.

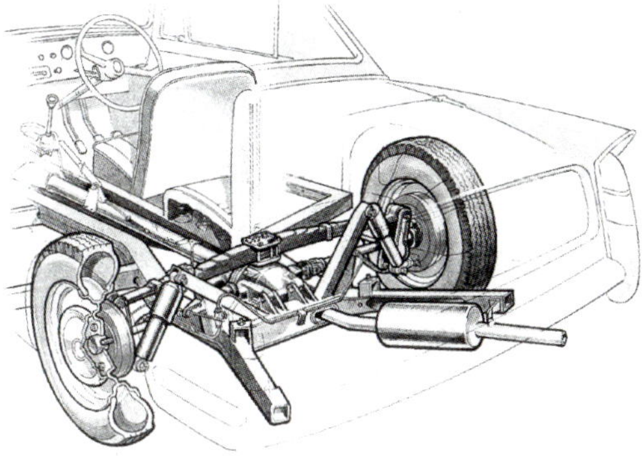

Only six years after the Standard Eight was announced, the revolution was complete. Not only did its replacement have a separate chassis frame, and smart Italianate styling, it was badged 'Triumph' instead of 'Standard.' There would be no going back ...

Open wide, please. One way to get at the Atlas' engine, transmission and front suspension area was to lift the entire bodyshell like this. Standard-Triumph seriously believed that dealers would be happy to do this – it was wrong!

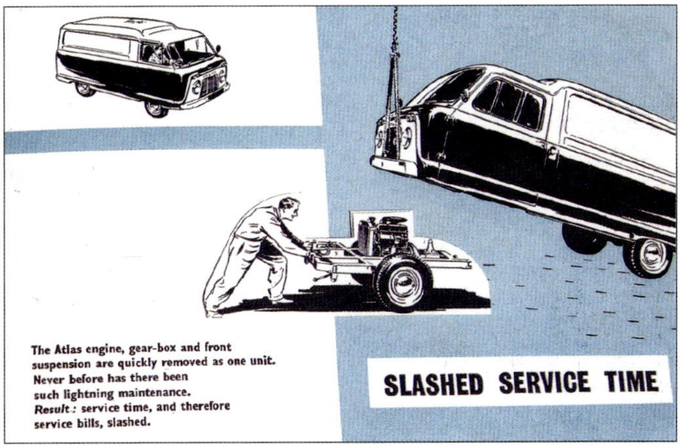

Although the original Atlas van proved to be under-powered, there is no doubt that the easy-access feature to the front-end for service and repairs was very valuable.

Few Atlas vans have survived to be preserved by Standard enthusiasts, but several have been repainted in the powder blue which was adopted by the 'Competitions Department' van in the 1960s.

If surviving Atlas vans are rare, the pick-up derivative is even more precious these days!

The work that went into rejigging the Standard business at this time was phenomenal, with the mental and physical workload on all concerned well over whatever might be considered normal. Not only was the 'divorce' from Massey-Ferguson to be accomplished, but the relocation of staff, engineering workshops and all from Banner Lane to Canley had to be carried out. The acquisition of various facilities – not least of which were the ex-Fisher & Ludlow factory at Tile Hill and the ex-Daimler 'shadow factory' at Radford/ Capmartin Road – had to completed, along with the re-equipment of both factories. Not only that, but the ambitious new Triumph Herald project had to be brought to fruition, and the cars shown to the public, as did the all-new six-cylinder engine which is described next.

Then, of course, there was the question of a successor to the Vanguard III, that of the refinement of the new Atlas van, and big decisions to be made about the completion of a (separate from Ferguson) tractor project. Busy busy? You could say that ...

Designed in the late 1950s, the new straight-six cylinder engine was introduced in 1960. First fitted to the Standard Vanguard Six, it became a Standard-Triumph staple for the next seventeen years. There were some design similarities (and shared components) with the small SC four-cylinder power unit.

Smooth straight-six

In October 1960, for Standard it was just like old times. For the first time in 30 years, Standard was about to start selling six-cylinder cars again – for the previous model had been the Flying Twenty of 1939. Yet, [and now this can be pointed out without an outbreak of sour grapes breaking into this description] the new engine arrived too late to reverse the fortunes of a company, already rushing inexorably towards bankruptcy. Even so, the new engine was a fine unit, which would live on, under new ownership, until the late 1970s, would power many important new models, starting with the Vanguard Luxury Six.

Even though it did not arrive for seven more years after the small four-cylinder engine was announced, too many people have assumed that the straight-six engine – as used in the Vanguard Six, and several later Triumph models – had always been planned when the little SC 'four' was being designed. Not so, says David Eley, who should know, as he also led the design team that laid down both engines!

"No, not at all. In fact it wasn't just a six-cylinder 'version' of the SC. Although we used all the knowledge gained, the front and the rear block faces were very similar, and there were some shared components, the length was always limited, and the cylinder bores were siamesed, for we had to design the new six-cylinder to go into the engine bay of the Vanguard. At first, incidentally, we always considered doing a 1600 and a 2.0-litre, but no more, no larger.

"There wasn't much common tooling, in fact the 'six' (20S, we called it) was entirely different, and the two engines were machined in different factory buildings. Well before we designed it, the Sales people had pressed very hard for this six-cylinder engine, because we were up against Rover, Ford, and Vauxhall. They said 'we cannot go on selling this big four-cylinder engine [the old wet-liner

Although Michelotti had little time, or budget, to make major changes to the Vanguard III, his 'Vignale' model of 1958 looked smarter than before. Then, from 1960, the arrival of the new six-cylinder engine helped prolong the life of the model even more.

unit] against that competition, we need a 'six' ...' – so we started laying out a straight-six."

Work seems to have begun in about 1957:

"And we had problems with it. What didn't work so well were the semi-downdraught Solex carburettors. For packaging reasons, that semi-downdraught layout was very useful, there was more room to play with, but we had so much trouble with them [cold starting was an early problem] that I'm sure this caused Harry Webster to have a go at doing a variable choke carburettor of our own.

"It always upset him that the SU was such a good carburettor, but that it was being made by the opposition. Well, we had this bright young man called Dennis Barbet at Alford & Alder, so Harry had a test bed brake installed down there, at Hemel Hempstead, and set Dennis to design and develop the original carburettor ..."

The concept of that carburettor, of course, was eventually handed over to Bendix-Zenith-Solex, where it eventually became the Zenith-Stromberg CD carburettor. Money changed hands, of course and, for sure, Standard-Triumph then got preferential treatment. As part of the deal, the company got exclusive use of this unit for a time before any other manufacturer could adopt it – after which the sales of SU carburettors began to eventually suffered considerably.

"We were all proud of the 2½-litre version which followed [such a size was only ever used in Triumph cars, never in Standards]. It had a very reasonable BMEP (Brake Mean Effective Pressure) and a good torque curve, which was ideal for saloon cars. It was quite light, too. You know, don't you, that the 2½-litre 'six' should also have gone into the Stag in the first place, but after Harry went off to Longbridge, the new V8 went in, instead?"

This was, in fact, one of the best legacies that could ever have been handed from one brand (Standard) to another (Triumph) which survived for another twenty years. Not only did it find its way into cars as various as the Triumph 2000, the Vitesse, the GT6 and the TR6 sports cars, but it was also sold in numbers to specialist manufacturers such as Marcos and TVR.

When it was new, however, Standard not only envisaged it as being useful in the Vanguard Six, in a new-generation Triumph TR sports car, and in the projected 'Zebu' saloon car project which is described next. It was, indeed, designed within the constraints of the Vanguard's engine bay, for it would have been ruinously expensive for the tooling of that car's shell, as provided by Pressed Steel, to be modified to make more space.

The new engine was a compact unit, with siamesed cylinder bores (which explains why absolutely no enlargement of the original 74.7mm bore dimension was ever attempted), and with a four-bearing (not seven bearing) crankshaft. Both cylinder block and cylinder head were in cast iron (Beans Industries, one of Standard's recent acquisitions, provided both), while fuel supply was by two semi-downdraught Solex carburettors.

Although the head incorporated individual inlet and exhaust ports to each of the six cylinders, history now tells us that the breathing was not originally very efficient. It was not until an entirely different cylinder head casting, with revised port shapes, was evolved for Triumph models in the mid/late 1960s, that its full potential was unlocked. Even so, it was a real advance over the dear old 'wet-liner' engine, which was nearing its development limits, as this comparison makes clear:

Model	Peak power	Peak torque
Vignale Vanguard (4-cylinder) (2088cc)	65bhp/4000rpm	113lbft/2000rpm
Vanguard Luxury Six (1998cc)	80bhp/4400rpm	116lbft/2500rpm

Wall-to-wall production and assembly of 20S six-cylinder engines, at Canley in the 1970s. Fuel-injection derivatives, for use in the TR6, are in the foreground.

Two important Standard-Triumph personalities alongside the new Herald when that car was launched in 1959 – stylist Giovanni Michelotti (left), and Managing Director Alick Dick.

The new Vanguard Six was launched in October 1960, its new six-cylinder engine fitting neatly into the Phase III/Vignale bodyshell. The 'SIX' badge can just be seen on the nose of this car, which was captured outside Stanford Hall, a stately home close to Rugby.

Once put on the market, little attention was then paid to the Vanguard Six, for at almost every level the emphasis went in to producing a replacement for it. After the automatic transmission version started production in early 1961, and optional front disc brakes followed in mid-summer, the only corporate move of note was that it was dropped from the home market for a time in the winter of 1961/1962 – then reinstated in June 1962!

By that time, the car that might once have replaced it – 'Zebu' – had already been cancelled, and a smart new 'Barb' (which would become the Triumph 2000) was on the way.

Zebu – a missed-opportunity?

At the end of the 1950s, in fact, Standard suffered the most disappointing reverse. It was just one of several cataclysms which thrust the company towards the financial crisis of 1960/1961. Yet it might all have been so different. If Ford had not announced the reverse-slope rear window Anglia 105E (and the Consul Classic 109E which followed it), Standard would probably have followed the same route. If Standard had still been making money in 1960, a 'new Vanguard' – the 'Vanguard IV' – might have appeared in 1961. In which case it is likely that there might never have been a Triumph 2000.

Work on a Vanguard III replacement – coded 'Zebu' – began in 1957, and unlike its predecessors it was always meant to have a six-cylinder engine. Project work began soon after the layout of the Triumph Herald had been fixed, so first thoughts were of a car with a separate chassis, with styling by Standard-Triumph, but advised by Michelotti, and with bodies to be supplied by Pressed Steel.

As originally planned, the newly developed six-cylinder engine would be in 1.6-litre or 2.0-litre form, the transmission was to be at the rear, in unit with the final drive, and there would be all-independent suspension. The first production cars were to be built in March 1960.

The UK target Basic price was to be £575, which was quite ambitiously low. This compared with the Vanguard III De Luxe's list price of £650, £610 for the current Ford Zephyr Six, and £580 for the Vauxhall Velox.

By the end of 1957, the Zebu design was forging ahead, and brimming with novelty: Not only had Technical Chief Harry Webster specified a separate chassis frame, but the new car looked totally different from any previous Vanguard, for it featured a reverse-slope rear window. Developed by Standard, with a little help from Michelotti, the body style had peaks over the headlamps, vestigial fins at the rear, and that amazing rear window style.

The transaxle – a combined clutch, gearbox and final drive assembly – was at the rear, connected to the engine

The 20S straight-six, originally introduced in 1960, was a mainstay of Standard and Triumph production until the mid-1970s. This excellent cutaway shows its final iteration – a 2498cc version, for use in the Triumph 2500TC in 1974.

by a one-piece open propeller shaft. The transaxle included a twin-plate clutch, and a four-speed gearbox casing in aluminium, while the axle casing was cast iron. The engine flywheel, complete with starter ring, was actually mounted at the front of the engine, with the starter motor positioned to the right side of the cylinder block, driving forward to that ring. This was to eliminate bulk and bulges around the front footwell of the body platform.

Triumph TR3-type front suspension was matched to a semi-trailing-link independent rear end, which had coil springs, and lever-type dampers. Steering was by rack-and-pinion, there was a lengthy remote-control gearshift linkage, the handbrake was positioned outboard of the driver's seat (like several contemporary Rootes Group

The 'Zebu' (the Vanguard replacement), as originally designed in the late 1950s, had a separate chassis frame, a straight-six engine, independent rear suspension, and a rear-mounted gearbox/final drive unit.

cars), and inboard brake drums were mounted on either side of the final drive unit.

"When we started designing it," Harry Webster once recalled, "I insisted on better weight distribution than normal. So we put the gearbox and back axle together, which gave us much more space in the front instead of a great big hulking lump between the footwells.

"Mick Bunker did the design of the rear suspension. It was one of the deepest regrets of my life that we never patented this, because it was the first car with it. BMW followed us slightly later."

George Jones, who ran the transmission design team for many years, remembers that the rear-mounted transmission was under the rear seat cushion, which made the padding under the third, central, passenger (if carried) very thin. The layout itself caused many development heartaches.

There were massive drive line vibration problems at first, and the engine tickover was very erratic, so to minimise it, a big rubber joint was placed at the front end of the propshaft and a Silentbloc joint was at the rear.

Even before the style settled down, Standard knew that they were not going to be world pioneers, for in America the 1957 Mercury Turnpike Cruiser had already featured a reverse-slope window.

However, although the front of 'Zebu' still looked uncoordinated, the side view was very smooth: this was a modern design, which would easily have overshadowed the opposition from BMC, Ford and Vauxhall.

Development problems

Standard-Triumph then struggled to make Zebu viable for two whole years, but fought an impossible battle. Not only did the engineers face driveline vibration problems, but there was also great difficulty in settling an acceptable style. Then there was also the enforced move of the entire design and development department (from Banner Lane to Fletchamstead North) to be faced, and the fact that the company then ran into severe financial problems.

Even so, five prototypes were constructed over a two-year period, one with Michelotti style changes, and the last with MacPherson strut independent front suspension. Michelotti advised on style refinement, and by mid-1959 it was all looking promising. But the schedule had slipped, by which time the Zebu could not have been launched before 1961. The company then invited the Editor of *The Motor* magazine, Christopher Jennings, to come along for a confidential preview.

Jennings, though as diplomatic as ever, had to comment that:

"I think it's beautiful, but confidentially I must tell you that you'll be accused of copying, because there is another British car coming which will beat you into production by quite a long way, and it has got a cut-back window just like yours."

That car was Ford's new Anglia Type 105E, and the

Standard began to develop a successor to the Vanguard III in 1957, with this astonishingly advanced Michelotti 'Zebu' proposal to run a reverse-slope rear window style. Unhappily for the long-term thinkers, it was abandoned.

Discouraged when Standard dropped his reverse-slope rear window style for 'Zebu,' Michelotti then offered this much more conventional alternative, which had a slight resemblance to the Herald of the day. It was not liked.

larger Classic 109E which was to follow it up. "It was a great shock," Webster recalled, "and because we knew we could rely on his word, we dropped the idea!"

Three further attempts were made to retrieve the situation. One was to re-shape the rear of the existing style, one was to produce a widened-lengthened Triumph Herald shape, and the third was to ask Michelotti to produce an entirely new style.

The face-lifted ('tail-lifted,' really) style was smart, but no longer outstandingly different, while the 'Herald' lash-up, which also dates from late 1959, was quite astonishing. Like a 'hot-cross-bun,' a Herald saloon shell was cut down the middle, and across the top, widened, lengthened, and given four passenger doors, but unhappily, the result was predictable – it still looked almost the same as a Herald. It was not a success.

By April 1960, the Vanguard Six (almost the final iteration of the Vanguard III) had been finalised, as a stopgap, so Standard allowed Zebu's projected launch date to slip to late 1962. The sales forecast had been reduced to 25,000/30,000 a year, and Pressed Steel estimated that it would cost £800,000 to tool up the structure for bodyshell production.

Finally, there was a completely revised chassis layout, with an utterly different type of backbone chassis frame, the gearbox now reverting to a conventional position behind the engine, and with MacPherson strut front suspension. Michelotti was commissioned to produce an entirely fresh style. Completed in the summer/autumn of 1960, this was something of a disappointment, angular where the original Zebu had been rounded, and brutal rather than delicate.

After that, the end came suddenly, and decisively. At the Board meeting of 19 September 1960, the Zebu project was cancelled. Prototypes were destroyed shortly afterwards – [certainly when I first visited the experimental departments in the spring of 1961, no trace of Zebu remained] – and the company was left without a successor to the Vanguard, which then had to soldier on until mid-1963.

The Rambler connection

There was another short-lived alternative to Zebu, which flared in 1960, but this project seems to have been bizarre.

Standard, it seems, was approached by American Motors of the USA, who offered it the use of the company's soon-to-be-revealed 1961 Rambler American shell, so that Standard could then transplant its own engines, transmissions and axles.

This approach was odd, because it was totally unexpected, and one which Standard had never even considered. Although Standard already had links with American Motors in Australia, AMC's only previous contact with a major British company had been when BMC (Austin) had assembled Nash Metropolitans in the 1950s.

AMC was much smaller than its neighbours in Detroit – GM, Ford, and Chrysler – and was making 422,000 Ramblers a year. The first version had been launched in 1957, when it had a 100in wheelbase and was no more than a warmed-over mid-1950s Nash, but for 1961 AMC had a completely new model almost ready.

This car had a unit-construction style, there were to be two-door and four-door saloons, coupes, a two-door convertible and an estate car, and in domestic form it was powered by 3.2-litre engines of 90bhp (side-valve) or 125bhp (overhead valve). Furthermore, in USA-made form, it weighed only about 2523lb/1144kg, which was actually 109lb/49kg less than the Standard Vanguard Six.

Alick Dick was interested enough to mention this proposal to his directors in September 1960, when he pointed out that such a car could replace the Vanguard Six at little, or no capital cost. Since Standard had recently begun to lose buckets of money this was a very attractive thought.

Even so, although the Rambler/Vanguard Six hybrid proposal was superficially attractive, no one warmed to it. During the winter of 1960/1961 one prototype irreverently dubbed the 'Vangler,' (or the 'Ramguard') was built up, photographs prove its existence, but no other trace now remains.

Although Dick and Tustin actually flew to the USA in October to discuss this proposal further, nothing came of it; and once Leyland made its takeover bid for Standard during the winter, the project was speedily buried. By the summer of 1961 a new project – the Barb/Triumph 2000 – was under way. Leyland [I am sure], made the right decision.

A new assembly hall – the 'Rocket Range'

In and around all these technical, financial and corporation developments in the 'frantic 'fifties,' it had become increasingly obvious that Standard needed more space to make more cars. Even so, wild ideas of turning the ex-Fisher & Ludlow plant at Tile Hill into a fully-fledged assembly hall, or pushing ahead with the erection of a brand-new factory on Merseyside (close to Hall Engineering in Speke, but quite separate from it – and not at all related to the 'Kirkby project' of a decade earlier) were soon abandoned.

With open space still available on the 'Canley Estate,' thoughts turned more and more towards the building of a new complex at Canley itself – and because so much capital was likely to come out of the 'divorce' from Massey-Ferguson, this became the favourite strategy.

The first official mention of such a scheme came in Board Meeting notes dated 25 April 1958 when, in a broad-ranging discussion regarding new model policy, reference was made to a New Assembly Hall/Basement Store/Body Store, which would accommodate up to 160,000 cars/year. This appeared to make economic and industrial sense, so six months later approval for its construction was given, to an estimate of £2,002,510: building work began almost at once.

The new hall, with final finish lines to be located at one end of it all, was located to the south-west of a mass of long-established buildings, which had been expended to their very

Started in the late 1950s when Standard was flush with money, but completed in 1960/1961 when the company came close to bankruptcy, the new assembly hall at Canley – nicknamed 'the Rocket Range' – was the most modern on the site when British Leyland took over. This study dates from 1963, when the Spitfire and TR4 sports cars had been launched.

limit in the 1930s, 1940s and 1950s. Those older buildings (which eventually included the sideways assembly sequence which, one believes, was near-unique in the British motor industry) had always been cheek-by-jowl with the palatial top-management offices, which had once been the pride of Sir John Black's working environment. The new building would free up the old halls for other purposes (eventually they would be involved in trim shop work, KD (Knocked Down) operations and rectification work of various types) and would be extremely close to the platforms of Canley railway station.

Because it looked so modern compared with other buildings on the site, the new block soon took on a nickname – the 'Rocket Range' – and was all set to have a floor area of 200,000ft^2. The new block operated on three floors, was much more spacious than the old halls, had three parallel final assembly lines, and was 1000 feet long. Completion was originally forecast for October 1960 (a deadline which was apparently met), which, hindsight now tells us, was almost exactly when the company's finances fell off the cliff, and when demand for Triumph Heralds and TR3As in particular were in steep decline.

By the early 1960s, when the 'Rocket Range' assembly hall had been completed – it is at the absolute centre of this shot – the Canley complex was almost full. The A45 Coventry by-pass crosses from left to right at the top, with Fletchamstead South and (far right) Fletchamstead North (which were both 'shadow factories' when built in the late 1930s) facing the road.

Looming financial collapse

While all this expansion was going ahead, Standard's management acted as if they were in 'La-La' land, seemingly deaf to their own fast-developing sales trends. Although Standard production was rapidly on the increase at this time, and UK car sales, nationwide, were still expanding too, Standard-Triumph sales suffered badly in 1960. The fact is that although the Herald was kindly received by the media in general, the public rapidly turned against it, as its selling prices were too high (significantly higher than Ten/Pennant prices), while the product quality did not seem to be up to scratch. At the same time – and this must have been terrifying to the company's financial officers – from mid-1959 there was no longer any guaranteed profit, or positive cash flow, from making tractors.

The following inter-related stats tell their own story.

Year*	Standard-Triumph production	UK car sales (all marques)	UK exports (all marques)
1959	85,926	657,315	568,971
1960	138,762	820,088	569,889
1961	78,735	756,054	370,744

* Standard-Triumph figures are for financial year (September-August)

In 1960, a year which had started in so promising a manner, everything suddenly seemed to turn against the company. Not only had the Triumph Herald struggled to establish its reputation, but tractor business had disappeared, and both the Standard Vanguard and the Atlas van seemed to be dead in the water. The USA market turned sharply down, which immediately left Standard with a mountainous stock of unsold TR3As. The decision to postpone the Zebu project really came as a final straw.

In the meantime, Standard had acquired a large tract of land in Speke, a suburb of Liverpool, which was close to the main railway line and the recently purchased Hall Engineering body plant, but connected to neither. A major new body pressings and body assembly plant, covering 300,000ft^2, on a 104-acre site, was projected – this, incidentally, being as well as, not instead of, the new 'Rocket Range' building at Canley, which was still not completed. Alick Dick cut 'the first sod' in March 1960, boasting that Standard would be the first motor industry company to start to build on Merseyside, and that he was committing £11 million to the scheme. Yet within four months, the company's mounting losses could not be ignored, all work had to be suspended, and would not re-commence until 1966, which was well after the Standard brand had been killed off.

Way back in 1958, management had forecast an ability to produce and sell 160,000 cars a year, all of them to be assembled in the 'Rocket Range,' and before long 'Liverpool No 1' (Hall Engineering), Tile Hill (ex-Fisher and Ludlow) and Mulliners/Forward Radiator in Birmingham were all gearing up to make that feasible.

By 1959, sales forecasts were already outstripping capacity, with the notional figure of 222,300 being quoted for 1961/1962, and more when 'Zebu' got going. Retooling and relocation of the Herald bodyshell was being considered with Pressed Steel, and an 1147cc version of the SC engine was on the way. In May 1960, the company went so far as to buy a Cessna 310 light aircraft, for £32,000, to ease the rushing to and from Liverpool, which looked likely. That was one asset which Leyland soon acquired, for its own use, after the merger was finalised!

Then, suddenly it seemed, all the green financial signals turned to red, sales fell off the end of a cliff, and losses began to mount. The principal problem was that the Herald, which had been launched only a year earlier, was not selling well. Always seen as expensive (compared with its rivals at Ford and BMC), it was rapidly building a doubtful quality record, too.

This, and the fact that the four-cylinder Vanguard was almost dead in the water, didn't help. Production, overall, was cut – Mulliners, for instance, chopped the building of TR3A shells to 200 a week in August, then to a mere 100 a week in October – and in parts of the empire, the workforce was put on a three-day week. Amazingly, though, it was time to announce post-tax profits for 1959/1960 – at £1,825,564 – but such profits had all been earned before mid-year.

By November 1960, Standard's financial position was becoming critical. Even though capital programmes were being cancelled at every turn, the company was now losing money at the rate of £600,000 every month. If a saviour could not be found, in short order, the company would have to call in the Receiver early in 1961.

Leyland Motors – 'White Knight' or predator?

Suddenly, and in the very nick of time, Standard received an offer from Leyland Motors, the prestigious Lancashire-based truck maker. Lord Tedder had retired from the chairmanship in November 1960 (he was 70 years old), Alick Dick had taken over from him – and within days Leyland swooped with a straight takeover offer.

Other historians have described what followed as a 'whirlwind courtship,' for certainly things moved ahead at a startling rate. By the end of November 1960 the two companies had agreed on terms – Leyland would offer two of its shares for fifteen Standard shares – and within a week the deal was announced in the Stock Exchange.

Although Leyland made no significant management changes at first, it was only after its finance team began to pore over the current position, and the immediate forecasts for 1961, the Standard's true financial crisis became clear. By January 1961 Alick Dick had to admit that his company might lose up to £3 million in the current financial year, the company's overdraft was £7 million, and more than 30,000 unsold vehicles were now in stock.

For Leyland, however, it was already too late to pull out. So what might it have to do, to restore Standard to its former glory?

One new, one middle-aged – Standard's new Herald-based Courier van poses alongside the updated Standard 7cwt van in 1962.

CHAPTER 12

LEYLAND TAKES OVER – THE FINAL YEARS

During the winter of 1960/1961, Standard had been extremely close to bankruptcy, with cash pouring out of the business at an alarming rate, but no sooner had Leyland made a successful takeover bid than things began to improve. It was not that the finances improved suddenly – they did not – but that the marketplace's perception of the company's likelihood of survival was transformed. Not that it was going to be easy, for Leyland was brutal in its assessment of Standard's commercial problems in 1961.

No sooner had Leyland taken control than the surgery began. General Manager Martin Tustin was immediately shipped out – to run the North American importing company, which he did until 1963, after which he resigned, and leaves our story. During the spring, Leyland's Sir Henry Spurrier became Chairman (thus demoting Alick Dick after a mere six months), while three Leyland executives – Donald Stokes, Stanley Markland and Sydney Baybutt – all joined the board. Within months, Standard followers knew that Markland was the typical north-country manager/engineer, Stokes the razor-sharp marketing man/salesman, and Baybutt a finance specialist.

Although Sir Henry reputedly read the riot act at his first Board meeting, demanding more economies, and a search for better product quality, in July he also approved a go-ahead to the Triumph Spitfire sports car project (which would be an enormous success in later years). It was agreed with Stanley Markland that the 'Barb' project (a six-cylinder car which effectively replaced the 'Zebu' project) should go ahead. Sir Henry also seemed to like what he saw in the potential of the vast Liverpool No 2 factory project, but briskly killed off the motorsport programme, and cancelled Standard's own 'Zero' tractor project.

Although Leyland had originally given Alick Dick free rein to spearhead the turn-around, its patience snapped at the beginning of September. Dick was abruptly and publicly fired, at which point Sir Henry Spurrier made this statement to the media:

"It was expected that conditions in the car industry would improve rapidly in the spring of 1961, and that Standard-Triumph International would have been operating at a substantial profit during that period. Unfortunately, losses continued to be made during those months, and it became clear to me and my colleagues of the Leyland board that it was essential to bring in drastic economies without delay, in order to meet effectively the intense competition now prevalent in the car industry throughout the world.

"The Leyland board, recognising its responsibility to Leyland shareholders, felt that this far-reaching exercise at

Leyland's Stanley Markland (left) receiving a trophy from a motor executive following Standard-Triumph's fine showing in the Le Mans 24 Hour race in 1961.

Stanley Markland

When Leyland Motors took control of Standard in the spring of 1961, it made haste to reinforce executive management with its own nominees. Three new directors from Leyland were appointed – Stanley Markland, Donald Stokes and Sidney Baybutt. Months later, when Alick Dick was abruptly fired, Stanley Markland became Standard-Triumph's managing director.

Markland was a bluff Lancastrian, had been born in 1904, and was a plain-speaking but extremely effective manager. After joining Leyland as an apprentice immediately after the First World War, by the 1950s he had become Leyland Motors's chief engineer, then the works director at the main factory close to Preston, but by the time of the take over he was also deputy managing director (deputy, that is, to Stanley Markland ...) of the Leyland Motors group, and managing director Albion, the Glasgow-based truck-making subsidiary.

Described as 'A Leyland man through and through ...' by his admirers (of whom there were many), and noted for his ferocious personal workload, along with his new Sales Chief, Donald Stokes, he set about turning round Standard-Triumph's fortunes. By 1962 the company was on the up, and by 1963 it was positively booming.

During that year, however, Markland and Sir Henry Spurrier quarrelled about the succession to the chairmanship of the parent company. At the end of the year, and after he had been passed over in favour of Sir William Black, he resigned from the company, and was not connected with any other industrial enterprise. He was only 59 years old, and many thought he was still at the height of his business powers.

Donald Stokes (later Lord Stokes)

Although Donald Stokes and Standard were only briefly connected – in fact from 1961 to 1963 – Stokes was very much the power behind the throne (on which Stanley Markland sat) in that period. It was Stokes who set about the whirlwind expansion involving Leyland, Standard, Triumph, Alvis and Rover, before the entire Leyland conglomerate moved aggressively into what was euphemistically called a 'merger' with BMC and Jaguar, to form the ill-fated British Leyland.

Donald Stokes joined Leyland Motors, the Lancashire-based truck manufacturer, as an apprentice in 1930, became an officer (eventually a Lieutenant-Colonel) in the Army during World War Two, became a successful salesman at Leyland Motors in postwar years, and joined Leyland's board of directors in 1953.

When Leyland rescued Standard from bankruptcy in 1961, Stanley Markland (see panel left) was drafted in as managing director, while Stokes also became a director of the revived company. During 1963 he became managing director of the entire Leyland Group then, from 1 January 1964 (just after the 'Standard' name had disappeared from private cars in the UK) he became chairman of Standard-Triumph.

Thereafter (and this post-dates a close connection with Standard) his rise was yet more meteoric, for he was knighted in 1965, became managing director (shortly chairman) of British Leyland in 1968, and was finally ennobled as Lord Stokes of Leyland in 1969. However, following the financial collapse of British Leyland in 1975, in the aftermath he was unceremoniously 'kicked upstairs' to become the nationalised company's non-executive president, but finally left the company in 1977.

In later years he had links with several concerns, notably a leading PR agency, retired to Sandbanks in Dorset, and died (at 94 years of age) in 2008.

STI should be borne entirely by the top Leyland executive, and that they should have a clear field in which to put their plans into practical effect.

"This requirement was discussed with, and made clear to, all members of the original STI board, who readily appreciated Leyland's point of view, and subsequently tendered their resignations, as has been reported.

"Mr Stanley Markland, Deputy Managing Director Leyland Motors Ltd, now appointed Managing Director STI, will introduce immediate measures designed to effect substantial economies in all overhead expenditure, and generally to run the organisation on lines similar to that of the parent company ..."

All except two of the existing Board (Frank Dixon and LA Woodall) were fired at the same time as Dick; Stanley Markland became a dictator without such a title. Frank

The new regime takes over after Leyland Motors rescued Standard from financial disaster in 1961. Managing Director Stanley Markland is at the wheel of this 1962 model Triumph Vitesse, while Harry Webster stands outside the car.

Dixon soon exited through the revolving door, followed by a whole host of senior managers, and it was not until May 1962 that Harry Webster and George Turnbull became full Board directors.

Although 1962 saw a remarkable turn-around in Standard's financial fortunes, much of the credit for that goes to the previous management. Not only had the new Michelotti-styled TR4 and Spitfire sports cars become instant favourites, and the Herald-based Vitesse soon made its mark, but the Herald 1200 transformed the fortunes of Standard-Triumph's 'mass market.' It was all very well (and partly true) that Leyland had underpinned the recovery, but all the models mentioned had already been conceived, and almost brought to market, by Alick Dick's Standard team.

In April 1962, a cut in British Purchase Tax offered a great boost to the market place, Herald sales leapt as a consequence, and the company was back in profit by the middle of the year.

Vanguard and Ensign – not a bang, but a whimper

Unhappily, the Good News was mostly 'Triumph'-inspired, for the long-running Vanguard was dying on its feet. In spite of its fine new engine, very few Vanguard Sixes were being sold, such that Pressed Steel pointed out it wished to withdraw from bodyshell supply, as it was becoming increasingly uneconomic to it. 16,000 of the sanction remained in October 1961, but Leyland were already looking for ways to reduce this.

In the early days, Leyland was so desperate to do anything – anything – to keep the Vanguard alive, that it asked for a Herald 1200-engined prototype to be built [the author knows this to be true, because he was working in the experimental department at the time and saw the dismal result].

Is it a boat? Is it a car? Actually it's both – or either – for the German Amphicar of the early 1960s used a mid-mounted SC engine of 1147cc, and was a true amphibian.

Don't panic, don't panic – the damage inflicted on this Ensign Estate in the 1960s was intentional – by MIRA in the course of testing motorway restraint barriers. Only a partial success, we reckon ...

This project was abandoned almost as soon as it had been suggested, but a much more viable alternative – of a revived and improved Ensign – took over instead. The Vanguard Six itself faded away in the winter of 1962/1963, which meant that in Britain at least, the very last new Standard model was to the Ensign De Luxe, a car designed with an eye to filling a gap in the price lists, and one for which some fleet business might be expected. It was a new project on which very little time needed to be spent – nor was it. As an observer in the engineering and development workshops, I can confirm that one single prototype car was built in 1961, briefly tested, pronounced viable, then almost immediately set aside to make way for more exciting work on cars like the new Triumph Spitfire and 2000 projects instead!

Think of the original Ensign (which had been abandoned in mid-1961), insert a 2138cc version of the famous 'wet-liner' engine, and the balance of the specification almost wrote itself. Four door saloon and estate car styles were on offer – these looking exactly like the previous Ensign – while the engine was effectively a detuned/single-carburettor version of that now standardised on the Triumph TR4 sports car, and was rated at 75bhp at 4100rpm.

The rest was wall-to-wall conventional. A four-speed gearbox was standard (though without synchromesh on first gear), and the old-type three-speed box was promised for some export territories: there was a central gear change, and Laycock overdrive was optional. Drum brakes were fitted all round, but disc brakes were optional. The cabin and fascia/instrument panel were simply trimmed, for this was not a car meant to compete with the Vanguard Six in any way.

Because the latest engine was 25 per cent more powerful than that of the original Ensign, the performance was enhanced, too – with independent road tests showing a top speed of 91mph, matched by overall fuel consumption of about 25mpg. Even so, this was never a Standard which was meant to stir up any emotion – the 'Triumph' badged machinery, from the same stable, did that job now – but it filled a useful gap while the next all-new 'Standard' – in fact it would be the new Triumph 2000 – was being developed.

Unhappily, as more and more glamorous new Triumphs appeared – Herald 1200 in 1961, Vitesse in the summer of 1962, and the cute little Spitfire later in 1962 – the Standard name began to drop out of the limelight. This was the rather feeble line-up of Standard private cars, which were still listed at the end of 1962:

Ensign De Luxe saloon	£745
Ensign De Luxe estate	£890
Vanguard Luxury Six saloon	£871
Vanguard Luxury Six estate	£967

By that time the writing was already on the wall – written in large letters – for the Standard brand. Triumph, backed with great enthusiasm, by the new owners, Leyland, was now certainly the glamorous marque in the stable, for the Triumph Herald 1200 family cars, the sporty Vitesses and TR4 sports cars, had just been joined by the jaunty little Spitfire sports car, too.

At Canley at least, the end then came quietly, with very little ceremony. In May 1963, the very last British-built Standard-badged private car – an Ensign De Luxe saloon (registered 2757 KV and retained on the company's own transport fleet for a time) – was produced. From then on, 'Triumph' took over completely.

Even so, for a few years after the very last Standard-badged car was built in the UK, there was residual involvement, and complication. On the one hand, although Standard private cars were no longer being produced, Standard Fifteen and Standard Twenty commercial vehicles (derivatives of the Atlas Major) carried on for a time, for Leyland were self-appointed experts in the CV (commercial vehicle) field, and were convinced that it could make good money out of this stocky machine, even though it had not designed it itself. As it happens, it was wrong – for this design never lived down its initial reputation for being under-powered, when it had used the Standard Ten/Triumph Herald engine.

After 1963, all the new British cars would be called Triumphs (though there would be Standards in India until the late 1980s), but spare parts would continue to be 'Stanpart.' In Coventry, the Canley and Radford factories became busier than ever (they survived through the British Leyland era, into the Rover Group period, and took on even more tasks), and were always affectionately known, locally and especially by its workforce, as 'the Standard.' However, although Leyland Motors now owned the business it seemed to be content to see the famous old name fade away.

Confused? Surprisingly enough, the workforce never seemed to have problems – I know this because I was a salaried employee of Standard-Triumph (or should I call it Leyland?) at that time – and certainly the motoring media soon settled happily on the use of the 'Triumph' brand instead. The problem – if ever there really was a problem – came from the old Standard diehards themselves.

So, what happened next? With Donald Stokes taking over as chairman of Standard-Triumph International Ltd at the end of 1963, the emphasis was soon heavily loaded on to two brands – Triumph, and Leyland itself. As already noted, because they were self-appointed experts in that motor industry market sector (though it had little experience to back that up), Leyland even dabbled with the idea of identifying several of its newly acquired products with its own corporate badge, and would become even more serious about that in the 1970s. In the end, this was never done on the cars, but it was certainly done on the one-time Standard Atlas Majors and their developments.

First of all, these became Standard Fifteen, and Standard Twenty models, but then, from the mid-1960s, they became Leyland Twenty types, with larger diesel engines and bigger payloads. UK assembly of these CVs ended soon after the formation of British Leyland in 1968, after which assembly of this design was transferred to India, where it carried on into the 1970s.

Even so, the Standard story was not yet over, neither in the UK nor overseas, for Leyland cherished a long-time intention to preserve the 'Standard' name on commercial vehicles. Behind closed doors, and in the proud and fertile minds of the paymasters at Leyland Motors, new projects would come and go throughout the 1960s. Not only the Atlas-based vans, but also the Standard Ten-based light commercial vehicles carried on into the mid-1960s.

Fortunately we have a fascinating record, provided from David Eley's reminiscences during his retirement. While other Standard engineers were playing happily around with Triumph Spitfires, 2000s, Spitfires, TR4As and Le Mans Spitfires in the early 1960s, David Eley actually found himself specialising in Leyland-inspired commercial vehicle projects:

"Once Stanley Markland of Leyland became managing director of Standard, he was interested in revitalising the Standard commercial vehicles, and needed someone to do that – so they picked on me ..."

By 1965 Standard had ceased making Standard-badged cars in the UK, and was concentrating on the Triumph brand instead. This was the still-born Triumph 'Fury' sports car project of 1965.

David's first task was to upgrade the Atlas Major van into the Leyland 15cwt van, and later the Leyland 20/1-ton van, with a choice of 2138cc petrol or the Ferguson-tractor-derived OE138 diesel engines, a four-speed Vanguard gearbox and a Vanguard rear axle. After that there was the Leyland 2-tonner, which was eventually built at the Tile Hill satellite factory:

"I wore a groove between Coventry and Leyland, pre-M6," David told the author, "working on that one! This machine featured a new Leyland-designed chassis, the basics of a Leyland 1-ton front-end, and the high-speed diesel engine [It all depends on what one means by 'High Speed,' of course]. The rest of the running gear was real 'bitsa' – with a Commer/Karrier gearbox, a BMC truck axle, and a front axle which Alford and Alder (a Standard-Triumph subsidiary) already had available."

Even though the diesel engine was enlarged to 87.74 x 107.25mm, 2611cc (thus becoming the OE160) – that was absolutely at the limit of that engine's capacity, yet the 2-tonner was still widely seen as under-powered. Even so, when re-launched as the 'Leyland 90,' for a time it was a commercial success.

Later – and what a pity this project was still-born – Eley also led a team which designed a radical 'walk-through' truck chassis for delivery vehicles, in which the Standard diesel engine, with automatic transmission, was mounted to one side of the frame, and placed on its side. As an engineer, David found this fascinating, but Leyland's marketing people eventually cancelled the idea.

Pony

One of weirdest Standard products, which never went on the market in the UK, was occasionally seen around the Canley factory complex in the 1960s, where a prototype, with a flat-bed truck back end was used for all manner of fetch-and-carry duties for years. As happened to often in the British motor industry, it was a machine which started life fulfilling one rather nebulous requirement, and ended up satisfying another! It is interesting to recall that if the front-wheel drive Triumph 1300 had not existed, then the 'Pony' would not have been developed.

"Leyland had a retired general on their marketing staff"- David Eley once told the author, "who in the early 1960s advised that the British Army's Parachute Regiment needed a small, narrow, forward-control 4x4 to fit into their aircraft. We built a prototype with a 5 or 6 cwt payload. It had a straightforward box-section chassis frame (everybody knew how to do chassis frames, but it was Ernie Jones who did that one ...), with half-elliptic springs. Because there was a differential in the sump, we had to design a crescent-shaped front axle beam around the front of the engine, to give clearance.

"Starting from the front-wheel drive Triumph 1300 engine/transmission, we added a two/four-wheel-drive transfer gearbox, but there was no centre differential, and there was a beam rear axle. The Paras tested it at Aldershot, where it performed well. Then, of course, wider-bodied aircraft like the Hercules came along, so the need for such a narrow vehicle (to fit old-type aircraft) disappeared.

"But all was not lost. We were already selling engines and transmissions to Autocars of Israel – and they were very keen to have a small, but normal-width 4x4 with a pick-up body for use in all the kibbutz settlements. Accordingly, we designed a new, normal-width chassis, sent the result out to Israel – but Autocars eventually went bankrupt and the project died out."

A few 'Pony' machines, they say, are still to be found in Israel.

The fate of Standard's historic factories

Banner Lane, of course, had dropped off Standard's radar abruptly in 1959, but the other major factories in Coventry – the Canley complex, and the Radford factory a few miles away (it was next door, of course, to the Daimler workshops, which were owned by Jaguar from 1960) continued to operate at full blast.

Once Leyland sank its teeth into the Standard-Triumph business, which gradually recovered stability, built more and more Triumph-badged cars, and became increasingly profitable, the old Standard factories remained immensely useful to Leyland. When the last UK-produced Standard-based car had been assembled in Coventry, this was the situation after 1963:

Canley. Continued as the Coventry HQ of the Triumph brand. Many new Triumph models would be announced in the next fifteen years. Design and development of new cars would continue, under different corporate names, at Canley until the mid-1990s.

Radford. Continued as an important factory complex building engines and transmissions for all Triumph (and, later, some British Leyland) models.

The operation finally closed down in the late '80s.

Allesley. Still very active as the factory-linked Service department, it eventually became redundant and was sold off.

In the meantime, of course, all contact had been lost with Banner Lane, and would never be re-established.

Standard – the name lingered on, but where?

The neat way to end this nostalgic story is to summarise what happened to the business in the years, which followed the building of the final cars in the UK.

Although the Standard branding disappeared completely after 1963, the Triumph brand that it had rescued in 1944 went from strength to strength. To confirm this, it is really only necessary to note the launch of the Triumph 2000 in 1963 (in many ways this was a lineal descendant of the last Vanguard), the front-wheel drive 1300 saloon in 1965, the GT6 sports coupé in 1966, and the original fuel-injected TR5 sports car in 1967. Then, already in the wings, there was a new family of overhead camshaft engines being developed, along with the very smart Stag drophead coupé.

From 1963 to the end of the century, however, it was the corporate developments, which were so complex and (ultimately) unsuccessful. First of all, Leyland Motors absorbed Rover (which had already bought Alvis) in 1967, then in January 1968 came the greatest (and most misguided) merger of all – the formation of British Leyland.

Although the basis of this was that the Leyland Group merged with British Motor Holdings (BMC-plus-Jaguar), the detail of the number of existing and near-moribund brands involved at that time was staggering. First of all, I should list those cars still on the market:

Austin
Austin-Healey
Daimler
Jaguar
Land-Rover
MG
Morris
Princess
Riley
Rover
Triumph
Wolseley
- along with these trucks:
AEC
Albion
BMC
Leyland
Scammell
– and those brands of cars quite recently closed down, but still trading in one way or another:
Alvis
Lanchester
Standard
Vanden Plas

Indian Standards

As already noted, even in the early days, Standard had been attracted to the commercial promise of the Indian continent. Standard cars dominated the transport facilities laid on for the Durbar Coronation ceremonies at the end of 1911 – which must, one supposes, have made companies like Daimler and Rolls-Royce very jealous.
The company, however, did not have the financial resources to build on this short-lived success, and no attempt was made to set up shop overseas until after the Second World War. Then, as I have already made clear, Britain's postwar financial plight made the idea of exporting cars in big numbers quite compulsory, and setting up local assembly operations (using parts supplied from Coventry) began to look attractive.

One day, no doubt, there is a complete book to be written about Standard's overseas enterprises, not only concerning cars, but commercial vehicles, but at this point I need only point out that cars like the Vanguard were built in Belgium (including a unique-to-that-country Vanguard convertible), Australia and Switzerland, Standard Tens were assembled in a variety of territories including Norway, South Africa, Southern Rhodesia, Australia, New Zealand, Brazil, Colombia and Peru, Ferguson tractors and diesel engines were made in France, while Vanguards, Tens and Pennants were all produced in India.

Before long there was a thriving CKD (Completely Knocked Down) department at Canley, where near-complete kits of cars, ready for assembly, were packed into huge wooden crates, for transportation to the far-flung assembly plants, where local assembly was usually confined to trim features. As 'Triumph' came more and more to prominence in the UK, so did the proportion of Triumphs sent overseas, which explains why, for instance, a limited number of TR sports cars were originally built in Australia, and in South Africa.

An afterlife in India

It was in India that the last flourish of cars carrying the Standard badge took place. Standard had set up the Standard Motor Products of India Ltd in 1949, this rapidly become one of the most important 'satellites' in the Standard empire. Stampro, as it was usually known, was equipped with a new assembly plant set up in Madras (the name has now been changed to Chennai) in south-east India. In the beginning, Vanguard kits were assembled for sale in India, and by the mid-1950s the Standard Ten had joined the Vanguard. Distributors all over the continent helped make Standard a well-known, and well-liked, British marque.

Early in the 1960s, the Standard Ten model died away, and was replaced in India by assembly of the Triumph Herald (the very smart two-door passenger car styled by Giovanni Michelotti, and which had gone on sale in the UK in mid-1959), though for persuasive marketing reasons it was inevitably rebadged as a Standard Herald and (retrospectively, at least known as the MkI. For the next two decades there would be a locally-assembled car whose inspiration (and mechanical basis) was the Triumph Herald), though it was always, but always, badged as a Standard.

[This rebadging process, of course, was neither unknown, nor difficult to carry out. As the author has already noted, there were territories where the Standard Ten was rebadged as a Triumph Ten, which has confused traditionalists ever since. Conspiracy theories abound, but all can be demolished by the simple process of noting that marketing imperatives were often considered more important than historic niceties.]

Maybe this looks familiar, like the Standard Pennant from which it was evolved, but in the 1960s this particular car was built in India, and badged as a Standard Ten.

As built in India, under Leyland control in the 1960s, the Standard Herald Companion was a unique blend of styling and naming. Much of the car was based on the Triumph Herald estate, but the four-passenger door layout, and the special tailgate, made it very different in detail.

Almost at once, however, the local Indian management, led by Mr K Gopalkrishna, requested major changes to the 'Standard' Herald, to make it more socially acceptable for the Indian market. No doubt if Sir John Black had still been in charge, he would have to tried to ride, roughshod, over the objections, but the later management (which included Donald Stokes and Technical Director Harry Webster) was more open to change.

The problem, Mr Gopalkrishna told him, was one of social status. In India, he insisted, it was not viable to sell as many two-door cars as he would like. Social mores made it clear that at this point in history, men had social superiority over women, and only they would be allowed to ride in the front seats of the car. On the other hand, an Indian woman in a sari might find it very difficult to clamber into the back seat of a 'Standard' Herald. In any case, it was often the case that the driver would be of a different (ie lower) caste than the owner, who would therefore refuse to use the same door as his chauffeur.

Astonishing? Ludicrous? Politically incorrect? Today, in the 21st century it certainly looks like that, but in 1960s India it was normal practice. Fortunately for all concerned, Standard-Triumph had already built a four-door saloon prototype version of the Herald, kept in the Experimental Department back at Canley, which might just be the answer to this conundrum.

The British-built prototype – there was only one car – carried the prototype number X696, and was first registered as 5099 HP in 1960-1961. Although it was never a cherished and loved one-off – certainly the car never seemed to be in mint-condition – it demonstrated just how easily the Herald's 'modular' construction could be adapted to a new purpose. X696 ran on the standard wheelbase, of the same length as that of other Heralds, and had all the usual features – 948cc engine, four-speed gearbox, rack-and-pinion steering, and all-independent rear suspension. The style of the four-door shell was much like that of the two-door, identical at the front, and with the same windscreen, and had the same rear end – the only major differences being the provision of four passenger doors and a more angular roof panel.

Although originally designed by Standard on the base of a Triumph Herald, the Indian-built Gazel was a Standard, not a Triumph, had a unique nose, four passenger doors, and a different rear-end shape.

Eventually, and after some delay, a deal was done. In 1967, when a revised Herald range was introduced back in the UK, this included the new 13/60, which had a revised bonnet style, including Vitesse pressings, but with only two headlamps. In India, the MkII was still a two-door car, but the MkIII had the four-door saloon shell, and from 1969 a four-door estate car, called the Companion, was also added.

After the Herald was dropped in Britain, all the tooling was sold to Stampro, and shipped to India. Shortly after, the car was comprehensively re-engineered, given a new chassis frame with a Triumph Toledo type of beam rear axle, and became the Standard Gazel. This was the point at which the rear end was restyled, the sharp-edged 'Michelotti' type fins were discarded, and a much plainer shape was adopted instead. This was the car that remained in production, in Madras, until 1982, only dropping out of the market when supplies of the dear old SC engine were no longer available from Coventry, where cars using that engine had not been built since 1980.

Many thousands – many tens of thousands, indeed – were undoubtedly made, but unfortunately detailed production figures are no longer available.

Standard Motors became independent of British financial capital in 1973. After the Gazel finally died off in 1977, the Standard 20 van, developed to an enormous degree from the original Atlas Major, which had become the Leyland 20 variety in the UK, but much changed to suit Indian conditions and market standards, carried on into the 1980s. It was during this time when Austin-Rover (the descendant of Leyland, then of British Leyland) startled the world by announcing that it would begin assembly of much-modified Rover SD1 hatchbacks, which would be badged as Standards.

The last Standard of all – really a Rover

Difficult to believe, right? The very last Standard-badged car, which was built in India, was a derivative of the Rover SD1 [SD = Specialist Division, a British Leyland title] , which had originally been designed and developed in Solihull in the 1970s. However, when I point out that the original Rover SD1 was partly engineered at Standard-Triumph (Spen King was technical director of the Rover-Triumph company at the time, for it had come into existence in 1972, to merge Rover and Standard interests), and that the original car's five-speed transmission was conceived at Canley, the complexities of this story (and, indeed, those of British Leyland), become yet more obvious.

The first of the Rover SD1s, the 3500, complete with V8 engine, went on sale, and in the next few years was also built with six-cylinder, four-cylinder petrol and finally with a four-speed diesel engine. However, it was not until 1983 that British Leyland began discussing the possibility of making modified Rovers in India, and badging them as Standards.

The Indian Standard 2000 of the mid-1980s was not quite mythical, but extremely scarce. Almost none survive to this day, this being a rare example. Except for the badging, there was virtually no visual difference between the last of the UK-built Rover SD1s, and the Indian assembled Standard 2000.

First thoughts were that SD1-type shells would be supplied in kit-form from the UK, and would be powered by Standard-derived 2.5-litre diesel engines (as already being used in Indian-built Leyland Twenty vans), but before assembly began in 1985, that option had been abandoned in favour of a Vanguard-derived 'wet-liner' power unit. For this application alone, it was mated to a special, Indian-built, four-speed transmission. In the beginning, the deal was that 12,000 body sets would be provided from the UK, and Stampro installed facilities at Chennai which enabled it to make up to 16 cars a day/4,000 cars a year.

The new car, badged as a Standard 2000, was sold only in India, and looked identical with the UK-built SD1 2000 type, but had a much-modified 1991cc engine, twin-SU carburettors and produced 85bhp. Compared with the old Vanguard engine, the Indian-modified unit had a 'Heron head' piston/head layout, with virtually a flat-faced head, and with combustion chambers in the top of the pistons.

Although this was a very brisk car by contemporary Indian standards, it was also one of the most expensive cars on the market (£12,000 at 1985/1986 currency levels), and sold only slowly. Although Stampro took over the body tooling after the UK-produced SD1 came to the end of its career in mid-1986, this car was not a long-term success: high fuel consumption and high prices were both issues. Production ended in 1987, the Standard 2000 died, as did the Standard badge, sadly this time for good.

The Standard story, therefore, was now complete, and the marque disappeared quietly, and without ceremony. Although the 'Standard' trade mark was then owned by the Rover Group, that concern had far too many troubles of its own to mark, or recall, the passing of a once-world-famous make of car. No British Standard, after all, had been produced for more than twenty years, and there seemed to be no chance that it would ever be revived.

When the last UK-manufactured Standard had been built in 1963, there were suitable nostalgic features in the regional and specialist motoring press, but when Indian manufacture ended, there was nothing. All that remained was for enthusiasts' organisations like the Standard Motor Club, the Standard Register, and a variety of thriving Triumph one-make clubs to keep the flame burning, which they have most successfully managed to this day.

These days, virtually no physical reminder of Standard's once dominant presence in Coventry remains – except at two locations. One is the magnificently placed, and maintained, Standard-Triumph Memorial, which the one-make clubs financed, and had erected, close to the Standard Social Club in 2000, and the other is a modest little plaque screwed to the wall of Coventry's Court building in Much Park Street, which proudly states:

"The Standard Motor Company was founded on this site in March 1903 by Reginald Maudslay ..."

Appendix A

Standard and SS – an important commercial link

Although Standard never took a major shareholding in Swallow Coachbuilding (the original owners of the SS brand), or in Jaguar (the company which replaced it in 1945), the two companies had close commercial links stretching from 1929 to 1948. In the first place, SS re-bodied the Standard chassis, then Standard supplied engines and complete rolling chassis to SS. Finally, it was Standard engines which kept some Jaguars going until 1948.

The two companies seem to have linked up immediately after Captain John Black arrived on the scene at Canley, so from 1929 onwards Black, and SS's founder William Lyons, built up a strong, if turbulent, relationship. Both were thrusting, determined and sometimes abrasive businessmen, but somehow they managed to found, maintain and preserve a relationship for almost twenty years. Although there was more than one occasion when a conflagration, and a commercial 'divorce' looked inevitable, the two stayed in contact throughout that time.

For William Lyons, it all began in Blackpool in September 1922, when he became a partner (with William Walmsley) in the Swallow Sidecar Company. Lyons, the stylist, soon progressed from shaping smart motorcycle sidecars to producing complete motor car bodyshells, the first of these being for the Austin Seven Swallow of 1927. Before long, demand for these innocuous, but pretty, little cars exceeded the factory space which SS had in Blackpool, so a move to the Whitmore Park estate, off Holbrooks Lane in Coventry, was completed in 1928.

One year later, the first Swallow-bodied Standard Big Nine was unveiled – Standard supplied the rolling chassis from Canley, with SS completing the job in the Whitmore Park estate – and the Swallow-bodied Standard Ensign 16 followed in 1931, priced at £275.

What followed, artistically at least, was inevitable. William Lyons, who had an unerring eye for a good line, realised that no matter how good his Swallow styles actually were, that it would always be constrained by the chassis on which it had to live. Those chassis were often too high off the ground, and their tracks too narrow, for an ideal basis. Something, he thought, would have to done.

Accordingly, in 1930, Mr Lyons set up a several-faceted programme – one being to commission the manufacture of a special, low-slung, long-wheelbase chassis frame from Rubery Owen in the West Midlands, while a related move was to approach Standard, to see if it would be willing to supply engines, four-speed transmissions, brakes, suspension, wheels and steering to equip this chassis, and to build up the rolling chassis, too. The third facet was to invent a new brand under which the cars would sell – SS.

This Swallow-bodied Standard was the first car to be produced by William Lyons' Swallow Sidecar concern, even before the SS brand was invented.

The choice of Standard's latest six-cylinder engines and running gear was a logical one – for the entire industry now recognised that this seven-bearing power unit was one of the smoothest and most reliable on the market. Not only that, but Mr Lyons knew that Capt Black was intent on expanding Standard's operations – and that the two companies were only a few miles away from each other, in different suburbs of Coventry. Even so, it took John Black and William Lyons some time to agree on the details of their deal– both were looking for the most profit, and the most prestige from this project – but by the spring of 1931 the arrangements were finalised.

As John Black laid out, in a letter to Mr Lyons:

"Following Mr Lyons's interview with the writer this morning, we are writing to confirm the points discussed, in order that any doubts and misunderstanding may be dismissed from our minds. The arrangement for the 1932 season is as follows:

"1. We agree to supply you with chassis of current production types, at net prices recently quoted to you.

"2. We agree to supply you with special six-cylinder chassis to suit special-body requirements.

"3. The chassis referred to under number 2 above, will be reserved exclusively for you."

Perhaps the commercially most important facet of the deal was that Standard also arranged for SS cars to be sold throughout its

William Lyons might have styled this SSII for production at his SS factory, but the early 1930s SSII was powered by a reliable, though unexciting side-valve Standard engine, and its associated chassis equipment.

Under the terms struck between Standard's John Black, and SS's William Lyons, Standard would assemble complete rolling chassis for SS, using a specially designed low chassis, which could not be fitted to any Standard model. Although every mechanical item in this SS Airline 20hp model was from Standard, the body style was pure SS.

dealer chain, which effectively gave William Lyons his first major distribution network without having to spend a fortune setting it up in the first place. One might say, in truth, that Mr Lyons never looked back after this.

In a later letter, also preserved in the Jaguar archive, we know that SS agreed to take 500 chassis up until the end of the Model Year (31 August 1932) at a price of £130 each, and that a different model – the chassis for what would become the SSII (which originally used no more, and no less, than an unmodified Standard Little Nine rolling chassis) would cost just £82. As it happens, SS had no difficulty in selling as many cars as it could build, for company records show that no fewer than 776 SS-badged machines were produced in that original Model Year.

As agreed, the new chassis, by Rubery Owen, was never used under a Standard, though all the running gear from current six-cylinder Standards was fitted to it, and assembled at Canley. No matter how much John Black fancied the idea of marketing a 'Standard' around that chassis, the agreement meant that he could not. He did, on the other hand, hold all the aces regarding the running gear, for at this time SS still had no machine shop of its own.

The original car was known as the SSI and was launched just before the Olympia Motor Show of October 1931.

It was available with a choice of 45bhp/2054cc, or 55bhp/2552cc Standard six-cylinder engines, which were currently used in the Standard Sixteen and Twenty models. Those power outputs, incidentally, were always as quoted by SS, who later became known for 'massaging' all such figures a little higher than the facts would support.

As launched in October 1931, the chassis itself had a wheelbase of 9ft 4in, and was allied to front and rear wheel tracks of 4ft 1in (purely for comparison, that of the equivalent Standard Sixteen was 9ft 1in/4ft0in), and the top speed of the complete car was about 70mph. The chassis was, of course, totally different from anything used by Standard, and much more low-slung. Because of this, and because of the exaggeratedly long and low lines of the first SS1 coupé, its roof was no less than 13 inches lower. This chassis, in fact, would be replaced by another SS-Jaguar designed item in 1935.

As far as production, in series, was concerned, Standard allocated special facilities at Canley. They took delivery of the new chassis frames from Rubery Owen (of Darlaston, north west of Birmingham, near Walsall), fitted them out with the complete

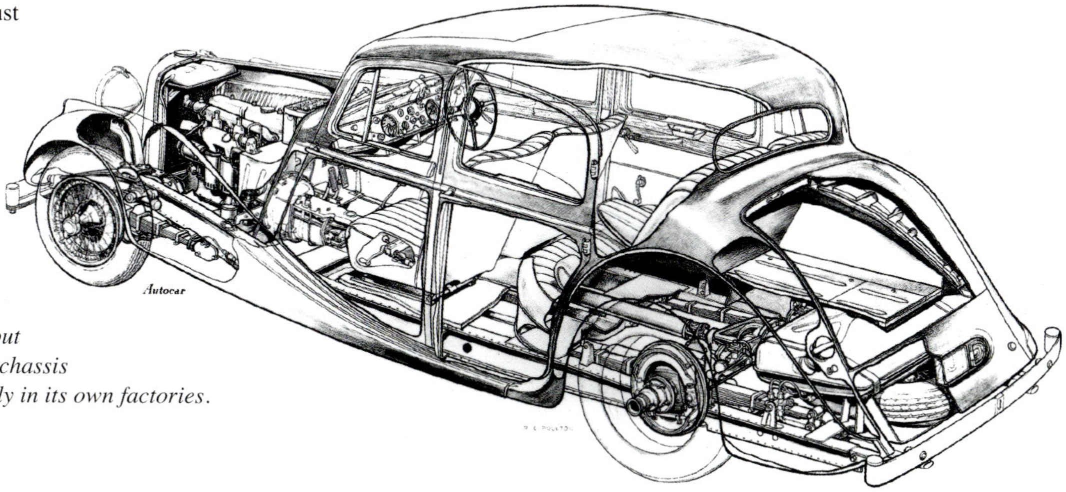

By the late 1930s, Standard still supplied engines and many chassis components to SS, for models like this 2½-litre model, but SS undertook its own chassis assembly in its own factories.

SS's 'Airline' saloon of the mid-1930s was a very smart car, complete with a Standard-built rolling chassis, including the side-valve six-cylinder engine and related gearbox.

Standard Sixteen/Twenty running gear, then delivered these, by truck to the SS factory in Whitmore Park, just a few miles away across the city, as complete running units, ready to have bodyshells fitted.

[Which brings me to the matter of the title – SS. What did it mean, was it Swallow Sidecars, Swallow Special, Standard-Swallow or Swallow-Standard? No-one, not even Mr Lyons himself, ever spelt out the implications – so let us just leave it at that.]

Details of how this far-reaching arrangement which Standard set up with SS have already been published, in great detail, in Jaguar marque histories. At this point, suffice it to say that the SS1 gradually evolved in the next four years, using enlarged engines of 2143cc and 2664cc (in both cases, when the corporate Standard six-cylinder engine was given a lengthened stroke of 106mm), while later SSIIs were built in 1343cc and 1608cc guise, too.

At the same time as the crank throw was increased to 106mm, Standard also introduced a new cylinder block. Originally these engines had featured a single carburettor, bolted to the right side of the block, with internal manifolding, but the '106mm' engines featured blocks with four inlet ports into the left side of the block, and much better breathing.

As already noted in chapter 5, Harry Weslake then worked together with William Lyons and SS, to develop an overhead-valve derivative of Standard's rugged side-valve engines, first on the six-cylinder block, and later on the four-cylinder block, too.

There was, however, one particular size of overhead-valve six-cylinder engine which was only ever used in SS-Jaguar and Jaguar cars, but never in a Standard of any type. This was the 3485cc power unit (82 x 110mm bore and stroke) which was found in SS-Jaguar 3½-litre, SS100 and Jaguar Mk V models. Although based on the original overall cylinder block dimensions, it was much-modified internally, developed 125bhp at 4500 rpm, and started life

From 1937 to 1949, every 1½-litre SS-Jaguar (later renamed, purely, Jaguar) was powered by a Standard 1776cc engine, with overhead-valve gear. The same engine, only lightly modified, was also used in postwar Triumphs – the 1800 Roadster and the 1800 saloon.

in the winter of 1937/1938. All in all, nearly 15,000 such 3½-litre engines would eventually be produced.

Not only was this deal extremely profitable as far as Standard was concerned, but the SSI and SSII cars were clearly very saleable, as more than 1700 cars a year were being produced by 1935. At this point, however, there was a further change of gear, with SS morphing into SS-Jaguar, with a different chassis frame being designed, and with the six-cylinder engines suddenly gaining overhead-valve cylinder heads (which had been designed for SS by Harry Weslake, but which would be manufactured by Standard).

SS began assembling its own rolling chassis at this stage – Standard, in other words, merely supplied engines and transmissions from Canley – all-steel SS-Jaguar saloon bodyshells

The SS100 of 1936-1939 was the sexiest of all prewar SS Jaguars, a rakish two-seater which was available with a Standard-built 2.5-litre or even a 3.5-litre six-cylinder engine. The larger-engined car's top speed was around 100mph – astonishingly fast for the period.

Jaguar's majestic MkV ran from 1948 to 1951, and was powered by the last of the overhead-valve six-cylinder power units which had originally been manufactured at Standard.

were introduced for 1938, and the badge was simplified to 'Jaguar' from 1945 onwards.

In drastically simplified form, this is the line-up of SS, SS-Jaguar and Jaguar cars produced with Standard or Standard-inspired running gear:

SSI (1931-1935): Made as a two-door saloon, a two-door coupé, Airline saloon, or Open Tourer. Built with 2054cc, 2143cc, 2552cc or 2664cc side-valve six-cylinder engines, rated at 45, 48, 53, 55, 62, 68 or 70bhp, depending on engine size or Model Year.

SSII (1931-1936): Made as a two-door saloon, a two-door coupé, or an Open Tourer. Built with 1006cc, 1343cc or 1608cc side-valve four-cylinder engines, rated at 28, 32, 34, 38, or 40bhp, depending on engine size or Model Year.

SS90 (1935): Made as a two-door open sports car. Built with 2664cc side-valve six-cylinder engine, rated at 70bhp.

SS-Jaguar 1.5-litre (1935-1937): Made as a four-door saloon, and a four-seater drophead Coupé. Built with a 1608cc side-valve four-cylinder engine, rated at 52bhp.

SS-Jaguar 1.5-litre (1937-1949): Made as a four-door saloon, and a four-seater drophead Coupé. Built with a 1776cc overhead-valve four-cylinder engine, rated at 65bhp.

SS-Jaguar 2.5-litre (1935-1949): Made as a four-door saloon, and a four-seater Drophead Coupé. Saloons had all-steel coachwork from 1938. Built with a 2664cc overhead-valve six-cylinder engine, rated at 102, later 104bhp

SS-Jaguar 3.5-litre (1937-1949): Made as a four-door saloon, and a four-seater drophead Coupé. Saloons had all-steel bodywork. Built with a 3485cc overhead-valve six-cylinder engine, rated at 125bhp.

SS100 (1936-1940): Made as a two-door open sports car. Built with a 2664cc or 3485cc overhead-valve six-cylinder engines, rated at 102bhp or 125bhp.

Jaguar Mk V (1948-1951): Made as a four-door saloon, and a four-seater drophead coupé. Built with 2664cc or 3485cc overhead-valve six-cylinder engines, rated at 102bhp or 125bhp.

Note: Standard built four-cylinder engines throughout this contract. However SS-Jaguar purchased all the six-cylinder engine tooling in 1942, and swiftly arranged for the machinery to be moved from Canley to Swallow Road in Foleshill – building its own engines thereafter. No engines were ever supplied to Standard from Foleshill.

SS (later Jaguar) bought the six-cylinder engine tooling from Standard in 1942, thereafter building its own six-cylinder power units. These are two under-bonnet views of the ultimate overhead-valve 'six' – the 3.5-litre – as fitted to a 1947 Jaguar.

Appendix B

'Works' rally cars in the 1950s

Standard appears to have been little interested in professional motorsport until it took over Triumph. Before and immediately after that, Standard cars were occasionally loaned out, almost entirely without success. There was no official or dedicated Competitions Department. After 1953 it was 'Works' cars like the Triumph TRs that took much of its effort, and made up most of its successes. There was a period, though, when the chunky little Standard Eights, Tens, and Pennants were useful in rallies, especially when the class handicaps were in its favour.

Before the mid-1950s, Standard occasionally loaned Vanguards to influential journalists, or to the most prominent of its dealers, but these cars were neither fast enough nor nimble enough to get into the awards lists. Purely as two examples, three factory-registered cars (KDU 718/719/720) started the 1951 Monte Carlo rally, but none finished higher than 37th, though a privately entered car took 19th place. Then, in 1953, of the 404 starters who competed in the Monte – where accurate time-keeping was far more important than high-performance – just six were Vanguards: dealer Dennis Done took 55th place, and no other example finished in the top hundred.

The only occasion in which a Vanguard troubled the scorers in the postwar Monte Carlo was in 1956, when Maurice Gatsonides' new Vanguard III took eighth place: this exploit has already been described in chapter 10.

On the other hand, the small Standards, latterly used as Pennants, were competitive little machines, sometimes made a lot faster in highly-modified form when regulations allowed. Every year from 1955 to 1958, one or other of these Works-prepared machines took awards at International level, after which the Triumph Herald took over instead. Competitions Manager Ken Richardson achieved much with very little resources, but finally had to concede that his machines could not consistently beat the much further-developed machines from BMC (Austin A35 and Morris Minor 1000), the Renault Dauphines, and particularly the front-wheel drive Saab 93s.

The story began in January 1955, when four new Standard Tens took part in the Monte Carlo rally. These were much-modified, with 46bhp engines from an early twin-carburettor setup, but the results achieved were modest. Strict regularity, and a great deal of pre-event practice, were both needed, but neglected – the result being that Standard took third and fourth in its capacity class.

Only two months later, however, a Standard Ten achieved a most remarkable outright victory – on the British RAC rally – when Lancashire-based confectioner Jimmy Ray, very ably

Leslie Brooke, Ninian Sanderson and 'Doc' Hardman drove this Works-prepared Ten in the Monte Carlo rallies of 1955 and 1956.

navigated by Brian Harrocks, kept the little car going in terribly icy and snowy conditions, when many other cars left the road, got lost, or otherwise failed to finish. Team boss Ken Richardson took third place overall, and to their joy the factory also won the Manufacturers' Team Prize.

In May, Maurice Gatsonides then entered an absolutely standard Ten in the Tulip rally, clearly chose his class with great care, and took fourth overall.

The Vanguard entry in the 1956 Monte Carlo rally (see page 158) was a shambles, but the Ten's performance in the 1956 RAC rally was another success. Four Tens (two of them privately-prepared) took the start, and at the end of another gruelling round-Britain week, Peter Cooper won his class (and took fifth overall),

Ken Gregory (at the time, Stirling Moss's manager) drives his Works-prepared Ten towards Hastings at the end of the 1956 RAC rally.

Tony Pounder's Sportsman decked out with Mobilgas Economy Run plates, next to his Works-prepared Standard Ten, as driven by Leslie Brooke in the 1956 Monte Carlo rally.

'Works' Pennants took second, third and fourth places overall in the RAC rally of 1958. Those particular cars were never used again in top-level motorsport.

while Johnny Wallwork won his class in one of the much-modified 'Works' machines.

That was good, but what followed in May, on the Dutch Tulip rally, was something else. Having looked very carefully at the regulations, Ken Richardson concluded that showroom-specification Standard Eights (not Tens, please note) had a good chance of victory, persuaded his management of this, and had no fewer than five brand-new machines prepared for the event. The result was astonishing. Although outright victory went to an Austin A30 (which was running in the same class), the 'Works' Eights finished second overall (John Wallwork), third (Paddy Hopkirk) and fourth (Denis Taylor), and also won the Manufacturers' team prize.

Even so, those Eights were never seen again in motorsport, and it was not until 1958 that there was another flurry of activity from the Tens, and the Pennants, which were succeeding them in the showrooms. John Wallwork took second in class in the Monte Carlo rally, but it was in the RAC rally of March 1958 that the little cars once again made headlines.

Standard's sales department was delighted to press Richardson to use the new Pennants on such a publicity-worthy event. Four brand-new cars – they carried consecutive registrations VWK 282, 283, 284 and 285 – were prepared, and were driven by formidable members of the 'Works' team, including Paddy Hopkirk, Tom Gold, Ron Gouldbourn (whose co-driver was Stuart Turner), and the newly-signed French Ladies' Champion Annie Soisbault.

To take advantage of the regulations, the Pennants ran in fully-developed form, complete with twin-SU engines, factory overdrive, and had to compete in the GT category. The weather was awful (with much snow in the Welsh and Lake District sections), so getting round the course, and completing the twenty special tests, was more important than doing it on time. The fact that Standard had Stuart Turner (already recognised as the country's most successful co-driver) in the team, helped considerably.

At the half-way halt, at Blackpool, both Goldbourn and Tom Gold had retained clean sheets for un-penalised runs, and were leading the rally, but as the route meandered north, conditions worsened, the Pennants sometimes got stuck behind other less-expert crews, and lost the lead to Peter Harper's Sunbeam Rapier. Even so, the gallant Pennants kept going strong, taking second (Goldbourn) and third (Gold) places overall. Paddy Hopkirk's team car was delayed with a damaged back axle, though the irrepressible Irishman kept going by visiting a Standard dealer at Tweedsmuir Motors, and begging a complete rear axle from a car in the showroom! Cyril Corbishley finished sixth in a 'Works' Standard Ten, the result being yet another Manufacturers' Team Prize success.

As Stuart recently told the author: "Please tell the story of the Pennants. Not many crews visited every control. The marking system was screwy, because even though we were not one of the 15 crews who scrambled over the Hardknott and Wrynose Passes (which meant that we missed a control up there), we still finished ahead of all, but one who did. There were 196 starters, but many retired. Ron did a great job in keeping our modified car on the road ..."

And that was the height of it. Within a year, the Herald had been launched, and in motorsport terms all attention went in to using the smart little Coupé instead of the old-style Pennant.

Clocking in at the Dover time control of the 1956 Monte Carlo rally is the Taylor/Tracey Standard Ten.

Stuart Turner, later to become famous for managing the BMC and Ford rally teams, was once a co-driver in 'Works' Standards. Many years later, he wonders how he could have been so brave ...

Appendix C

Series-production petrol engine 'family' dimensions

The following listing starts with the Model S of 1913, which was the first Standard to use what we might call a 'series production' power unit:

'S' -derived four-cylinder units – 1913-1926 (side-valve at first, progressively overhead valve from 1920)	
1088cc	62 x90mm (introduced for S of 1913).
	- 2-bearing crank, iron block, iron head,
	L-head side-valve at first.
1307cc	68 x 90mm
	Overhead valve, derived from ohv 1088cc power unit.
1328cc	62 x 110mm (long-stroke version of original 'S')
	- for use in the SLS model (L = Long stroke ...)
	Side-valve.
1598cc	68 x 110mm (derived from SLS), but with larger bore and now with overhead valves from late 1921.

'Big Four' of mid-1920s-vintage period	
1944cc	75 x 110mm (three bearing crank, aluminium crankcase)

Six-cylinder engine, produced only 1926-1928 (related to V4 four-cylinder unit)	
2223cc	68 x 102mm (seven-bearing crankshaft, overhead valve)

1930s small-car six-cylinder side-valve) (Closely related to the small four-cylinder engine of the early 1930s period)	
1337cc	57 x 87.3mm (really 88mm) – 4-main bearing crank (introduced July 1932)
1497cc	60.3 x 87.3mm (quoted as 60.25. Was 87.3 really 88?). Same basic engine as above, with four main bearings (introduced July 1932)

1930s – 1940s four-cylinder engine Standard, SS-Jaguar and Triumph (originally side-valve, later overhead valve for SS-Jaguar and Triumph)	
1153cc	60 x 101.6mm (announced in Nine of late 1927)
	- 2 crankshaft main bearings
1287cc	63.5 x 101.6mm (also available from 1927/1928)
1343cc	63.5 x 106mm (introduced, Ten, late 1933)
	(3 crankshaft main bearings)
1608cc	69.5 x 106mm (introduced, Twelve, late 1933)
	(3 crankshaft main bearings)
1776cc	73 x 106mm (3 crankshaft main bearings, overhead valves on SS-Jaguar
	'1½-litre' and Triumph 1800 models)

1920s – 1930s six-cylinder (originally side-valve)	
1930cc	63.5 x 101.6mm (same dimensions as 1287cc 'four')
	- seven (7) crankshaft main bearings
	(announced in late 1928)
2054cc	65.5 x 101.6mm
2143cc	65.5 x 106mm
2552cc	73 x 101.6mm
2664cc	73 x 106mm (overhead-valve on SS-Jaguar engines only)
3485cc	82 x 110mm (overhead-valve only, engine exclusive to SS-Jaguar)

Postwar (1947 introduction) 'wet-liner' unit (4-cylinder, overhead-valve)	
1670cc	76 x 92mm (Standard Ensign and Atlas Major commercial vehicle)
1850cc	80 x 92mm (Ferguson TE20 tractor and prototype-only Vanguard)

Postwar (1947 introduction) 'wet-liner' unit (4-cylinder, overhead-valve)	
1991cc	83 x 92mm (Triumph TR series, Vanguard Sportsman, 'Standard 2000' in India)
2088cc	85 x 92mm
2138cc	86 x 92mm (TR3A option from 1959, TR4 from 1961)
2188cc	87 x 92mm (exclusive to Ferguson tractors, from 1956 onwards)

Postwar (1953 introduction) SC unit (4-cylinder, overhead valve)	
803cc	58 x 76mm
948cc	63 x 76mm
1147cc	69.3 x 76mm (only in Triumphs – Heralds, Spitfires, etc)

Postwar (1953 introduction) SC unit (4-cylinder, overhead valve)	
- and, in later Triumph models as follows:	
1296cc	73.7 x 76mm (Spitfire, 1300, Toledo, Dolomite 1300, etc)
1493cc	73.7 x 87.5mm (Spitfire 1500, 1500, Dolomite 1500, etc)

Six-cylinder engine, introduced 1960 (6-cylinder overhead valve)	
1596cc	66.75 x 76mm (used only in Triumph Vitesse 1600)
1998cc	74.7 x 76mm (Vanguard 6, Triumph 2000, GT6, Vitesse 2-litre, etc)
2498cc	74.7 x 95mm (Triumph TR5/TR6/2500 and 2.5Pi applications)

Appendix D

Standard and Triumph model launches

No sooner had Standard bought up the remains of Triumph than it began to develop a new and rationalised model design and launch programme. This list shows how the two brands developed after 1945, what production cars were launched in which years, and how Triumph eventually came to dominate Standard:

Year	Standard model	Triumph model
1945	Eight	
	Twelve	
	Fourteen	
1946		1800 Saloon (later Renown)
		1800 Roadster (later 2000 Roadster)
1948	Vanguard	
1949		Mayflower
1953	Vanguard II	
		TR2
	Eight	
1954	Ten	
1955	Vanguard III	TR3
1957	Pennant	
	Ensign	
1958		TR3A
1959		Herald
1960	Vanguard Six	
1961		TR4
1962	Ensign de Luxe	
		Vitesse
		Spitfire
1963		2000
1965		1300 (front-wheel drive)
1966		GT6
1970		Stag
		Toledo
		1500
1972		Dolomite
1975		TR7
1979		TR8
1981		Acclaim

The last British-built Standard private car was produced in 1963, the last Triumph in 1984.

Appendix E

UK-produced Standard production models 1903-1963

Year introduced	Model	Engine size (cc)*	Comment (including production Figures)
1903	6hp ('Motor Victoria')	965, sv, 1-cyl	Commission No 1
1904	12/15hp ('Motor Victoria')	1930, sv, 2-cyl	
1905	16hp	3142, sv, 4-cyl	
1905	18/20hp	4714, sv, 6-cyl	
1905	Model 8 – 16/20hp	3530, sv, 4-cyl	
1905	Model 9 – 24/30hp	5295, sv, 6-cyl	
1906	Model 10 – 10hp	631, sv, 2-cyl	
1906	Model 14 – 30hp	5589, sv, 6-cyl	
1906	Model 11/Model 12 – 50hp	11,734, sv, 6-cyl	
1906	Model 13 – 10hp	1262, sv, 4-cyl	
1906	Model A – 15hp	1894, sv, 6-cyl	
1906	Model 30 – 30hp	5589, sv, 6-cyl	
1907	Model 15 – 15hp	1894, sv, 6-cyl	
1907	Model B – 20hp	3322, sv, 6-cyl	Commission No 500
1907	Model C – 40hp	6227, sv, 6-cyl	
1908	Model D – 30hp	4032, sv, 6-cyl	
1908	Model E – 16hp	2688, sv, 4-cyl	
1909	Model G – 29.5hp	4032, sv, 6-cyl	
1909	Model J – 12hp	1656, sv, 4-cyl	Commission No 2000
1909	Model K – 15hp	2413, sv, 4-cyl	
	Unlabelled – 15hp	2235, sv, 4-cyl	
1909	Model L – 20hp	3620, sv, 6-cyl	
1911	Model M – 23.6hp	4629, sv, 6-cyl	
1912	Model O – 20hp	3335, sv, 4-cyl	
1912	Model Q – 15.5hp	2413, sv, 4-cyl	Commission No 3000
1912	Model X – 15.6hp	2373, sv, 4-cyl	
1913	S (rated at 9.5hp)	1087, sv, 4-cyl	

Private car assembly then ceased from 1914 to 1918. Except for the prewar Model S of 1913, no prewar cars were ever revived in postwar years.

Year introduced	Model	Engine size (cc)*	Comment (including production Figures)
1918	S	1087, sv, 4-cyl	2134
1919	SLS	1328, sv, 4-cyl	498
1920	SLO	1598, ohv, 4-cyl	
1921	'8hp' (actually rated at 9.5hp)	1087, sv, 4-cyl	c500
1921	SLO4	1598, ohv, 4-cyl	
		1944, ohv, 4-cyl	
1923	V2/V3	1307, ohv, 4-cyl	
1925	V4	1944, ohv, 4-cyl	
1926	V6 (18-36hp)	2223, ohv, 6-cyl	
1927	Nine	1153, sv, 4-cyl	
		1287, sv, 4-cyl	c10,000
1928	15hp	1930, sv, 6-cyl	
1929	Envoy (became Sixteen and Twenty for 1932)	2054, sv, 6-cyl	
		2552, sv, 6-cyl	
1930	Big Nine	1287, sv, 4-cyl	
1931	Little Nine	1006, sv, 4-cyl	
1932	Little Twelve	1337, sv, 6-cyl	
1932	Big Twelve	1497, sv, 6-cyl	
1934	10/12 Speed Model	1608, sv, 4-cyl	
1933	Nine	1052, sv, 4-cyl	
1933	Ten	1343, sv, 4-cyl	
1934	10/12 Speed Model	1608, sv, 4-cyl	
1934	Twelve	1608, sv, 4-cyl	
1934	Sixteen	2143, sv, 6-cyl	
1935	Twenty	2664, sv, 6-cyl	
1935	Flying Twelve	1608, sv, 4-cyl	
1935	Flying Sixteen	2143, sv, 6-cyl	
1935	Flying Twenty	2664, sv, 6-cyl	
		2143, sv, 6-cyl	
1936	Flying Nine	1131, sv, 4-cyl	
1936	Flying Ten	1267, sv, 4-cyl	
1936	Flying Light Twelve	1343, sv, 4-cyl	
1936	Flying Fourteen	1608, sv, 4-cyl	
		1776, sv, 4-cyl	
1936	Flying V-Eight	2686, sv, V8	
1938	Flying Eight	1021, sv, 4-cyl	30,040 (prewar)

Private car assembly then ceased from 1940 to 1945, after which the 'Flying' part of the titles was dropped.

Year introduced	Model	Engine size (cc)*	Comment (including production Figures)
1945	Eight	1009, sv, 4-cyl	Reintroduced prewar model 53,099 (postwar)
1945	Twelve	1608, sv, 4-cyl	Reintroduced prewar model 32,188 (postwar, incl 14hp)
1945	Fourteen	1776, sv, 4-cyl	Reintroduced prewar model
1948	Vanguard I	2088, ohv, 4-cyl	184,799
1953	Vanguard II	2088, ohv, 4-cyl	86,000 (which includes 1885 Diesel-engined versions)
		2092, ohv, 4-cyl Diesel	
1953	Eight	803, ohv, 4-cyl	136,317
1954	Ten	948, ohv, 4-cyl	172,500
1955	Vanguard III	2088, ohv, 4-cyl	Later, 'Vignale,' from 1958 37,803, plus 26,286 Vignale
1966	Vanguard Sportsman	2088, ohv, 4-cyl	901
1957	Ensign	1670cc, ohv, 4-cyl	34,664
		2088cc, ohv, 4-cyl	
		2092, ohv, 4-cyl Diesel	
1957	Pennant	948, ohv, 4-cyl	42,910**
1960	Vanguard Six	1998, ohv, 6-cyl	9953
1963	Ensign II (De Luxe)	2138, ohv, 4-cyl	2318

From 1931 to 1940, Standard provided engines, transmissions, and some chassis components to SS-Jaguar, as follows:

Engine size (cc)*	Comment
1343cc, sv, 4-cyl	For the SSII
1608cc, sv, 4-cyl	For the SSII
	For the SS-Jaguar 1.5-litre
1776cc, ohv, 4-cyl	For the SS-Jaguar 1.5-litre, with specially designed overhead-valve cylinder head
2054cc, sv, 6-cyl	For the SS1
2143cc, sv, 6-cyl	For the SS1
2552cc, sv, 6-cyl	For the SS1
2664cc, sv, 6-cyl	For the SS90 sports car
2664cc, ohv, 6-cyl	For the SS-Jaguar 2.5-litre, with specially-designed overhead-valve cylinder head.
	Also for the SS100
3485cc, ohv, 6-cyl	For the SS-Jaguar 3.5-litre. This engine was never used on a Standard product.
	Also for the SS100

Jaguar purchased the six-cylinder tooling in 1942, and transferred all such engine manufacture to its own premises.

Triumph-badged cars built under Standard ownership

Year introduced	Model	Engine size (cc)*	Comment (including production Figures)
1946	1800 Roadster	1776, ohv, 4-cyl	
1946	1800 saloon	1776, ohv, 4-cyl	
1948	2000 Roadster	2088, ohv, 4-cyl	
1949	2000 (later Renown)	2088, ohv, 4-cyl	
1949	Mayflower	1247, sv, 4-cyl	
1953	TR2	1991, ohv, 4-cyl	
1955	TR3	1991, ohv, 4-cvl	
1957	TR3A/TR3B	1991, ohv, 4-cyl	Optional 2138cc from 1959
1959	Herald (several body styles)	948, ohv, 4-cyl	
1961	Herald 1200 (several body styles)	1147, ohv, 4-cyl	Including 12/50
1961	TR4	2138, ohv, 4-cyl	
1962	Vitesse (saloon and convertible styles)	1596, ohv, 6-cyl	
1962	Spitfire	1147, ohv, 4-cyl	
After 1963 all private cars built in Coventry, and on other sites, were badged as Triumphs.			

* Where appropriate, cubic capacities have been recalculated from official bore and stroke dimensions.
** Other historians dispute these figures as being too high, though they were indeed issued by the company in the 1960s and 1970s.

Appendix F

Production figures – year-on-year

How many cars did Standard build after 1945? The following figures were provided by Standard-Triumph Product Planners in the 1970s, and are now thought to be less than accurate in some details. In the absence of any later sources, however, they are offered on the 'best guess' basis. In all cases, the Triumph-badged models are included, but tractor production is not:

Model Year*	Total production	
1946/1947	37,363	
1947/1948	36,923	Vanguard started production
1948/1949	41,004	
1949/1950	54,490	
1950/1951	65,444	
1951/1952	50,693	
1952/1953	42,697	Vanguard Phase II announced
1953/1954	72,926	Eight/Ten range started production
1954/1955	96,941	
1955/1956	86,466	
1956/1957	48,835	
1957/1958	76,539	Pennant started production
1958/1959	85,926	Triumph Herald started production
1959/1960	138,762	
1960/1961	78,735	
1961/1962	78,383	
1962/1963	100,764	Last Standard private car built

– after which the Standard brand disappeared, and all future cars were badged as Triumphs.

The same sources, which can no longer be authenticated, claim that approximately 200,000 Standards had already been built in the 1903-1939 period.

*August to July, ie August 1950 to July 1951.

ALSO FROM VELOCE ...

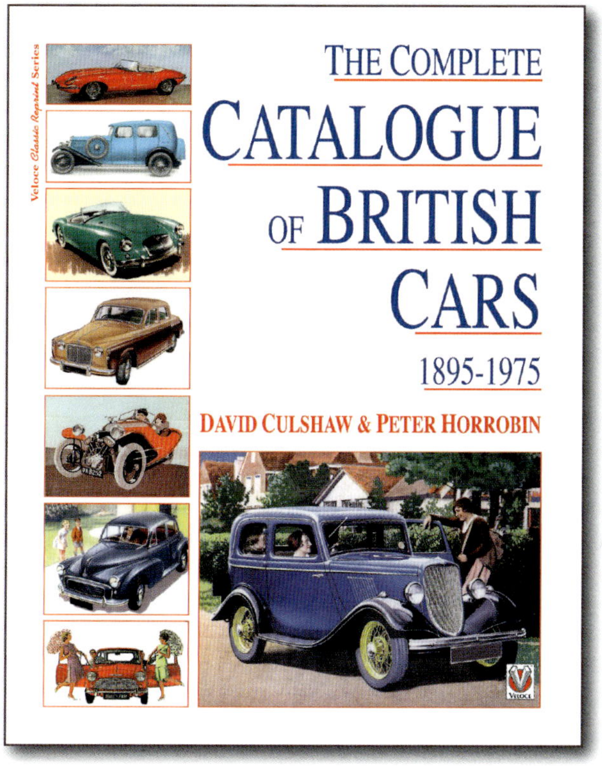

Hardback • 21.5x27.8cm • £30.00* UK / $54.95* US • 496 pages • 1000+ pictures • ISBN: 978-1-874105-93-0

The famous Culshaw and Horrobin. The most comprehensive account of British cars ever published in one volume, this book presents a huge amount of information - historical as well as technical - in a way which will serve the needs of the dedicated enthusiast, automotive historian and the general reader.

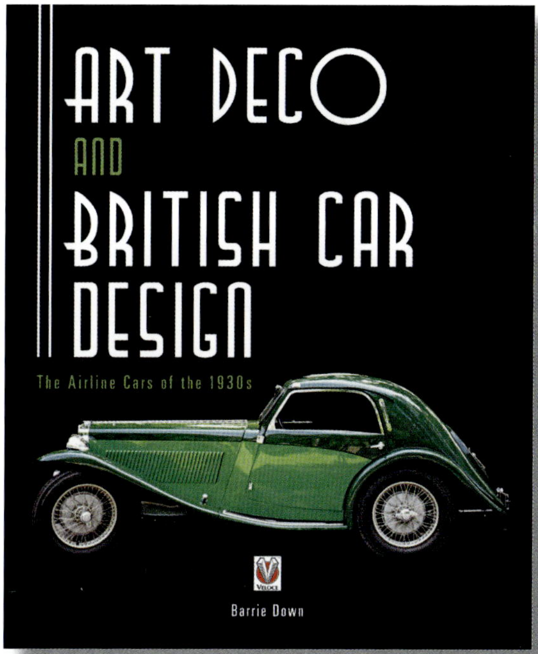

Hardback • 20.7x25cm • £22.50* UK / $44.95* US • 144 pages • 215 pictures • ISBN: 978-1-845842-52-9

The Art Deco movement influenced design and marketing in many different industries in the 1930s, and the British motor industry was no exception. This fascinating book is divided into two parts; the first explains and illustrates the Art Deco styling elements that link these streamlined car designs, describing their development, their commonality, and their unique aeronautical names, and is liberally illustrated with contemporary images. The book then goes on to portray British streamlined production cars made between 1933 and 1936, illustrated with colour photographs of surviving cars. This is a unique account of a radical era in automotive design.

For more info on Veloce titles, visit our website at www.veloce.co.uk
email info@veloce.co.uk • tel: +44 (0)1305 260068 • *prices subject to change • p+p extra

Index

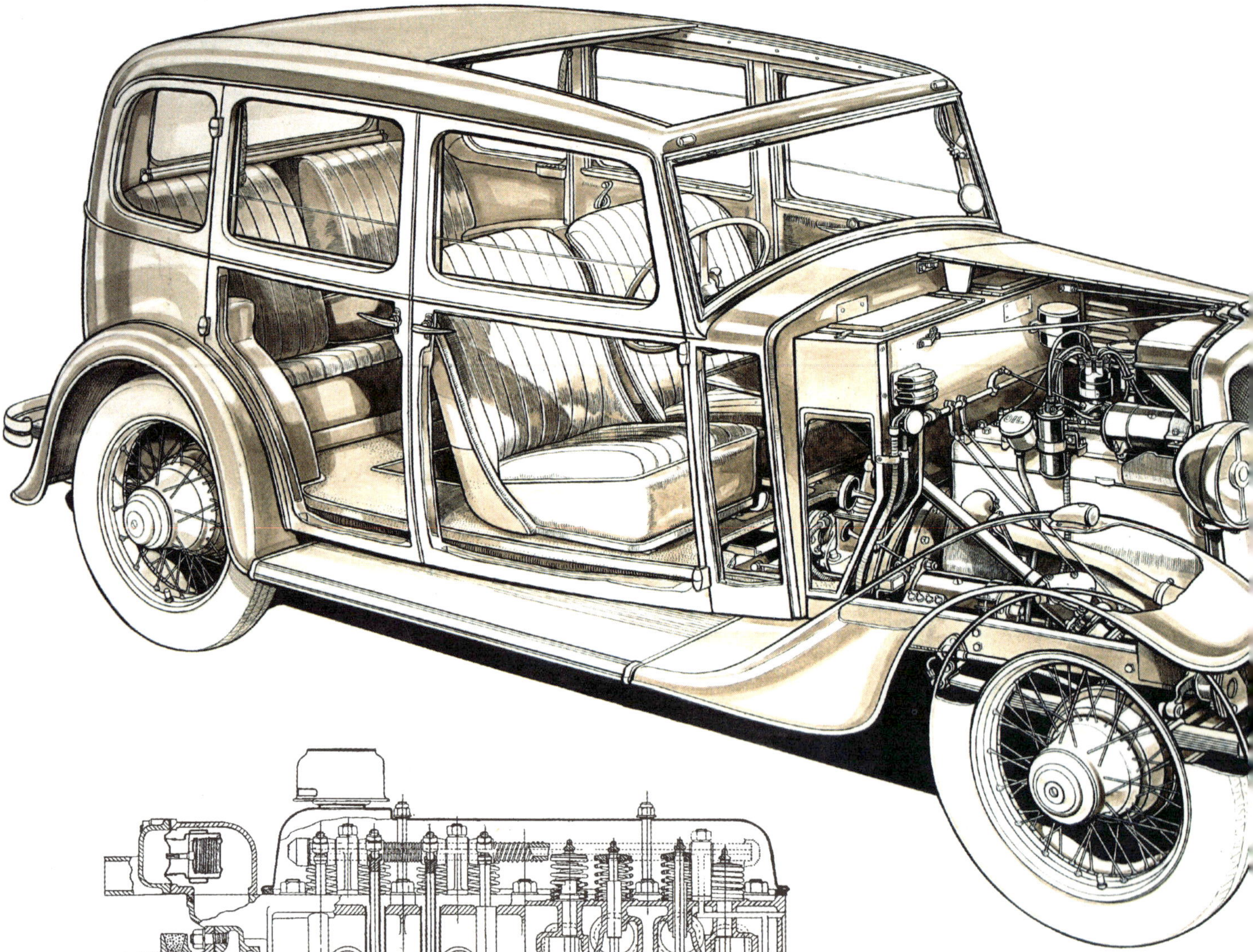

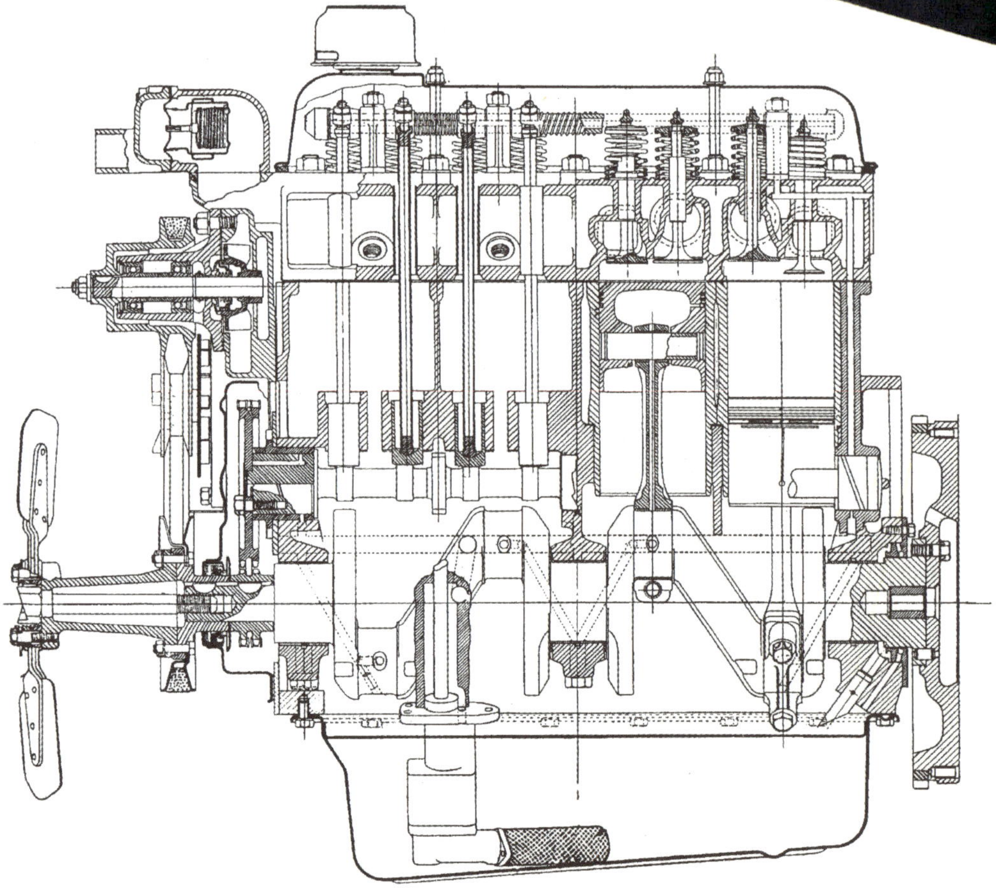

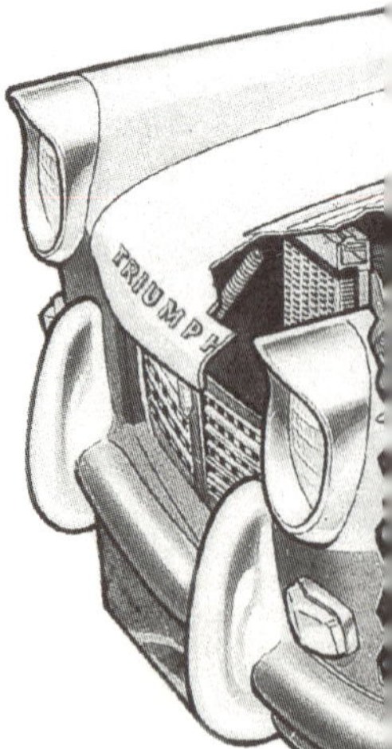